HILL COUNTRY ECOLOGY

Essays on Plants, Animals, Water, and Land Management

Jim Stanley

HUGO HOUSE PUBLISHERS, LTD.

Hill Country Ecology: Essays on Plants, Animals, Water, and Land Management

ISBN: 978-1-936449-74-3

Library of Congress Control Number: 2017948518

Cover Design & Interior Layout: Ronda Taylor, www.rondataylor.com

Hugo House Publishers, Ltd.

Denver, Colorado
Austin, Texas
www.HugoHousePublishers.com

To Priscilla,
still the love of my live and a passionate advocate for all living things,
and to everyone who appreciates and
conserves our native habitat.

ACKNOWLEDGEMENTS

Of all the people and organizations I am indebted to I have to list first the Texas Master Naturalist program and the executive director of that organization, Michelle Haggerty, and specifically, my fellow volunteers in the Hill Country Chapter, most of whom are my very best friends.

There are many people who have been especially helpful to me in learning about the Hill Country ecology and whose work has made a major contribution to preserving and restoring native Hill Country habitat. I especially want to acknowledge the following: Bill Armstrong, J. David Bamberger, Robert Edmonson, Rebecca Flack-Neill, Joe Franklin, Donnie Frels, Scott Gardener, John Herron, Bill Carr, Jason Singhurst, Sky Jones-Lewey, Mike Kreger, David K. Langford, Ricky Linex, Bill Lindemann, Bob Lyons, Christie Muse, Bill Neiman, Steve Nelle, Barron Rector, Katherine Romans, Rufus Stephens, Roy Walston, Brad Wilcox.

Among the many organizations that I want to acknowledge for the good things they do for the Hill Country are the Hill Country Alliance, Hill Country Land Trust, Bamberger Ranch Preserve, The Nature Conservancy, Riverside Nature Center, Cibolo Nature Center, Fredericksburg Nature Center, and the Native Plant Society of Texas chapters in Boerne, Kerrville and Fredericksburg.

I also want to make special mention of Steve Nelle, retired NRCS agent and certainly one of the most knowledgeable experts on all aspects of land management, for all the help and guidance he has given me on everything from simple plant identifications to complicated scientific issues and even ethical and philosophical dilemmas.

And a special thanks to John Huecksteadt for being a great friend and fellow learner of all things natural in the Hill Country.

INTRODUCTION

This book is a labor of love for me because it is about the Hill Country, or at least the native, natural part of the Hill Country. And my purpose for writing it is to teach others about the natural part of the Hill Country.

I grew up in the high plains of Texas without any hills and virtually no real native trees. But when I was a kid my family visited the Hill Country many times, and those visits became imbedded in my mind as what a beautiful landscape should look like. And that vision has persisted through the decades when I lived in the Midwest, in Louisiana, and in the Northeast, all places with a natural beauty of their own.

So 17 years ago, when my wife and I decided to retire while we were still young enough to enjoy it, the Hill Country was where we chose to live. Within a year of moving here we became involved with Riverside Nature Center in Kerrville and the local Native Plant Society of Texas, and then when the Hill Country Chapter of the Texas Master Naturalist held its first training session in 2002, we were in that class. Being a Master Naturalist has truly been a life-changing experience for us. The mission statement of the Texas Master Naturalist, "To develop a corps of well-informed volunteers to provide education, outreach and service dedicated to the beneficial management of natural resources and natural areas within their communities," has become my full-time "job" in retirement.

In the intervening years, I have spent many hundreds of hours attending presentations, seminars, symposia, field days, and other gatherings, listening to numerous experts (mostly university and governmental agency biologists and other scientists) talk about the ecology of the Hill Country. And I have spent several thousand hours volunteering in various capacities, helping over 400 landowners better understand their property and their land management issues, helping train over 450 new Master Naturalists, and working to educate the general public about land management issues.

In 2009, my first book, *Hill Country Landowner's Guide,* was published by Texas A&M Press, and I was awarded the Carroll Abbott Memorial award by the Native Plant Society of Texas for that book in 2012. In 2014 I published my second book, *A Beginners Handbook for Rural Texas Landowners. How to Live in the Country Without Spoiling It.* Since 2010, I have been writing a weekly column, *The Hill Country Naturalist,* for the Kerrville Daily Times, and, more recently, also for the Mason County News and the Sansaba News.

Many of those seven years of weekly columns, edited and arranged by topic, make up most of the essays in this book. They were originally written to help the average reader better understand the ecology of Hill Country, the plants, the animals, the hills, the water, and the soil, and the issues of managing rural land and preserving and improving our native habitat. In addition, I have tried to instill in my readers a greater love and respect for nature in general and for our native community in particular, which includes the soil, the water, the plants, the animals and the people, and for the true joy of observing and interacting with nature. And I hope I have managed to entertain the reader as well.

This is not a book for professional biologists, range scientists, or land management experts. It is a book for laymen, written by a layman. As such, I have tried to describe the various biological principles and land management issues as simply, but accurately, as possible without resorting to too much scientific jargon and/or more detail than most folks are likely to be interesting in. There are professional textbooks and publications for those wishing a higher-level discussion.

I have been fortunate to have the opportunity and the time to spend many, many hours learning from experts, in person and via books and other writings, and spending time with nature throughout the Hill Country. I feel an obligation to share what I know with everyone else in the Hill Country in the hopes that in the end it will be conserved, and that landowners will develop what Aldo Leopold called, an "ecological conscience." I believe in the essential truth of the following quote, from Baba Dioum, "In the end, we will conserve only what we love, we will love only what we understand, and we will understand only what we are taught."

I hope this book will serve to help readers learn more ABOUT the Hill Country ecology. It is not necessarily a book to be read from front to back, but rather to be read one topic at a time in the order of the reader's choosing. The essays within each section were originally written at different times under possibly different conditions and each essay may have a slightly different emphasis on the subject. By necessity, there is some repetition in the discussion of certain issues among the different essays, so that any given essay can be understood alone without the reader having read other related essays.

I believe strongly that the best hope for the future of the Hill Country, given the continuing loss of native habitat to development and land fragmentation, and the projected increasing human population, is for all of us to become good land stewards. Once native habitat is lost or destroyed, it is pretty much lost forever, or at least for many decades, but once it is conserved or protected, it still has to be continually protected or it could still be lost.

Finally, I have to borrow a quote from Aldo Leopold in his introduction to his great book, *A Sand County Almanac,* "There are some who can live without wild things, and some who cannot. These essays are the delights and dilemmas of one who cannot."

CONTENTS

— SECTION I —

HISTORY OF THE TEXAS HILL COUNTRY

I don't know if there is an "official" definition of where the boundaries of the Texas Hill Country are. It is frequently defined as the area north and west of I-35 from north of Austin to west of San Antonio (or north and west of the Balcones escarpment which parallels I-35 in that area), but that doesn't exactly define the northern and western boundaries. For want on any better definition, I will go with the counties the Hill Country Alliance generally considers the Hill Country: which would be all or part of Uvalde, Medina, Bexar, Edwards, Real, Bandera, Kerr, Kendall, Comal, Kimble, Gillespie, Blanco, Hays, Travis, Mason, Llano and Burnet counties.

Whatever definition you chose, the Hill Country is a large piece in the center of what geologically is considered the Edwards Plateau as well as part of the Llano uplift, the latter being a largely circular area centered in Llano county.

Most of central Texas was under shallow seas during the Cretaceous geologic period (100 +/- 35 million years ago) during which time limestone, from the shells of various organisms, as well as from chemical processes in the sea, was deposited on the ocean floor as the sea level repeatedly advanced and retreated. As sea levels finally receded for good and the land began to be uplifted, the limestone became the bedrock of most of the Hill Country. Some of the Llano uplift area being the exception as the limestone has been eroded off of that area exposing a granite base.

Slowly, as rivers and streams began to flow over the relatively flat landscape and erode the soft limestone, valleys were formed and as the valleys became deeper and wider the appearance of the Hill Country began to look more like a collection of hills rather than valleys. The valleys and riparian areas were in fact accumulations of sediment eroded from the highlands and tend to have deeper, less rocky soils.

Moving forward to much more modern times, say the last 200 or so years, when we have numerous written records, the Hill Country might have looked somewhat like it does today. To greatly oversimplify and generalize what the early European explorers and settlers wrote about the Hill Country, it would be that, compared to what we see now, there would have been somewhat fewer trees, more open grasslands and savannas, particularly on the flatter, higher elevations. There would have been, generally, more of the taller grass species than we see today and less cedar. There would also have been more numerous springs, seeps and small creeks than we see today.

There would have been herds of bison migrating around eating most all of the grasses and forbs (weeds or wildflowers) in the prairies and savannas, but not returning to any given area until the vegetation had grown back. There would have been more numerous wildfires in the grasslands and these fires would have covered much larger areas than is the case today. Along with the bison were elk and pronghorn, as well as their predators, wolves, bears and mountain lions and many smaller animals.

I have to emphasize, that while the above picture is, I believe, generally true, it doesn't mean that it applies to every single parcel of land. Not every upland acre was devoid of cedar brakes, not every acre saw huge herds of bison very often, or was burned regularly.

As the Hill Country began to be populated by European settlers, their footprint on the land began to be apparent. The settlers brought with them cattle, sheep, goats, pigs and chickens, all of which were vital to their survival, and they kept these animals close to their houses to protect them from predators, the latter of which they shot at every opportunity to protect their livestock. This resulted in the land being grazed by livestock continuously year round instead of only occasionally by migrating herds.

As the population of Europeans increased, the Native Americans were increasingly driven out, died of European diseases and/or were killed. The Native Americans were partly responsible for setting some of the wildfires that burned through the Hill Country.

As the human population began to increase, and especially after barbered wire became available in the 1880s, many ranches became quite large encompassing tens of thousands of acres with vast herds of livestock. In the first half of the 1900s, several factors including drought, the dust bowl, the depression and two world wars caused all landowners, large and small, to severely overgraze their land just to make a living.

Thus virtually all of the Hill Country, along with most of the rest of the state has been overgrazed in the past. In addition, the overgrazing coupled with the reduction in wildfires led to an increase in the woody plant cover over much of the area. (Wildfires burning through grasslands would kill most all woody plant saplings before they could grow to a size to withstand the fires.)

Now, most Hill Country properties probably have more mature hardwoods growing on them than was true 100 or so years ago. The white-tailed deer population has increased dramatically in the past 80 or so years, because of fewer hunters and many fewer predators, hunting regulations, and better forage availability due to the increased number of hardwoods. Now, however, because of the increased number of deer, many Hill Country properties are pretty much devoid of young hardwood saplings to replace the mature trees—they are being eaten before they can become mature. Most Hill Country properties have a distinct browseline below which the deer have eaten most all vegetation.

Thus, the number of hardwood trees in the Hill Country has probably begun to decline. The same is not true, however, of cedar (Ashe juniper and redberry juniper), the reasons being that cedar is about the last thing deer prefer to eat if anything else is available, as well as the fact the cedar reproduces prolifically and grows very fast. Less grass cover caused by continual overgrazing and fewer wildfires, and no natural limits on its growth, has allowed cedar to become invasive on many properties.

So to summarize the main changes to the Hill Country landscape since the beginning of European settlement, one would say that most properties today have somewhat more trees, fewer open grasslands, less grass, less soil, possibly fewer springs and seeps, and maybe more cedar than would have been there 200 years ago. There is also the fact that today we don't have migrating herds of bison, the wolves are gone, the populations of bear and mountain lions is almost infinitesimal, and we have fewer, smaller wildfires than in the past. And of course we have all of the obvious alterations we have caused by all of us living here.

Having said all of that, because it is important for everyone to understand the changes that have occurred in the Hill Country, it is also true that the Hill Country is probably less altered by modern man than any other part of the state (with the possible exception of some parts of the Trans-Pecos region of far west Texas). Because of the steep terrain and rocky soil, the vast majority of the Hill Country landscape is unsuitable for plowing and farming. So for most properties, the only sustained use of the land has been for ranching on native grass ranges—the native habitat may have been altered by too many grazers and browsers, but it is still native habitat.

Please note that I am not being critical of farmers and timbermen, we all like to eat and we all like to live in wooden houses. But plowed fields and row crops are not habitat for any native species to speak of. Nor are replanted forests with single species of trees or "improved" pastures with non-native grasses such as bermudagrass, kleingrass, Willmann lovegrass, buffelgrass, Guinea grass or Old World bluestems, etc.

So the Hill Country is, without question, closer to its "native state" than most parts of the state, or the nation for that matter. Yes, I am certainly well aware there are places in the Hill Country that are being farmed and there are "improved" pastures as well, but the acreage covered by most of those properties in a very small part of the total acreage in the Hill Country.

From a naturalist standpoint, the Hill Country is an ideal place. Sitting in the middle of the state and having much of the area largely unaltered, the Hill Country has vegetation from all the adjoining areas, the wetter east, the drier west, the coastal plains of the south and the cross-timbers and high plains to the north. This gives us a longer list of species, both plant and animal, than most of the other areas. We also sit in the middle of major bird migration routes as well as the monarch butterfly migration route.

As I was growing up in the near-treeless high plains, my family took most of their vacations to the Highland Lakes area as well as several hunting trips to various parts of the Hill Country. All my life my vision of a beautiful landscape has always been the Hill Country. And I suspect that is a major reason for many of our current residents being here as well. The climate, the hills, the trees, the creeks and rivers, the native habitat all make this area an extremely desirable place to live.

The Hill Country, however, faces several serious challenges. Here is a partial list: water supply, distribution and use, loss of rangeland to "development," land fragmentation as larger ranches are broken up into smaller "ranchettes," and increasing numbers of residents. As more and more residents demand more and more services it degrades the "small town/rural" lifestyle which attracted many of us to the Hill Country in the first place. These are challenging problems that need to be addressed, but probably can't be eliminated. The Texas Hill Country. Let's hope we don't love it to death!

LIFE IN TEXAS BEFORE WE GOT HERE

Before we can assess where we are and where we want to go, it helps to know where we came from. And in terms of the land, it helps to know what the Hill Country was like before we got here and how settlement and human population growth have affected the landscape. And it is also somewhat humbling to learn that the people that came before us understood a lot of things that we are still learning.

The following are some examples of what early Texans described that they saw. The first few essays describe what we think most of the Hill Country looked like before European man arrived in significant numbers as well as what some early visitors observed. The latter essays deal with the ecological changes caused by modern man. There is a section in Appendix I which lists many recommended books by early Texans.

What The Hill Country Was Like Before We Got Here

People often ask, "What did the Hill Country look like in the past?" The answer of course depends a lot on how far back in time you want to go. During the last ice age, there were mastodons, saber-tooth tigers and spruce/pine forests, but that is probably not what most people have in mind when they ask the question.

The time many people have in mind is before many European settlers had arrived in Texas, before European man had much effect on the land. And this is a very good time period to refer to, because not only was it the time just before man-made great changes were beginning to take place in Texas, but also the first time that we have the detailed descriptions of the Hill Country by numerous educated explorers. They arrived in Texas at a time before the settlers of European ancestry had been here for a sufficient time or in sufficient numbers to have had major effects on the countryside—the early to middle 1800s.

Various explorers made forays into different parts of the Hill Country at different times. No single account can be taken as best describing the Hill Country, but each description is a snap-shot in time and place. It is only after putting together all of their accounts that a relatively accurate picture emerges of the early 19th century Hill Country.

In general, the Hill Country of the early 1800s had considerably fewer trees, including cedar (Ashe juniper), than we have now and more open grasslands and savannas. The most densely wooded areas were along creeks and streams and the steep valleys thereof, where mixtures of various hardwoods and cedars were common. Most of the flatter uplands contained considerably fewer trees of any kind, although occasional live oak mottes and scattered cedar brakes did exist.

In many areas, especially in areas with the deeper soil, the grassland would have looked different because of a greater proportion of taller grasses, especially what we call the Big Four of the tall grass prairie, big bluestem, yellow indiangrass, switchgrass, and little bluestem. These grasses put up seed heads that, in wet years, could be taller than a man's head.

Bison ranged widely in great herds which migrated long distances. The southern part of the Hill Country may not have seen the really large herds seen further north in Texas and the Great Plains, but the bison did range beyond San Antonio. Elk and pronghorns also grazed these lands.

When a large herd of bison passed through an area, they left virtually nothing uneaten. Fortunately, the herds seldom passed through the same area more than once during the growing season or maybe not again until the grass had recovered, so the heavily grazed grasses could recover and, with the fertilizer left behind by the animals, grow back vigorously. Some of the early explorers reported that on attempted trips of some distance, they sometimes had to turn back because coming along just after the bison had been through the area, there was nothing for their horses to eat.

The other major occurrence in the early 1800s was fire. The early explorers described encountering numerous prairie fires that burned huge areas, sometimes burning for weeks at a time. Some of these fires were certainly caused by lightning, but many were set by the Native Americans, either accidently or on purpose. (They knew that soon after a fire, the new green grass shoots would attract game animals.) These fires in the grasslands are the main thing that kept more trees from growing, because before a sapling could get big enough to withstand a fire, it would be burned up.

Because there was much less grass for fuel in the wooded areas on the slopes, these areas seldom burned. The white-tailed deer probably spent most of their time in the wooded areas, because there was less for them to eat on the grasslands.

With all of the large prey animals around, it is not surprising that there were many large predators as well. The last wolf and black bear in Kerr County were killed in the early years of the 20th century.

A Glimpse of the Hill Country in 1846

A German geologist, Ferdinand Roemer, traveled through the Hill Country from early 1846 until the spring of 1847, and chronicled his observations in great detail in a book, since translated into English by Oswald Mueller, called *"Roemer's Texas."* Roemer was actually employed to study the area by a German company interested in developing some German settlements in the Hill Country.

Roemer described in detail the difficulty in traveling in Texas back then, which was just after Texas became a state. It took them 17 days in January and February of 1846 to travel from Houston to New Braunfels, a distance of 250 miles. Much of the time was spent trying to get wagons unstuck from muddy trails.

In New Braunfels, Roemer made the acquaintance of Ferdinand Lindheimer, a naturalist and newspaper editor, now known as the Father of Texas Botany. Roemer described a trip he made with Lindheimer to Mission Hill, which is on the outskirts of present day New Braunfels, as follows," Our path led us again past the springs of Comal, but suddenly ascended the steep, wooded slope of the hill.... The cedar trees which covered the slopes exclusively, formed an impenetrable thicket through which a path had to be cut.... As soon as we reached the summit of the hill, the cedar forest ended. An open, grassy plain, only broken here and there by brushwood and scattered live oak trees, spread out before us. It extended to Mission Hill about two miles distant..."

Roemer described a trip to Fredericksburg from New Braunfels, the "road" going first southeast from New Braunfels to the Cibolo River and then north 90 miles to Fredericksburg. It was a four-day trip, and on the second night they were concerned about a prairie fire that seemed to be approaching them from several directions. They burned the grass around their camp to protect them from the fire and then they enjoyed a "beautiful spectacle... the strips of fire, several miles in extent appeared as fiery brands...flames shooting up high or just glimmering..." This is just one of several of Roemer's observations that included prairie fires.

Roemer reported that the herds of buffalo seen in the New Braunfels area by earlier settlers had disappeared by the time of his visit, although he did observe buffalo herds as well as some pronghorn on a trip to a trading post on the Brazos River. He had numerous encounters with Native Americans of various tribes during his visit, most were intentional contacts initiated by people Roemer was traveling with for the intention of doing business with the Native Americans. But Roemer was also fearful of unintentional contacts while traveling in small groups.

Although Roemer's training was in geology, and he described the geology of each area he visited and took fossil samples, he also made numerous comments about the fauna and flora he encountered. He commented on flowering plants several times including windflowers, blue tradescantia, trumpet creeper and rough-leaf dogwood, and he particularly admired the Texas mountain laurel. He also noted the live oaks, cedar, cypress, post oaks and mesquite trees. He was fascinated by our cacti and succulents, noting three genera of cacti (*Echinocereus, Mammillaria*, and several species of *Opuntia*)

Roemer reported that while bears were common in the general area, they had left the area of New Braunfels after settlement began. He did observe mountain lions, wolves, deer, bobcats, ocelots, javelinas, skunks, opossums, rabbits, and squirrels (including flying squirrels). He noted with some interest that raccoons, common in other parts of Texas, did not seem to be common around New Braunfels.

Roemer observed many rattlesnakes, also water moccasins and the rough green snake. The birds mentioned included the mockingbird, cardinal, bluebird, roadrunners, hummingbirds, whip-poor-wills and vultures. He also saw catfish (up to 4 feet long) gar, soft-shelled turtles and alligators (at least one 11 feet long).

As Roemer pointed out, his visit was not primarily for the purpose of cataloging all the plants or animals in the area, so the ones he mentioned probably caught his eye for some reason, and the lack of mention of any species certainly doesn't imply they were not seen or identified.

To get a more accurate picture of what early Texas was like, you have to read the accounts of many people.

Americans Before Columbus: What They Had, What They Didn't

After watching a TV documentary about conditions in the Americas before Columbus, I thought a few observations about the larger area would be of interest.

Those of us who think mainly about the history of our area tend to think about what the Hill Country was like before and after people of European ancestry moved in, and we envision Texas as being peopled by small nomadic tribes of Native Americans who moved with the buffalo, lived off the land, and had relatively little impact on the local ecology.

But that is a rather parochial view. There were Indian "villages" in east Texas that were farmers as well as hunter-gatherers, as there were in much of the Eastern half of North America. And to think about the larger scale, there were the huge cities and civilizations such as the Incas of South America, the Aztecs and Mayans of Central America, and the Pueblos of our Southwest. All of these civilizations had huge farms, many irrigated, where they grew corn, potatoes, tomatoes, peppers and squash. Some domesticated turkeys, many fished streams and rivers. The ruins of their cities reveal sophisticated civilizations with advanced knowledge of mechanical and civil engineering, astronomy, and agriculture. Neither the North American or South American people were aware of each other or of the Europeans before Columbus.

So the Americas were not "empty" when Columbus sailed, nor were they peopled by only "ignorant savages" as some explorers referred to them.

But there was a lot that the Europeans had that no-one in the Americas had. Two related things were a written language that could be understood by many people and the printing press. This allowed knowledge to be disseminated much more widely and quickly in Europe than in the Americas.

Some of the most important things Europeans had that the Americans did not have were domestic livestock; horses, cattle, sheep, goats, pigs and chickens. These livestock all contributed greatly to the ability of Europeans to live in cities and still have plenty of food available. Raising livestock instead of hunting meant people did not need to spend as much time just in the pursuit of food. Being able to plow fields with horses instead of human power, and to thus raise many grain, vegetable, and fruit crops was also a great advantage for the Europeans.

The only things close to domesticated livestock in the Americas before Columbus were llamas, which can't be ridden, can't pull a plow, and can't carry much, and the turkey. Americans also didn't have most of the vegetables that are familiar to us today.

What Americans did have was lots more land and lots more game than the Europeans, especially since much of the forests had been cut down in Europe for lumber and farming. But hunting in the Americas was difficult because Native Americans lacked guns and horses, so hunting buffalo involved stalking by foot or crawling through the grass and using bows and arrows or spears.

One of the important things Americans did not have was small pox, cholera and measles, and thus the American populations did not have the immunity to these diseases that Europeans had. Some estimates are that as high as 90 percent of Native American populations, both north and south, died from these diseases.

Early Settlers to the East coast brought with them the livestock listed above, but also European cereal grains (wheat, barley, oats, rye), and many vegetables and fruit trees. Although they didn't know it at the time, they were lucky that they also brought European honey bees (for honey) that pollinated their fruits and vegetables, because native bees did not recognize those plants as food sources. Unfortunately, Europeans also brought many non-native "weeds" with them as well.

Not everything was transferred from Europe to the Americas. Native Americans gave the Europeans corn, potatoes, tomatoes, sugar, and later cotton and tobacco. And they gave them syphilis.

The horses and guns brought by the Spanish Explorers greatly changed life in early U.S. It made possible the near elimination of the buffalo and made skirmishes among different tribes of Native Americans and between them and the settlers much more deadly. Iron objects such as axes and plows greatly accelerated the destruction of many prairies and forests for lumber and farmland.

So early America was not "empty" and without man-made alterations, but the pace of change accelerated greatly after the Europeans "discovered" America.

Lessons from the Old Timers

Ever hear the phrase, "The older I get, the smarter my father gets"? I have always been in awe of how much folks in the 1800s and early 1900s knew and understood about the world around them. When you think of how much time most people back then had to spend every day just raising, gathering and preparing food, building shelters, and hundreds of other essential daily activities, it is amazing how much they learned about the world around them.

A friend recently sent me a copy of a Forestry Bulletin from 1904, entitled "The Timber of the Edwards Plateau of Texas: Its Relation to Climate, Water Supply and Soil," by William Bray. It is not that I learned that much about the Edwards Plateau from this 30-page report that is not well known to many people today, but that it was as well understood by some folks over a century ago. We tend to think that we are so much smarter than people back then with all of our modern education, books, electronic gadgets and all the time to read and learn.

Bray described the geology, topography and boundaries of the Edwards Plateau (EP) as thoroughly and accurately as anyone I have ever read. He considered the EP as the rainwater catchment area for all of the rivers that flow from the EP into south Texas and that make the latter region as productive as it is.

Bray understood the importance of vegetative cover, both grassland and woodland, in preventing erosion and discussed several places where trees, including cedar, were overharvested on the slopes of canyons which led to severe erosion, as well as the drying up of local springs and creeks. He described the sources of all of the rivers in the EP and even published the flow rates for a dozen springs and rivers as measured in December 1895!

Bray provided a general description of the EP as wooded canyons and grassland plateaus. He described the transformation from "prairie to timberland" in these words, "These ranges have been overpastured and the grass...has become unable to wage an equal fight against the shrubs...settlement has stopped the periodic burning of the grasses which...prevented the timber from gaining on the prairie."

Bray discussed cedar at some length, including its value for posts, poles, and building material as well as for firewood. In terms of cedar brakes, he wrote, "The writer knows of no region in which any species of cedar is so uniformly abundant and dominant as is the cedar in the limestone country of Texas."

Bray also quoted Howard Lacey, a rancher/naturalist on Turtle Creek in Kerr County, "Some of my own cedar was burned about five years ago and the ground is now covered with shin oak and Spanish oak sprouts…There is a vast quantity of cedar on the upper waters of the Frio, Nueces, Llano, Guadalupe and Medina rivers."

Bray discussed the importance of timber as a commercial product, saying, "A large part of the support of the hill country population comes from the sale of wood for fuel….Much is still handled at Marble Falls, Kerrville, Boerne" He was concerned that some places were being overharvested, saying, "So long as small owners depend…for their income upon the sale of wood, the temptation will be strong to denude rough, thin-soiled hillsides which would far better be kept with a protective timber covering."

We know that most of the cedar in the Hill Country today has grown up since the significant harvesting that took place in the late 1800s and early 1900s, or since the latest fire. Bray was concerned about fires too, saying, "There are few types of forest which more invite destruction by fire than the cedar brakes of dry central Texas."

Bray's biggest concern for loss of "timber," from either fire or harvesting, was that wherever trees are destroyed, the bare ground would be very much susceptible to erosion, loss of soil and therefore, loss of water holding capability. He said, "In the first place…trees break the force of the rain...further, debris of the forest floor holds back the fallen water…the spreading and interlacing network of roots…binds the soil fast against erosion."

What seems incredible to me, is that experts today are still working to teach and put into practice all of the lessons that were known to their predecessors over a century ago.

Fire in the Hill Country, the Good, the Bad and the Dangerous

Back before Europeans settled the Hill Country in the 1800s, there were two forces that dominated the landscape. Huge herds of migrating bison and wildfires that swept across the prairies periodically. It is estimated that these wildfires burned the grasslands on average every 5 to 7 years.

The fires were caused either by lightning or the Native Americans, who set fires because they knew that the new grass that would come up in a few weeks would attract lots of game.

These fires were the reason there were fewer woody plants back then because young woody saplings were killed in the grass fires. The recent encroachment of juniper is the result of having fewer fires than in the past. Fires also cause an increase in some species and a decrease in others, adding to the biodiversity. In addition, there is a fertilization effect as the ashes contain essential nutrients that would otherwise be limited.

Modern land managers are rediscovering fire as a tool to keep ashe juniper in check and to improve and maintain native habitat. These modern pasture fires are called "prescribed burns," and they are conducted only under certain conditions.

Prescribed burns are conducted by groups of people with training and experience under only certain weather conditions and only after thorough preparation of the site, including removing vegetation from the perimeter. Most people don't appreciate the fact that the intensity of a fire, the flame height, and the speed with which it moves are all greatly affected by the weather conditions.

High winds and low humidity make for exceedingly dangerous fires, while low winds and high humidity make for much more easily-managed fires. Prescribed burns are conducted only under conditions of low wind and high humidity and only after thorough preparation and planning and only with a team of experienced people. Anything else is not a prescribed burn.

Unfortunately, there are a lot of brush piles burned in the Hill Country, usually by the landowner or someone working for the landowner, frequently with only one or two people around to light the fires, and too frequently with little attention paid to weather conditions. We read about it in the newspaper when they get away from people and burn large areas, often their neighbor's property. Unfortunately, these wildfires are usually called "controlled burns" that got away. Well, if it got away, it wasn't "controlled!" But worse, many people confuse the term "controlled" with "prescribed." There is a huge difference between a prescribed burn and someone burning a brush pile; "controlled" burns are not "prescribed" burns.

What may surprise many people is that a large brush pile that has burned down to a pile of ashes and charred logs can still be smoldering for days, even weeks. It is not uncommon for someone to burn a large pile with no problem, only to go back to the ashes and stir it up with a tractor on a windy day and have the flying embers start a grass fire.

So how should brush piles be burned? The main thing is that it should only be done when the wind is low and predicted to stay that way. High humidity days are better than dry days. During a light rain or drizzle, or just after a heavy rain is best. A cell phone, a source of water, and a helper are nice to have also.

Even better, but more work, is to make a small pile of brush, light it, and feed it with the remainder of the brush one limb at a time. That way you have complete control of the size of the fire and if the wind comes up, you can stop feeding it. Finally, remember that a pile of ashes may still have live coals for many days after the fire.

Be careful out there.

The Effects of Modern Man on the Ecology of the Hill Country

Previously, I discussed what the Hill Country looked like before European settlers arrived in significant numbers. Now let's look at what changes have occurred since the arrival of these settlers of European ancestry.

Prior to 1800, Texas was populated mainly by Native Americans with only a very few early settlers. The Native Americans certainly had some effects on the Hill Country ecology. They started, intentionally or accidentally, grass fires, hunted many wild animals and cultivated a few small farms here and there. But their effects on the landscape were relatively minor, because of their relatively small numbers and their rather subsistence lifestyle.

Most of the settlers arriving in the Hill Country in the mid-1800s were either immigrants coming directly from Europe, mainly Germany, or people of European ancestry from the Southern US. They brought with them their knowledge and habits of agriculture based on land that had much deeper soil and higher rainfall than the Hill Country. And they brought with them their exotic animals, ones we now call cattle, sheep, goats, pigs and chickens.

Most of the early settlers were homesteaders who had little or no money, few possessions, only a few head of livestock, and relatively small plots of land, from which they had to provide everything for their families. It was not an easy life.

The few animals they had were crucial to their food supply, what little money they earned and to their quality of life in general. These animals were grazed continuously on their small plots of land and guarded carefully from predators. The animals' only food was what was grown on their land.

This continuous grazing changed the nature of the landscape, greatly reducing the amount of grass and changing the kinds of grass to lower quality species. The settlers also did everything they could to prevent or contain grass fires as fire not only threatened their homes and barns, but also burned up their animal feed.

The combination of continuous grazing and suppression of fire put in motion a change in the landscape as shorter grass, more bare ground and fewer fires gave rise to more woody plants becoming established in areas that were previously largely grasslands.

The settlers also cleared land for crops and gardens, hunted all sorts of wildlife to supplement their food stores, and killed every predator they could to protect their livestock.

As the number of settlers and livestock increased, their effects on the ecology became greater. The grass was overgrazed because of too many livestock allowed to graze the same areas continuously. With the introduction of barbed wire, all of these conditions became even more common. At the same time as the population of Texas was growing, there were commercial hunters operating from Texas to the Dakotas slaughtering the bison in large numbers, mostly just for the hides.

By the beginning of 20th century, raising livestock was intense and widespread in Texas, and economic conditions, including the depression and the dust bowl caused severe overgrazing of most of the state and the accompanying loss of soil in many areas. The result of all of this is that the land in most of Texas is considerably less productive than it was even as recently as the early 20th century.

Two things that did not happen in the Hill Country to nearly the extent they did in other parts of the state, are lumbering and farming. Because of the thin rocky soil, steep slopes and unreliable rainfall, the major activity that the Hill Country has seen has been ranching, and other than shorter, poorer quality grasses and more trees and cedar, it looks a lot like we think it did 150 years ago.

We will never get back to conditions of 150 years ago. That would require taking down all the fences, bringing back the bison, the wolves and other large predators, allowing fire to burn unhindered and, maybe most difficult, replacing the lost soil. But we are fortunate to live in an area less altered by man than most of the country.

I should also state that nothing I have described should be considered a criticism of our ancestors and their activities. They had a very hard life that required them to be constantly concerned about surviving the next winter. And they didn't have the knowledge we have gained in the last 50 years about how to best manage land in the Hill Country.

— SECTION II —

PLANTS

If asked to describe the Hill Country, I think the first thing most people would mention would be either the hills or the plants, with the other being the second thing they mention. It is not so much that the plants growing in the Hill Country are unique or that, for the most part, the plants growing native here cannot also be found in adjacent ecosystems in Texas. But there does seem to be something about the combination of trees, shrubs, forbs and grasses, together with the hills that defines the Hill Country as unique not only to Texas but to the rest of the country as well.

When Hill Country landowners talk about things they are doing to "manage" their "land," it is really the plants thereon that they are managing. Ranchers main activity, other than animal husbandry, is really growing grass. New small landowners nearly always want to grow new trees or shrubs and/or wildflowers, and maybe even more grass as part of their initial plans for their new property. Everyone is concerned when any of their mature trees appears to be dying. And of course, ever since Aldo Leopold wrote in the first half of the twentieth century, most writers define the "land" as the community of the soil, the water, the flora, the fauna and the people.

PLANT BIOLOGY

It helps to understand something about how plants work, how they carry out their functions, what their requirements are, what their limitations are, and what we can do to "manage" them. Most of us only see our native animals for fleeting amounts of time and then only occasionally, but we see the plants around us all the time. Plants are important.

Before I proceed, I should warn the readers that I am certainly not a professional biologist and the discussion here is decidedly the simplified, amateur version of biology. As alluded to in the Introduction, this section is intended as a "layman's" guide to basic biology, but I hope I have provided enough detail to help everyone understand the basics of Hill Country native habitats.

The Organization of All Life on Earth

Given the tremendous number of species of living things on Earth (about two million have been identified and scientists believe there are many more millions not yet discovered), it may seem surprising that all life can be grouped into only five or six categories, called Kingdoms.

You might be surprised to learn that the experts are not in total agreement as to how many different kingdoms of life there are—some lump different organisms into one kingdom while others put them into different kingdoms. And this layman is certainly not going to get into that discussion.

So for our simplified purposes most (but not all) life on earth can be thought of as being either a plant, an animal, a fungus, an alga, or a bacterium.

A single bacterium is a cell which is defined as a unit of living matter encased in a membrane which separates it from the outside world. All living things are composed of cells, but bacteria cells do not have a nucleus.

Algae are plant-like organisms that produce their own food by photosynthesis. Alga cells also contain chloroplasts where photosynthesis occurs.

Fungi include molds, yeasts and mushrooms. Fungi cannot make their own food like plants because they do not have chloroplasts with chlorophyll. Instead, most decompose the remains of dead organisms to obtain the food they need. Their cells also lack the cell wall structure that characterizes plants.

Plants are multi-cellular organisms that can photosynthesize carbohydrates from carbon dioxide in the air and water. Their cell walls are relatively rigid and made of cellulose, which makes for strong support, but a general lack of mobility.

Animals eat other organisms to obtain their food and energy and their cell walls are more flexible. This flexibility allows for easy movement, and most animals are mobile in search of food and mates.

Below each of these kingdoms is a hierarchy of subsequent classifications. One such classification system is a taxonomic rank from division, phylum, class, order, family, genus and finally species. For example, most of the plant kingdom is divided into the mosses, the ferns, the gymnosperms and the angiosperms.

The mosses (or Bryophytes) look somewhat like other plants, but structurally they are different in that they lack the vascular tissues xylem and phloem that transport water, minerals and sugars up and down all other plants. They do not form seeds and require moisture to reproduce.

Ferns have the vascular tissues of other plants and can support themselves. They also do not produce seeds and require moisture for reproduction, which is why both ferns and mosses are almost always found in moist, shady areas.

Ninety percent of all plant species produce seeds. A seed is an embryo and a food supply packaged into a protective covering, and because the seed can survive drier, harsher conditions than mosses and ferns, seed-producing plants have colonized most of the land. Seeds are produced after pollen fertilizes an egg.

Gymnosperms are non-flowering plants that produce seeds in cones. The name comes from Greek words for "naked" and "seed," and the seeds of conifers (cone-bearing plants) are not encased in a fruit. Think pines, firs, cypress, junipers, etc.

By far the largest group of plants, and the youngest in evolutionary history, are the angiosperms, which are all of the flowering plants. These plants produce their seeds in a "vessel" (Greek "angeion"), which we would call some kind of fruit (seed, berry, bean, acorn, nut, etc).

Both the gymnosperms and the angiosperms require pollination, in which pollen from a male part must be transported to a female stigma. This requires either wind or insects or other animals, but it also allows for a greater probability that the pollen will come from a different plant than the egg, thus giving rise to greater chances for genetic diversity.

The more we know, the more amazing Mother Nature is.

Ecological or Plant Succession: How Mother Nature Rearranges Her Landscape, and How We Are Involved

Think about a volcano emerging from the surface of the ocean and forming a new island, new land. At first there is no life of any kind on the island. Eventually, however, after the lava has cooled, there may be some bacteria or algae begin to grow on the lava at the edge of the water, and these microorganisms begin a very long, slow process of breaking down the rock.

As the algae and other simpler forms of life grow, die and decay, organic matter is added to the decomposed rock and we have the beginnings of soil. This is followed by the higher plants, some arriving at the island by sea, some in bird droppings. As the amount of vegetation increases, insects blown by the wind and other small animals arriving on drifting seaweed begin to colonize the island. The pace of change increases as larger and larger plants and animals become established and the amount of soil increases, and eventually you have Hawaii, or Trinidad or Puerto Rico, with trees and jungles.

This process is called "primary plant succession," and it has gone on and continues to go on everywhere. Plant succession is the natural process by which one group of plants succeeds or takes over from another group. When this process stops and the plant composition remains stable, it used to be referred to as the "climax plant community." That plant community will continue until some major event (climate change or major natural or human activity) occurs in the environment that changes which plant(s) are favored over others. If this occurs, secondary plant succession will begin and may take the community in a different direction.

Before Europeans arrived in large numbers in the Hill Country, we had more open grasslands with fewer trees than we do now, at least on the flatter highlands. The grasslands were made up of a larger percentage of taller grasses such as little bluestem, big bluestem, yellow indiangrass and switchgrass, and these grasses were grazed by large herds of bison on a regular, but infrequent, basis. These grasslands also burned every few years, caused by either lightning or the Native Americans. This was the climax plant community prior to the early 1800s.

When the European settlers moved in, they brought livestock with them which grazed the same area constantly, thus greatly reducing the amount and species composition of the grass, and they fought fires with all their might. This changed the area from one where the grasses were denser and larger and burned every few years, which kept the numbers of trees and shrubs controlled, to one of smaller, less dense grasses with fewer fires, thus allowing woody plants to increase in number. This human-induced change in the environment caused secondary plant succession to take the Hill Country from one with many areas of open grasslands to more savanna-like areas with significant woody plant populations.

But it turns out that cedar is more capable of expanding into this new environment than hardwoods are, and so the percentage of cedar has increased, relative to hardwoods. And to exacerbate things further, in more recent times, say the 1960s to the present, the significant increase in white-tailed deer populations, again caused by man's activities, has shifted the plant succession yet again to slow the regeneration of hardwoods, but allow the cedar to increase largely unchecked, thus our current cedar overabundance.

But we have found that the cheapest and most effective way to keep cedar under control, once an area has been cleared of the larger bushes, is to conduct periodic (every 5-10 years) prescribed burns. Prescribed burns are very effective in killing small (3' or less) cedar bushes and keeping once-cleared areas free of cedar, and to a lesser extent, hardwoods also.

In other words, man's activities caused the encroachment of cedar in the first place by altering the environment, allowing plant succession to take the landscape in a different direction, and now we are reversing the process by reintroducing fire where it had once been largely eliminated and again allowing plant succession to change the landscape more to our liking.

You may argue whether all of this is good, bad, or inevitable, but it does tell us a lot about how to manage land to achieve our desired result. Or as Aldo Leopold famously observed, habitat "can be restored by the creative use of the same tools which have heretofore destroyed it- ax, cow, plow, fire and gun."

The main point being that this is just one example of where man can work with Mother Nature to achieve our desired result.

How Does a Tree Work?

Have you ever stopped to think about what goes on inside a tree? We know that the roots of a tree take up water and minerals from the soil and transport them to the leaves where some of the water is used in photosynthesis to combine with carbon dioxide from the air to make sugars, starches and cellulose.

But the roots are 30 feet below the top of the average Hill Country tree, and there are many trees that are several times that tall. How does the water get up to the leaves? Trees don't have hearts. They don't really even have a closed circulatory system. So how does it work?

Just under the bark of a tree are three structures that are involved with the transportation of fluids within the tree. The outermost structure is the phloem (pronounced flow-em), just inside of that is the cambium and then the xylem. The xylem and the phloem structures are made up of many long cells connected end to end in a chain that reaches from the roots to the leaves and which form rings of living tissue just under the bark.

The xylem, running from the finest root hairs to the tallest leaf is where water and minerals from the soil are transported to the leaf. But how does it get there? If we were designing such a system, we would use a pump, which would require an external energy source. The tree doesn't have a pump.

It turns out that there is an unbroken column of water from the roots to the top leaf, from one xylem cell to another all the way to the top. The water molecules are attached to each other in this column of water by adhesive and cohesive molecular forces. On the underside of the leaves are microscopic structures called stoma which open and close with temperature and humidity and from which droplets of water evaporate.

When a water molecule evaporates from a leaf, in a process called evapotranspiration, its place is taken up by the next molecule below it, which pulls up the molecule below it by capillary pressure and so on and so on all the way down to the roots. Thus water flows from the roots to the leaves through the xylem cells.

When the leaves make carbohydrates from carbon dioxide and water, not all of this material is used to make starches and cellulose for the leaves. The roots have to grow too, and they can't make their own carbohydrates. So sugar solution made in the leaves (sap) is transported down to the roots through the phloem structures under the bark. The sugar molecules are the building blocks for starches and cellulose, the former being energy stores and the latter being structural components (wood) of the plant.

How does a tree make its first leaves of spring when it doesn't have any leaves as yet to carry out photosynthesis? The answer is that sugars are transported from where they were stored in the roots for the winter back up the phloem to make the new leaves. So at different times, sugar solution can flow both directions in the phloem. How does it do that?

The energy to drive that process is called osmotic pressure, in which water in the xylem flows into cells with high sugar concentrations, forcing the sugar solution into the phloem which then flows through the phloem into cells with lower sugar solutions. Thus sugar is transported from areas of high concentration to areas of low concentration. In the summer and fall the leaves have higher concentrations of sugar than the roots, but in the early spring the roots have the higher concentration, and these concentration gradients drive the flow of sap from where it is not needed to where it is.

By the way, the process of storage of starches in the roots is where we get our potatoes, carrots, radishes, turnips and beets, and the sap flow in early spring gives us maple syrup.

Most of the growth of trees is at the tip of the branches as the tree grows taller and longer branches. But the trunks also grow a little in diameter each year as older xylem becomes sapwood and older phloem becomes bark and are replaced by new layers produced in the cambium. This process is revealed in the growth rings of trees.

The Chemistry of Photosynthesis and the Carbon Cycle

Photosynthesis

$$6\,CO_2 + 6\,H_2O + \text{Sunlight} = C_6H_{12}O_6 + 6\,O_2$$

Carbon Dioxide | Water | Glucose | Oxygen

Combustion or Decay

$$C_6H_{12}O_6 + 6\,O_2 = 6\,CO_2 + 6\,H_2O + \text{Heat}$$

Chemical equations for photosynthesis and combustion and decay.

Don't be alarmed by the chemical equations accompanying this column, you don't need to understand the chemistry. But it is important that everyone understand the basics of photosynthesis and how carbon is cycled and recycled in the ecosystem.

First photosynthesis:

All green plants have a form of chlorophyll. It is a chemical compound that enables (or catalyzes) the conversion of carbon dioxide in the air and water plus sunlight into carbohydrates. The chlorophyll isn't used up in the process, but without it carbon dioxide and water would not react to form carbohydrates.

You will notice in the chemical equation for photosynthesis, oxygen is the byproduct of that chemical reaction. In fact, this is the process that produced oxygen for the first time on the young Earth, and the reason why animals could not have evolved until enough green plants produced enough oxygen for animals to live.

The chemical equation I have included shows the product of photosynthesis to be glucose. Glucose is a simple carbohydrate also known as a sugar. It is also a major building block for all other carbohydrates; sugars, starches and celluloses. All of these larger and more complex molecules are made up of glucose and glucose-like molecules strung together in different ways.

Sunlight is essential to make photosynthesis work—plants can only produce glucose in the daylight. And it is the light energy from the sun that is stored in the carbohydrate molecules that drives just about all living ecosystems. It is the energy stored in the carbohydrate molecules (cellulose) in the trunk of a tree that is released when the tree is cut down and burned.

Burning, or combustion, is a process of reacting oxygen with carbon-containing materials to produce carbon dioxide and water, plus the heat that is produced when burning. You will note that the reaction for combustion is exactly the reverse of the photosynthesis reaction.

So the simple carbon cycle is for green plants to capture the energy from the sun to produce carbohydrates from carbon dioxide and water, using chlorophyll to enable the reaction. Then the stored energy in the carbohydrates can be released when a carbohydrate is burned (combusted) or even digested or decayed. Digestion and decay are the same reaction as combustion, just slower and more controlled.

When a corn plant grows from a seed it uses photosynthesis to make the stems and leaves and kernels. When we eat the corn, our bodies get energy by the digestion process in which the starch is converted back into glucose and then into carbon dioxide and water. When the corn plant dies and decays, the same process takes place, although at a much slower pace. If the farmer burns the corn stalks in a still to make moonshine, he gets the energy trapped in the carbohydrates of the stalks.

The corn is thus a source of what we would call renewable energy, because the carbon dioxide and water produced in the burning process (well, not exactly the same molecules) can be used next year in the photosynthesis process to grow more corn, and this process can continue, theoretically, forever.

But if instead of using the corn stalks for fuel, the farmer uses coal, or oil or natural gas, then the farmer is using a non-renewable fuel. Non-renewable because the formation of these "fossil fuels" required millions of years and complex geologic activity to convert carbohydrates from ancient plants and animals into these carbon-based fossil fuels. This long-term heat and pressure over millions of years caused a chemical transformation in which the carbohydrates were stripped of much of their oxygen, forming what we call hydrocarbons, a different class of compounds that are not found in significant quantities in living organisms.

Since the formation of these fossil fuels takes many orders of magnitude longer times than anything on a human time-scale, they are not considered renewable and thus their use is a one-time thing. Once they are burned, they are gone, but the carbon dioxide and water formed in the combustion is added permanently back to the Earth's atmosphere.

This is obviously an over-simplified picture of the carbon cycle. It doesn't account for conversion of small amounts of carbohydrates into proteins, fats and other compounds in plants and animal bodies. We use all of these food types to provide the energy to run our bodies and keep us warm, and then we exhale carbon dioxide and water with every breath as we "burn" our calories.

Seeds: The Most Important Part of the Plant

Think about this. A very tiny (sometimes as small as the period at the end of this sentence) collection of chemicals arranged in certain ways somehow manages to survive without rotting, degrading or decomposing for very long periods of time, but when conditions become just right, changes occur in the structure of this tiny seed and a living green plant is produced. More specifically, here is what happens.

The seed coat which has kept water from entering the seed and causing it to rot while in its dormant state has to crack, weaken, thin or otherwise begin allowing water to seep into the seed. As the seed adsorbs water and the cells begin to expand, chemical reactions begin to take place to rearrange the molecules in the seed into other types of chemicals that make up roots and shoots.

The seed must push aside some soil and produce a tiny root to allow it to adsorb even more water before it can begin to form a shoot. It must then produce a small shoot which it sends through the soil up to the surface and then produce one or two tiny green leaves.

It is true that under certain conditions truly ancient seeds have been discovered in dry caves and tombs that have been found to be viable hundreds or even thousands of years later. Those are of course extreme examples, but it is not unusual to observe grasses or forbs sprouting in areas where the seeds must have been several years old. Considering the amount of genetic material, food and energy reserves stored in those tiny seeds, you have to marvel at how truly amazing Mother Nature is.

It also means, however, that if we want to have this kind of bounty in the future, we should do whatever we can to make sure that this year's seeds are allowed to mature and survive. In order for seed production to result in successful germination, several things must happen. First the flower has to be pollinated, otherwise the seed will not be fertile. Then the seed must stay on the plant until it is mature. Then the seeds must be distributed around to different locations. Finally, the seed must come in contact with mineral soil and survive without being eaten by birds or insects, or rotting, until conditions are right for germination.

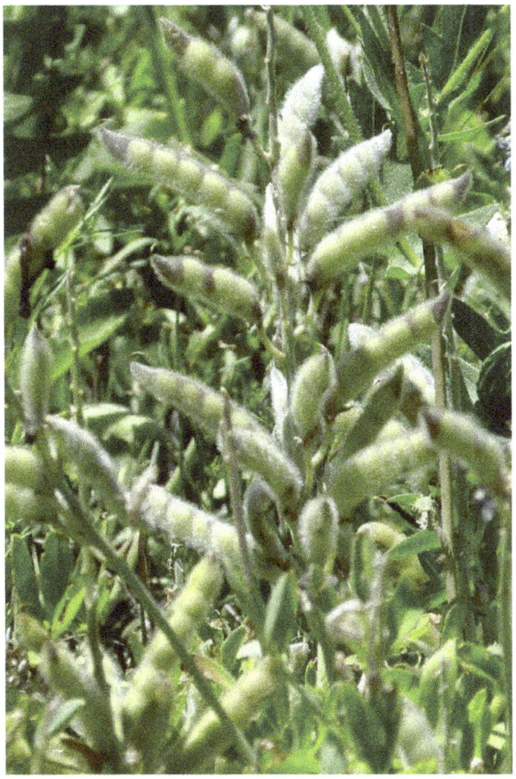

Immature bluebonnet seeds maturing in the sun. They are legumes in the pea family.

There is not much that we can do about the latter steps, but we can have some influence on the early steps. For those many species of flowers that require pollination by insects, we can refrain from using excessive insecticides so that there will be plenty of insects around to do the work. Some plants can be pollinated by hummingbirds and other animals.

We can refrain from mowing or cutting off seed heads before the seeds are mature, but we don't always know how long that takes. In May some of the early-blooming plants such as bluebonnets and Texas wintergrass are about finished blooming and have set seed, but the seeds are not mature yet. So the safest thing to do is to let the seeds mature on the plant until they appear to be ready to fall off naturally. For many wildflowers, this may mean late in the year when the leaves of the plant are turning brown and falling off, which may be later than many people are willing to tolerate. But the longer the seeds stay on the plant, the greater probability that the seeds will be mature. Furthermore, the longer you leave the plant unmowed or uncut, the greater chance birds or other small animals will harvest the seeds for you and, best of all, distribute them widely.

Of course, if you want to distribute seeds over certain areas to get more of the plant where you want it, the most successful way to do it is to watch the seed head and when the seed structures appear to readily come off, you can gently pull them off and then scatter the seeds where you wish. This works well with grasses as well as most wildflowers. When you are scattering seeds, it is important to get the seeds to make direct contact with mineral soil (by putting them on bare soil and stepping on them), not just throwing them onto dried leaves, as the latter will just rot or be eaten.

Mother Nature is always interesting and never boring.

Leaves: Common, Complex, and Essential to Life as We Know It

Ask someone what the first word is that comes to mind when you say the word "leaf," and the great majority will say "green." And with good reason. When you look at the countryside, when you look at the trees, the shrubs, the grass, the forbs, what you see is green, at least for most of the year. When you think of spring, you think of brown turning to green.

The substance in the leaves that gives them their green color is chlorophyll. And the chlorophyll is important not because it is green, but because of the function it performs within the leaves, which makes it essential to virtually all life on earth as we know it.

So even if you never eat any green leaves, or if you are an obligate carnivore, your life still depends on leaves and their chlorophyll to make carbohydrates which power most all life on earth.

Even in a simple Texas redbud leaf, complex processes are occurring all the time.

The underside of most leaves contains microscopic structures called "stoma" which are tiny openings into which carbon dioxide from the air can enter the interior of the leaf and also excess water can evaporate in a process called evapotranspiration. The excess oxygen produced in the photosynthesis reaction also escapes from the stoma. Essentially, leaves can "breathe."

The size of the openings can be controlled by the leaf to let more or less carbon dioxide in and to release more or less water, depending on what the plant needs at any one time. So leaves may be smarter than you thought they were.

In the fall, when deciduous plants stop making chlorophyll, the green of the leaf will disappear. For many trees and other plants that show fall color, the color of other components in the leaf will then dominate and the leaf may appear to be yellow, red or some combination of those colors. Once those colors also disappear the leaf will usually appear some shade of brown.

The final step in the life of most deciduous leaves is for the attachment of the leaf to the twig or stem to break and the leaf will fall.

Then in the spring, for woody deciduous plants, when the conditions for that plant to resume growth occur, carbohydrates stored throughout the winter in the roots will be brought up the phloem structures in the trunks and branches to swell the buds formed the previous year and the growth of new leaves begins.

All of this happens in an organism with no brain or nervous system and with no help from us. Just another wonderful example of Mother Nature at work, without which virtually all life on Earth would cease.

Trees Losing Their Leaves in the Fall: A Natural Life Cycle of Plants

Our native woody plants (trees and shrubs) fall into two categories: evergreen and deciduous, the latter means they lose their leaves in the winter and then put on new growth on last year's stems. The majority of our woody species are in fact deciduous, but that doesn't mean they all behave the same.

The timing of leaf drop and of growing back new leaves varies from species to species as well as with the length of daylight, temperature and moisture, and even within those conditions, there is some variation among individual plants.

Some examples of species differences: Buckeyes (Texas, red and yellow) usually lose their leaves in August or early September. Walnuts start losing their leaves in September and are bare before most of our other trees begin to lose leaves. Then in the spring, elbowbush usually blooms in early February and puts out leaves shortly after that, which is why it is also called spring herald.

Spanish oak (Texas red oak) leaves turning red in the fall before falling off.

Of course, most of our deciduous trees lose their leaves in November and December with a lot of overlap among the species depending on weather conditions. The leaf color changes are caused by hormones reacting to length of daylight causing a reduction in chlorophyll production. When the green chlorophyll production ceases, the yellow pigments that are always in the leaf begin to show and a new red pigment is produced, thus giving us our fall colors. Once photosynthesis stops because of the absence of chlorophyll, other processes are triggered which cause the leaves to break away from the branches.

Of course, not all of our native trees and shrubs lose their leaves in the winter. Cedar (Ashe juniper) is obviously evergreen. Evergreen native shrubs include Texas mountain laurel, evergreen sumac, yaupon, cenizo, agarita, Texas madrone, and, some years, Texas persimmon and willow baccharis.

I left off live oak from the above list because, technically, it is not evergreen, but is semi-evergreen. It does lose its leaves every year, but in the spring, not in the fall, and the new leaves begin emerging at the same time as the old leaves fall, so the tree is leafless for only a very short time if at all. Mexican white oak is likewise semi-evergreen, although it undergoes leaf exchange a little earlier in the spring than do live oaks.

One might ask why are some trees deciduous and others evergreen? In areas farther north where the ground freezes, roots cannot grow to find water, and if the trees kept their leaves and continued to lose water from their leaves, the trees would wilt and die. Also, the cells of most tree leaves would be damaged if the water in them were to freeze. And finally, most deciduous trees are shaped in such a way that if they had leaves on in the winter, the weight of the snow would break their limbs.

So that raises another question: how do evergreen trees survive the winter? They have several characteristics which enable them to do so. Many evergreen trees have a waxy coating on the surface of the leaves to prevent loss of water during the winter. Others have cells with high concentrations of sugar which act as an antifreeze to prevent the cells from being damaged. Most of the evergreen trees in more northern locations are gymnosperms (pines, spruce, etc.) which have very fine needles with coatings and a limb structure that sheds snow.

The really amazing part of all of this is that it is the DNA within each cell of the tree that is programmed to produce certain structure types and certain hormones, and the hormones react to conditions of light, temperature and moisture, thus triggering changes in different cells that stop the production of certain chemicals and start the production of others. And, apparently, all the cells in every leaf of the tree undergo these changes at about the same time in an organism that has no brain and no nervous system.

And in the spring, the little bud produced last year has all the programming in its DNA to "know" when and how to begin making a new leaf and begin the process all over again. And for some trees, this process has been going on for literally hundreds of years—all programmed by the DNA in the original acorn or seed.

What Makes the Leaves Change Color?

People frequently ask, "What causes the leaves to change color?" It turns out it is a really complicated sequence of events that cause deciduous trees and shrubs to turn from various shades of green to yellow, orange, and/or red, or just brown.

Throughout most of the spring, summer and early fall, most leaves have high amounts of a group of chemical compounds called chlorophyll. All of this group of compounds are green which give the leaves their color. The general structures of chlorophyll molecules are somewhat similar to the hemoglobin molecule except hemoglobin contains iron while the chlorophyll has magnesium in its place.

In the fall, as the length of daylight decreases and nighttime increases, something in the leaves of plants causes the photosynthesis and the manufacture of chlorophyll to slow down and to eventually stop.

As the green color fades, the color of another group of compounds, called the carotenoids, which have been in the leaves all the time, become visible, and these compounds are yellow or orange. These are the pigments that make corn and bananas yellow and carrots orange.

As the chlorophyll production declines, it triggers the production of another group of compounds, called the anthocyanins. These compounds are various shades of red, and are what gives color to red apples, strawberries and cherries.

So, to greatly oversimplify the whole process of fall color change, as the hours of nighttime increase, it signals to the leaves it is time to start shutting down photosynthesis and chlorophyll production and increasing the production of anthocyanins. This changes the color of the leaves from green to some mixture or combination of yellow, orange and red, and the relative amounts of these other colored pigments determine the exact shade of a leaf.

It is a common belief that weather, freeze dates, and/or rainfall determine the time of fall color. In fact, the predominant determinant of the timing of both fall color and of leaf drop is the length of daylight and darkness. Temperature and rainfall can have a secondary effect on timing and on the exact balance of the fall color pigments, and thus cause slightly different colors in different years. Also, different species of trees and shrubs have different relative amounts of these pigments, and so react slightly differently to increasing nighttime hours.

So in a woodland with different species of trees, you can expect to see different colors on any given day and perhaps a few days later see another collection of different colors. Bright sunny fall days with cool nights tend to give rise to more vivid colors. Also, there is always a slight variation among individual trees in terms of both timing and color.

Because day length is a function of latitude, the days get shorter in the north earlier than they do here, (In the late fall we have over an hour more daylight than Minnesota) which is the main reason leaves turn colors earlier in the north.

As the process of shutting down photosynthesis and chlorophyll production continues in the leaves, the veins of the leaves begin closing off, and at some time the structure at the base of the leaf petiole (stem that attaches the leaf to the twig) dries up and that is what causes the leaves to fall. As the pigments fade, the leaves turn brown when there are no pigments to give color.

How Do Trees Without Leaves Make New Leaves in the Spring?

When a tree begins to produce the first small leaves of spring, where does the material for these first leaves come from? Before there are any leaves, no photosynthesis can occur and thus no carbohydrates are being produced. So how can a tree without leaves make leaves?

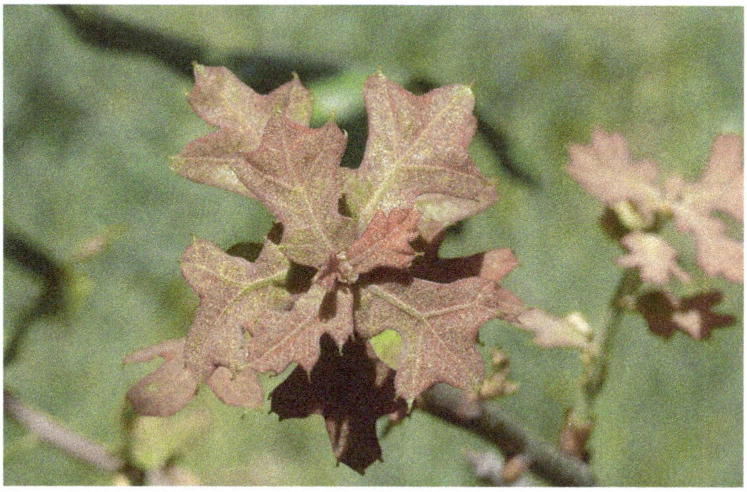

Tiny new spring leaves on a blackjack oak.

The answer is that some of the smaller carbohydrate molecules such as sugars and starches were stored in the tree, mainly in the roots, during the previous summer and fall, and it is these stored non-structural carbohydrates that travel up the tree and out into the buds to become the first green leaves of spring. And for species that bloom early in the spring, much of the material of the blooms also comes from this same source of stored sugars and starches.

This process is not unique to trees either. Similar processes occur in all other perennial deciduous plants including grasses, forbs and shrubs.

This also explains why droughts during the summer and fall limit the amount of sugars and starches produced (remember, water is essential for photosynthesis), but the effect may not be obvious in the plants until the following spring.

It is important to note that photosynthesis is the source of energy that makes all of our lives possible. The raw materials for photosynthesis, carbon dioxide and water, are low energy compounds that cannot be used by plants or animals to maintain life. Only when energy from the sun is captured to make high energy compounds (carbohydrates), using chlorophyll as the catalyst, do we have an energy source that can sustain plant and animal life on Earth.

So everything you had for breakfast this morning either came directly from a plant via photosynthesis (the carbohydrates) or via subsequent conversion to fats and proteins either in the plant or, if you ate an animal product, in the animal that ate the plants.

And when you take a deep breath, it is only because of photosynthesis that there is oxygen in the air.

The Underground World of Roots

I have written before about the inner working of leaves, the most obvious part of plants that we are most familiar with. Here I want to discuss roots, the least familiar part of plants for most of us.

In general, roots have three functions: holding the plant firmly in the ground, absorbing water and minerals for the whole plant, and producing hormones. Without the first, trees and flowers and even grass would fall over and be blown around by the wind. Without the second function, none of the normal biological processes the plant needs to live, grow and reproduce would be possible. Among the hormones produced by the roots are cytokinin and gibberellin, necessary for shoot growth and development.

One specialized function of roots in some species of plants such as carrots, beets and radishes, is the unusually large amount of carbohydrate storage in the roots—the parts we eat.

Roots of different species of plants tend to have different structures. Most dicots (broad-leaved woody and herbaceous plants) tend to have a single root that grew from the embryo as the seed germinated, and that is called the taproot. Some taproots are much larger than all other branching or lateral roots, while some are no larger than the lateral roots. In many such plants, the underground root system has a structure similar to the above-ground portion of the plant with a main stem and branches.

For monocots (grasses, lilies, palms) the growth of the roots begins at the base of the leaves, not with the embryonic root, and these roots do not in general branch, but each grows down from the surface of the ground. These roots are called "adventitious roots" which make up a fibrous root system with a mass of roots extending from the ground deep into the soil.

Most of the adsorption of water and minerals that occurs in the root system of a plant does not take place in either the taproot, the lateral roots or the fibrous roots, but rather in the tiny root hairs that branch off from the other, much larger, roots. These tiny root hairs can be one tenth or less the size of the larger roots. They may also have a much shorter lifespan and are replaced often.

In order for roots to grow, the tips must push their way through the soil, mostly into the pores between soil particles. This "movement" through the soil occurs because a section of root cells just behind the root tip absorbs more water and expands in size, pushing the tip forward. The very tip of the growing root has hardened cells that can keep it from wearing away as it is pushed through the soil.

The roots of most species of plants have a symbiotic association, called mycorrhizae, with soil fungi. The fungi grow tiny thread-like cells called hyphae into the roots which carry phosphorus into the roots, which gives the roots much more of this essential element than they could absorb from the soil without the fungi. The fungi get sugar produced by the plant which it needs to live.

Another symbiotic relationship exists in the root zone of legumes such as beans, peas, mesquite, alfalfa and clover. These are frequently called nitrogen-fixing plants, but it is not the plants that have the unusual ability to "fix" nitrogen. (Elemental nitrogen is obviously omnipresent in the air, but plants cannot utilize nitrogen in that form—only in the forms of nitrate, nitrite or ammonia.) But there is a soil bacterium, called Rhizobium, that can indeed "fix" nitrogen and supply the plants with which they associate with useable nitrogenous compounds. It does so by invading parts of the roots of legumes and forming nodules in the roots that contain nitrogen in forms the plant can use. And the bacterium receives sugars from the plant.

From the foregoing it should be obvious that healthy soil fungi and bacteria are essential, along with other soil organisms, for healthy plants, and in turn healthy plants are essential for a healthy soil. If we do what we can to help the above ground vegetation, we will also help the below-ground parts as well.

Legumes: An Interesting, Important, Diverse Family of Plants

The Legume family has many interesting properties and is represented by over twenty different species of Hill Country plants.

The scientific or Latin name for this family is Fabaceae, and is also known as the Pea family. In Texas, Legumes are the third largest plant family after the Aster or Sunflower family and the Grass family. Flowering plants are classified and placed in families by scientists according to the, sometimes minute, structures of the flowers so the general appearance of the plants as a whole may have little in common with other members of the family.

The most easily recognized characteristic of the Pea family is that its seeds are enclosed in a "pod" composed of two halves which split apart when dry. Think sweet peas, black-eyed peas, or green beans.

From an agricultural and nutritional standpoint, the most important characteristic of almost all legumes is that they have associated with their roots bacteria called Rhizobia that have the ability to "fix" nitrogen.

This ability of the bacteria associated with the roots to make nitrogen readily available to the plant explains why legumes tend to have a higher protein content than other plants. We, and all other animals, need plant protein to survive, obtained either directly from the plants or indirectly by eating animals which eat plants.

When legumes die, the nitrogen "fixed" by the bacteria in the soil, as well as the nitrogen in the plant's tissues becomes available for subsequent plant growth in crop rotation. This is how legumes enrich the soil for subsequent crops, saving on the use of synthetic fertilizers. Legumes are sometimes called "green manure" for that reason.

Most anything we would call a bean or a pea or a lentil is a legume, including all of the different peas and beans we find in the grocery store, but also including soybeans (worldwide the species produced in greatest amount). Likewise, the very closely related species of clovers, vetches and alfalfa are legumes.

A single odd pinnately compound leaf of a Texas mountain laurel with 9 leaflets.

One, perhaps surprising, member of the legume family is the peanut. The plant blooms above ground, but then forces the growing fruit below ground where it matures to contain, usually, two "seeds" which we call peanuts, inside a "pod" which we call the shell.

Some native wildflowers that are legumes include, but are certainly not limited to the following: Illinois bundleflower, sensitive briar, two-leaved senna, Lindheimer's senna, partridge pea, Texas bluebonnet, scarlet pea, scurf-pea, black dalea, purple dalea, milk vetch.

Other than the pea-like "pod," the other characteristic of Legumes that is easy to note is that most, but certainly not all, have compound leaves. The leaves of plants are classified as either simple or compound. A simple leaf is a single leaf that is attached to a stem or twig. A pinnately compound leaf has the appearance of many pairs of simple leaves attached to opposite sides of a stem, usually with a single leaf at the end. In fact, these are leaflets and the whole collection of these pairs of leaflets along the stem is part of a single compound leaf. Think mesquite or Texas mountain laurel.

One has to keep in mind that everything in biology or botany doesn't fit in neat little boxes with no exceptions. Not all legumes can fix nitrogen. Not everything that bears a fruit called a pod is a legume.

Not every legume has compound leaves, and not everything with compound leaves is a legume. But if I see something that makes what looks like a bean pod, I am certainly going to suspect it is a legume, and if it has compound leaves the odds are even better.

Lichens and Other Things That Grow on Trees

Lichens, made up of fungi and algae can come in many different shapes and colors. These are on a live oak branch.

Lichens are composite organisms made up of a fungus and usually a green alga, or sometimes a cyanobacterium. Many different species of fungi and different species of algae may combine into a number of different shapes and colors of lichens. They can be found in rainforests, on the arctic tundra, and in deserts. They can be found growing on rocks, trees, soil, and even roofs.

Fungi are characterized as organisms that lack chlorophyll and thus cannot carry out photosynthesis. Think molds, mildew, mushrooms and yeasts. Algae, on the other hand do contain chlorophyll and can convert carbon dioxide from the air into carbohydrates, but unlike higher plants, they do not have leaves, stems or roots.

When this complex association is formed, the alga produce the carbohydrates needed for life for both partners, and the fungus surround the alga protecting it and helping to capture and retain water. The resulting lichen may then take on shapes, forms, colors and characteristics different from either of the two partners.

Most of the lichens seen growing on rocks are flat, thin growths that sometimes can be mistaken for patches of paint, and they can be many different colors. Growths on tree limbs and trunks tend to look like flat wavy leaves, highly-branched fine hair-like bunches or any of many different shapes and colors as well.

Lichens need sunlight, but not necessarily full sun. They are not only able to tolerate extreme ranges of temperature, but also can survive being severely desiccated and then recover when wetted again. Lichens can be very long-lived. They are epiphytes, meaning they obtain all of their requirements from rain and the air and get no nutrition or water from the substrate on which they are growing. When growing on rocks, however, they may decompose small amounts of rock in an extremely slow process which can be the beginnings of converting rocks into soil. Their presence on tree trunks or limbs does not harm the tree in any way. When viewed close-up, some of them can be quite beautiful and interesting, and I think add character to our oak trees.

Speaking of epiphytes, the common ball moss found usually on the lower limbs of trees is another plant that does not get any nourishment or water from the tree. It likes areas with low sunlight, protected from the wind and areas of high humidity, which is why it is frequently found on the lower limbs of oak trees. Many people see the ball moss growing on dead or dying lower limbs and assume the ball moss killed the limb, but this is a mistake of assigning cause and effect. Lower limbs of big trees are so shaded from the sun that the lower limbs frequently die from lack of sunlight, just as all of the limbs close to the ground when the tree was a sapling died.

Once you see ball moss growing on fence wires and telephone wires it is easier to understand that the plant does not get anything from the tree limb except a place to grow. Ball moss is not actually a moss, but a flowering plant. Spanish moss, its cousin, and some other bromeliads are also epiphytes, not parasites.

Mistletoe, on the other hand, is not an epiphyte, but what is classified as a hemi-parasite. Mistletoe grows a root-like structure called a haustorium directly into the limb of a tree and absorbs water and some minerals from the host tree. However, it is also capable of making its own carbohydrates by photosynthesis, so it is not totally dependent on the host for all of its nutrients.

Mistletoe has smooth, opposite, leathery, evergreen leaves. Male and female flowers are produced on different plants and the female produces white to translucent berries. The plant is poisonous to humans if eaten, but birds seem to like the berries, and then participate in dispersing the seeds.

While mistletoe can damage a limb to the point of killing the limb, it would be a very unusual event for the parasite to kill a whole tree. Just cutting off the green part will not necessarily kill the mistletoe; but cutting the limb off some distance from it will. (Don't forget to immediately paint an oak limb)

This past Christmas season, I heard that because of the drought mistletoe was in short supply and was selling for $25 for a little piece!

Galls: Strange Growths on Trees and Other Plants

I have discussed lichens, ball moss and other things that grow on trees. Galls don't fit in that category because they are not things that grow ON trees, but rather abnormal growths that are part OF the tree.

A collection of several different galls found on local trees.

The most commonly seen around here are small round brown balls on oak tree twigs, but there are many different forms and colors of galls and they are not limited to oaks or even to trees—galls can be found on flowers, shrubs and even vegetables.

Galls are not like tumors that are caused by an abnormality in the cells of the plant such as caused by a cell mutation. Galls are caused by external agents. Most often galls are caused by insects, although fungi and bacteria can also cause some galls.

Most commonly, galls are caused by a tiny (1-8 millimeters) gall wasp or gall fly of the genus *Cynipidae*. When the wasp pierces a part of the tree in order to lay its egg, something in this process apparently induces the tree hormones in the locality of the sting to cause abnormal growth, and it is this abnormal growth that results in the gall. The insect is really looking for a host on which to lay its egg, and the egg becomes encased in the gall.

Galls are generally composed of resins, tannins and cellulose, and it is this material that becomes the food for the growing larva. The larva will eventually emerge from the gall as a gall wasp and the life cycle will repeat itself. When fresh, galls are solid and fairly hard. Once the larva emerges what is usually left is a light, hollow shell.

The gall wasps usually find fast-growing tissue such as new spring growth to lay their eggs. This may be because the new growth is softer, but it is also the part of the plant that is growing the fastest and thus has the most growth hormones. There are an estimated 800 species of gall wasp in North America. Most of them only form galls on specific tree species and only on specific parts of that tree. And it appears that the size, shape and color of the gall is unique to a particular species of wasp laying eggs on a particular part of a particular species of tree.

The accompanying photograph shows several different types of dark brown galls. The small gall on the underside of a live oak leaf was obviously formed this year, as was the large (1-inch diameter) light-tan galls. One of the latter was split open (it's quite hard) and you can see the small larva in the center.

Interestingly, a few years ago, for the first time in 12 years, we had a large number of the large light tan galls growing on blackjack oaks. They were large enough and light enough in color to be conspicuous. Many are now falling off. They are all growing on the cup of the much smaller (next year's) acorns—not on twigs or on the acorns, just on the cups.

There are tiny parasitic wasps that find galls and deposit their own eggs in the gall. The new larva then consumes the original larva and the rest of the gall as well.

While most of the galls I have seen in this area were on oak trees, and oaks are apparently more likely to have galls than other trees, it would be misleading the leave the impression that all galls are on trees. The next most common place to find galls is not on twigs (or acorns) but on the underside of leaves. This type of gall can be found on just about any kind of vegetation and usually looks like a collection of bumps or warts or balls stuck to the underside of the leaf. They can often be mistaken for a bunch of insect eggs, but if you try to scrape them off you will find the are indeed not something attached to the leaf, but are part of the leaf—galls.

While it may appear that these growths are detrimental to the plants, most galls, and certainly those on trees, represent such a tiny fraction of the biomass of the tree that their effect is insignificant. Some galls, formed by fungi, especially on crops, are indeed destructive.

CEDAR (ASHE JUNIPER)

Probably one of the first land management decisions many new landowners make is what to do with cedar (Ashe juniper). This is likely because by the time someone spends much time in the Hill Country looking for a property to buy, they have seen a lot of places that are overgrown with cedar and have had several people tell them how awful and invasive cedar is and how if they get rid of it the land will revert to its natural state and they will have springs begin to flow.

This leads some new landowners to do things they may regret later when they find out that much of the things they have heard are exaggerated, distorted, over-simplified views about cedar. It is a more complicated subject than many people realize. Hopefully the following will help everyone understand cedar better.

The Myths and Reality of Hill Country Cedar

There is no topic of land management in the Hill Country that is so much discussed, and about which there are so many myths, as for Ashe juniper, what most folks call cedar. Let me first try to dispel the myths.

To begin with, cedar is not really a cedar, but a juniper. The one that is most common in the Hill Country is Ashe juniper (*Juniperus ashei*), or blueberry juniper. Growing primarily north and west of most of the Hill Country is Redberry juniper (*Juniperus pinchotii*). Like all junipers, they belong to the Cypress Family of Gymnosperms (meaning "naked seed"), which brings us to the second myth.

The blue berries we see on the female trees are not really berries, although everyone refers to them as juniper berries, but they are actually classified as "fleshy cones."

Blueberry cedar (Ashe juniper), perhaps the most common woody plant in the Hill Country.

Another myth is that cedar is not native. But here we have hundreds of references in the writings of early explorers and settlers describing cedar and junipers in great detail. And there is fossil evidence of pollen being here since the Pleistocene Epoch (more than 12,000 years ago).

So, cedar is native, natural, xeric, and evergreen, it has very few diseases or pests, and grows in most all habitats in the Hill Country, except for permanently wet areas. Its berries are eaten by many birds and small animals, and it provides cover and winter protection for birds, deer and other creatures. All desirable traits for a tree or shrub. So what is the problem?

The problem is not with any individual cedar tree, but with the prolific way it reproduces and forms new trees and thus becomes too numerous for a healthy habitat and crowds out other native grasses, forbs and woody plants. And large dense stands of cedar are poor habitat for anything.

In the old days, before European settlers arrived in the Hill Country, periodic grass fires and wildfires killed small cedar bushes and thus kept its numbers in check. After Europeans drove off the Native Americans and grazed the grass short, fewer fires meant more cedar. Then after barbed wire was invented in the 1880s, there was a huge demand for fence posts and a lot of the early cedar was cut. But beginning in the mid-1900s, the demand for cedar posts declined and T-posts became available. Since neither deer nor anything else likes to eat cedar, and we have many fewer fires, there is no natural control on the spread of cedar in the Hill Country.

While it is true that some people have found springs returning to their land after removal of a lot of cedar, it does not mean that it works everywhere. Whether new springs are created depends on what replaces the cedar, the topography and the underlying geology, and the size of the property in question.

At the Kerr Wildlife Management Area near Hunt, a 96-acre savanna was high fenced with no animals inside the fence in the 1960s. Today there is virtually no grass and the area is a total cedar brake (dense stand of cedar).

Since there is no natural limit to the expansion of cedar, any bushes on a property now will continue to get bigger and most small cedar bushes will continue to grow, unless the owner conducts some kind of management program.

Fortunately, of all of the plant species that can become invasive, ashe juniper is the easiest to kill, because it does not resprout from the roots. Once cut off below the lowest green leaf, it will die, or, if the trunk is sufficiently burned, it will die. Most other species people want to get rid of will sprout back from the roots.

After weighing the options, just about everyone resorts to some form of mechanical control, including bulldozers, skid-loaders with shears, or chain saws. The first can be the most destructive to the land, the next less so and chain saws much less destructive. Most folks seem to be opting for chain saws for smaller properties and bobcats with shears for larger acreages.

Aside from the disruption of the land, the other two potential problems are to prevent erosion and what to do with the cut cedar. Most experts recommend never attempting to remove Ashe juniper from steep slopes as this almost always results in severe erosion. Laying cut branches over bare ground areas helps prevent erosion on flatter areas and helps grasses become established.

Most people resort to burning brush piles when burn bans are lifted and there are times of low wind and light rain or high humidity, but it is also true that many wildfires are started by people burning brush piles, so be very careful. For smaller properties, the cut limbs can be chipped into cedar mulch.

The Water-Cedar Connection: It's More Complicated Than You Think

I recently attended a conference on the future of water in the Hill Country, one of many sponsored by the Hill Country Alliance, Schreiner University, Texas Tech University and Texas Public Radio. During a question and comment period there were two individuals who made comments regarding the role cedar may play in our water supply.

One person commented that it was obvious that cedar uses or captures an inordinate amount of water and getting rid of it will give us more water. The other person responded that that was a myth, that there are good reasons to manage cedar, but eliminating it won't give us significantly more water.

It turns out that both of these two views are common, and both have some truth to them. But, like a lot of things when you get right down to it, the real truth is somewhat unsettled and probably a lot more complicated than most folks like to think.

It is true that there are instances where people have cleared cedar from their land and have subsequently found springs flowing that were not flowing before the clearing. It is also true that some folks have done exactly the same thing and seen no such result.

It is true that some early studies indicated that cedar trees catch rainwater on their leaves and keep it from reaching the ground and that the water then evaporates back into the air after the rain. There is one early study that was widely interpreted (probably erroneously) as finding that 80 percent of the rainfall over cedar never reaches the ground. But several subsequent studies have indicated that the amount of rainwater interception by cedar is probably more like 40 percent, and grass intercepts 15 percent.

It is also true that all vegetation (including oak trees and grass) intercepts rainfall that never reaches the ground, and the amount of such rainfall captured on the surface of the leaves depends on the size of the plant, the texture of the leaves, and the amount of rainfall. In very light showers, most of the rain is intercepted by vegetation; in heavy rains, only a very small percentage is caught by the vegetation.

There is also historical data that shows that the flow rate of the Pedernales River over the past 100 years or so is about constant, in spite of the fact that the amount of cedar cover in the watershed in that time period has greatly increased as well as the human population.

It seems logical to assume, based on those instances where people have removed cedar and found new spring flow, that if everyone were to remove cedar we would have more water in the aquifers and greater river flow. But what works on a small landowner scale may not be duplicated on a watershed scale. There are, however, government programs that subsidize landowners to remove cedar based on that assumption.

We want water to soak into the ground, where some of it nourishes vegetation, some of it flows downhill underground to replenish local water tables and springs to feed the base flow of creeks and rivers and some may infiltrate deep underground to recharge aquifers. We want there to be enough vegetation to slow down the overland flow of water so that it has time to soak into the ground. We don't want water to run off the land, except in very hard rainfall events where it flows down rivers to help fill lakes.

Rainwater falling on bare ground dislodges soil particles and as it runs off it carries away the soil, permanently reducing the amount of water the soil can hold and the amount of vegetation it can sustain. Clearing cedar without replacing it with something else like grass will result in more erosion and more runoff and the silting of lakes.

Too much cedar is not good habitat for wildlife and is wasted grazable land for livestock. Less cedar and more native shrubs, grasses and wildflowers is preferable from the standpoint of the rancher as well as the habitat for wildlife. So there are certainly reasons to manage the amount of cedar in the Hill Country. Small amounts of cedar are good for diversity and small cedar brakes are good shelter for wildlife, but too much of any one species is undesirable.

So my advice to landowners is to work to manage the amount of cedar, reducing or preventing large monocultures of cedar, work to maintain good stands of native grasses by not overgrazing the land, and work to develop a diverse native habitat. Doing so may or may not result in more springs.

The Backyard Cedar Tree

When we built our house, the exact location and orientation seemed obvious, except the view from the back porch would have been into a patch of cedar mostly clustered under a few nice post oaks. So one of the first things we did was to remove most of them so we would have a less obstructed view of the pasture beyond.

But we left one cedar. Unlike all of the cedars that we removed, which were what is usually referred to as "regrowth" cedar, multi-trunk bushes mostly less than 12-15 feet tall, the one we kept was what most people would call an "old growth" cedar. It has a single trunk, about 18 inches in diameter with the lower branches being about 6 feet off the ground. It is between 30 and 35 feet tall.

It is not what most people would describe as an attractive tree. It is not symmetrical. It has some bare spots, some broken limbs and a few dead branches. But it has become, along with an equal-sized post oak, the dominant feature in our back yard and we are quite fond of it.

On one side, the cedar's outer branches are almost over the low end of the recirculating creek I built a few years ago and which attracts many birds as both a source of drinking water and also a place to bathe in. The squirrels seem to drink from it several times a day. We have a suet feeder hanging from the cedar, a bird feeder for sunflower seeds hanging from the post oak (well, the squirrels think it is a squirrel feeder sometimes), and we have a platform feeder for sunflower seeds not too far from both trees. So there is a lot of wildlife activity in the area of the old cedar tree.

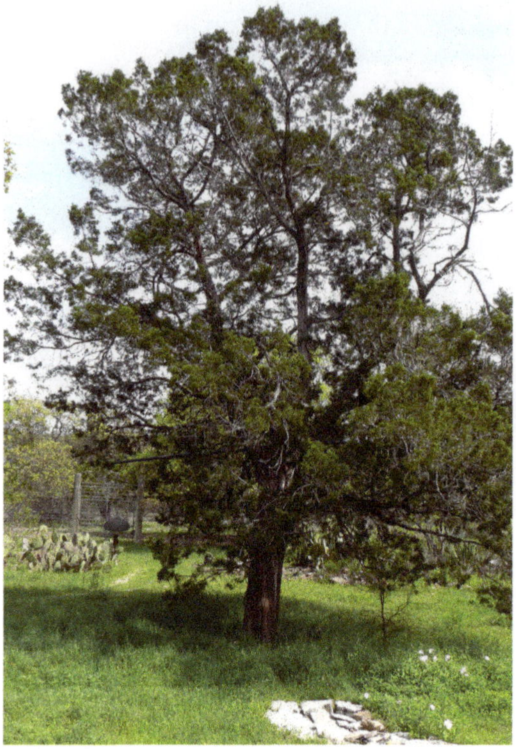

The backyard cedar—part of wildlife habitat.

The birds, especially the shy ones, like to sit in the cedar and scout the area before coming down to drink or bathe, and especially after bathing, most birds with wet wings just want to get somewhere safe to dry off their wings, and the cedar is the perfect place for that. In the summer, the few dead twigs here and there make ideal perches for hummingbirds to sit between trips to their feeders.

The outermost limbs of both the cedar and the post oak come to within about two feet of overlapping, but this just makes it fun for the squirrels to jump from one tree to the other so they can travel without getting on the ground. Because of the overlapping limbs of the post oaks and blackjacks to the north, squirrels can travel through the trees well over a hundred feet to reach the cedar and come down to get a drink without being on the ground for more than about 6 or 8 feet.

Underneath the cedar we have a collection of volunteer, native woody plants. These include a hackberry, a gum bumelia, an escarpment black cherry, a live oak and a greenbrier. These have all appeared since we built the high fence and no longer have any deer or other browsers to eat them. Since the cedar is a male, we have not had any small cedars come up under it, as we might have if it were a female.

We don't have any lawn grass under the tree, just whatever Mother Nature puts there on her own. In the winter, it is usually rescue grass, a common non-native annual cool-season grass, as well as some vetch. Later in the year these will be replaced with a mixture of native grasses and a few wildflowers.

The most important aspect of this big old cedar, and the post oak next to it, is that we can sit on the back porch in the morning with a cup of coffee, or take an ice-cream break in the afternoon and enjoy both seeing and hearing numerous birds and watching the antics of the squirrels almost constantly. This is really the reason we wanted to live in the country in the first place. It wouldn't have been nearly as enjoyable or interesting if we had removed that old cedar when we removed the others.

Be careful what you get rid of, you might regret it later.

How Much Brush is Too Much Brush?

Most all property owners in the Hill Country will, sooner or later, have a brush problem. But before I can talk about a brush problem, I have to define what a brush problem is, and before I can discuss that, I have to define what "brush" is.

My definition of brush is woody vegetation, especially shrubs and vines, but not including tall mature trees, that grows in a dense-enough manner that would make it difficult for a person to walk through it. Some might refine the above definition to include only "unwanted" woody vegetation with those characteristics, but I don't make that distinction.

So, what species do folks consider "brush" that might create a problem? Depending on whom you talk to and which species they have more of than they would like to have, it could be ashe juniper (cedar), redberry juniper, mesquite, willow baccharis, prickly pear, agarita, greenbrier, shin oak, Texas persimmon, huisache, bee-brush, or acacia. And it is kind of like the way different people view Mexican hat—if they like it, it is a wildflower and if they don't, it is a weed.

Let me make one point very clear. Everything in my list above is a native plant that has been here for eons, that has evolved with all of the native trees, grasses, forbs and animals to be a part of the Hill Country habitat. Everything in the list has beneficial properties and can contribute to the diversity of the native habitat. There is nothing inherently bad or undesirable about any single plant of any of the above species and a healthy, sustainable, diverse native habitat would be expected to contain a number of the above species.

Old Ben Franklin said, "Moderation in all things." I don't think he was thinking about habitats, but it does seem to apply.

What constitutes "too much" of any one species, or even of a collection of several species is something every landowner has to decide for himself or herself. Cattle and sheep ranchers will probably want less brush and more open grassland than someone managing their property for black-capped vireos or deer.

The reasons to manage brush might be for fire protection (cedar trees within 20 or 30 feet of a home can be a problem), improved rangeland (less brush, more grass for grazers), wildlife habitat (a diversity of species and habitat types), to capture more rainwater (more grass, less brush—although this is still a bit controversial), or a combination of the above.

I have to point out that everything I have said so far applies to native plants only. Exotic, non-native plants, even if not present in large numbers, can be a problem and may contribute nothing to the native habitat, so they should be controlled at the lowest level possible.

It is also important to emphasize, that if nothing is done to control the numbers of the more invasive species of native brush (e.g. cedar) they will continue to increase in numbers and size and crowd out other native species, thus degrading the habitat. Large areas of cedar brakes (thickets too dense to walk through easily) are very poor habitat for any native animals. Unfortunately, much of the Hill Country is in this condition because of few fires and no human control. If man doesn't control cedar, in the absence of a wildfire, nothing will.

Owning a piece of rural native habitat in the Hill Country is not something you buy and then just sit back and enjoy. You have to manage and maintain it.

FORBS

Forbs are important components of any native habitat and provide food for many vertebrates and invertebrates. They tend to be early successional plants on bare or disturbed soil.

I recommend the following book to help anyone with the names of common Hill Country flowers, *Wildflowers of the Texas Hill Country*, by Marshall Enquist,

Is it a Weed or a Wildflower?

We have probably all heard, or asked that question ourselves. What is the difference? Does it matter? Is there a true distinction or is it subjective—in the eye of the beholder?

One of the major categories of land plants are woody plants (trees, shrubs and vines) which keep their woody stems even in winter and grow new growth on previous year's wood. Grasses can be annual or perennial and are characterized by having long narrow leaves with parallel veins, usually starting near the ground. Forbs are broad-leaved (as opposed to grasses) herbaceous plants (do not form persistent woody tissues) that can be either annual or perennial, things most people call wildflowers or weeds.

So now that we have come full circle and I have totally confused you, what is the difference between a weed and a wildflower? The one I hear most often is that a weed is a wildflower that is growing where you don't want it.

Of course, that definition means that you and I can look at the same plant in the same place and disagree on whether it is a weed or a wildflower. Also, you can consider a bluebonnet growing in an area where you planted it as a wildflower, but when it grows up in your lawn, then it becomes a weed.

It is really interesting the strong feelings many folks have about flowers and plants in general. I guess we all have flowers we like and those we don't, and some of those feelings date back to our childhood. If your mother grew this or that and commented favorably on it, then chances are that you will like it too. But if she fought a certain plant to keep it out of her yard and cursed its existence, then chances are that you hate it too.

Or if you were raised on a farm or ranch and a certain plant grew up in the fields, or accumulated around the stock tank and nothing ate it, then chances are you have pretty strong feelings about it too. The very fact that something grew in the pasture that the cows wouldn't eat was reason enough to hate that flower and to feel that it was crowding out the good grass that the cows needed.

Since bluebonnets are the state flower of Texas and sort of a Texas icon, just about everyone thinks of them as a wildflower and would like to see more. Same thing with several of the other spring bloomers that grace our roadsides in good years such as Gaillardia, (aka Indian blanket or firewheel), Indian paintbrush and winecup, followed later by the many yellow flowers, such as Engelmann daisy, coreopsis and greenthread. Most everyone would consider all of these to be wildflowers, almost anywhere they grow.

But equally common and noticeable are Mexican hat and white prickly poppy. Some people hate Mexican hat for reasons I don't fully understand, except that cattle don't eat it. Some years it is very common and other years it is less so. Many folks mistake white prickly poppy for a thistle because of the prickles on the leaves and stems. So it is common for folks to consider these wildflowers to be weeds.

My personal definition is that native forbs are wildflowers and non-native forbs such as Malta star thistle, musk thistle, bastard cabbage, purple loosestrife, ox-eye daisy and periwinkle are weeds. For that matter, I would also consider any of the "cultivars," "hybrids" or "varieties" of native plants such as "New Gold" lantana and "Henry Duelberg" salvia as noxious weeds as well. We don't need our real native Texas lantana or mealy blue sage to have to compete with non-natives.

So the bottom line is some weeds are wildflowers and some wildflowers are weeds, depending on your point of view—you can have your own opinion about anything and so can I. But I would hope most folks would learn to appreciate natives and not non-natives.

My Favorite Fall Flowers

When the subject of Native Hill Country Wildflowers comes up, most folks think about bluebonnets, Indian blanket, Indian paintbrush, winecup—all things that bloom in the spring. While I certainly like our spring flowers, I happen to like fall even more. Here are some of my favorite fall flowers, in no special order.

Gayfeather or liatris (*Liatris mucronata*) grows as a multi-stem perennial with erect stems up to 2 to 3 feet tall. The leaves are very numerous, narrow and long, and the flower head is a spire-like structure up to about a foot long. The flower head is made up of many small purple flowers with tiny purple threads or filaments sticking out, giving the flower head an interesting texture. It can often be seen along roadsides from August to October.

Maximilian sunflower (*Helianthus maximiliani*) is a very showy, large perennial plant that can grow up to about 6 feet tall. It tends to spread from a single stem to a round clump of stems that may be over six feet in diameter. The leaves are narrow and long (lanceolate), usually 2 to 4 inches long. In September and October, the stems elongate and put up flower heads that open to individual 2 to 3 inch yellow flowers with yellow-orange disk (center) flowers. Interestingly, the flowers begin blooming from the top bud of the stalk first and progress to the lower buds—opposite from most flowers with multiple buds on a single stalk. Maximilian sunflowers are frequently seen as large green round hemispheres along road sides. It may be grazed by cattle and deer.

Tall goldenrod (*Solidago altissima*) is an impressive, erect plant up to 6 feet tall. The leaves are long and narrow, tapering to a point at both the tip and the base. It blooms in September and the flowers are composed of numerous small flowers along many branches off the stem, giving the whole 6 to 10 inches of the top of the plant a bright yellow color. There is also the smaller cousin of tall goldenrod, prairie goldenrod (*Solidago nemoralis*) which usually does not get over 2 feet in height. Both plants are perennials. These flowers have a bad reputation as being a cause of hay fever, but the flowers are not wind-pollinated and thus not the culprit.

Common sunflower (*Helianthus annuus*) is usually 2 to 3 feet tall, but can be larger. It has thin, heart-shaped leaves on very rough, dark-colored stems. The flower heads can be 3 inches or more across with yellow petals and brown disk flowers. These are annual flowers that reseed themselves every year.

Anyone who loves butterflies should certainly have Gregg's mistflower, (*Conoclinium greggii*) in their garden. The plants are usually 2 to 3 feet tall with triangular-shaped, deeply incised leaves. The flower heads are a multi-branched umbrel of very small blue flowers with blue filaments making for a somewhat flat-topped, fuzzy, blue appearance. Butterflies really love this plant for nectar, especially the queen butterfly. As I was writing this, I went out and looked at one of our clusters of Gregg's mistflower and counted 5 queens and a monarch actively nectaring on the plants. It blooms from July to October.

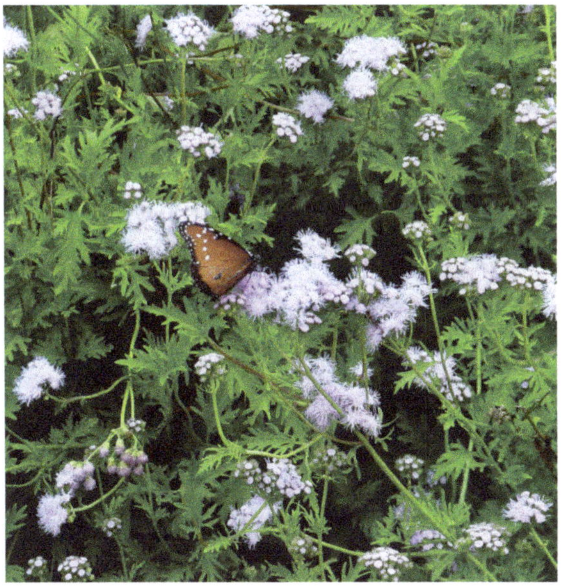
A Queen butterfly nectoring on Gregg's mistflower.

Damianita (*Chrysactina mexicana*) is a small shrub-like, basketball-sized plant with dark green needle-like leaves and small yellow flowers at the tip of the branches. The contrast between the yellow flowers on top and the dark green underneath is striking. It is a very xeric plant requiring little water, and it blooms after rains beginning in April into the fall.

Cowpen daisy (*Verbesina encelioides*) produces 2 to 3-inch yellow daisy-like flowers with toothed petals. It has 2 to 3-inch heart-shaped, toothed leaves. It is an annual that reseeds itself quite well. It is often seen on dry, disturbed land and in areas where animals are fed, because it appears that nothing, including deer, eat it! It is also a larval plant for the bordered-patch butterfly.

Mealy blue sage or mealy sage (*Salvia farinacea*) is a sprawling perennial up to three feet tall with one to three-inch-long leaves that have wavy or toothed margins. It produces a flower head up to a foot long with many congested purple or violet-blue flowers. It can bloom from spring through November with rain. It is not generally grazed by animals.

Fall aster (*Symphyotrichum oblongifolium*) (Say that three times quickly!) is a 2 to 3-foot-tall plant with oblong toothed leaves. The flower on the end of stalks has purple to light purple petals with a yellow center.

Frostweed (*Verbesina virginica*) is a perennial 2 to 4-foot-tall single or multi-stem plant with large (up to 6 inches) leaves. They usually have what are referred to as "wings" or "ribs" (flat appendages) up and down the length the stems. Frostweed blooms in the late summer to fall with large clusters of off-white or greenish white ray and disk flowers at the top of the stems. Frostweed is almost always found growing in the shade of large trees—almost never totally out in the open. It is not usually grazed by livestock or deer.

Another name for frostweed is iceplant and the reason for that is that on the early morning of the first hard freeze, the sap in the stems will freeze and burst the stem near the base and ooze out looking like the purest possible white old-fashioned ribbon candy with sparkling crystals.

Snow-on-the-mountain (*Euphorbia marginata*) is an upright 2 to 3-foot-tall perennial that usually branches about half-way up the stem or higher, frequently with several branches at the same point on the main stem (think of a candelabra). The leaves are 1 to 3-inch-long ovals attached directly to the stem. It blooms in late summer and early fall with white clusters at the tip of the branches and several bracts (leaf-like structures) with white margins and green centers just below the flower heads.

It is in the Spurge family, not a milkweed, but it does produce milky sap which contains euphorbium, a poisonous substance that can be irritating to the skin of some people and very irritating to the eyes and mouth. Snow-on-the-mountain is not usually eaten by anything.

Two-leaf senna, two-leaved senna or twin-leaf senna (*Cassia roemeriana*) is usually an upright or somewhat spreading perennial about a foot or so tall with unique paired leaflets in the same arrangement as fingers when making the "victory" sign. It can bloom as early as the spring or as late as September, depending on rainfall. The one inch blooms consist of five yellow pedals with visible veins. It is a legume and produces small bean-like pods. Two-leaf senna contains chemicals that have been used as laxatives. It is not usually grazed by animals.

The "Big Four" Native Perennial Forbs of Texas

It is common in range science, land management and naturalist circles to hear references made to the "Big Four grasses of the tall grass prairies," which were the dominant grasses of the prairies from Texas to Canada in the 1800s. These grasses not only made up the bulk of the vegetation, but each one is among the tallest grasses as well as the most palatable and nutritious for grazers. The Big Four grasses are little bluestem, big bluestem, yellow Indiangrass and switchgrass, all grasses that are desirable and species that land stewards strive to establish on their properties.

Grasses were certainly not the only vegetation growing on the prairies. There were numerous forb species as well. But I had never heard a similar "Big Four" term applied to forbs until Ricky Linex, NRCS agent, used it in his recent book, "Range Plants of North Central Texas." According to Linex, the "Big Four "native perennial forbs in Texas are: bush sunflower, Engelmann daisy, Illinois bundleflower, and Maximilian sunflower.

These species are not necessarily the tallest or largest forbs found in native prairies, but what they have in common is that they are all highly palatable to all classes of livestock and deer, they are high in protein, attractive to pollinators, and the seeds are used by quail, dove, turkey, and many songbirds. They are thus all very desirable species to have in any native grassland habitat.

Bush sunflower (*Simsia calva*) is a native, perennial, warm-season forb in the *Asteraceae* or sunflower family. It grows as a multi-stemmed bush about 1 to 3-feet in height and diameter. The leaves are oppositely arranged, 1 inch to 1.5 inches long, triangular, with small lobes. Both the leaves and stems are rough to the touch. The flowers are 1 to 1.5 inches in diameter on the end of a stem with 10 or more yellow petals and a slightly orange center. With moisture, it can bloom from April to October.

Engelmann daisy (*Engelmannia peristenia*), also called cut-leaf daisy, is a native perennial cool-season forb, also in the *Asteraceae* family. It grows about 2-feet tall with long (6 to 12 inches) deeply pinnately-lobed leaves (thus the name "cut-leaf"). The flowers appear from March to July and are about 1.5 inches in diameter with 8 yellow petals.

Illinois bundleflower (*Desmanthus illinoensis*) is, in spite of the name, a perennial warm-season legume native to Texas. It grows up to three feet tall, usually with several stems. Typical of many legumes, the leaves are twice pinnately compound with 6 to 12 branches each containing 20 to 30 tiny leaflets (1/8th inch or less), giving the plant a fern-like appearance. Flowers are a whitish spherical puff-ball less than 1/2 inch in diameter from May to June, or later with moisture. The seed pods are bunched together in a distinctive tight spherical cluster or "bundle" up to 1 inch or so in diameter.

Maximilian sunflower (*Helianthus maximiliani*) is a native perennial warm-season forb. It grows in large colonies of unbranched stems that can reach 6 feet tall under ideal conditions. The leaves are alternate, lanceolate, pointed at both ends and average about 4 inches long. The bright yellow flowers, up to 3 inches in diameter, grow along the upper part of the stems at the axils of the leaves in September and October. The colonies expand over time and can be 8 to 10 feet across.

Maximilian sunflower, one of the Big Four of native forbs

The irony of the big four grasses and the big four forbs, which are all highly desirable in any grassland or savanna, is that in many cases, they are among the hardest to find—for the very reason that they are highly desirable. They are the most often eaten by grazers and/or browsers and therefore the most likely to be the first species lost on overgrazed or overbrowsed properties.

Some of the Most Common Wildflowers of the Hill Country

Mexican hat, a common native wildflower, especially in overgrazed pastures.

If you ask folks to name the most common wildflowers of the Hill Country, many people will name the most famous, showy wildflowers, especially spring blooming ones such as bluebonnet, Indian blanket, Indian paintbrush, Engelmann's daisy, Plains coreopsis and maybe a few others.

But if instead the question is to name the wildflowers that are found on the most properties, a completely different list will likely be produced. The flowers on this list are not necessarily the most showy and most are not found covering huge areas like we often see bluebonnets and Indian blankets in the spring. Some are hardly noticeable at all.

One reason why many of the flowers that would be on the most common list can be found on nearly all properties with native habitat is that they are not generally eaten by white-tailed deer. So they survive even on properties with high deer populations.

In the last 15 years, I have visited several hundred different properties in the Hill Country, and many of the flowers that I have seen most often are listed below. You may not have all of them, but if you have any natural area, you probably have some of them.

Mexican hat or upright prairie coneflower is a multi-stemmed, erect brown and yellow coneflower that can grow up to 3 feet tall. It is common in overgrazed pastures. It can be a biennial or perennial and it blooms from May through August.

Mealy blue sage is a perennial erect multi-stemmed 2 to 3-foot shrub-like forb that puts up multiple spires of violet-blue ½ inch to 1 inch flowers. It blooms from April through July.

Prairie verbena is a perennial, low-growing forb with two-inch clusters of light-purple blooms at the end of multiple stems. It blooms from March to October.

Frostweed is an erect 2 to 5-foot perennial that produces single or only a few stems. Leaves are simple, toothed, oval with pointed tips from 2 to 6-inches long and 2 to 4-inches wide. The stem has prominent "wings." Clusters of dull-white to greenish-white flowers form large flower heads from August to November. It is usually found growing in the shade of trees. On the first hard freeze of the year, the stem will split and exude pure white ribbon-candy-like frozen sap at the base.

Queen's delight forms rounded clumps up to two feet in height and across. This perennial forms inconspicuous spikes of tiny yellow-green flowers from April to September. It is a perennial.

Cowpen daisy is an annual that efficiently reseeds itself. It generally grows to 2 to 4-feet tall with 4-inch-long triangular toothed gray-green leaves. It puts up 1 ½-inch wide sunflower-like blooms with, usually, 12 petals from April to November.

Rabbit tobacco is a very short (1-4 inches) semi-shrubby perennial with tiny leaves covered with white hairs that give the plant a gray appearance. The tiny flowers are white to pale pink. It blooms from April to June.

Silver-leaf nightshade is a one to three-foot perennial forb. The leaves are 1 to 4 inches long, lanceolate and covered with white hairs giving the appearance of being gray or silver. The blooms have five petals, violet to purple, with yellow centers. The fruit is a ½ inch yellow berry.

Snow-on-the-mountain is a single-stem four-foot tall annual with branching in the top half resembling a candelabra. The leaves are green with white margins. Flowers are inconspicuous in clusters at the end of the stems. The sap of this plant can be very irritating to the skin and eyes, so be careful around it.

Here are several more common forbs: bluets, damianita, frogfruit, skeleton plant, 4-nerve daisy, Texas vervain, and zexmenia.

Gardeners should take note that none of these plants listed here are really what we would call deer favorites. In reality, deer eat what is available to them, and if nothing better is available they will eat at least some of nearly everything. But in most areas, you should be able to grow most of these plants without deer being a problem.

GRASSES

Grass is, arguably, the most important category of plants to be growing on the land, not that woody plants and forbs are not essential for a healthy native habitat. But a Hill Country landscape with just grass can still have healthy, functioning soil and capture rainwater as necessary for the operation of the hydrologic cycle. A landscape with just forbs or just trees would not function as well.

The property of grass that makes it so essential to a healthy Hill Country habitat is the root system of grasses and the complex relationships with soil organisms which maintain a fertile, functioning soil structure.

Grasses were the primary component of the tall grass prairie that once stretched from central Texas to Canada, although forbs were certainly an important component of those prairies as well.

The first book I would buy to help identify Hill grasses is, *Grasses of the Texas Hill Country*, by Brian and Shirley Loflin.

Watching Grass Grow—It's More Interesting Than You Think

Of the over 700 species of grasses found in Texas, probably only about 75 would be considered really common in the Hill Country. Grasses are classified as either "bunch" grasses or "turf" grasses; the latter being low, spreading lawn grasses. The vast majority of all native grasses in Texas, however, are bunch grasses, meaning they grow from a common base at ground level, with the leaves growing up and the roots growing down from that point.

If you could reach down and grab a bunch grass at the base and pull it totally out of the ground with all roots intact, you would see something very different from what you would see by doing that with a forb (weed or wildflower) or a small tree. Instead of a branching structure in the roots like a forb or a woody plant, all of the roots of the grass would originate at the plant base near the surface of the ground, and there would be at least as much biomass below the ground as above the ground. Mature bunch grass plants can easily have root systems 6' or more long.

Within this mass of roots lives a whole community of insects, nematodes, bacteria and fungi. About a third of these roots die every year and are replaced, and these microorganisms feed on the dying roots as well as on secretions from the living roots. In return, these microorganisms help to solubilize minerals and fix nitrogen that the roots take up. This symbiotic relationship not only helps the grass grow better, but it also makes the soil more porous and actually contributes to building more and better soil.

This porous soil acts like a sponge to allow rainwater to soak into the soil rather than run off. Native bunch grasses do a better job of this than forbs, woody plants, or, for that matter, bare ground.

When one-third of the roots die each year, they are replaced by new roots made from carbohydrates that are produced by photosynthesis in the leaves. In turn, the roots bring water and nutrients from the soil up to the leaves so that the photosynthesis can take place. All of this is a long way of saying "It takes leaves to make roots and it takes roots to make leaves."

But what happens if Bossy comes along and wraps her long tongue around that grass plant and pulls off a lot of the leaves? The answer, like so much in biology, is "It depends." If after Bossy has had her bite, no other animal comes along to take another bite for some time, then the stored energy in the roots and the remaining leaves can make more leaves to replace those that were eaten and the plant regains its original vigor. However, if Bossy and her sisters stay in the area and repeatedly take a bite out of our bunch grass, and if the amount of leaves they take represents 50 percent or more of the original bunch, there will not be enough leaves left to regrow the leaves and replace the roots that have died, and the plant will eventually decrease in size.

If this process happens repeatedly throughout the pasture, eventually all of the bunch grasses that Bossy likes to eat will decrease in number and size and may eventually die out completely, leaving mainly grasses that are either smaller, shorter or less palatable than our original grass plant. And guess what, it doesn't take Bossy to do this to the grass; other species, including John Deere and Toro can do it too.

The bottom line is that repeated grazing or mowing of native bunch grasses that removes 50 percent or more of the original foliage will eventually cause the better, more palatable grasses to decrease. They will be replaced by those species that the animals can't or don't like to eat or the mower can't reach (such as grassburs), which will then increase.

On the other hand, if enough rest period between Bossy's visits is provided, Mother Nature will be able to restore that grass plant so Bossy can enjoy another bite again in the future.

The Big Four Grasses of the Tall Grass Prairie

Two hundred plus years ago there were somewhat fewer woodlands, fewer trees scattered on the savannas, and more grasses in the Hill Country than we see today. Back then the prairies that stretched from Canada to Texas (the southern end of which was in the Hill Country) supported huge herds of migrating buffalo, as well as grazing elk and antelope. This area was called the "Tall Grass Prairie," and the reason for that name was that the dominant grasses that grew back then were indeed "tall." There are many reports of early explorers referring to the grass as "as high as a saddle horn."

The four grasses that made up a large part of that grass community were little bluestem (*Schizachyrium scoparium*), big bluestem (*Andropogon geraridii*), yellow indiangrass (*Sorghastrum nutans*), and switchgrass (*Panicum virgatum*).

Of the four, little bluestem was probably the most common and wide-spread of all the grasses. In central Texas it is believed that, historically, over half of all grass plants were little bluestem. It is characterized as a bunchgrass about the size of a basketball with leaves 2 to 4 mm wide and 12 to 18 inches long. It puts up multiple stems in late summer which are usually 2 to 4 feet tall, but can be up to 6 feet tall. Between the nodes, the stems are alternately red and green. Fluffy seeds are produced along the top half of the stem. In late fall the stems turn a reddish brown and remain standing throughout the winter.

Little bluestem is often used as an indicator of the range condition: healthy ranges will almost always have significant amounts of little bluestem, whereas overgrazed ranges may have little or none. Little bluestem is often seen as the first of the tall grasses to return to recovering ranges.

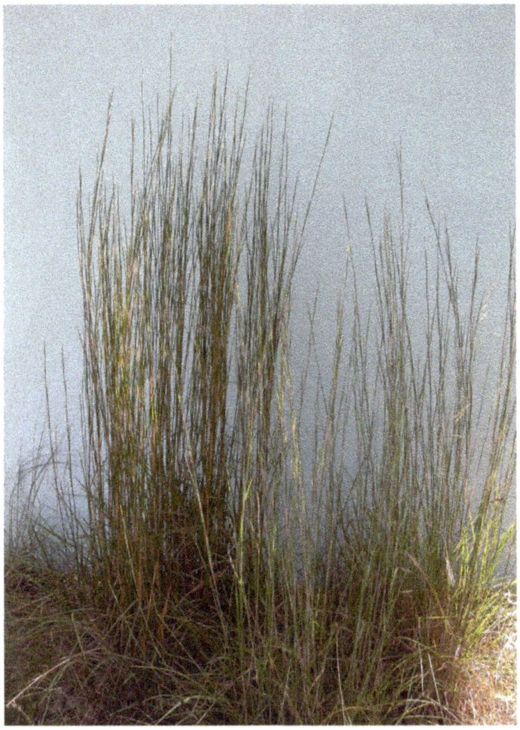

Little bluestem, historically the most common grass species in the Hill Country prior to settlement.

Big bluestem, one of grazers favorite grasses, not as common now as in the past.

Big bluestem, in contrast, looks nothing like little bluestem. It has wider leaf blades (4 to 8 mm), and longer blades (18 to 24 inches) and it puts up many fewer stems. Seeds are produced on two to four branches near the top of the stem, the angle between the branches being about 30 to 45 degrees. It is sometimes referred to as the "turkey foot grass" because the common three seed branches remind some folks of a turkey foot. These stems can be very tall (over 8 feet) although in our part of the Hill Country I have never seen any over about 6 feet.

Big bluestem is probably the least common of the big four grasses to be found in the Hill Country—finding it is an unusual event. In my personal experience growing it, it seems to be the hardest to propagate and the one that requires the most water.

Yellow indiangrass has blades that are 10 to 15 mm wide and taper to a narrow base and to a long tip. The several stems can be from 6 to 10 feet tall, although most often in this part of the country are around 6 feet or less in poor rain years. The leaves are rough when rubbed backwards (toward the base). When in bloom in early fall, parts of the flowers are bright yellow, thus the name. These grasses are sometimes planted as ornamentals in landscapes.

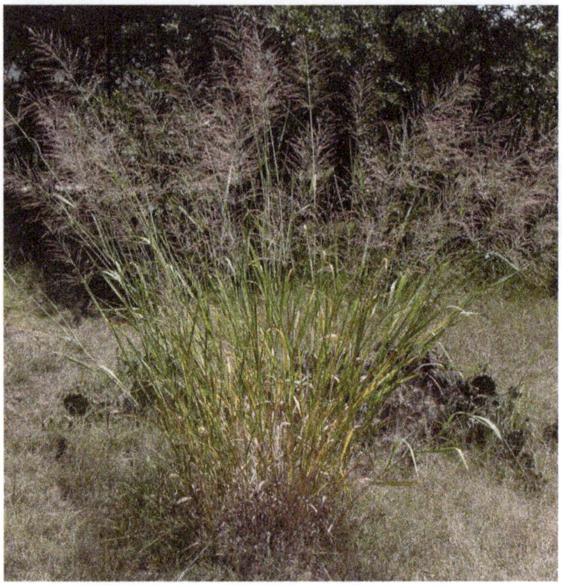

Switchgrass produces more foliage than just about any grass.

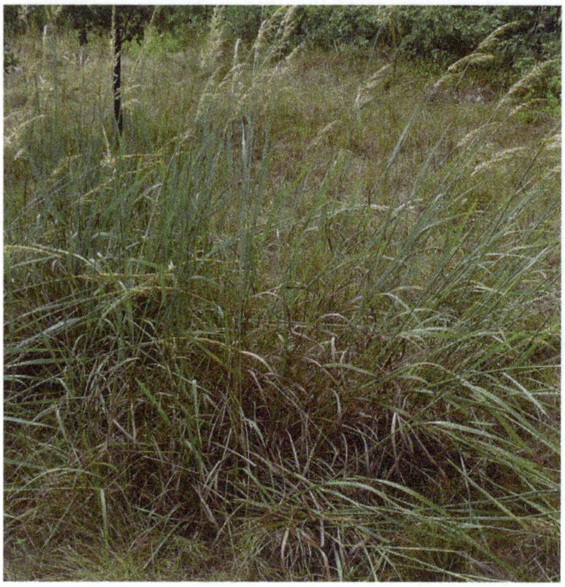

Yellow indiangrass, a desirable grass to have in a rangeland or in any landscape.

Switchgrass is the biggest grass of the big four and it produces significant growth earlier in the year than the others. The blades are 1 to 2 cm wide and it produces many stems that can be from 6 to 10 feet tall, usually closer to 6 feet in this part of the country. It produces an open multi-branched seedhead that somewhat resembles the invasive Johnsongrass (the latter, however has a white stripe down the length of the leaf blade, switchgrass does not). It may also be found growing in riparian areas.

Because it is easy to grow, requires little extra water in most areas, and produces a large amount of biomass, it has been considered as a source of renewable energy if the technology of converting cellulose directly to ethanol ever becomes a reality.

All four of these grasses are good forage grasses for grazers and good grasses to have on any healthy rangeland or native habitat. These grasses, with their deep, massive root systems and the microorganisms that live in the soil among these roots are largely responsible for the fertility of the Great Plains which we have turned into the breadbasket of the world.

Grasses, Soil, Erosion, Water Catchment—All Connected

Native bunch grasses are a critical component of our Hill Country habitat, so much so that it is hard to have a discussion about any issue associated with our native habitat without discussing grasses. And a discussion of any of these issues necessarily begins with a discussion of the characteristics and growth processes of grasses.

Native bunch grasses germinate from seed by producing a single green blade, at the base of which is a tiny root. As the plant grows, more blades of grass and more roots are formed in an ever-enlarging circle, or "bunch," with the mass of roots below ground resembling the above-ground leaves.

Our native grasses evolved to be grazed periodically by migrating herds of herbivores, but when the grasses had been grazed, the herds moved on and would not return to any given location until the grass had grown back. So even though the migrating herds ate the grass down to near nothing, it was not "overgrazed" in the sense of the health of the grass, as in time the plants could grow new leaves and roots and restore the grass plant to its original condition.

When European settlers moved in with their livestock, which were not migratory, but grazed the same piece of land continuously, the grass never had time to recover. And as the above-ground leaf area was reduced its ability to supply the roots with the necessary carbohydrates was diminished and the result was that the grass plants became smaller and weaker.

The smaller and weaker grass plants not only meant there was less above-ground vegetation but also less below-ground root systems, and all of the micro- and macro-organisms that live in a symbiotic relationship with the plant roots were also reduced as well as the total organic matter content of the soil. So continuous grazing not only reduced the amount of available forage above ground, but it also reduced the health of the soil and its fertility and future ability to grow more grass.

Soil is a mixture of finely eroded rock of different textures from large-particle sand to fine-particle clay. In addition, healthy soil has organic matter, both living bacteria, fungi, nematodes, earthworms, beetles, ants, etc., but also dead, decaying organic matter such as dead roots and leaf litter. The other components of soil are air and water.

In the Hill Country, the component of soil most lacking is organic matter. Dead organic matter contains components the living plants need for healthy growth, and it also gives the soil a lighter texture which makes it more porous for water to infiltrate. And the greater the amount of organic matter, the greater the amount of water the soil can hold, all else being equal.

So healthy grasslands have healthier soil which not only is capable of growing more new vegetation, but it can also hold more soil moisture. The soil under native grasses is more porous than that under bare ground, so more water soaks into the ground and less runs off in healthy grasslands than on land with sparse grass cover and more bare ground. Furthermore, dense grass cover slows down the flow of water, giving it more time to soak in and to drop any sediment the water might be carrying.

Erosion usually starts with raindrops striking bare soil, dislodging tiny particles of soil and carrying them off. Good stands of native grasses not only reduce the amount of bare ground, thus preventing as much soil from being dislodged, but by slowing down the flow of water across the land and making a porous soil these grasses greatly reduce the amount of erosion and store more water in the soil.

So, healthy grasses make for healthy, fertile soil which can grow more vegetation; grass as well as forbs and woodies. It also reduces the amount of erosion from both wind and water, and allows for the infiltration of water into the ground to both nourish vegetation but to also seep deeper underground to replenish local water tables and even sometimes an aquifer.

Excessive mowing or grazing reduces the ability of native grasses to function as discussed above, and thus leads to poorer soil, more erosion and less soil moisture. Well-managed land with low stocking rates and rotational grazing can give the grasses time to recover and function as they have historically.

Native Grasses, The Most Important Thing Growing in the Landscape

A healthy, productive and sustainable habitat should have many different species of all types of plants; woody plants (trees and shrubs), forbs (weeds and wildflowers) and grasses, all growing together. Diversity is good. Each type of vegetation has different characteristics and performs a different function in the ecosystem, and most of us, if shown pictures of different landscapes, would choose scenes where all three types are evident as the most beautiful.

The big four grasses of the tall grass prairie were discussed above. While the population of these grasses in this area is much smaller than it used to be, all four can still be found. Little bluestem is believed to have dominated grasslands in this area before settlement and is still quite common and a good indicator of a well-managed grassland. Switchgrass is most often seen along creeks and streams and helps protect stream banks from erosion.

Other very desirable grasses from the standpoint of forage quantity and quality include sideoats grama (the state grass of Texas), eastern gamagrass, silver bluestem, plains lovegrass, Canada wildrye, Texas wintergrass (speargrass), blue grama, buffalograss, green sprangletop, southwest bristlegrass and meadow dropseed. All well-managed ranches in this area will have at least two of the Big Four plus half of the above grasses in abundance.

In contrast, there are many grasses that are either too small to produce significant amounts of forage or are unpalatable for various reasons. Finding many of these grasses in a pasture is an indication of overgrazing. This list includes Texas grama, red grama, windmillgrass, purple threeawn, oldfield threeawn, Japanese brome, hairy tridens, red lovegrass and common sandbur.

Grasses which are frequently found around water and may help stabilize riparian areas include: bushy bluestem, Lindheimer muhly, switchgrass, aparajograss (plus numerous species of sedges and rushes that look like grasses but aren't).

Grasses which grow early in the year are called cool-season grasses and include Texas wintergrass, Canada wildrye, rescuegrass, Scribner's dichanthelium, perennial ryegrass.

Introduced grasses that compete with natives and become problems either because they are invasive and/or because they prevent better-quality grasses from growing include (but, are not limited to) the following bermudagrass, johnsongrass, kleingrass, KR bluestem and related species (Kleburg bluestem and old world bluestem), downy brome (cheatgrass), buffelgrass, Guinea grass, and dallisgrass, and Willmann lovegrass.

Most native grasses are bunch grasses, which means that they form a clump of foliage in a bunch, usually round, instead of growing spread out like a lawn (turf) grass. Some exceptions are buffalograss, which is frequently grown as a lawn grass, and curly mesquite, both of which spread by runners (stolons) just like Bermuda or carpet grass.

Mowing: Time to Rethink Old Habits?

I have not seen any figures, but I bet the gardening/land management activity most often practiced by landowners is mowing. When the early English noblemen began the practice of running a few sheep in front of their mansions to keep the grass short, they started a custom that has become synonymous with being a homeowner—mowing the lawn.

With the spread of suburbia and the marketing departments of John Deere and Scotts and Toro, the practice has become almost mandatory. In fact, many municipalities require homeowners to keep their grass mowed. But do lawns really make sense? And is frequent, close mowing good for the grass? What about the use of water?

It is important in any discussion of lawns and mowing to make a distinction between two different types of grass. Lawn grasses are what are called turf grasses and naturally grow short. Most have stolons (runners) above ground and/or rhizomes below ground which cause the grass to spread out and cover an area. The non-native turf grasses most commonly used in this area are St. Augustine and Bermudagrass. Native grasses that grow similarly are buffalograss and common curly mesquite.

Lawns in general, but especially grasses like St. Augustine and Bermudagrass, use an inordinate amount of resources. First, St. Augustine requires many times more water than we usually get in a normal year, so lots of watering is required for it to survive. Bermudagrass requires less, but still requires frequent watering. These non-native grasses also require frequent applications of fertilizer which uses lots of resources to manufacture. Lawn mowers are some of the most polluting gas engines around. Furthermore, monocultures of these grasses are poor habitat for anything except perhaps grackles. In short, these lawns are not very environmentally friendly.

One could minimize some of these problems by mowing less frequently and with the mower set as high as possible. Doing this allows the grass to shade the soil better and thus allows the soil temperature to be lower. This not only reduces water evaporation from the soil but keeps the soil microorganisms healthier. One of the easiest things homeowners can do to reduce the impact of lawns is to mow less frequently. During the drought of 2011, I saw folks running a lawnmower over short, dormant lawns where nothing was sticking up to mow and instead they were raising a huge cloud of dust. Just because it is Saturday and it is your usual mowing day doesn't mean you should mow if the grass doesn't really need it (actually the grass really never "needs it" for its own good, it is just our sense of aesthetics that seems to require it).

Not catching the cuttings but allowing them to be mulched and kept on the lawn, at least some of the time, returns nutrients back to the soil and thus reduces the need for fertilizer, plus it reduces the amount of waste going to our landfills.

Obviously the biggest saving of all of these resources would be to not have a lawn, or to have one of native buffalograss. Buffalograss requires far less water than the two non-native grasses discussed above, and it requires no fertilizer at all. Once established, it can live without water—going dormant in droughts and greening up after a rain. Buffalograss also usually needs mowing only once or twice a year. Reducing the size of lawns and replacing them with vines, other ground covers, or perennials all help mitigate some of the problems discussed above.

For those folks that don't really have regular turf grasses, but keep the native grasses mowed short, it is important to understand that mowing bunch grasses frequently and too low will eventually weaken and kill the plant and it will be replaced by various weeds and grassburs that tolerate frequent mowing. The best times to mow native bunch grasses, if it is required, are in late June or July and again in December or January, and most do better if they are mowed to a height of 4 to 6 inches.

I can tell you from personal experience, that giving up the weekly suburban ritual and instead allowing native grasses to grow and mowing them only twice a year has sure freed up a lot of my time, and I don't miss the mowing one bit.

The Universal Beneficence of Grass

When I was a kid, I was active in 4-H, an organization for kids sponsored by what is now called the Texas AgriLife Extension Service. During my time in 4-H, I raised several 4-H animals, and at one time I was on the 4-H grass judging team for our county. To call it "grass judging" was kind of a joke because it was really just grass identification contests, and I was really awful at it.

But it did instill in me a deep appreciation and interest in grass that has continued throughout my life. I now know a lot more about our native grasses and I certainly consider them the most important class of vegetation to have on the land, both because grass is best at holding water and preventing erosion as well as building a fertile soil.

So when I read the following essay, written well over 100 years ago, probably sometime after the civil war, I immediately wanted to share it with you.

"GRASS"

"Next in importance to the divine profusion of water, light and air, those three physical facts which render existence possible, may be reckoned the universal beneficence of grass. Lying in the sunshine among the butter-cups and dandelions of May, scarcely higher in intelligence than those minute tenants of that mimic wilderness, our earliest recollections are of grass and when the fitful fever is ended, and the foolish wrangle of the market and the forum is closed, grass heals over the scar which our decent into the bosom of the earth has made, the carpet of the infant becomes the blanket of the dead.

"Grass is the forgiveness of nature—her constant benediction. Fields trampled with battle, saturated with blood, torn with the ruts of cannon, grow green again with grass, and the carnage is forgotten. Streets abandoned by traffic become grass grown like rural lanes, and are obliterated; forests decay, harvest perish, flowers vanish, but grass is immortal.

"Beleaguered by the sullen hosts of winter, it withdraws into the impregnable fortress of its subterranean vitality and emerges upon solicitation of spring. Sown by the winds, by wandering birds, propagated by the subtle horticulture of the elements, which are its ministers and servants, it softens the rude outline of the world. Its tenacious fibers hold the earth in its place, and prevent its soluble components from washing into the sea.

'It invades the solitude of deserts, climbs the inaccessible slopes and forbidding pinnacles of mountains, modifies the climates and determines the history, character and destiny of nations. Unobtrusive and patient, it has immortal vigor and aggression. Banished from the thoroughfare and field, it bides it time to return, and when vigilance is relaxed, or the dynasty has perished, it silently resumes the throne from which it has been expelled, but which it never abdicates.

"It bears no blazonry of bloom to charm the senses with fragrance or splendor, but its homely hue is more enchanting than the lily or the rose. It yields no fruit in earth or air, and yet, should its harvest fail for a single year famine would depopulate the world."

John James Ingalls, (1833-1900), Author, orator, lawyer and Kansas senator. My thanks to Ricky Linex, of the USDA/NRCS, for bringing this essay to my attention in his book, *Range Plants of North Central Texas.*

I assume, from the location and time that the author lived, that he was primarily thinking about the native prairie grass that would have been growing in the Tall Grass Prairies of Kansas during his time. This grass kept the soil in place and made for the most fertile land in the country. Unfortunately, most of the Tall Grass Prairie is gone and the non-native lawn grasses most folks have around their houses have few if any of the beneficial properties of our native prairie grasses.

WHY NATIVE PLANTS

We couldn't have healthy, functioning native habitats without native plants. The habitat we have in the Hill Country today evolved to be here over hundreds of thousands of years, meaning the native animals, insects and plants all evolved to be here together with our soil and climate. So when we work to manage a native habitat, we should be working to conserve and/or restore the native plants and animals in a relationship as nearly similar to what was here before European man arrived in the Hill Country as is possible in the 21st century.

By definition, no exotic or non-native plants would be here in an ideal case, and any native plants that have become extinct would be restored. We cannot, of course, attain such an ideal condition, but that doesn't mean that we shouldn't do as much as we can. The fact that the goal is unattainable, doesn't mean it is not a useful target or that we shouldn't always favor native plants over non-native ones.

Why Native Plants and Not Exotics?

Several of the Native Plant Society of Texas chapters in the area, Boerne, Fredericksburg, and Kerrville, have a program to promote native plants called NICE, **N**atives **I**nstead of **C**ommon **E**xotics. They highlight and publicize a new native plant each month or quarter and work with local nurseries to make sure people can find that plant for sale.

I have had many discussions with people either about the plants they have on their property or plants under consideration for planting, and often when I mention that this or that plant is or is not a native, I get kind of a blank stare as if to say, "What difference does it make?" It is a good question, and to anyone wishing to conserve, restore or improve our native Hill Country habitat, it makes a significant difference. Here is why.

To state the obvious, native Hill Country plants grew up here. They have been part of the natural ecosystem for hundreds or thousands of years. They have been successfully living, growing and propagating through droughts, floods, severe thunderstorms, insect and other animal predation, fires and whatever else Mother Nature dishes out. They have been coexisting with all of the other native flora and fauna of the Hill Country and have obviously survived. And, and this is important, they have done so up until the past 150 years or so without any help or interference from man.

What does this mean? It means that the native plants have evolved to live here with our variable weather patterns, our caliche soil and our early and late freeze dates without any human giving them extra water, or fertilizer, or pesticide, or pruning, or pollinating. In other words, they can take care of themselves, thank you very much.

Another characteristic of native plants is that they seldom become invasive (spread uncontrolled into areas outside of where they were planted) as many exotic plants do. Some exotics that do become invasive and cause serious problems for the native habitat include Chinaberry, Chinese pistache, Chinese tallow (are we beginning to see a pattern here?) ligustrum, nandina, giant reed, bamboo, vitex, Johnsongrass, KR bluestem, giant salvinia, and tamarisk (salt cedar).

The astute reader might wish to point out that cedar, although a native plant, can also become invasive. This is true. However, they have become invasive only because of disturbances caused by man, specifically overgrazing and the removal of frequent fire.

Most all of the exotics listed above were brought into this country for what seemed like a good reason at the time, and no one expected this would lead to the invasion we now experience. The law of unintended consequences comes into play here. We didn't intend for these plants to take over and destroy or alter the native habitat. But given the huge number of imported plant species, the chances were very high that some of them would find the Hill Country very much to their liking and with nothing to inhibit their propagation.

When non-native species crowd their way into native habitats, they disrupt the many interrelationships among all the native species of plants and animals, sometimes causing the extinction of native species.

Many of the exotic plants brought to the Hill Country, even those that do not ever become invasive, still require more water than similar native plants. This is especially true of lawn grasses such as St Augustine and Bermudagrass as well as many ornamentals. So for areas such as ours where water is a precious commodity, having native plants that do not need extra water is a very important feature. (It should be noted here that newly planted native plants, like all others, need extra water to become established.)

Finally, another reason to plant native plants is that because of the increased deer populations in our area in the last few decades, many native plants are becoming scarce because of deer predation, especially on the new young trees. Where will the replacements for the mature hardwoods come from? Planting native plants and caging them from the deer helps restore the native plant balance that we formerly had.

So, it would be NICE if everyone would take these points into consideration and work to conserve what native plants you have and plant only natives for a more natural landscape.

Invasive Plants to Avoid in the Hill Country

World-wide, invasive species are second only to habitat destruction (for development and farming) as the cause of the loss of species. It is estimated that the US spends over 100 billion dollars a year fighting invasive species. The Hill Country has, so far, been spared some of the worst examples of invasives experienced by other parts of the country.

We don't have, in large amounts, the kudzu of the southeast, the Asian carp of the Midwest, the zebra mussels of the Great Lakes, the Buffelgrass and Guineagrass of the Rio Grande Valley, the Cheatgrass of the western plains, or the Tamerisk of our western rivers. So far as I know, Giant salvinia has not made it to any of our local lakes, yet.

The legal definition of an invasive species is, "An alien species whose introduction does or is likely to cause economic or environmental harm…." Exotic, or alien, plants are introduced into this country either for the nursery trade, for agricultural purposes, or accidentally. Most of these plants do not become invasive, or are not invasive in the part of the country in which they are originally introduced. But certain species, and it is impossible to predict which ones, do become invasive and they grow and reproduce so prolifically that they escape where they were originally planted and crowd out native vegetation.

This invasion of introduced plant species results in a decrease in the population of certain native species, thus changing the balance of vegetation in the ecosystem. Species of insects or other animals that depended on the displaced plant species may disappear. Or the introduced plant may be utilized by different species, thus upsetting the balance of nature, so the diversity, the health, and the productivity of the ecosystem may be diminished.

A non-native plant found growing anywhere it was not originally planted is, or likely will become, invasive and should be avoided for the protection of our native habitat. Here are some of the worst offenders.

For trees and shrubs, the worst are Chinese tallow, Chinaberry, ligustrum, tree of heaven, paper mulberry, golden raintree, salt cedar, and vitex. Chinese tallow and Chinaberry are already taking over large stretches of the Guadalupe River banks and are increasingly seen throughout our area. Ligustrum is nearly ubiquitous in and around our cities and is a very strong competitor with our native plants. The tree of heaven is a very fast-growing tall tree which produces huge quantities of seeds, many of which produce numerous shoots in the landowner's lawns, but worse yet, are beginning to move out into the country. Vitex has almost totally choked off access to parts of upper Lake Buchanan.

For some years, it was thought that Chinese pistache, while it grows well here, was not invasive. There has been some recent evidence, however, that that is not the case and we may be seeing it escape from people's yards into natural areas. It is not uncommon for plant species to take many years to become invasive, as first the trees must reach reproductive age and the population necessary to become invasive.

Among the other worst invasives in this area are the giant reed (Arundo donax), which has taken over large stretches of many creeks in the area, crowding out all other vegetation. Other offenders include cocklebur, castorbean, bamboo, nandina, Japanese honeysuckle, musk thistle, Malta star thistle, Johnsongrass, and Bermudagrass.

Probably the most wide-spread invasive plant in the Hill Country, one that is present on nearly every ranch and ranchette, is King Ranch bluestem. In past years TXDOT planted lots of KR bluestem along roadsides to prevent erosion (fortunately, they now mostly use native grasses). Whether or not KR is better at that than some native grasses is questionable, but at any rate, it has spread from roadsides to almost everyone's property. It is most prevalent in moderate to heavily grazed pastures where it takes over from native grasses and is exceedingly difficult to remove.

So, the bottom line here is to avoid exotic plants that are known to become invasive and be cautious about any newly-introduced species as we never know what can become invasive. There are lots and lots of native plants which grew up here, belong here, and never cause any problems. So let's stick with these natives; they are easy to grow, don't cause problems, and don't need extra water or fertilizer.

Learning to Identify Native Plants

I am sometimes asked, "How do you learn to identify plants?" I suspect that it is like learning anything else, there is certainly more than one way to do it. What worked for me might not work for you.

But before we talk about how to learn the names of plants, we might ask why learning the names of plants is important. The plant would be the same whether we gave it a name or not, but having a name gives us something to associate everything else we know about the plant. Think of it like the name of a folder, either on your computer or on the tab of the old manila folders you keep in a file cabinet. The name on the tab allows you to know where to put all the information you have about that plant.

You could of course make up your own name for plants, but then you couldn't talk to other people or find information in books about the plants under your made-up name.

Learning plant names has to start by learning how to distinguish the differences among different plants, and that requires you to learn what characteristics to look for. For laymen, the characteristics one uses are different for trees, grasses and forbs.

For trees, one looks at the type of leaf, the arrangement of leaves, the shape of the leaf, the type of margin (edge) of the leaf. For some trees, other clues are important, like bark, leaf size, texture, fruit, etc. For grasses, the most used characteristics are the size, shape, and arrangement of the seed head. For forbs, one most often looks at the color, size, shape, and arrangement of the blooms, but also with attention to the leaves. Most books for plant identification have sections that discuss these characteristics and the names used to describe them.

My friend Bill Lindemann, in discussing how to learn to identify birds, talks about looking for the important characteristics such as relative size, shape, bill, color, markings, etc., and identifying plants is the same process.

Unfortunately, most books which describe plant characteristics have the plants listed by scientific family name. If you are just beginning to learn plant names, and you don't know the name, you certainly won't know the family it is in, so finding your plant in a book can be tedious. It is kind of like the schoolboy complaining if he doesn't know how to spell a word, he can't look it up in the dictionary.

There are keys published in some books which allow you to go through a series of questions about the plant you are interested in (e.g. Are the leaves arranged on the stems alternately or oppositely? Do the leaves have smooth margins or toothed ones?). But keys to grasses and even forbs can be difficult to use.

See the Tree and Shrub Identification subsection below.

For people just starting to learn our native plants, I would recommend the following books: *Trees, Shrubs, and Vines of the Texas Hill Country*, by Jan Wrede; *Grasses of the Texas Hill Country*, by Brian and Shirley Loflin; and *Wildflowers of the Texas Hill Country*, by Marshall Enquist. The advantage of these three books over the many other good books on these topics is that each of these books lists only those plants that commonly grow in the Hill Country, so you don't have to leaf through pages of pine trees or swamp flowers looking for your plant.

Learning to identify our native plants is not an easy task, but it can be a fun one, something you can do whenever and wherever you are. You start with what you already know (I'll bet you can identify a cedar, a live oak, a cypress, a mesquite, a bluebonnet, a Mexican hat, etc., so you don't really start from scratch. The more you learn, the more fun it is and the more you begin to appreciate our beautiful Hill Country. Good luck.

Non-Native Plants and Animals Can Be a Real Problem

"A monoculture of exotic invasive grass in Laguna Atascosa National Wildlife Refuge, home of the endangered ocelot."

Recently, on a trip to the Texas Coast and South Texas, I saw, again, the problems presented by many invasive plant species. Most people in the Edwards Plateau, and most of the rest of Texas for that matter, are aware of the exotic, invasive grass, King Ranch or KR Bluestem and it is a problem most all landowners have to deal with.

But in South Texas, some other non-native, invasive grasses, buffelgrass, Guinea grass, and Klegberg bluestem, are taking over vast areas and completely crowding out native grasses and forbs. See the next essay for more on the South Texas situation.

People often point out, correctly, that most of the food we eat is in fact not native to North America. All of our livestock (cattle, sheep, goats, pigs and chickens) was introduced by early settlers; none are native to the Western Hemisphere. The same is true with most of our vegetable crops, fruit trees and most all cereal grains (wheat, oats, barley).

So it is logical to ask, if all of these food-producing species are OK, why isn't every other newly introduced species? The answer is simple. All of the animals listed above are domesticated; they can be herded, moved, managed, handled, kept in a given area, and their population can be controlled by man. And all of our main food crops, (vegetables, fruits and grains) can likewise be controlled so they don't become invasive.

For an exotic plant or animal to become a serious problem, three things have to happen. First, the plant or animal must be able to reproduce without man's help and/or in spite of man's attempt to control it. Second, the plant or animal must be able to escape wherever it was introduced and colonize other properties or areas. And third, it must be able to out-compete native species in a way that alters the native habitat.

The majority of introduced species, plant and animal, do not fit those characteristics, but many do and we don't know enough to be able to predict in advance which species will become a problem. Exotic ungulates (Axis, fallow, sika deer, blackbuck antelope) are not much different from goats, so why are they a problem? IF one of these exotic species were introduced into a ranch to replace cattle or sheep or goats and IF they never escaped from that ranch, and IF their population were controlled so they did not outcompete white-tailed deer for food, then they could be considered just another livestock species and not a problem.

But when axis deer escape and become feral, as feral hogs did many years ago, they are no longer under the control of man. Their population can increase above the numbers the habitat can handle, and we have a problem.

When a rancher plants a non-native forage grass that can then escape his property and invade other properties, including National Wildlife Refuges, and that grass crowds out native grasses and forbs to the detriment of wildlife, we have a problem.

Some of you may be asking yourselves, don't white-tailed deer and cedar fit the three criteria I listed above for an invasive species? The answer is that yes, they do. But the reason they do is not because they were introduced from another ecosystem, but that man altered our ecosystem, and habitat, to allow deer and cedar to increase in numbers to the point of being invasive. We killed most all of the large predators, removing population control of the deer. And we eliminated or stopped most prairie fires, which had previously controlled the numbers of cedar. So we created those problems and we have to fix them.

We didn't introduce white-tailed deer or cedar into our habitat, but we did introduce KR bluestem, buffelgrass, Guinea grass, Kleberg bluestem, Chinaberry, ligustrum, axis deer, feral hogs, and the list goes on and on.

We have enough problems with invasive exotics already, let's not introduce any new ones.

Invasive Exotic Grasses Are Reducing the Diversity of our Native Habitat

I have written in previous essays on different aspects of exotic plants, trying to make the case that exotic species are detrimental to our native habitat and flora and fauna. But there is a difference between non-natives like crape myrtle, and rosemary and even St. Augustine lawn grass, which are not invasive and plants that are invasive. (Yes, St. Augustine is a poor choice for a lawn grass in an arid area like this, but it can't grow successfully here without man's help and thus is not invasive in the Hill Country.)

An invasive species is one which escapes cultivation and propagates on its own into other areas, usually crowding out native vegetation and taking over an area. Things like Chinaberry, ligustrum, *Arundo donax* (giant reed), KR bluestem, vitex, Kleberg bluestem and the other "old world bluestem cousins," buffelgrass and Guinea grass all fit the definition of invasive.

A recent article in Texas Wildlife on this subject caught my eye. Forrest Smith, of the Caesar Kleberg Wildlife Research Institute of the Texas A&M University-Kingsville, wrote an article entitled "Are Arthropods the Canary in the Coal Mine?"

Arthropods include insects, spiders and crustaceans that have external shells and segmented bodies. Smith described several studies in South Texas in which researchers counted the numbers of arthropods as a measure of the biodiversity of the area, and compared the numbers found in native grass pastures to those found on sites containing exotic grasses.

In one study, the researchers found 60 percent more arthropods in native sites than in sites containing exotic grasses, and, perhaps most surprisingly, the amount of grass cover ascribed to the exotic grasses was less than 20 percent. In another study the researchers found 73 percent less forb cover on sites containing more than 25 percent exotic buffelgrass. In yet another study, the number of species of arthropods on native grass sites was found to be ten times that found on sites with exotic old world bluestem grass.

Because of the nature and growth habit of most exotic grasses, they take over bare ground between native bunchgrasses and prevent the germination of native forbs (wildflowers), which in turn are necessary for many species of insects to live. In fact, it works both ways, some species of forbs need a certain species of insect to pollinate them and some species of insects need a certain species of forb for their larva to feed on.

So when the invasive grass chokes out the forbs, the greatly-reduced number and diversity of forbs affects the insect populations and diversity, which in turn further reduces the number of forbs.

So why do we care about the number of arthropods and insects? Because the effects don't stop there. In fact, that is just the beginning. Without the forbs, ground-nesting birds like turkey and quail, plus dove and many other prairie birds, will lose a vital food source. Without insects most all types of birds will have a hard time raising their young as even seed-eaters and hummingbirds need insects for protein. Lizards, amphibians and small snakes also live on insects. Higher up the food chain the predators of the quail, dove, sparrows, lizards, toads, etc., are also deprived of their normal food source.

Previously, I wrote about invasives we had observed in two South Texas National Wildlife Refuges, saying, "invasive grasses, buffelgrass, Klegberg bluestem and Guinea grass, are taking over vast areas and completely crowding out native grasses and forbs. In many affected areas, these grasses have formed a tangled, two-foot-high monoculture of grass with larger shrubs being the only other vegetation. These areas are useful habitat for very few species of birds, mammals or other animals."

The ranchers who planted these grasses, because they are somewhat more productive as forage for cattle, may not have intended that the grass escape into the wildlife refuges, but it did. Now the cattle raisers are left with good cattle forage but poor wildlife habitat, including deer habitat, and the wildlife refuges are now also poor habitat.

This is the danger that Smith was referring to in his reference to reduced arthropods as being like the "canary in the coal mine." And it is going to be hard for us to get back to the "fresh air" of native habitats.

GROWING NATIVE PLANTS

The Why, What, When and Where of Tree Planting

Why should we be planting trees? There are several reasons. Because the high deer populations prevent the natural replacement of older trees and they eat all of the root sprouts and saplings that are within their reach. Some small trees and shrubs are becoming scarce, so planting them ourselves helps assure the survival of the species. Planting new trees and shrubs adds to plant diversity and thus the quality of the habitat. Then there is carbon sequestration and lowering the temperature in the local environment. And of course, there is just the fact that most of us really like trees and like to live among them.

What kind of trees should we plant? There is a short answer: NATIVE, NATIVE, NATIVE. Native trees are adapted to our thin, high pH soil and drought-prone climate, and once established, need little or no care or maintenance. They grew up here, and they know how to make it on their own. Many non-native trees require more water, fertilizer, or other extra care than native trees. Also, some non-native trees become invasive by spreading uncontrollably and crowding out native vegetation.

Specifically, what kind of trees should you plant? I have reduced a number of longer lists of recommended trees to two groups of reasonably available, successful and desirable trees you might consider. All of these trees are native to the Hill Country or to adjacent areas.

The trees followed by a W need to be in relatively wet areas, those with a D need deep soil, those with a G need good drainage, and those followed by an E are evergreen. If no letter follows the name, they can grow most everywhere.

For large trees: bald cypress (W), bigtooth maple, bur oak, cedar elm, chinquapin oak (D), escarpment black cherry, gum bumelia, Lacey oak (G), live oak (E), Mexican white oak (Monterrey oak) (E), pecan (D), Spanish oak (Texas red oak), sycamore (W), Texas ash, and Texas (little) walnut.

For smaller trees and large shrubs: Anacacho orchid tree, buttonbush (W), Carolina buckthorn, cenizo (G, E), desert willow (G), Eve's necklace, flameleaf sumac, goldenball leadtree (G), hop tree (wafer ash), Mexican buckeye, Mexican plum, Mexican redbud, Mexican silktassel (E), possumhaw, rough-leaf dogwood, rusty blackhaw, Texas mountain laurel (E), Texas persimmon, Texas redbud, and yaupon(E).

When should we plant trees? That's easy. The most-preferred month is October. After that the preferred months, more or less in descending order, are: November, December, September, February, March and April. Don't even think about planting in May through August; even if you manage to keep a tree wet enough so that it doesn't die, it won't be growing many roots until cooler weather anyway. This of course is contrary to the advice given in colder climates, where the winter is the most stressful period and the preferred planting time is in the spring.

Where should you plant your trees? There are two answers to that. First, plant it where IT wants to be. Don't try to plant a tree that wants some shade and moist soil out on a bare, south-sloping, caliche hill. Find out what type of environment a tree needs before buying it, and if that doesn't match your lot, don't waste your money. If it is going to be a large tree, before you dig a hole, look up. If you see a power line or other obstruction, you should move to a different location.

The second answer to the above question is to plant the tree where you can take care of it. If you try to put a tree way out on the corner of your lot up on a hill, and the only way to get water there is to carry it, you are not likely to be very successful. Finally, no tree (other than a cedar) will survive outside of a fence or enclosure on most properties, at least until it has most of its leaves above the deer browse line (about 5').

How to Plant a Tree—There's More to It Than You Think

I know that most people think they know how to plant a tree. But it is also true that a major cause of the loss of newly planted trees and shrubs is improper planting. Here is a 12 step procedure based on directions from Robert Edmonson of the Texas Forest Service.

1) **Select an appropriate location for the tree.**
   Use a tree that will grow well under local environmental conditions and provide it with plenty *of* space to grow and mature. This includes both vertical and horizontal space for the canopy and plenty of room for root growth. Don't try to grow water-loving plants on rocky, sunny slopes, or xeric plants next to water.
2) **Dig the hole at least twice as wide as the root ball (wider is better).**
   Wide areas give roots a place to spread and grow. Dig the hole no deeper than the root ball to keep the tree from settling too deep and dig square holes to allow for root penetration out of the hole and into the surrounding soil. (Round holes tend to cause the roots to grow in a circle inside the soft fill dirt.)
3) **Fill the hole with water and check the drainage.**
   If it takes longer than 24 hours to drain, select another site. A tree will die if its roots are underwater for long periods of time. Tree roots need air.
4) **Prune the tree sparingly only if necessary.**
   Remove dead, broken and diseased branches and crushed and girdling roots only. Removing even a small portion of the healthy canopy actually slows root growth and delays establishment. A well-selected tree requires no pruning.
5) **Remove all foreign materials from the tree.**
   This includes wires, twine, cords, containers, tags and especially non-biodegradable bags. If planting a balled and burlapped tree, remove as much of the burlap as possible to allow for water infiltration into the bag and root penetration out of the bag.
6) **Set the tree in the hole with the root collar flush or slightly above natural grade.**
   Planting too deep is a leading cause of mortality of newly planted trees. Do not pick the tree up by the trunk. Always handle by the container or root ball.
7) **Gently backfill with the same soil that came out of the hole.**
   Create a natural environment, not an artificial one. Do not add soil amendments or fertilizer. Too much nitrogen will burn tender young roots, slowing growth and delaying establishment. Settle the soil with water. Tamping the soil causes compaction and damages roots.
8) **Stake the tree only if necessary.**
   Staking is required only for very flexible, floppy young trees. Stakes should not be left in place longer than 1 year.
9) **Mulch the tree out to the drip line. Spread mulch 1-2 inches deep up to but not touching the trunk. Wood chips, pine bark, leaf litter, hay, etc. are great mulches. Mulch keeps soil**

temperature fluctuations to a minimum and increases soil moisture retention. Mulch also suppresses weed growth and organic mulch adds nutrients to the soil.

10) **Water the tree for at least one year, preferably two.**
A newly planted tree requires 6-8 gallons of water per diameter inch of trunk per week, less often in late fall or winter. A thorough soaking is much better than light, frequent waterings.

11) **Protect the tree from animals (this includes humans).**
A wire-mesh cage at least 3 feet in diameter and 4 feet tall staked to the ground works miracles. Deer and livestock will eat your tree if it is not protected and weed-whackers will kill your tree in an instant.

12) **Perform routine maintenance for at least two growing seasons.**
This includes biannual weed control, yearly mulch replacement, weekly watering, and protection maintenance.

Choose a Tree for the Site, Not a Site for the Tree

A friend of mine, Robert Edmonson, of the Texas Forest Service, is an expert not only on oak wilt, but also on planting and growing native trees and shrubs. One of the messages he likes to convey to people is to "choose a tree for the site, not a site for the tree."

At first this might not make sense to you, it may seem like two ways to say the same thing, but Robert explains it this way. Many people go to a nursery and look over the available trees and shrubs, find something they like, then take it home and then start looking for a place to plant it. But often the tree that they bought is unsuitable for the site they had in mind, and the outcome is usually poor.

They would have better luck if they first chose a site where they want a tree and assess the characteristics of that site (space, sunny or shady, deep soil or shallow), and then go find a tree that grows well in that type of environment. Just because you have decided that you want a "such and such tree" because your sister or a guy down the block has one does not mean that you have a place where it will grow.

I heard a story about a neighbor down the road who saw cypress trees growing down the road from his house so he bought some and they promptly died. Then he noticed there were sycamores down the road too, so he bought some and tried them—with the same result. The problem was that cypress and sycamores are trees that grow in riparian areas with deep soil and some moisture, but the neighbor lived on top of a nearby hill with shallow, rocky soil.

The point Robert tries to make is to know the kind of environment a tree or shrub likes to grow in and then only buy species that are compatible with the kind of sites you have available. In fact, that advice applies to perennials and wildflowers as well.

I can tell you from personal experience that the same species growing even in close proximity to one another can exhibit very different growth characteristics. Soon after we moved into our house we planted a possumhaw out in full sun. It grew slowly and had unhealthy-looking leaves, but it did produce berries. After a few years we found volunteer possumhaws growing in various places under mature trees in the yard and we now have a half dozen of the shrubs, all much larger and healthier than the original.

We have a number of mature blackjack oaks and post oaks growing around the yard, and we have quite a few volunteers of both species, either from root sprouts or acorns. Most are growing under larger mature trees and are healthy, but growing slowly. But two blackjacks growing in a fairly open space are much larger and growing faster than any growing in the shade. It is hard to find blackjack oaks for sale in nurseries because they are hard to grow from acorns into healthy trees. I have planted and caged several small blackjacks over the years only to watch them grow very, very slowly.

Several years ago I planted and caged several fairly similar-sized cedar elms, and watered them regularly for the first three years. Most of them made beautiful trees, but two are alive and growing, but very slowly, and don't appear to be very healthy.

The point of these examples is that even when we do pay attention to the environment and plant species known to grow in a certain environment, success is not always assured. So to improve our success rate, it is important to know the growth requirements of trees and shrubs and to only buy species that fit the sites we have available.

The best way to find the growth characteristics of native trees and shrubs is to go to the Lady Bird Johnson Wildflower Center website, www.wildflower.org/plants/. What you learn there will not guarantee you will have 100 percent success with new plantings, but it will make sure you won't waste your money trying to plant a cypress or a buttonbush or a pecan on a rocky hilltop.

How to Tend Our Gardens More Like Mother Nature Would

We have all seen the fertilizer ads and the lawn mower ads, and many of us have lived in suburbs where everyone had manicured lawns that looked like the ads. It is not clear how modern Americans have come to regard such unnatural monocultures as the ideal, but it is clear that such landscapes are not natural.

Mother Nature doesn't grow single species of grass in wide expanses, devoid of other grasses, weeds or flowers. She doesn't own a lawnmower either. Sure, there are grazing animals, but they each pick and choose what to eat, leaving some plants and nibbling others, all of which increases the diversity of flora in Mother Nature's "lawn."

You don't see any dead limbs or oddly-shaped shrubs in those TV ads either. Our sense of "neatness" forbids that too. But Mother Nature doesn't own a chain saw or pruners either. Dead limbs, strange-shaped trees, and irregularly spaced trees are all part of natural landscapes.

And guess what. Mother Nature doesn't own a leaf rake either. So in the fall when all the humans are franticly raking up every single leaf that falls on that beautiful lawn, Mother Nature gets to rest and enjoy the colors.

If we humans had the same sense of aesthetics as Mother Nature, the fertilizer companies might be in trouble, but we would have a lot less yard work to do.

Of course, this isn't all about how much work we should do, but what is best for the landscape and the habitat around us. Spreading chemical fertilizer on lawns, and then giving the fast-growing lawns the additional water they require, is a waste of natural resources. But then the weekly mowing of the new growth and disposing of the clippings amounts to stuffing the leaf bags with dollar bills, since that is where the fertilizer nutrients and even some of the water goes. This might all be worth it if the result were a healthier habitat, but in fact the reverse is true. Large expanses of weed-free St. Augustine are home to almost no wildlife. And the soil below isn't that healthy either.

If pruning every dead limb, felling every dead or misshapen tree, or raking up every leaf and twig and hauling them away or burning them were so beneficial, how is it that the trees and the shrubs and the weeds and the grass evolved to thrive in this country before we arrived and invented riding mowers, weed-eaters, and chainsaws.

Obviously, none of us wants to live with a dead tree in our front yard, but a dead tree or a pile of dead limbs out in the "back 40" is just good wildlife habitat. And does it really make sense to rake off live oak leaves from a flower bed, and then go to town to buy mulch for the bed? Leaving leaves, limbs, and last year's grass where they lay helps to return the nutrients contained in them to the soil, after they have served as much-needed mulch for a time, and while it may not be neat, it is nature's way.

Mother Nature doesn't own any bug spray either. I have been impressed with the minimal amount of insect damage we have observed around our house on our native flowers, shrubs, and trees. I think I can count on one hand the number of times in the past 16 years that we have used any insecticide outside our house. And even some of those times, we have since learned, if we had just waited a few more days, the caterpillars would have turned into a cocoon and the plants would put up new leaves and all would be right with the world.

I know some people will disagree with much of what I have said here. But I also know that if more people practiced the kind of yard maintenance described here we would be using fewer natural resources and making a smaller footprint on the ecology of the Hill Country. If everyone would at least think about these ideas before doing what they have always done, that would be a start.

Native Forbs You Can Grow in Your Garden

There are many beautiful, perennial, native forbs that you can grow in your garden. Being native means they can generally get by on somewhat less water than many non-natives, and they can tolerate our native soil (although most like good drainage). Here is just a partial list.

Big red sage is a 2 to 4-foot-tall plant endemic to the Hill Country. It produces bluish-red blooms that stand out from the upper stems and that attract hummingbirds. It blooms from June to October.

Blackfoot daisy is a bushy 6 to 18-inch-tall perennial with classic daisy-like blooms of white petals and yellow centers. It is quite drought tolerant and likes well-drained soil. It blooms from April to October.

Cedar sage is a one to two-foot-tall perennial with round fuzzy leaves that prefers shade to half-sun. It produces spikes with many brilliant red tubular flowers from March to July. Hummingbirds love this plant also.

Damianita is a small, much-branching evergreen shrub (not actually a forb), seldom much over a foot tall. It has ½ to ¾ inch yellow flowers at the tips of the stems periodically from April to September. It is very drought tolerant and requires good drainage. Not a deer favorite.

Engelmann daisy or cut-leaf daisy is a common roadside perennial from ½ to 2-feet tall with fuzzy long deeply-lobed leaves. It blooms with 1-inch yellow blooms from March to July.

Four-nerve daisy is a one-foot-tall plant with gray-green leaves that grows in sun or half-sun. Its yellow daisy-like blooms are 1 to 2 inches in diameter at the top of stems. It blooms from March to June and again in early fall.

Gregg's mistflower is one of the best butterfly plants around. It is usually from 1 to 3-feet tall and grows best in half sun. The blooms are light blue and feathery from July to October.

Lance leaf coreopsis is a 1 to 2-foot-tall plant with long narrow leaves that likes sun to half-sun. It produces yellow 1 to 2 inch flowers from April to June.

Maximilian sunflower grows in colonies which can attain several feet in diameter with numerous stems from 2 to 6-feet tall. Large yellow flowers are produced up and down the top portion of the stems in September and October. It grows best in full sun with normal amounts of moisture.

Mealy blue sage is a 1 to 2-foot-tall perennial with narrow leaves and blue flowers. It blooms in the spring and is sometimes confused with bluebonnets. The deer don't eat it. It can grow in sun to half sun.

Tall goldenrod is an erect plant from 3 to 6 feet tall with numerous clusters of small yellow flowers in an open flower head at the top of the plant. Blooming occurs from September to October. It grows best in full sun.

Yellowbells, or esperanza, is a spectacular, large, 3 to 6-foot plant that produces many 3 to 5 inch clusters of bell-shaped flowers from April to November. It can grow in full sun.

Wild red columbine prefers shaded to half-sun locations that are at least slightly moist. It grows as a rounded shape less than a foot tall but puts up flower stalks 1 to 2-feet tall in the spring. The blooms are reddish with spurs in back and yellow centers in front that attract hummingbirds.

Zexmenia is a very xeric (drought-tolerant) bushy, 1 to 2-foot-tall plant of open pastures. It produces many small yellow daisy-like blooms from May to September. Deer don't eat this plant.

Plants with Prickles Are Not All Bad

I know a lot of people who think that any plants that can poke you are bad and who set out to eliminate them from their property. Like everything else in Nature, it is more complicated than that.

Let me start with the most common one, prickly pear. The long "thorns" on a prickly pear are technically called spines because they are modified leaves (thorns are modified limbs or twigs), and the fine hair-like structures are called glochids. Some folks wage war on prickly pear while others seek out different varieties as landscape plants. Prickly pear do have some important functions in a native habitat, primarily as cover and protection for quail and small animals, as well as "nurse plants" to protect forbs and woody plants that would otherwise be eaten by deer and livestock.

Several years ago my wife and I heard loud screams coming from a large prickly pear in our front yard. If you have ever heard the screams of a rabbit in distress, you will always know it when you hear it. When we went to investigate, I found the back end of a large Texas Rat snake sticking out of the prickly pear. I grabbed it and pulled it out, fearing what I would find when I could see the head, but it didn't have anything in its mouth and hadn't swallowed anything either. I let the snake go about 100 yards or so away and later we saw a mother cottontail moving babies from the prickly pear—her hiding place had been discovered.

It is not uncommon to find plants such as young hackberries, escarpment black cherries, Carolina buckthorns, etc., growing up in the middle of a large prickly pear, which is protecting these otherwise deer-favorite trees from being eaten. The purple tunas produced by prickly pear are food for just about every native animal including deer, coyotes and most all of the smaller furry critters we have.

In the drought of the '50s, ranchers burned off the spines of prickly pear so their cattle, sheep and goats could eat the pads. Interestingly, I am told by most all range scientists that if cattle are eating prickly pear with the spines on, they are severely malnourished, and there isn't much nourishment in the pads anyway. But I have observed some cows that apparently have developed a taste for pear and are eating prickly pear pads with the spines on (It hurts just to watch that!), and they seem to actually relish them.

Agarita bushes are interesting in that they have neither thorns nor spines, but because of the extreme stiffness of the leaves and the very sharp points on the leaves, they are certainly well-armed. What good are agarita? Well, in the early spring their yellow flowers attract native bees and later the red berries feed birds, raccoons and other critters. And they provide the same kind of nurse-plant service that I described above for prickly pear. While walking people's property, I frequently find clusters of several species of woody plants growing together, and agarita is almost always one of the species.

The greenbrier vine is another plant many landowners try to eliminate. It can have many spines on the leaves and thorns on the stems, although sometimes neither are all that prevalent. It turns out that the leaves contain up to about 20 percent protein, and deer will eat them, especially in the winter.

Yuccas and agaves have sharp-pointed leaves that provide protection from predators for quail and other small animals. Mesquite beans are an important food source for just about all herbivores and omnivores, and mockingbirds like to nest among their thorn-protected branches.

Dr. Dale Rollins, probably the state's best known expert on quail, tells a story about his speaking to a group of ranchers on a field day about how every plant has some beneficial function in the habitat, if we are just smart enough to understand it. He said an old rancher came up to him and held a grassbur up in his face and said, "Oh Yeah, what is this good for?" Dale said he was almost ready to give up when a friend of his spoke up and said, "They slow down quail dogs don't they?"

So, just because there are some plants you may not want growing in places around your house doesn't mean they are not important to the native habitat.

Dead Plant Material is Valuable: Don't Throw It Away

When it comes to deciding about how to manage a native habitat, I always try to think about how Mother Nature did things before humans arrived and started to "manage" things and to "improve" the landscape. One thing I know for sure, Mother Nature didn't throw things away.

Humans, on the other hand, tend to want to get rid of things they consider to be "unattractive," especially dead plant material. But dead plant material is an important component of a healthy, functioning ecosystem, and it takes many forms from many different sources.

Let's start with lawns. Lawns are not my favorite landscape feature, being wasteful of resources and poor habitat. But this is one place where many folks don't just collect dead plant material, they make it dead in order to collect it. Mowing and collecting the clippings is removing some of the fertilizer and any other nutrients that were contained in the leaves as well as some of the water and, at least in the case of many folks, the clippings are simply thrown away.

Dead plant material contains the organic matter so vital to a healthy soil as well as many minerals. A host of insects and microscopic creatures help to break down this organic matter into tiny particles which are then incorporated into the soil. Organic matter is the most commonly lacking component of Hill Country soils.

The subject of raking leaves is covered in the next essay.

Downed limbs not only provide a habitat for some insects and microorganisms and the critters that feed on them, but they also provide a "nursery" area for grass, forbs and woody plants to grow up and get established inside the protection of the dead limbs. Downed limbs also slow down water runoff and reduce erosion.

And then there is the issue of dead trees. Of course, if you live in town, there may be a lot of peer pressure for you to remove a dead tree in your front yard. But certainly for those of us in the country, there is the option of leaving dead trees alone and allowing them to decay and fall naturally. Standing dead trees provide food for woodpeckers and other animals seeking the insects under the bark. In addition, holes drilled by woodpeckers not only provide nest sites for themselves, but for other species as well. Many living, as well as dead, trees have large hollow limbs and trunks that provide homes to squirrels, ringtails, owls and a number of other native critters.

Downed wood in the form of large limbs, as well as tree trunks, will rot slowly, providing nutrients to mushrooms, microorganisms and various insect larvae. The slow decomposition of dead wood, facilitated by these species, provides a long term source of organic matter and minerals to the local soil.

And finally, in riparian areas, downed tree trunks are an important feature to help to slow down flood water, dissipate energy and provide habitat for riparian fauna such as frogs, toads and turtles.

The bottom line is that throwing away dead plant material is taking away an important component of the fertility of future soil and thus the plants that will be growing in that soil. In addition, removal of all dead plant material is also removing an important component of a healthy native habitat that cost us nothing, but is important to the functioning of your local ecosystem. So try not to throw it all away.

Leaves: Nature's Renewable Resource

Fallen leaves as Mother Nature recycles her resources.

When I was a kid growing up in the High Plains of the Permian Basin, where there are no real native trees, all we had was one Chinese elm in the yard. So I didn't grow up with the habit of raking leaves in the fall. Then when I moved to the Northeast, we lived in and were surrounded by a forest of very tall oaks, hickories and maples, so we had lots of leaves fall on our lawn, driveway, and flower beds. We had two choices back then, haul them all up a pretty steep driveway to the street and let the city haul them away or take care of them on our property.

Partly because we knew that throwing the leaves away was throwing away much needed organic matter and nutrients and partly because hauling them up to the street would have been a lot of hard work, we chose to use them on our property. Most of the time, we would rake the leaves into rows or small piles and run the lawnmower over them several times to chop them up into smaller pieces, and then use the chopped up leaves to spread on flower beds to prevent freeze damage to some of the plants and return organic matter to the soil. What we didn't use in that way we put in a huge pile to compost.

Since we moved back to Texas, we don't have near the volume of leaves that we had back in the NE, so it is never that much of a chore. Usually in areas under trees where there is little if any "lawn" because of the deep shade, we just leave the leaves under the trees. Sometimes we rake some of the leaves up to spread over flower beds to help keep the soil from freezing and keep moisture in the soil during the winter. This also returns organics and nutrients to the soil for the microorganisms in the soil to help return to the plants in the spring. (If you have a low faucet or anything else you want to protect from freezing, a pile of leaves makes a pretty good insulator.)

My philosophy of gardening is to try to mimic Mother Nature as much as possible. Mother Nature doesn't rake leaves. In fact, the health of the woodland part of our Hill Country is partly because of leaves falling under the trees, covering the ground to protect the top inch or so from freezing and from drying out, shading the soil in the summer, and providing habitat for all kinds of beneficial insects, skinks, lizards and toads.

Of course, if you have a city/suburban type lawn, especially if it is St. Augustine, you don't want leaves covering it during the winter as this might allow mold to grow on your lawn. In some cases, where the leaf cover is thin, if you can set your lawnmower to mulch you can grind up the leaves fine enough to fall down between the grass blades which should be OK. Or you can make compost piles with the leaves, chopped up or not, to give you compost next year. Most of the time to be successful around here, compost piles should to be watered occasionally and to have some different kinds of plant material.

Think of keeping leaves on your property as one more thing to recycle, along with cans, bottles, newspaper and cardboard. None of our natural resources are so abundant that we can afford to waste them. Buying ground up trees to use as mulch doesn't seem to make as much sense as using free, recycled, natural leaf mulch.

Surviving Another Hot, Dry Summer

As I was standing out in the afternoon sunshine (Don't ask why I didn't do this in the early morning!) using the last of my rainwater supply to try to keep our trees and shrubs from wilting, it occurred to me that this was an annual battle to keep everything we want to grow alive and well while at the same time not using too much of our scarce natural resource.

It also occurred to me that there are a lot of things landowners can do to help their trees, shrubs and perennials survive another summer while also keeping an eye on the amount of water we use. Here are some thoughts.

The first thought is that we have to get into our heads that this is going to be an ongoing struggle for the foreseeable future, as it is not going to get any cooler and we are not going to have any more water, at least not on a long-term basis.

Since most of the water used by the average homeowner for at least six months a year is for lawn care, the lawn is the first place to concentrate one's effort. Many people have concluded that trying to keep a large, water-hungry, introduced-grass lawn looking picture-book perfect is not only a losing battle, but perhaps one that we should not be trying to win. Greatly reducing the size of the lawn and replacing St Augustine or even bermudagrass with some of the newer native grass mixtures of buffalograss will save a lot of water. Mowing infrequently and at a high mower setting and leaving the clippings on the lawn are all water- and time-saving practices as well. If the lawn ain't growing, don't be mowing!

Installing drip irrigation on all flower beds and around shrubs is the most efficient way to water these plants. Sprinkler systems of all kinds are the least efficient as much of the water evaporates before it even reaches the plants, or blows off in the wind, or just wets the leaves or mulch, none of which helps the plants at all.

The most dependable drip systems utilize what are often referred to as "in-line emitter" tubing, ½ inch or ¼ inch plastic tubing with built in emitters every several inches. How the tubing is laid out in the beds, in terms of how close together the tubing is as well as how close to the individual plants is important, but the systems allow for a lot of flexibility in this regard. Trees should be watered to a depth of 6 inches so that a 6-inch screwdriver can be pushed in all the way. Ideally, one would want the drip tubing to be under mulch.

One of the biggest mistakes many people make in laying out drip tubing around trees and shrubs is running the tubing too close to the trunks. Trees and most shrubs have most of their feeder roots at least as far out from the trunk as the outer limbs are, so that is where most of the drip tubing should be.

Mulch is critically important. The temperature of bare soil can be 20 to 40 degrees hotter than the soil under mulch and that causes much of the water in the soil to evaporate and kills soil organisms as well. Many people recommend 3 or 4 inches of mulch. My personal opinion is that two inches are optimal. More mulch won't keep the soil much cooler, but it will intercept water from rain or sprinklers thus preventing some of the water from reaching the soil.

Plant selection and location have a lot to do with the success of plants surviving the summer. In general, and there are obvious exceptions, plants that grow predominately east of here require more water and plants that grow west of here require less water. Plants that you see growing natively (not planted by anyone) in areas similar to your location are your best bet.

Most perennials, small shrubs and vines can grow in at least partial shade and will do much better when planted under trees than when planted where they are exposed to full western or southern sunlight.

Finally, you will always have a few things that require some hand watering on the hottest days. That is OK, it gives you a chance to get out and enjoy your yard—but don't wait until mid-afternoon like I did.

How to Make Your Garden Look "Natural"

A few weeks ago I was walking the property of new landowners, helping them identify the trees, grasses and forbs on their land. At one point I observed a medium-sized pecan tree, but upon approaching it I noticed two other pecans and I told the owners that these had been planted several years ago.

They wanted to know how I knew they were planted instead of being natural. The answer was that they were in a perfect straight line and exactly equally spaced and about the same size. The probability of Mother Nature doing that is very remote.

Humans plant things in rows, evenly spaced, or in some other recognizable pattern—the result, I guess, of our innate sense of order.

In Nature, there is no such pattern as to where plants are located. What we see in a walk through a natural area is the result of the plants that have survived growing in the place where we find them. I am reminded of the difference between humans and Mother Nature in the placement of new plants every time I walk around our yard and observe all of the volunteer plants that have come up in the past 12 or 15 years.

With the exception of a few grasses and forbs here and there, the great majority of the volunteer plants in our fenced yard are under trees. Since we didn't plant any of the things I am referring to, Mother Nature must have been involved. Why would Mother Nature show a preference for the areas under trees? Probably for a couple of reasons: first, the areas under trees are shaded and therefore the soil is more moist and the new sprouts will be shaded and not baked in the hot sun. Secondly, most of the volunteer woody plants that have come up in our yard that are clearly not root sprouts from a mother tree are of species that produce berries—hackberry, escarpment black cherry, possumhaw and prairie flame-leaf sumac. Birds like to eat berries. Birds like to sit in trees. The bird droppings under the trees thus contain seeds.

Most people have driven down country roads and noticed the unusually high populations of numerous plant species along the fence rows—all for a similar reason. Birds like to sit on fences too.

One of the things I do find surprising is that a larger percentage of the volunteer trees under our trees are growing up close to the trunk. I wouldn't expect birds to spend more time up next to the trunk than out among the outer limbs, so I have no explanation for the volunteers being close to the trunks.

But it is certainly true, that in nature it is not uncommon to find young trees growing near the trunk of a much older tree of a different species. We humans would never walk up to a mature tree and try to dig a hole to plant a young tree just a few feet from the trunk. It is just not logical to us and would limit the growth of the new tree anyway.

Likewise, it is common to find multiple native species growing all intertwined together. Common examples are agarita, hackberry, grape, and greenbrier all intermingled together, the hackberry and grape getting some protection from the agarita and greenbrier. At another time you might find an escarpment black cherry and cedar elm growing up in the middle of a prickly pear.

Most all native grass areas are a complicated mix of up to a dozen species of grasses and sometimes even more species of forbs. In fact, when recommending reseeding of a grassland, most experts will recommend planting mixtures of grasses and forbs with at least a dozen species, because the odds of getting something to grow and to mimic Mother Nature are better with mixes.

So the next time you are out in your garden and thinking about adding some native plants, think mixtures and diversity, not straight lines and uniformity. You will be surprised at how "natural" your garden will look, and the birds and the butterflies will love it too. But don't get me wrong, if it best fits your sense of aesthetics, native plants will grow in neat rows too.

TREE AND SHRUB IDENTIFICATION

In spite of the fact that I believe that grasses are the most important plant group on Hill Country properties, I have to admit that the dominant plants most people notice the most, pay attention to the most, and are the subject of many of our management activities are the trees and shrubs. And I also have to admit that I have a real love affair with trees and shrubs. So it is not by accident that this is a large part of this book. Trees are, quite simply, important to the lives of many of us. They are also a major component of the native habitat of the Hill Country

It helps to know the identity of a tree, and something about it, before one can know how to manage, care for, or in some cases get rid of any given tree. This is why a significant part of this chapter is devoted to learning how to identify common Hill Country trees.

In addition to the following section on Tree and Shrub Identification, there is a more detailed tree key as well as photos to aid in tree identification on my website, www.hillcountrynaturalist.org. On the "HC Ecology" page you can find my "Tree ID Key," a collection of photos for the species in the key on "Tree ID Photos," a collection of leaf photos on "Leaf Photos Sorted by Leaf Type," and a number of individual leaf photos on the "Photos" page.

My recommendation for the single best book on this subject is, *Trees, Shrubs and Vines of the Texas Hill Country*, by Jan Wrede.

Guide to Tree and Shrub Identification: Part I

Here I begin the first in a series of essays aimed at helping people identify the woody plants they find on their property and elsewhere in the Hill Country. This is a topic that can easily occupy whole volumes of academic books, but which I hope I can simplify in a way that will be useful to most people.

First, I want to explain why I think knowing the names of our native plants is important. I like to think of the name of a plant as the name you write on the tab of a file folder into which you put everything else you know about that plant, whether that file folder is in your metal file cabinet, on your computer, or, more likely, in your brain.

Knowing the names of our native plants helps you better understand the complexity of our native habitat, to appreciate the species diversity we have, and as you do that you will come to value nature even more. It also helps in talking with others about plants. My experience in visiting peoples' properties is that there are usually many more species of plants than the owners ever suspected they had.

The problem in teaching plant identification is that it is much easier for people to distinguish plants visually than from a verbal or written description, and that obviously poses a problem due to the constraints of space in a book.

The first thing that one needs to know in order to learn how to identify plants is what things to look for. Most of us do this already in identifying birds. When you see a bird, you may not think about it consciously, but you note its size, color, markings, and maybe beak shape, because these characteristics are useful in identifying the bird. What you don't think about is that the bird has a beak, two eyes, two feet and feathers—because those characteristics don't distinguish one bird from another. The same thing is true in identifying trees.

What is important in tree identification, at least for non-professionals, is the characteristics of the leaves: their size, shape, type, margin, and arrangement. Next I will discuss these characteristics that you need to learn and understand in order to be a able to identify trees and shrubs.

Tree and Shrub Identification: Part II

I began this series with a description of how to learn to identify native trees and shrubs using some documents on my website. Today I want to discuss what characteristics one looks for in identifying woody plants. I hope to describe these characteristics well enough that those who do not wish to go to the website can still follow the discussion.

A single, compound leaf of a Texas mountain laurel with 9 leaflets on the left and a stem with simple leaves of an escarpment black cherry on the right.

The five characteristics one needs to study in order to identify a woody plant all have to do with the leaves. These five characteristics are leaf type, leaf arrangement, leaf shape, leaf margins, and leaf size.

Leaf type may be the most difficult property for beginners to master. There are two basic types of leaves; those that are considered "simple" leaves and those that are considered "compound" leaves. Don't confuse "simple" with "uncomplicated" simple leaves, which are the most common type, can have many different shapes, sizes and arrangements.

Simple leaves are composed of the leaf itself, or "blade" attached to the twig or branch by a stem that is called the "petiole," and the part of the petiole that extends into the blade is called the "midrib." Just above the point of attachment of the petiole to the branch, there will be a bud (sometimes almost invisibly small) which will become next year's leaf.

A compound leaf is made up of what may appear to be several leaves, but are in fact "leaflets" that are all part of a single leaf. In the accompanying photo, the photo of a branch of an Escarpment black cherry (on the right) is made up of several (8) individual simple leaves, but the photo of a Texas mountain laurel on the left is a single compound leaf composed of 9 leaflets.

The arrangement of the leaflets that form a compound leaf can be a group of three leaflets (trifoliate) with the center leaflet usually longer (poison ivy, agarita, box elder), or a group of five leaflets (palmate) all attached at a central point (Virginia creeper, Red buckeye), or they can be in pairs on opposite sides of a central stem called a "rachis," usually with a single end leaflet (the Texas mountain laurel in the photo, pecans and walnuts). These latter leaves are called pinnately compound leaves. Just to complicate our lives further, some pinnately compound leaves are further branched with the leaflets on the outermost branches (mesquite, mimosa, Chinaberry).

Leaf arrangement refers to the location of the attachment points of the leaves up and down the stem. If the leaves (either simple or compound) are more or less randomly attached up and down the stem but not attached directly across the stem for each other, then the arrangement is called "alternate." If, on the other hand, the leaves are attached directly across the stem from each other, then the arrangement is called "opposite." Alternate arrangements are more common than opposite.

Since the leaflets of a pinnately compound leaf are almost always arranged along the rachis opposite one another, it is sometimes difficult to tell the difference between an opposite arrangement of simple leaves and a pinnately compound leaf. In the latter, all of the leaflets will be in approximately the same plane and separated from each other by the same distance, whereas simple leaves arranged oppositely will be in different planes and at different distances. Also if a bud can be seen where the petiole attaches to the stem, everything from there outward is a single leaf.

Leaves can be many shapes from long and narrow, round, heart-shaped, or oblong to pointed at the tip or pointed at the base.

The term for the characteristic of the edge of a leaf is the "margin." If you can run your finger along the edge of the leaf and it is smooth all the way around, it is said to be "entire" (live oak, ligustrum). If the edge has tiny teeth along the margin, it is called "toothed" (escarpment black cherry, elm). If there are bumps here and there it is called "lobed." Some species have very shallow lobes (shin oak, Lacey oak) and some have deep lobes (Spanish oak, bur oak).

Guide to Tree and Shrub Identification: Part III

In the previous essay, I discussed the main features of woody plant leaves that one uses to identify different species, and today we will begin using those characteristics and my key to identify some trees.

Depending on how large a collection of plants is covered, keys can be many hundreds of pages long and extremely detailed. The one I have written to use here only covers 60 or so of the more common Hill Country species and is less than 6 pages long. It can be found on my website.

Keys are written in the form of a series of paired questions (*e.g.* Is it black? If so go to xx. Is it not black? If so, then go to yy). You proceed through a series of questions until you eliminate everything else a plant could be and you come to a matching description of the plant in question.

I will skip over the first two categories in my key (those plants with needles or minute scaly leaves—cypress and junipers respectively) and also those with parallel veins that are yucca-like—sotol and twist-leaf yucca.

The next category consists of plants with a vine-like growth habit. It is important here not to think of only things that climb up the house or a tree. While the five species we will consider can all do that, one most often sees them growing along the ground or over small bushes. In my list of common Hill Country vines, I have five species of vines. Here are the descriptions of each of those vines using primarily the leaf characteristics discussed in the previous essay of leaf size, type, arrangement, margin and shape.

Four native vines: Clockwise from the top, greenbrier, Virginia creeper, trumpet creeper, and grape.

Greenbrier is a vine with simple leathery leaves arranged in an alternate pattern and with entire margins. The leaves are usually 2 to 4 inches long, triangular- or heart- or egg-shaped. The stems have sharp thorns and the leaves sometimes have spines along the midrib or margins as well. In spite of the spines, it is a favorite deer food.

Grapes have simple, alternate, roundish 2 to 6 inch leaves that can either be toothed and/or palmately lobed. (Lobes are protuberances along the margin of the leaf which can be either rounded or pointed—the grape leaf in the accompanying picture has 3 lobes and is also toothed). There are at least 60 species of grapes in Texas. The above description will fit most of them. Mustang grape leaves have a white underside and a cupped leaf shape which distinguishes them from most others.

This is a good time to point out that Mother Nature is never uniform. The leaves on a single plant can have slightly different shapes, and smaller, newer leaves can be different from older leaves. Native grape vines may show several different leaf shapes on the same plant.

Poison ivy has compound trifoliate leaves (three leaflets attached to the end of a petiole) arranged in an alternate pattern along the stem. Leaves are 1 to 4 inches long usually with a single lobe on the side of each leaflet. If box elder trees are in the vicinity, small shoots of that look very much like poison ivy, except the leaf arrangement for box elder is opposite.

Virginia creeper is a vine with 2 to 6 inch alternately arranged palmately compound leaves (five leaflets attached to the end of the petiole) with the longest leaflet in the center. The leaflets are coarsely toothed. The leaves turn bright red in the fall.

Trumpet creeper is unusual in that its leaves are pinnately compound and attached in an opposite arrangement. The photo shows 13 coarsely toothed leaflets on the single leaf.

It is important to note that leaf characteristics are not the only clues to help identify woody plant species. Bark color or texture can sometimes be helpful, the texture of the leaves can be useful, flowers, fruit, the environment, and many other things can also aid in identification.

Guide to Tree and Shrub Identification: Part IV

I discussed how to identify some common Hill Country vines by their leaf pattern in the previous essay. Here I will discuss how to identify some common trees and shrubs that all have a simple leaf, alternate arrangement, and an entire margin. If you don't remember the definitions of those terms, go back to PART II of this series.

Everything I will discuss here will have a simple leaf type, the leaves will be arranged along the branch in an alternate arrangement and the leaf margins (edge) will be smooth or "entire." But as the accompanying photograph shows, there are big differences in the leaves even within the above description.

Starting with the smallest leaf and progressing to the largest, cenizo has the smallest leaves, usually less than an inch long and they tend to be oblong or elliptical in shape. The leaf arrangement is alternate, although the tiny leaves tend to cluster so closely together that it may be difficult to determine that. Cenizo stands out from most other native shrubs in that it is gray-green in color—some think of it as silver-gray. It is a rounded shrub usually 3 to 10 feet tall. Cenizo is evergreen and flowers throughout the spring, summer and fall after a rain.

The leaves of Texas persimmon are seldom much more than an inch long, oblong or oval in shape, usually wider at the tip. The leaves are frequently slightly inrolled (convex from the top) and have a velvety feel. Its leaves can be persistent in mild winters. Persimmons are dioecious, meaning there are male and female plants, and only female plants produce fruit. The round fruit can be up to an inch in diameter and turns from green to black in the fall. Persimmons are usually shrubs to small trees and tend to have peeling bark showing smooth trunks and limbs.

Gum bumelia (also known as chittimwood or gum elastic) has 1 to 3-inch-long oblong leaves that are narrow at the base and wider at the tip. It is a medium-sized tree that has long straight thorns. It produces small white blooms in July.

Simple, alternate, entire leaves: From the smallest on the right, clockwise, cenizo, Texas persimmon, gum-bumelia, live oak, hackberry, Carolina buckthorn, Texas redbud.

After cedar, live oaks are probably the most common woody species in the Hill Country. The leaves are oblong, usually 1 to 4 inches long, dark green on top and lighter green underneath. They are referred to as semi-evergreen because they keep their leaves throughout the winter, then drop their leaves in the spring and regrow new leaves immediately. New leaves or leaves on small shoots may have sharp lobes or points on the leaves.

Hackberry leaves are usually 2 to 5 inches long, tapering to a point, and rough in texture. Hackberries may have some leaves with teeth on parts of the leaf. Hackberries can often be identified just from the bark that usually has conspicuous bumps or "warts." These trees produce berries that birds and other animals like and are a good wildlife habitat tree. There are two species hackberries in the Hill Country; netleaf hackberry and sugarberry.

Carolina buckthorns are large shrubs with elliptic 2 to 4 inch leaves that are characterized by having very prominent veins and midrib, visible from both the top and bottom. The surface of the leaves is smooth. In spite of the name, Carolina buckthorns do not have thorns.

Texas redbud is a small tree with large, 2 to 6 inch nearly round or heart-shaped leaves that grow on a long petiole (stem). Pink blossom clusters come out before new leaves in the spring. There are two other closely-related species of redbuds; eastern redbuds which do not grow well here and have generally larger leaves, and Mexican redbuds which have smaller, thicker leaves with wavy margins.

Again, all of the trees and shrubs discussed here have simple leaves with an entire margin, arranged in an alternate manner. Other trees and shrubs that have the same type of leaf but are less common include the American smoketree, spicebush, bois d'arc and the exotic, invasive Chinese tallow.

In identifying trees and shrubs, it is important to never just look at one leaf or one branch, but to look at several parts of the plant as Mother Nature doesn't always make everything the same. Also, feeling of the leaves gives clues of texture, thickness or stiffness that can also help to distinguish different species.

Guide to Tree and Shrub Identification: Part V

I described a number of species that have simple leaves, alternately arranged with entire (smooth) margins in the previous essay. Now I will discuss species that have simple leaves, alternately arranged, but with toothed margins.

The tree that fits the above category with the smallest leaves is the cedar elm. Its leaves are usually 1 to 2 inches long, oblong or oval, very stiff and rough. It is sometimes described as being "double-toothed." Cedar elms are common, strong trees which flower in late summer or fall, attracting many bees. It can turn yellow in the fall.

Willow baccharis or poverty weed has long (1 to 4 inches) linear, very narrow (1/4 inch or less wide) leaves which usually have a few teeth on the margins. The surface of the leaves has a sticky substance on them. This is usually a multi-trunk shrub 3 to 10 feet tall with an erect growth habit. It is often seen along roadsides and can be invasive on disturbed soil areas. In riparian areas it serves to hold the soil in place. It is dioecious meaning it has male and female flowers on separate plants—female plants are conspicuous in October or November with clusters of white flowers. Baccharis is not a true willow, but is in the Aster family.

Escarpment black cherry is our most common native member of the *Prunus* genus of cherries, plums and other fruits. It can be a very large tree that can be found growing almost anywhere, but most commonly in or near riparian areas. Its 2 to 4 inch leaves are shiny on top, oval with a pointed tip and very small-toothed margins. Like most fruit trees, when young the bark is smooth, somewhat silvery with horizontal stripes, but when mature the bark becomes almost black.

The black willow is a true willow found growing almost exclusively along creeks and lakes. It has 3 to 6-inch-long linear dark green leaves that are usually only about a ½ inch wide. The leaves are finely toothed.

Note: Some of the leaves in the photo have such small "teeth" that they may not show in the photo.

Slippery elm and American elm are closely related elm trees, neither of which are very common in our area. These elms both have 3 to 6 inch oblong leaves with pointed tips, and both have "double-toothed" margins and a somewhat rough texture to the leaves. These trees are most often seen in deeper soils in lowland areas. The two species can be distinguished by small differences in their seeds, called "samaras" and by the color pattern of the interior of the bark. The numbers of these trees were greatly reduced by Dutch Elm disease in the middle of the 20th century.

Two other related tree species that fit the category of simple, alternate, toothed are the creek plum and the Mexican plum. Both are native to our area, but not very common. The creek plum is more likely to be found along creeks as multi-trunk shrubs which very often form thickets. The Mexican plum is more of a small tree and does not as readily form root sprouts or thickets. The latter is more likely to be found in the nursery trade. Both have leaves that are oblong with pointed tips. The creek plum may have slightly narrower leaves that are smooth and shiny on top whereas the Mexican plum's leaves are duller with a softer feel due to fine hairs on the surface. The latter's leaves may also be somewhat inrolled. Mexican plum fruits are usually larger than creek plum fruits.

Simple, alternate, toothed leaves: From the smallest leaf on the left clockwise, cedar elm, willow baccharis, escarpment black cherry, black willow, slippery elm, Mexican plum.

Other simple, alternate, toothed species include Texas madrone, Carolina basswood, Anaqua and Cottonwood.

Just to remind everyone how we are going through the tree key, first I covered woody plants with a vine-like growth habit, then trees and shrubs with simple, alternate, entire leaves, then here those with simple, alternate, toothed leaves.

Guide to Tree and Shrub Identification: Part VI

Here I will discuss species that have simple, alternate leaves with a lobed margin. Lobes are bumps, points or other protuberances along the margin of the leaf. This category covers all of the common Hill Country oaks except for live oaks which have leaves with an entire margin.

Shin oaks, also known as white shin oaks, are generally the smallest oak trees in the Hill Country and they also have among the smallest leaves, 1-4 inches long simple leaves that have only small irregular bumps (lobes). They are also characterized as having peeling bark, being usually less than 20-feet tall with trunks less than one foot in diameter. Shin oaks are very frequently found growing in groups and they root-sprout prolifically.

Lacey oaks, also called blue oaks, have leaves that are also slightly lobed and similar to shin oaks but have a waxy coating on the leaves that gives them a blue-green or grayish cast. Lacey oaks are medium-sized trees with a bark showing a pattern of small rectangles. Lacey oaks are endemic to the Hill Country. They are named after their discoverer, rancher/naturalist Howard Lacey, who owned a ranch near Kerrville in the late 1800s and early 1900s.

Spanish oaks, or Texas red oaks, have 3 to 5-inch deeply incised, prominently lobed leaves with sharp points. As is characteristic of both red oaks in the Hill Country (Spanish oaks and blackjack oaks), the tips of the lobes have short hair-like bristles and the surface is smooth. Spanish oaks are among the first oaks to green up in the spring and they frequently turn red in the fall.

Simple, alternate, lobed leaves:. Clockwise from the largest leaf on the left, bur oak, shin oak, Lacey oak, Spanish oak, post oak, Monterrey oak, chinquapin oak, blackjack oak, sycamore.

Post oaks have 3 to 5 inch leaves that frequently show two prominent rounded lobes that give the leaves a cross-like shape. The leaves are dull and slightly rough to the touch. They tend to have very straight trunks with large branches and a lighter colored bark than most trees.

Monterrey oaks or Mexican white oaks are not really native to the Hill Country, but are known to grow natively in Val Verde County. The leaves are 3 to 6-inches long with small lobes or large teeth on the tip end of the leaf. The leaves have a thick, leathery feel. Mexican white oaks are semi-evergreen in the same way live oaks are, keeping leaves through the winter and then doing leaf-exchange in the spring. This oak is commonly sold in nurseries.

Chinkapin oaks or chinquapin oaks have 3 to 6-inch-long elliptic leaves with a wavy pattern of lobes around the margin. The veins show a pinnate (feather-like) pattern ending at each lobe. These are large trees that are most often found growing in deep soil in lowlands or in riparian areas.

The blackjack oak has 3 to 7-inch-long and wide leaves frequently shaped like a duck foot. Being a red oak it has bristles at the end of each lobe, sometimes referred to as the "duck's toenails." The leaves are shiny and smooth. The bark of blackjacks tends to be darker than most other trees.

The bur oak is most often found in the north and east parts of the Hill Country, but is commonly planted elsewhere. It has the largest leaves (6 to 12-inches long, up to 6 inches wide) as well as the largest acorns (golf ball size). Its leaves are usually deeply incised with multiple rounded lobes.

Sycamore trees have leaves as wide as they are long and can be from 3 to 8 inches in both dimensions. The leaves usually have three main lobes with smaller lobes between the main ones. This pattern is called palmately-lobed. The bark of sycamores tends to be light-colored and peeling. They are usually found near water and can be very important trees for holding the soil of creek banks and beds in place.

Two other species that have simple, alternate, lobed leaves are mulberries, which are well-known for having multiple-shaped leaves on the same tree, and Vasey oaks, a small West Texas/Trans Pecos species.

Guide to Tree and Shrub Identification: Part VII

Resuming our tree and shrub identification, after the last category of simple, alternate, lobed leaves, I have one species that is considered simple, alternate, crenate (rounded teeth). The shrub possumhaw has this leaf type, with 1 to 2 inch leaves that are oblong with the base narrower than the tip, the latter of which may be notched. Possumhaws are dioecious (male and female flowers on different plants), and the female plants produce red berries that usually survive throughout the winter. Its evergreen cousin, yaupon holly, has smaller leaves and is more common in the wild east of the Hill Country.

This completes our list of simple leaves with an alternate arrangement along the stem. The next category is one with simple leaves, oppositely arranged, as shown with the pairs of leaves in the photo.

An elbow-bush is a rounded shrub with ½ to 2-inch oval leaves that usually have a fine-toothed margin. Elbow-bush is also called Spring-herald because it blooms the last of January or first of February and is the first species in our area to do so. It generally shows an opposite pattern to the small branches. It is also dioecious and female plants produce blue-black berries.

Mexican silktassel is a medium to large shrub that has 1 to 3-inch oval leaves that have a leathery, thick texture and are hairy below. The leaves have an entire margin and a wavy shape instead of being flat. This multi-trunk shrub is evergreen.

Ligustrum or Japanese privet, is an invasive, non-native shrub to small tree. The leaves are 2 to 5-inches long, oval with a somewhat sharp tip, shiny and dark green. The margins are strikingly entire and uniform, almost giving the leaves the appearance of a plastic plant. Ligustrum is evergreen and produces poisonous black berries. It can form thickets and often escapes cultivation and becomes a serious problem to control.

Coral honeysuckle is a vine but was not included in the vine category discussed earlier because it is less commonly encountered, except for where it has been planted. It is an evergreen twining vine with 1 to 3-inch-long oval leaves which are about one-inch-wide with entire margins. It produces bright red or orange tubular flowers in good rain years from early spring to late fall that are much visited by hummingbirds.

Rough-leaf dogwood can be a small tree or large shrub. It has 1 to 4-inch oval leaves that are pointed at the tip with an entire margin. They are rough on the upper surface and the veins are parallel and prominent on top and raised on the bottom. These dogwoods produce cream-colored clusters of flowers in April and May which make waxy white berries in the fall. Rough-leaf dogwoods root-sprout rather prolifically and can form dense thickets which are good wildlife cover, but can be a nuisance in your yard.

Clockwise from the single leaf in upper left, possumhaw. Remainder simple opposite leaves elbow-bush, Mexican silktassel, ligustrum, rough-leaf dogwood, American beautyberry, rusty blackhaw viburnum, bigtooth maple.

Other simple, opposite, entire species include white-bush honeysuckle, invasive Japanese honeysuckle (non-native), beebrush, flame acanthus and canyon mock-orange.

Less common simple opposite toothed shrubs are American beautyberry and rusty blackhaw viburnum.

American beautyberry is a 3 to 8-foot-tall multi-trunk shrub with oblong, pointed, toothed leaves. The leaves are usually three to seven inches long. Beautyberries are distinctive in the way they flower and produce berries in tight clusters at the nodes of the stems forming striking bunches of purple berries up and down the stems. The birds seldom allow them to last into the winter.

Rusty blackhaw viburnum is a large shrub or small to medium-sized tree. It has 1 to 3-inch glossy leaves with toothed margins. The center vein usually has red hairs along the underside of the leaf. It produces clusters of white blooms in early spring and dark blue berries.

The bigtooth maple, the famous fall-color tree of Lost Maples State Natural Area, is a large tree with simple, opposite, lobed leaves. The leaves are about 2 to 3-inches long and wide with three main lobes and several smaller ones, but no teeth. While it grows natively today only in isolated areas like the Lost Maples SNA, Big Bend National Park, and Guadalupe National Park, it is commonly planted and does well in many areas.

Guide to Tree and Shrub Identification: Part VIII

Here I will begin describing woody plants that have compound leaves, and in fact all of the plants to be discussed today are classified as being "pinnately" compound, meaning they have leaflets arranged opposite each other along the central axis called a "rachis." Both the leaflets and the rachis are lost in the fall and regrow in the spring. The accompanying photo shows nine compound leaves, all with several leaflets. All of the species discussed today have leaves arranged in an alternate manner along the main stems.

Kidneywood has the smallest leaves of this category with leaves only 1 to 2-inches long and with tiny leaflets. It is usually a medium-sized, multi-trunk shrub with an airy appearance. Kidneywood produces white flowers in clusters on spikes at the end of branches after rains. Kidneywood does not have thorns.

Eve's necklace is a small tree with 4 to 9-inch compound leaves with oblong leaflets an inch or less long. It produces pink flowers and bean pods (it is a legume) that are constricted between the beans giving the appearance of a necklace.

Compound, alternate leaves: Clockwise from the smallest leaf on the lower right, kidneywood, Eve's necklace, evergreen sumac, prairie flame-leaf sumac, Texas mountain laurel, toothache tree, Mexican buckeye, little walnut, pecan.

Note: for the photo, the smallest leaves of most species were chosen to better fit into the photograph, most leaves you see will be larger.

Evergreen sumac can make a large shrub or small tree with 3 to 5-inch leaves. The leaflets are oblong, about one-inch-long, and are shiny on top. It is, as the name implies, evergreen.

Prairie flame-leaf sumac has 6 to 12-inch leaves with 2 to 3-inch-long, narrow "lanceolate" (long, narrow with a sharp point) leaflets. The leaflets are sometimes unsymmetrical at the base, giving the leaflet a curved or sickle-shape. Prairie flame-leaf sumac can be distinguished from most other compound-leaf species by a flattened or "winged" rachis near the end of the leaf. This large shrub produces cream-colored clusters of flowers and red berries on spikes at the end of branches.

The Texas mountain laurel is a large multi-trunk shrub with shiny 4 to 6-inch leaves containing oblong shiny, one to two inch leaflets. It is best known for its very showy purple flower clusters in the spring that smell like grape Kool-Aid. This legume produces red-orange seeds in a pod. Both the seeds and leaves are poisonous. Texas mountain laurel is evergreen.

The above five species are all categorized as being compound, alternate, and entire. Other species in this same category include Texas pistache, western soapberry, wafer ash (hop tree) and the non-native Chinese pistache.

The next four species have compound, alternate, toothed leaves.

The toothache tree, also known as prickly ash or tickle-tongue, is a spiny shrub with 2 to 5-inch leaves containing one inch wrinkled, toothed leaflets. It has thorns on the stems and also on the rachis. The leaflets are known to numb your mouth.

The Mexican buckeye is a multi-trunk shrub with 6 to 12 inch leaves, each with 2 to 4-inch-long lanceolate, toothed leaflets. It makes pink blooms in clusters before the leaves emerge in March or April. The fruit are large, dark brown, spherical seeds which are encased in three-chambered pods.

Walnuts and pecans are in the same family and have similar leaf characteristics. Both have long (12 inches or longer) leaves with 3 to 7-inch-long lanceolate leaflets that sometimes are unsymmetrical and sickle-shaped with toothed margins. Generally, pecans will have larger leaves and larger leaflets, but their sizes overlap.

There are two species of walnuts in the Hill Country. The smaller, more common little walnut or Texas walnut, and the less common larger black walnut. (Some would add the Arizona walnut, which I believe is even less common.)

Pecans have 4 part husks that split off from a smooth nut. Walnuts have round, smooth husks that degrade away from rough, irregular nuts. Black walnuts have 2 inch husks and 1 ¼ inch nuts, little walnuts have 1 inch husks and ¾ inch nuts. Arizona walnuts are in between in size. Pecans and black walnuts will likely only be found growing natively in deep rich soils in creek bottoms, while little walnuts can grow in poorer soil away from creeks.

Guide to Tree and Shrub Identification: Part IX

Here I will cover species with other types of compound leaves.

The first species is Agarita, a shrub with trifoliate compound leaves (three leaflets attached to a central point). Agarita is a small to medium-sized shrub which has leaflets that are very stiff with five lobes that are extremely sharp so that touching any part of the shrub is difficult. The leaves are green with grey or blue edges. Agarita is evergreen, seldom eaten by deer or livestock, and produces yellow flowers that attract bees in early spring, followed by red berries for the birds.

The next category is plants with twice-pinnate compound leaves arranged alternately along the stem. Twice-pinnate, sometimes called bipinnate, refers to the fact that the leaflets are not attached to the main rachis, but to branches off of the main rachis.

The species with the smallest leaves in this category is the fragrant mimosa, also known as pink mimosa or Lindheimer mimosa. These usually short shrubs have small, 1 to 2-inch-long leaves, with numerous tiny leaflets on several paired branches. These native mimosas produce pink spherical flowers. The shrubs are armed with numerous short thorns on the stems.

The goldenball leadtree is a small tree with twice-pinnate compound leaves 3 to 8-inches long with 3 to 7-pairs of branches. The oblong leaflets are ½ to ¾ of an inch long. The tree produces bright yellow spherical blooms in spring and sometimes later in the year as well. It is a legume. It does not have thorns.

Mesquite, or honey mesquite, is another species with bipinnate compound leaves with two branches of the rachis at the end of the main rachis, giving a wishbone shape to the leaves. The leaflets are about an inch-long and very narrow. The stems have long straight thorns. Mesquite is another legume that produces a yellowish slender bean pod much favored by many animals. It can be a large tree or a multi-trunk shrub. Mesquite prefers deep soil for its long tap root and it can become invasive under certain conditions.

Clockwise from the smallest leaf on top: twice pinnately compound, alternate fragrant mimosa, goldenball lead tree, Chinaberry, compound opposite box elder, bipinnately compound, opposite mesquite, trifoliate, opposite agarita.

The Chinaberry is a large, invasive exotic tree that has escaped cultivation and colonizes many areas, especially riparian and adjacent areas where it crowds out native vegetation. Its leaves are 1 to 2-feet long with several branches off the main rachis. The dark green leaflets are 1 to 3-inches long and are deeply-toothed or lobed. It produces lavender bloom clusters and ½ inch yellow round fruits which are poisonous.

Other twice-pinnate, compound, alternate trees and shrubs are Roemer's acacia, catclaw acacia, huisache and retama, all well-armed with thorns.

Our final category of woody plants is compound, opposite and lobed, and the species that fits that category is the box elder. It has light-green, usually drooping leaves 6 to 15-inches long. The leaflets are frequently trifoliate with three lobed leaflets at the end of the rachis, but sometimes with other pairs of leaflets on the rachis as well. The three leaflets resemble those of poison ivy, but the opposite arrangement on the stem distinguishes box elder from poison ivy. Box elder is most often found in or near riparian areas and it can be a prolific root sprouter as well as seed producer.

This concludes the plant identification guide of the 70 or so most common woody plants I have seen in the Hill Country.

To review, we started with plants with a vine-like growth habit, then species with simple leaves, alternate arrangement and entire margins, then toothed margins, then lobed margins, then crenate margins. We then considered species with simple leaves with an opposite arrangement. This was followed by compound, alternate, entire leaves, then toothed leaves, followed by the categories discussed today.

So the main thing to remember when looking at an unknown tree or shrub, is to determine the leaf type, arrangement and margin in order to place the species in the right category. From there, one has only a relatively small number of possible Hill Country species to consider.

It is important to keep in mind that all of this series of plant ID columns pertain to Hill Country woody plants ONLY. These columns and photos will not be as useful in other parts of the state.

HILL COUNTRY TREES AND SHRUBS

Where Are All the Little Trees?

A while back a neighbor of mine asked me, "Where are all the little trees? I just realized there are no little trees around my house, they are all mature oaks." It was an accurate observation, and a good question.

Almost everywhere in the Hill Country, if you look closely at the hardwood trees, you will see that they are all mature trees, live oaks with trunk diameters of 6 inches or more, and the same holds for Texas red oaks (Spanish oaks), post oaks, Lacey oaks, chinquapin oaks and blackjack oaks. And it is not limited to oaks either, you probably won't find any young escarpment black cherries, cedar elms or hackberry trees either. You may find shin oaks that are less than 6" in diameter, but they are naturally small and a 4-inch diameter tree is mature.

So where are the replacement trees for when these mature oaks die? Why are there no 3-feet tall live oaks, 6-feet tall Spanish oaks, or -inch diameter cedar elms? There is a one-word answer, deer. White-tailed deer are browsers, which means they eat mainly the leaves of woody plants and some forbs (weeds and wildflowers). As the deer population began to increase after the eradication of the screw-worm fly in the 1960's, they began to eat a larger and larger percentage of young tree sprouts until by the 1990's there were very few young trees surviving. So, to paraphrase an old song, "Where have all the little trees gone/ Gone to white-tails, every one."

You may ask how do we know that it is the deer that are responsible, and not goats, or climate change, or lack of fire, or something else. The evidence can be summarized as follows. We see a lack of young trees even on properties that have not been grazed with any livestock or exotics for many years, so these animals are certainly not the sole source of the problem (though they may contribute). We do see young trees of many species that happen to be growing on steep rocky slopes or over steep stream banks where deer cannot reach them. On properties where the population of white-tailed deer has been controlled to relatively low numbers for a long time, such as the Kerr Wildlife Management Area outside of Hunt, we do indeed see young live oaks and other hardwoods, both in areas where prescribed burning has taken place and where it has not.

Finally, if you will allow me a personal observation, since building our house about 16 years ago and enclosing about an acre around it with a fence to keep out the deer, we now have some 3-foot high live oaks, two 8-feet tall blackjacks, several prairie flame-leaf sumacs, many 5 to 8-feet high escarpment black cherries and one over 10 feet, a 6-feet high hackberry—none of which can be found on the property outside the fence.

You may have noticed that I have been referring to this as a problem for hardwoods. This is because the same problem does not exist with cedar (Ashe juniper). You can find all sorts of young cedar trees, from a few inches to a few feet high almost everywhere. So why is this problem observed for almost every other species, but not for cedar? Because cedar is very far down the list of plants deer most like to eat; they will eat most any hardwood plant before they will nibble on a cedar tree, and even then, they tend to leave the very young cedars alone.

So what does all of this mean? I expect that we have probably seen the maximum hardwood population in most of the Hill Country and that over the next few decades we will begin to see fewer and fewer of these trees. Having fewer trees is not necessarily catastrophic, there were fewer hardwoods 150 years ago than there are now.

But part of the problem is that a piece of the natural habitat is now missing, the mid-story vegetation, the shrubs and small trees that would naturally grow from the ground up to about 6'. This is the natural habitat for lots of birds and some other small animals, the endangered black-capped vireo being one example. So basically, the white-tailed deer have not only destroyed a part of their own habitat, but they have also destroyed the habitat, cover and food source for a lot of wildlife.

The deer have caused one other change in the appearance of our landscape; they have changed the shape of our trees. They have made them into lollypops, with nothing but trunk showing below about 5' (the browse line), and all of the leaves in a round ball above that. That is not the way our native trees would grow naturally.

The Ubiquitous Live Oak: Symbol of the Hill Country

A favorite, if misshapen old live oak tree on the author's property.

Ask most people what words come to mind when you say Hill Country, "hills" may be the first word they think of, but "live oaks" will likely be a close second. No other tree symbolizes the Hill Country as well. I feel confident in saying that the number of live oaks in the Hill Country is second only to cedar (Ashe juniper).

The live oak in this area (*Quercus fusiformis)* is sometimes called the Texas live oak, or the Plateau live oak or Escarpment live oak. These names distinguish it from the Southern live oak or Virginia live oak (*Quercus virginiana*) which grows more along the Texas coast and east all the way to the Atlantic. Some experts believe the Plateau live oak is not a separate species, but a sub-species of the Virginia live oak, and others believe there are hybrids of the two. For our purposes here, I will just call our trees live oaks.

Live oaks are classified as semi-evergreen because they do lose their leaves every year like other deciduous trees, but they do so at almost the same time as new leaves are beginning to form, usually in March or April. So the tree is actually never without green leaves or is only without green leaves for a few days—which is why it is called a "live" oak.

The tree flowers at the same time as the new leaves are forming. The male flower parts are the catkins which are a string of loosely attached structures that hang down from the twig. The female flower parts are tiny inconspicuous structures attached to the twig. As are most trees without showy flowers, they are wind-pollinated. Acorns mature in the fall.

Live oaks are fairly prolific root sprouters. That means that new plants come up around the "mother" tree and grow from the roots of the mother tree. These sprouts have the advantage that they derive their water and minerals from the root system of the mature tree and thus have an advantage over a plant sprouting from an acorn. The new sprout may have points on the margins of the leaves somewhat like a holly leaf, which confuses some people into thinking it is not a live oak (it is not uncommon for the leaves of newly-sprouted plants to have points or be stiffer than mature leaves—probably a protection mechanism to keep them from being eaten).

It is common to find a group of mature live oaks of the same size growing close to each other. While these may appear to be separate trees, they are more likely to be all connected through a root system that was originally the "mother" tree (which may be long gone). That means all of these trees are really clones of the original and are all part of a single plant.

The fact that live oaks in close proximity to each other are probably interconnected through the roots also explains why oak wilt kills many more live oaks than any other species. The oak wilt fungus, once infecting one tree through a wound, can travel through the vascular system and the roots to other connected trees.

Live oaks are pretty slow growing, even when compared with other oaks. Slow growing trees usually are the strongest. I know of three or four live oak root sprouts on our place, all protected from browsers since they were discovered, that are between 10 and 16 years old, and none of them are over 3 feet tall!

After the 2011 drought, I have personally witnessed several hardwoods and cedar (Ashe juniper) trees that died and have heard of similar experiences from many other folks as well, but it seems that, given the number of live oaks around, we have lost a smaller percentage of them than most other species.

On the deer-food favorability lists, live oak is only moderately preferred. That, plus the fact that they are such prolific root sprouters (shin oaks also produce lots of root sprouts) means that on properties with only moderate populations of browsers (goats, exotics and white-tailed deer) it is possible to find small live oak saplings.

Hill Country Oak Trees—More than Just Live Oaks

How many different species of native Hill Country oaks do you think there are? Well, depending on how far you think the Hill Country extends, I think the answer is eight, counting live oaks. Here they are:

Blackjack oaks (*Quercus marilandica*) are one of two species (the other being Spanish oaks) in the Hill Country that belong to the Red Oak family. All the other oaks are classified as White Oaks, except that live oaks are sometimes considered a class by themselves. Blackjack oaks tend to have darker bark than most other trees in the area and the leaves are thin, shiny, smooth and tend to have a shape like a duck's foot. At the tip of the leaf where the "duck's toenails" would be you can usually see a very small hair-like point sticking out.

Chinquapin oaks, also spelled chinkapin, (*Quercus muhlenbergii*) are large trees usually found in the deeper soils along creeks and streams. They have oblong leaves with scalloped edges.

Lacey oaks (*Quercus laceyi*) were first described by an Englishman, Howard Lacey, who owned a ranch south of Kerrville in the late 1800s. They are also called blue oaks as the color of their leaves tends to be somewhat blue-green, which means they can be picked out from other trees at a distance. They are usually medium-size trees that often grow in rocky areas along the edge of hilltops, but they seem to be able to grow almost anywhere.

Post oaks (*Quercus stellata*) tend to have the lightest-colored bark of all the other trees. They also tend to have very straight trunks (*i.e.* like a post). Their leaves are often described as cross-shaped with large bulges on either side of the leaf near the top. The leaves also have a somewhat rough feel when rubbed between the fingers and lack the "points" found on blackjack oaks, with which they are sometimes confused.

Shin oaks (*Quercus sinuata*) are also known as White shin oaks and Bigelow oaks. They tend to be the smallest oak species in this area, usually no more than 12 to 15-feet tall. They have a fairly light-colored bark that looks shaggy as though pieces of the bark are flaking off. These trees frequently grow close together in groups and it is common for them to produce many root sprouts near the base of the trees, although if you have many deer, you may never see them.

Spanish oaks (*Quercus buckleyi*), also known as Texas red oaks, have deeply lobed leaves (deep indentations between fingers with points) and tend to give the most fall color of all the oaks in the Hill Country. They also green up early in the spring with very light-colored leaves which contrast nicely with the deep green of the cedars. Spanish oak bark frequently, but not always, has whiteish patches of lichen on it. Spanish oaks are very closely related to Shumard oaks which are found east and north of the Hill Country, but the latter do not do as well here as the native Spanish oaks.

Bur oaks *(Quercus macrocarpa)* are more common in the northern and eastern part of the Hill Country. These tough, strong trees have, as the name implies, the largest acorn, sometimes almost the size of a golf ball, with a large, shaggy cup. They also have the largest leaves, up to a foot in length and deeply incised with large lobes.

Some Native Hill Country Trees Other Than Oaks

There are a number of common, large, native trees in the Hill Country that are not oaks. Here are some of them.

Bald cypress (*Taxodium distichum*) is common along the banks of the Guadalupe and its tributaries as well as many other streams in the Hill Country. It is unusual for a conifer (cone-bearing) tree to be deciduous (loses its leaves in the winter) which is why it is called a bald cypress. These trees were highly prized for the durability of the wood for making shingles, which led to the settlement of Kerrville. They are fast growing, and generally the largest trees in the Hill Country.

Cedar elm (*Ulmus crassifolia*) is an elm with very small, stiff, rough leaves. It is common throughout the Hill Country where it appears to be equally at home on limestone soils or acidic soils. It flowers and sets seed in late summer, which is unusual, and, because not much is blooming then, it attracts many native bees when flowering. Its leaves turn yellow in the fall. Two other species of elms grow in the Hill Country, although they are not nearly as common as cedar elms. American elm (*Ulmus americana*) and Slippery elm (*Ulmus rubra*) are both large trees with large leaves and are more likely to be found in riparian areas.

Escarpment black cherry (*Prunus serotina* var. *eximia*) is a Hill Country native cherry with thin, soft leaves that turn yellow in the fall. The tiny white flowers are produced on stalks in the spring, followed by tiny cherries for the birds. Young stems and branches have light grey bark, but large trees have almost black bark with grey patches.

The ranges of two species of hackberry overlap in our part of the Hill Country, sugar hackberry (*Celtis laevigata* var. *texana*), which predominately grows east of here, and netleaf hackberry (*Celtis laevigata* var. *reticulata*), which predominately grows west of here. Both have rough bark with bumps, frequently called "warts." The upper leaf surface of netleaf hackberries is usually rougher than for the sugarberry species. Both trees are excellent sources of food for many species of wildlife and are considered beneficial to have in the habitat.

Pecan (*Carya illinoinensis*) is the native pecan of the Hill Country. It requires deeper soils than are found in most of this area which is why it is predominately found growing in the "pecan bottoms" of alluvial soils along creeks and rivers. Thomas Jefferson gave George Washington some pecans from the Midwest (they were unknown on the east coast) and they are now the oldest trees in Mount Vernon! The thinner shell varieties that are grown commercially are all derived from the native pecans.

Sycamores (*Platanus occidentalis*) are the large trees with large leaves and white bark that are usually seen along river banks and creeks. They have large five-lobed leaves. They are fast growing and have the ability to take root and grow to maturity in a gravel bar in the middle of a creek, conditions where most trees would be swept away in a flood. Large trees such as cypress and sycamores are desirable along riparian areas where they help to stabilize stream banks and prevent erosion.

Walnut: There are three species of walnuts native to Texas, and all three can be found in the Hill Country. Black walnut (*Juglans nigra*) is the largest tree and also has the largest fruit with husks 1 ½ to 2 ½-inches in diameter. Little walnut or Texas walnut (*Juglans microcarpa*) is the smallest of the three and also has the smallest fruit (less than 1-inch in diameter. Arizona walnut (*Juglans major*) is intermediate in both tree size and husk size between the other two. Black walnuts grow in deep soil along streams and can grow quite large, although generally not as large as pecans, but little walnuts can also grow in shallower soil away from any permanent water.

Mesquite (*Prosopis glandulosa*) is a tree everyone is familiar with. It is not nearly the invasive pest in much of the Hill Country that it is in other areas, because it really likes deeper soil than we have in most places.

Other, less common Hill Country trees are black willow, bois d'arc, gum bumelia, Texas ash and western soapberry.

The More Common Native Shrubs and Vines of the Hill Country

The following list represents shrubs and vines that I have frequently observe in the Hill Country.

Agarita (*Berberis trifoliolata*) is one of the most common shrubs in the Hill Country. It is usually a multi-branched shrub to 6 feet in height and diameter. Its trifoliate leaves are blue-green or gray green, with each very stiff leaflet having, usually, three lobes that are very sharp and very strong. Its yellow blooms in early spring attract many different insects and the red berries feed many species of wildlife, and humans sometimes make jelly from them. Agarita are good to have because they are excellent nurse plants that protect the young leaves of other plant species from being browsed by deer, and they provide cover for quail and rabbits and nest sites for birds.

Texas persimmon (*Diospyros texana*) is a multi-stem shrub with small simple oval leaves that are slightly inrolled (edges turn down) and feel like velvet. The bark peels off revealing a smooth gray surface. Female trees produce one-inch diameter round fruits that turn black when mature. Most all wildlife enjoy these fruits which also make good jelly. Deer usually do not browse the leaves.

Virginia creeper (*Parthenocissus quinquefolia*) is a common vine, especially in shady places under trees where it may form a complete ground cover. It has palmately compound leaves (five leaflets attached to the end of a stem) which make it easy to identify as do the leaves when they turn red in the fall. It produces small light-blue berries. Virginia creeper is readily browsed by deer and livestock.

Texas mountain laurel (*Sophora secundiflora*) is a common shrub frequently planted in gardens. It has pinnately compound leaves with 1 to 2-inch-long leaflets that are wider at the tip. It blooms with a very showy purple cluster of flowers that smell like grape Kool-Aid in the spring. It is an evergreen legume. The red seeds are hard and round and encased in a pod—they are toxic to humans and animals. It is not usually browsed.

Possumhaw (*Ilex decidua*) is a branching shrub with simple 1 to 2-inch leaves with rounded-toothed edges. Female plants produce red berries that usually persist throughout the winter after the leaves have dropped. Deer and livestock will browse this shrub.

Sumacs: There are quite a few species of sumacs in Texas, and three that are common in the Hill Country: Flameleaf sumac, Fragrant sumac, and Evergreen sumac. Flameleaf sumac, or Prairie flameleaf sumac (*Rhus lanceolata*) usually grows as a multi-trunk small tree with long compound leaves composed of 10-15 or more pairs of narrow leaflets. Its small white flowers are clustered on the end of branches which produce berries that turn from red in the fall to brown in winter. Many species of birds and mammals eat these berries. The leaves sometimes turn a brilliant red in the fall.

Fragrant sumac, aka Skunkbush sumac or Aromatic sumac (*Rhus aromatica*) is a small shrub, usually less than about 8 feet, with trifoliate compound leaves (leaves composed of three leaflets growing from the end of a petiole). The leaves give a pungent odor when crushed, thus the name. Its small flowers appear as clusters at the end of branches before the leaves appear. The fruit is clusters of small red, fuzzy berries that ripen in the summer.

Evergreen Sumac (*Rhus virens*), is another plant with shiny green compound leaves. It produces tiny white blooms in clusters in the summer, especially after good rains. It can attain a height up to 12 feet, but may have leaves down to the ground. It may not be eaten by deer.

Desert willow (*Chilopsis linearis*) is a small tree from the western edge of the Hill Country and westward. Desert willows are airy trees with long, narrow leaves that grow in full sun, even in the West Texas desert. They bloom throughout the summer after rains with beautiful pink and purple orchid-like flowers and produce long, very thin bean-like pods. It is a good landscape tree for well-drained areas.

Roughleaf dogwood (*Cornus drummondii*) is a spreading shrub or small tree with a pronounced tendency to produce root sprouts which can mature into thickets. The simple leaves are 1 to 4-inches long and about half as wide, with a pointed tip. The leaves are somewhat rough with prominent veins. Roughleaf dogwood blooms in the summer and produces white berries which ripen in late summer or early fall. This fast-growing shrub usually does best as an understory plant. The more showy flowering dogwood which grows throughout the eastern US does not do well here.

There are three species of Redbud in Texas. The Eastern redbud grows from just east of here and throughout the eastern half of the US. The Mexican redbud grows natively in the Trans-Pecos region, although it will grow just fine in this area if planted. The redbud native to this area is the Texas redbud (*Cercis canadensis* var. *texensis*). It has the same general appearance of the Eastern redbud except the leaves are smaller and somewhat thicker. It blooms with pink flowers in early spring before the leaves come out, giving areas where they are common a beautiful pink hue. They produce reddish-brown leguminous seed pods. This is a popular fast-growing landscape tree. The Eastern redbud does not grow well in our limestone soils.

Texas kidneywood (*Eysenhardtia texana*) is an irregularly-shaped shrub with compound leaves with many tiny (about 1/4-inch-long) leaflets. Its flowers are small white blossoms in spikes at the end of branches that attract native bees. Flowering can occur anytime summer or fall after a rain. During drought periods, the kidneywood can drop its leaves and then regrow them after a rain. The seed pods produced are very small. This shrub looks like something that should be growing in South Texas and have thorns, but it doesn't have any thorns.

Most of the above shrubs will be eaten by hungry deer.

Some Less-Common Native Hill Country Shrubs and Small Trees

The following shrubs and small trees, while not rare, seem to me to be less common than the ones described above.

Rusty blackhaw (*Viburnum rufidulum*) is an understory tree or shrub with glossy green opposite leaves with tiny red hairs on the leaf stems and center vein. Large white flower clusters are formed in early spring. The leaves turn maroon in the fall. It produces small blue berries that are edible.

The Goldenball leadtree (*Leucaena retusa*) is a leguminous airy small tree with bipinately compound leaves. They are very drought tolerant and grow best in very well-drained soil. They are common on hillsides around Junction and Leakey. The flowers are conspicuous one inch yellow balls which are produced from spring to fall and form long thin bean-like seed pods.

Fragrant mimosa, or Pink mimosa (*Mimosa borealis*) is one of many mimosas that grow in Texas, but it is the most common in this area. It is usually a small shrub with compound leaves with tiny leaflets and many small prickles or thorns. It produces very showy ¾-inch pink spherical blooms in the spring which attract butterflies. It grows in dry limestone hillsides.

Blanco crabapple blooms attract local bumblebees.

Eve's necklace (*Sophora affinis*) is a shrub or small tree with compound leaves with one inch oval leaflets. It produces pale pink blossoms in the spring which in turn make dark seed pods that are constricted between each seed, giving the appearance of a bead necklace, thus the name. There are many Eve's necklaces growing in South Llano River State Park outside of Junction.

Mexican silktassel or Lindheimer silktassel (*Garrya ovata*) is a multi-trunked evergreen shrub with two inch dark green leathery leaves. It is dioecious, meaning male and female flowers are on separate plants. Because it is evergreen and makes dense foliage, it provides birds with good winter protection.

Elbowbush or spring herald (*Forestiera pubescens*) is a shrub with arching branches and leaves and twigs arranged on opposite sides of the branch. It is dioecious. Flowers are produced before any other trees or shrubs in late winter, thus the name Spring herald. Small, blue-black berries are produced on female plants which are eaten by wildlife.

Blanco crabapple, or Texas crabapple (*Malus ioensis* var. *texana*) is a shrub with a very limited range (Blanco, Kerr and Kendall counties) and, because it is a favorite of deer, it is threatened with extinction. It is a beautiful native crabapple with pink flowers in April and small green apples in October. It has substantial thorns. Landowners are encouraged to grow this plant, in protected areas, to help maintain the species.

Toothache tree, tickle tongue, or lime prickly ash (*Zanthoxylum hirsutum*) is a fairly common, interesting shrub with small crinkled leaves and thorns that look like rose thorns. The leaves contain a substance that will numb your mouth if chewed and produce a citrus odor when crushed. Wildlife like the small red fruit. This is a larval host plant for the giant swallowtail butterfly. It is not usually eaten by deer.

American smoke tree (*Cotinus obovatus*) is an unusual shrub that grows primarily in Kentucky, Tennessee and adjoining states with a disjunct population here in Bandera, Kerr and Kendall counties. It has oval leaves with reddish leaf stems. In the spring it produces small blossoms on long red or purple hair-like stems in crowded clusters that give the shrub a smoke-like appearance.

There are numerous other native shrubs that I haven't discussed, mainly because they are not that common. Not all of the species of shrubs that I have discussed in these essays would be appropriate for any given place in your yard, but among all of these native shrubs everyone should be able to find several that work for them.

Most of the shrubs I have discussed can be found in local native plant nurseries, and I encourage everyone to plant as many as possible to contribute to the diversity of the Hill Country habitat.

Native Hill Country Vines: A Nice Addition to the Landscape

Somehow, when one mentions vines, a jungle comes to mind, but not our semi-arid region. Maybe it is just too many Tarzan movies when we were kids. Anyway, we have lots of vines here as well, and here are some of them.

One of my books lists 60 species of grape (*Vitis* spp.) known in Texas. Not all grow in the Hill Country, but many do. The most distinctive species is Mustang grape (*Vitis mustangensis*), which is more common in some parts of the Hill Country than others. It is distinguished by having inrolled (curved downward) leaves that are somewhat duller green than other grapes on top but totally white from minute hairs on the bottom. Because the underside of the leaf sometimes shows, one can identify this grape driving down the road. They sometimes cover fence lines and small trees with their dense foliage.

The other local grape species have common names such as Spanish grape or mountain grape and have the characteristic wide grape leaf with jagged edges and no white hairs underneath. All native grapes produce fruit, but in nearly all cases it is much smaller and in smaller bunches than you would buy in the grocery store, but the birds and small animals love them.

Virginia creeper (*Parthenocissus quinquefolia*), also in the grape family, is a very distinctive vine with palmately compound leaves (think of spreading the fingers of your hand, each finger representing one of the five leaflets, with all the leaflets attached at your palm). It produces small blue fruits and the leaves turn bright red in the fall. Considered a good understory plant.

Greenbrier, (*Smilax bona-nox*) is a common understory vine with triangular or heart-shaped leathery leaves. It usually has thorns or prickles, sometimes all over, including the leaves, but sometimes only a few along the stem. The leaves stay on well into the winter and are good high-protein deer food. Berries in clusters turn dark blue in the fall. Because of the thorns and the tangled way the vine grows, it is considered a nuisance by many people.

Southern dewberry, (*Rubus trivialis*) is a low-growing vine with compound leaves with oval leaflets. It blooms white in the spring and makes black berries that are edible in early summer. This is a common shade-loving low vine that grows throughout the eastern US. The stems have short thorns.

I would judge the above vines to be the most often encountered around our area, but there are several more native Hill Country vines.

Poison ivy (*Toxicodendron radicans*) doesn't seem to be nearly as common around here as it is in most of the US north and east of here. It is often confused with box elder tree sprouts which also have "leaves of three," or with Virginia creeper which has five leaflets. When climbing a tree, it often puts out tiny "rootlets" from the stem that attach themselves to the bark. In spite of its toxic properties, deer eat it and birds like the berries it produces.

Coral honeysuckle (*Lonicera sempervirens*), is a great landscape plant that has red tubular blooms from very early spring into late fall and attracts hummingbirds. Other birds like the fruit as well. Please don't confuse this native honeysuckle with the exotic invasive Japanese honeysuckle.

Another good landscape plant is cow-itch vine or ivy treebine (*Cissus incise*). This vine has thick leathery leaves with two deep indentations that give some the impression of three leaves. This vine, which is also in the grape family, has unusual foliage texture and produces berries that the birds like.

Scarlet leatherflower (*Clematis texensis*) is endemic to the Hill Country, known to grow only in 7 counties. This somewhat delicate vine grows in dappled shade and produces small red bell-shaped flowers. Its cousin, Purple leatherflower (*Clematis pitcheri*) likes to grow in moist, shady areas.

Pearl milkweed vine (*Matelea reticulata*) is a thin-stemmed vine with heart-shaped leaves that produces a small greenish five-petal flower with what looks like a pearl in the center.

Carolina snailseed (*Cocculus carolinus*) looks very much like Greenbrier, but without the thorns. There are several Passionflower vines (*Passiflora* spp.) that produce spectacular ornate blooms. Finally, there are three Pipevine species that are host to the pipevine swallowtail butterfly larva.

Native, Evergreen Shrubs of the Hill Country

If you are looking for evergreen shrubs to plant, here is a list of the more common evergreen Hill Country shrubs. Most shrubs are multi-trunked although some can appear to be single-trunked small trees.

Texas mountain laurel (*Sophora secundiflora*), also called mescal bean, is an evergreen shrub usually 4 to 8' tall with compound, dark-green leaves with shiny leaflets 1 to 2-inches long. (A compound leaf is a leaf divided into two or more leaflets with each leaflet resembling a small simple leaf.) It has large showy purplish flowers in the early spring that smell like grape Kool-Aid. It produces a gray seed pod with red seeds which ripen in late summer. Both the leaves and the seeds contain an alkaloid that is toxic to livestock and humans when ingested. Deer will avoid this plant.

Cenizo, or Texas sage (*Leucophyllum frutescens*) is a 4 to 10' shrub with very small silver-grey leaves. It usually flowers around 7 to 10 days after a good rain, covering the whole shrub with lavender blooms that attract hordes of native bees. More common in the west, they require little if any extra water. Cenizo is not a deer favorite.

Evergreen Sumac (*Rhus virens*), is another plant with shiny green compound leaves. It produces tiny white blooms in clusters in the summer, especially after good rains. It can attain a height up to 12 feet, but may have leaves down to the ground. It may not be eaten by deer.

Agarita (*Berberis trifoliata*) is a common Hill Country shrub with compound leaves consisting of three very stiff leaflets, each with 3 to 5 very sharp points. They produce small, fragrant, yellow flowers in early spring that are a favorite with native bees. The red berries ripen in late spring and some people make jelly from them. Agarita shrubs make good "nursery plants" by keeping browsers away with their sharp leaves, thus allowing young hardwood trees to grow up inside the shrubs without being eaten. It is common to find hackberry and cherry trees growing up inside an agarita. Mature leaves are not eaten by deer.

Texas madrone (*Arbutus xalapensis*) is the distinctive shrub or small tree with the peeling bark revealing a smooth reddish or tan bark. Its leaves are dark green and leathery; its flowers are white clusters in early spring followed by small red berries. It's native range in the Hill Country is limited to Real, Bandera, Kendall and parts of adjacent counties. It can be very difficult to grow. In Big Bend's Chisos mountains there are places where madrones grow into large spectacular trees. Because of deer browsing, one usually only finds small madrones growing up inside cedar bushes or other protective vegetation.

Cedar, Ashe juniper, (*Juniperus ashei*) is certainly the most common evergreen shrub in the Hill Country. It is dioecious, which means male and female flowers are produced on separate plants. The female plants bear the blue berry-like cones which are eaten by many species of wildlife. Cedar is eaten by deer only when there is little else for them to eat. Many species of wildlife use cedar thickets for cover, especially in winter.

There are two common Hill Country shrubs that are not strictly speaking evergreen, but are classified as having persistent leaves, meaning they survive into the winter, and in mild winters or in slightly more southern locations, may indeed be evergreen. They are the Texas Persimmon and Willow Baccharis.

Texas persimmon (*Diospyros texana*) is a common shrub of central, south and west Texas. It was discussed in a previous essay.

Poverty Weed, Roosevelt weed or willow baccharis (*Baccharis neglecta*) is a common, somewhat-invasive multi-trunked shrub with airy fine foliage. It is commonly seen colonizing disturbed areas of bare soil and can become an invasive pest, but along riparian areas it can be beneficial in holding soil in place. Baccharis is also dioecious, and the female plant flowers in early fall with large bunches of whitish flowers. It is not eaten by deer.

Native Shrubs That Grow in Wet Shady Areas

The following native deciduous shrubs are usually, but not exclusively, found in shady, wet areas in canyons and along creeks.

False Indigo, or Amorpha (*Amorpha fruticosa*) is a medium-sized shrub with compound leaves with oval leaflets about one-inch long. It puts up flower spikes in the spring that can be 2 to 4 inches long and vary from dark blue to purple, resembling a bottle brush with yellow stamens. Very small seed pods are formed in the summer.

Buckeyes: There are four species of native shrubs in Texas with common names of buckeye. Three closely-related species are the Texas buckeye or white buckeye (*Aesculus glabra* var. *arguta*) found from this area to NE Texas and beyond, the Yellow buckeye (*Aesculus pavia* var. *flavescens*) the most common one in the western Hill Country, and the Red buckeye (*Aesculus pavia* var. *pavia*) found predominately in the east part of the Hill Country. Mexican buckeye (*Ungnadia speciosa*), not related to the others, is common throughout a large part of central and west Texas.

The three Aesculus species have palmately compound leaves (having 5, sometimes 7 to 9 or more) leaflets radiating from a central stem tip like fingers on a hand), and all three produce seeds in a semi-triangular, three compartment seed pod. The three species are most easily distinguished by the color of their flowers. All three species are very poisonous if ingested. Mexican buckeye is in a different genus and is distinguished by having pinnately compound leaves (leaflets arranged in pairs along a leaf stem) and showy pink blossoms in early spring. It has a seed pod similar to yellow and red buckeyes. The seeds of this species are also poisonous if ingested.

Carolina buckthorn (*Frangula caroliniana* or *Rhamnus caroliniana*) is a large shrub or small tree with 2 to 4-inch-long, very shiny green leaves with prominent veins. It produces very small inconspicuous flowers in the spring and red to black 3/8-inch berries. It is usually seen growing where it is protected from the deer.

Creek plum *(Prunus rivularis)* is a small shrub (to 6 feet) prone to thicket-forming shoots. It is inconspicuous except in early spring when it is covered with cream-colored fragrant flowers. Its fruit is usually less than ¾ inch in diameter. There are several other plum species native to different parts of Texas.

Buttonbush (*Cephalanthus occidentalis*) is found almost exclusively adjacent to or actually in creeks. It has 2 to 6-inch leaves that are usually partially folded along the center and arranged along the stems in pairs opposite each other. Its striking summer fragrant flowers look like 1 inch round pincushions or, if you are a certain age, Sputniks, which turn into rough brown balls. Not, apparently a favorite deer food.

American beautyberry (*Callicarpa americana*) is a 3 to 10-foot tall shrub with 2 to 6-inch egg-shaped pointed leaves in an opposite arrangement along the stem. They have white or pink flower clusters along the stem that form an eye-catching bright purple ring of berries around the stem. They grow naturally at least as far west as Kendall Co.

Wafer ash or Hop tree (*Ptelea trifoliate*) is a medium-sized shrub in the citrus family. It has trifoliate compound leaves (leaves in clusters of three). It has inconspicuous sweet-smelling flowers which eventually form flat wafer-shaped winged seeds. Legend has it that early settlers used the seeds in place of hops for making beer. Not a real deer favorite.

Common Spice-bush *(Lindera benzoin)* is a rather unremarkable multi-trunked shrub which grows in moist areas from central Texas north and east to Maine and Michigan. It has small yellow flower clusters attached to the stems before the leaves come out. The fruit is very small berries. The leaves, when crushed, have a citrus aroma. Deer will nibble it.

It should be noted that almost nothing in Mother Nature is absolute. I have collected the shrubs discussed here as ones found along creeks and in cooler canyons simply as a unifying feature of these shrubs. But while it is common to find these shrubs in these areas, it should not be assumed that they cannot be found in drier, sunny areas, or that they cannot be grown in areas removed from water. And conversely, it doesn't mean that other species, not discussed here, will not sometimes be found along creeks in shady canyons.

Some Hill Country Trees and Shrubs of the Legume Family

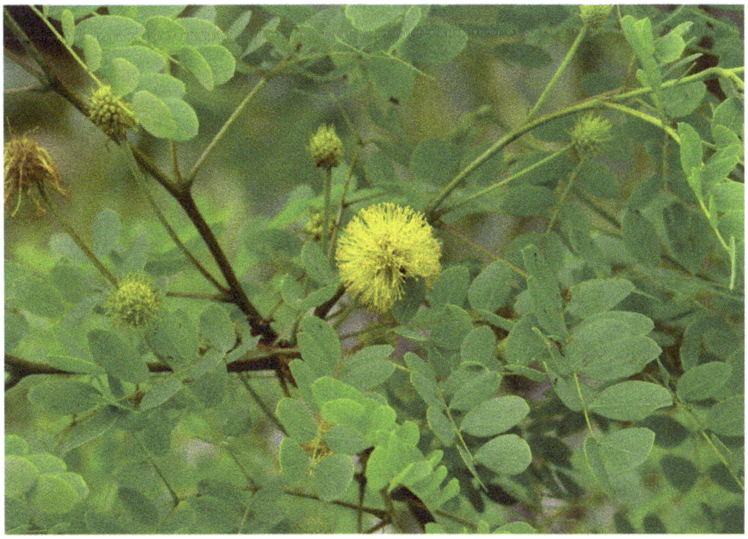

Goldenball lead tree, a beautiful, drought tolerant Hill Country native.

As discussed earlier, the legume or pea family of plants produce seeds in "pods" like beans or peas, most are capable of "fixing" nitrogen from the air to use by the plant, and most have compound leaves. Here are a number of the more common Hill Country native trees and shrubs that belong to that family.

There are many species of Acacias, including Huisache (*Acacia farnesiana*), a large shrub or small tree with tiny leaflets, long thorns in pairs at the leaf nodes and ½-inch golden-yellow spherical flowers in the spring. Roemer acacia or Catclaw acacia (*Acacia *roemeriana)*, is a shrub with small, rounded leaflets, short curved thorns, and cream-colored ½ inch balls on red stems in the spring. There are several other acacia species, most of which are more common to the south and west of here.

Anacacho orchid tree (*Bauhinia congesta*) grows on the western part of the Edwards Plateau. It is a shrub to small tree with two ½ inch leaflets attached to the end of a petiole and ¾ inch wide five-petal white flowers in spring.

Black dalea (*Dalea frutescens*) is a low (1 to 3 feet) rounded bush with gray-green leaflets and bright purple flowers from summer to fall.

Eve's necklace (*Sophora affinis*) is a small tree with one-inch-long oval leaflets. It has pink pea-like flowers in early spring and the seed pod is constricted between seeds giving the appearance of a "necklace." It makes a nice, airy landscape tree.

False indigo (*Amorpha fruticosa*), is usually a multi-stem shrub growing in shade near creeks. It has one-inch oblong leaflets and puts up 2 to 6-inch-long flower spikes composed of many tiny purple flowers.

Golden-ball lead-tree (*Leucaena retusa*) is a bipinnately small tree with ¾ inch elliptic leaflets and bright yellow 1 inch spherical blooms in the spring

Kidneywood (*Eysenhardtia texana*) is a thorn-less multi-trunk shrub with tiny leaflets. It puts up small white blossoms that the bees love on flower stalks at the end of branches. It is a favorite of deer.

Our native mimosa is fragrant mimosa or Pink mimosa (*Mimosa borealis*) which is a low multi-branched shrub. It produces ½-inch pink round balls in early spring and small flat pea-like pods. This shrub has many short prickles along its branches.

Probably the most well-known legume in Texas is the Mesquite or Honey mesquite (*Prosopis glandulosa*). Because it can be invasive under certain conditions in certain areas, it is often considered to be a nuisance. However, in moderate density in many places it is a valuable tree providing nectar for bees and highly nutritious beans for livestock and wildlife. In much of the Hill Country the soil is too shallow for mesquite to grow well. Its flowers are yellow-green clusters on long drooping spikes.

Retama (*Parkinsonia aculeata*) is a small tree or large shrub with unique foot-long leaves sporting tiny leaflets. At the base of each leaf are small sharp thorns. In drought times the retama will drop its leaves and then grow them back after rains. The bark is smooth and green and can carry out photosynthesis like leaves. It blooms throughout the spring and summer with bright yellow flower clusters.

Texas mountain laurel or mescal bean (*Sophora secundiflora*) is a stunning evergreen shrub or small tree with shiny, dark-green oval leaflets 1-2 inches long. It blooms in early spring with large showy clusters of purple-blue pea-like flowers which smell like grape Kool-Aid! The leaves and seeds of this plant are toxic to livestock and humans if ingested. Deer seldom nibble this plant.

Texas redbud (*Cercis canadensis* var. *texensis*) is a showy small tree with 2 to 3-inch simple leaves that are heart-shaped to round (this is the only Legume discussed here that does not have compound leaves). It produces pink blooms before or at the same time as the leaves are emerging in the spring. This is a popular landscape plant that grows well, but be certain you are not buying an Eastern redbud which will not do well here.

The above is just a small fraction of the total number of woody leguminous plants known in Texas.

The Basics of Oak Wilt

I suspect everyone who has lived for any length of time in the Hill Country has heard of oak wilt, but I also know there are a lot of myths and misinformation about it. Here are some of the more important facts about this disease.

Oak wilt is a disease that primarily affects live oaks and red oaks (blackjack oaks and Spanish oaks in the Hill Country). It is caused by a fungus that grows in the vascular system of a tree and plugs up these systems thus preventing the natural movement of water, nutrients and carbohydrates which usually kills the tree. (A tree's vascular system provides a similar function for the tree that our circulatory system does for us.)

Live oak leaves showing the characteristic "fishbone" pattern when infected with oak wilt.

For landowners, the most important things to know are: first, how does the fungus get into the vascular system of the tree and second how can it be prevented from getting into the tree. Once a tree has the disease, there is no cure.

The fungus gets into the tree in one of two ways. When red oaks become infected and are dying, the fungus occasionally forms a fungal mat just under the bark that is full of spores. Tiny sap beetles, which live on sap, are attracted to these fungal mats and get the spores on their bodies. As the beetles fly off looking for another source of sap, if they find an oak tree that has just been cut, pruned or had a limb broken or the bark skinned off, they will land on that wound and the spores will spread into this fresh sap and thus infect a new tree. This is how new oak wilt centers are started.

The second way is if an infected tree is attached to another oak tree by their roots. This can occur if one tree sprouted from the root of the other or if the roots simply grew together and grafted. If this occurs, then the fungus can travel from the roots of one tree into the roots of an adjacent tree. This is much more likely to occur with live oaks than with red oaks. It is common to find groups of adjacent live oaks killed by the disease and that is why the vast majority of oaks killed in the Hill Country are live oaks.

The most effective way, by far, of preventing the fungus from infecting a healthy tree is to paint all wounds, cuts, scrapes, etc., on all oaks immediately, thus preventing the sap beetles with spores on them from getting to fresh sap. There is a lot of evidence that a large proportion of all new oak wilt centers are in fact started by people pruning or wounding trees and not painting the wound immediately.

If oak wilt has already infected neighboring live oak trees, there are two possible ways to prevent it from infecting others nearby. The timing and the distance between the trees is very important in determining the probability of success. If it is determined that a tree you wish to save is apparently healthy and is likely to be connected to a diseased tree, then injecting the fungicide Propiconazole 14.3 into the vascular system of the healthy tree, at the right time, has a relatively good chance of killing the fungus before it damages the tree. Note that this is not like a vaccination; trees don't have immune systems. You are simply placing the fungicide where it can contact the fungus before the latter has a chance to damage the tree. The fungus does not live in the ground.

An alternative procedure that can protect several trees at once may work if all the conditions are right, and that is trenching which involves digging a deep trench between the diseased tree(s) and the healthy ones to sever the root connections between them.

There is not enough space here to discuss the details of when and how these possible treatments might be applicable, but these details can be obtained at the very excellent website of the Texas Forest Service, www.texasoakwilt.org.

White oaks (post, shin, chinquapin,) are very much less frequently affected by oak wilt than red oaks and live oaks. Recently, some Lacey oaks have been found to be infected with oak wilt.

Hypoxylon: The OTHER Oak Tree Disease

Whenever anyone in this part of Texas thinks of a disease of trees, or just thinks of trees dying, they always think of oak wilt. And with good reason. Oak wilt is probably the proximate cause of the death of more mature oak trees in the Hill Country than any cause, other than man.

But there is another fungal disease, called hypoxylon or hypoxylon canker (*Hypoxylon atropunctatum*) that infects and kills oaks. Both oak wilt and hypoxylon are caused by a fungus, both cause a destruction of the vascular tissue of the trees. Red oaks are the most susceptible and quickest to die from both diseases.

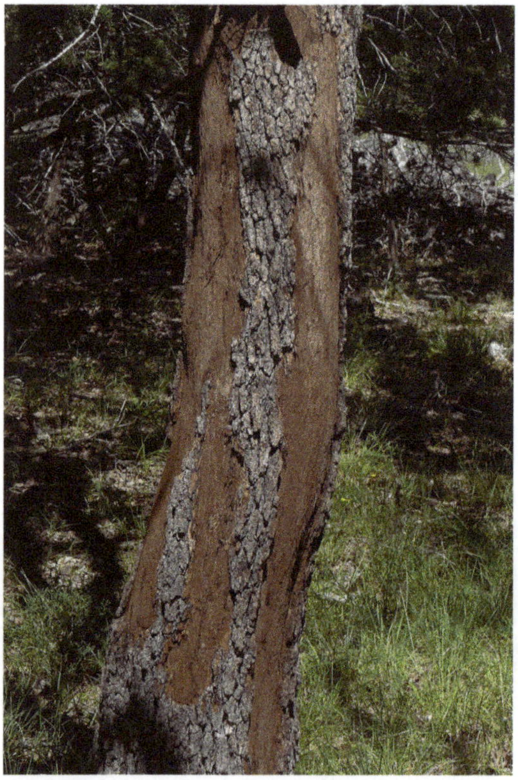

A post oak tree recently infected with hypoxylon showing the brown fungus after the bark fell off.

That is about where the similarity ends. Oak wilt is a primary pathogen which means it can infect a perfectly healthy host. Hypoxylon is an opportunistic pathogen which means it is always or usually ever-present but only infects the host when the host is stressed.

Oak wilt fungi can travel from tree to tree via interconnected roots and thus can kill many live oaks in an area from a single initial infection. Hypoxylon never moves through the roots from tree to tree, so only individual trees are infected rather than a whole grove. The spores of oak wilt fungus are transmitted to new sites by sap beetles seeking fresh sap on wounded trees. The spores of hypoxylon fungus are airborne and are thus everywhere.

The consequences of the above characteristics are that most trees in Texas killed by oak wilt are live oaks infected by the fungus moving from an infected tree to a healthy tree through the roots. Red oaks infected with oak wilt usually die quickly but, being less likely to be connected to other trees through their roots, usually only one tree dies. Perfectly healthy trees can become infected with oak wilt.

Hypoxylon, on the other hand usually only kills stressed trees. Stress can come from being watered too much, compacted soil over the roots, fill soil placed over the roots, or, usually, drought. Red oaks appear to be the most susceptible, although all oaks can be infected and indeed, at least in some states, hypoxylon has been found in elms, pecans, sycamores and other trees. I have observed hypoxylon in post oaks and Lacey oaks, but mostly in blackjack and Spanish oaks. Sometimes hypoxylon will be seen on only a single limb or on only part of a tree and it may take a year or two to totally kill the tree. Rarely the tree is not totally killed and may give rise to new growth.

Unfortunately, the symptoms of hypoxylon infection are generally not evident until the tree is mortally infected. The symptom then is sloughing bark down to the cambium and a brown velvet-like coating of spores on the trunk where the bark once was. This brown color usually eventually turns light grey with dark tar-like patches on the bare trunk.

There is no known method to prevent hypoxylon except to keep the tree from becoming stressed by watering during droughts and not damaging the root zone. Like oak wilt, there is no cure for hypoxylon either.

All of the above was brought home to me recently when I took a walk around a part of our property comprising about 4 acres and counted a half dozen blackjack oaks with hypoxylon, none of which showed any symptoms a year previously. The drought of 2011 clearly stressed these trees, some of which lost their leaves last fall. Previously, over the ten-year period prior to last year, I had only observed about the same number trees with hypoxylon on over 20 acres of woodland-savanna consisting mainly of live oaks, blackjack oaks and post oaks.

If you have a tree showing the signs of hypoxylon, its chances are not good, but I wouldn't be in any hurry to give up on it. I would give it plenty of time, at least until late spring or early summer of the following year, to put out some new green leaves and root sprouts, before I would give up on it. I have at least two blackjacks that obviously lost limbs or even the main part of the tree to hypoxylon, but still have healthy living parts several years later. A little water wouldn't hurt. If a dead tree can't fall on you, your house or your car, you can let Mother Nature take care of it in due time.

"Mighty Oaks from Little Acorns Grow"

Many people place oaks in a somewhat more revered category than other trees. Mighty oaks are used as a symbol of things that are strong, long-lasting and reliable. There are about 400 species of oaks that grow to tree-size worldwide, 58 of which grow in the U.S., and 38 of those grow in Texas. There are at least 8 species of oaks that grow in the Edwards Plateau.

Oaks are generally classified as in the white oak or red oak group; the names themselves are not really meaningful.

White oaks are characterized as having leaves with either smooth edges or, usually, rounded lobes (bumps along the edge of the leaves) without bristles at the tips of the lobes. Their acorns grow to maturity in one year, and usually sprout in the fall. The acorn cups have a knobby appearance on the outside and are smooth on the inside. Next year's buds on white oak branches are not sharply pointed.

Red oaks, by contrast, have lobes with points along the edge of the leaves and bristles at the tip of the points. Their acorns take two years to mature (become mature in their second fall) and usually sprout in the following spring. Red oak acorn cups are smoother than white oaks on the outside and are densely hairy on the inside. Their next year's buds are usually sharp pointed.

White oaks have plugged cells or vessels which prevent flow of fluids and are therefore the wood of choice for making wine barrels. Red oak heartwood is permeable and therefore not suitable for wine barrels, but can be treated with wood preservatives utilizing the open channels.

Oaks are wind-pollinated with the female flowers tiny and inconspicuous at the junction of the leaves and the stem. The male flowers are in dangling, bead-like strings that hang from the twig and are called catkins. They appear as the leaves are forming in the spring.

Of the common oaks in the Hill Country, only Blackjack oaks and Spanish oaks (also known as Texas red oaks) are in the red oak family. All of our other oaks; Lacey oaks, Chinquapin oaks, Shin oaks, Post oaks and Live oaks are in the white oak family. (Some experts put live oaks in a separate group altogether, but most call them white oaks). If we stretch our area a little to include the rest of the Edwards Plateau, we can add to the above list Vasey oak to the west and Bur oak and Shumard oak to the east. Vasey and Bur oaks are white oaks and Shumard oak is a red oak.

Oaks in general are slow growing, and slow growing trees tend to be the strongest, although Spanish oaks seem to be brittle and break off in wind storms more often than most of the others.

It is possible to grow oaks from acorns, although many acorns are not viable because a small wasp has laid its eggs in the acorn and the worm thus hatched eats the inside of the acorns. Put a handful of acorns in water and those that float are not viable.

Root sprouts, which are little trees that are connected to the roots of a mature "mother" tree usually grow faster and have a better chance of making it than trees growing from acorns. That is largely because the former are growing from a network of mature roots much larger than itself and so it can withstand drought and any other stress much better. If you see root sprouts coming up under and around a mature tree, if you cage them before the deer find them, you will have a much better chance of having a healthy new tree than planting an acorn or planting a nursery tree either for that matter.

Our Oak Population is Declining

One of the first things I noticed on a recent walk was a large dead limb that had broken off of a blackjack oak. On closer inspection, I discovered some other dead limbs on the tree along with about half of the limbs looking fine. But the dead limbs showed signs of hypoxylon.

On reflection, we have lost an inordinate number of blackjacks since buying our property in the 1990s. Most of these oaks were probably at least 50 years old and many were probably significantly older than that. This represents a large percentage of these great oaks dying in the last 15 years. In the same time frame, we have lost an even greater percentage of a much smaller number of Spanish oaks, (some to hypoxylon and some to wind), a few post oaks, but no live oaks.

Death is part of nature, so it is not surprising that trees die, but in the normal order of things, young sprouts and saplings will grow up to replace the older trees and the habitat remains unchanged. The problem is that there are no young sprouts or saplings of any of these trees. None anywhere except in areas protected from the deer. Deer love most all tree leaves, but especially blackjacks and Spanish oaks. And the increasing deer population in many areas in the past few decades has meant that no future oak trees are allowed to grow to maturity.

The above, coupled with the loss of live oaks from oak wilt, means two things. First, we are moving into a time when the hardwood tree population of the Hill Country is declining, meaning we will have fewer trees per acre in areas of high deer populations. Secondly, the scenic views in the Hill Country will reveal more dead trees and dead limbs than in the past.

Basically, what is happening is that as man has eliminated most all predators of white-tailed deer, the excessive deer numbers are altering the native habitat in a way that reduces new hardwood tree growth.

But because juniper (cedar) is not something that deer like to eat very much, the deer are not preventing new juniper trees from becoming established, so that although the hardwood trees with be declining, the junipers will not.

There is no doubt that drought is part of the cause of the death of many trees, but it is also true that many of these trees survived the drought of the 1950s and everything since then.

How Fast Are We Losing Our Trees?

I discussed above about what I believe to be the declining numbers of hardwood trees in the Hill Country. The reasons for this are mainly the excessive numbers of white-tailed deer, although in some areas the number of exotic ungulates may have also contributed as may the current or past presence of large goat herds

It is a simple fact that finding any replacement hardwood sprouts or saplings within the reach of deer on most properties is a rarity. If there are no replacement hardwoods surviving to become mature trees with most of their leaves above the reach of the deer, then as the older trees die the numbers of these trees will necessarily decline.

What I never had any idea about was just how fast is decline occurring? So I recently decided to see if I could get any indication about that by counting trees, both alive and relatively recently dead. And because it was as good a place as any to start, and because I knew the area and had a memory of many of the individual trees, I did my survey on our property in an overgrazed, overbrowsed woodland/savanna.

I walked the property counting all hardwood trees (everything except cedar) on an approximately 10-acre plot. It turns out that all of the hardwood trees in this plot were oaks; live oaks, post oaks, blackjack oaks and shin oaks. I counted 392 living mature oaks. At the same time, I counted 29 trees that had died in the past 12 years or so, most all of which were blackjacks, a lesser number of post oaks and only a very few live oaks. None of the oaks died of oak wilt, but mostly drought stress and/or hypoxylon. There were perhaps a half dozen trees that were counted as living because they had at least one significant limb with leaves, but most of them showed signs of hypoxylon and will likely die in another year or so.

That means that about 7 percent of the trees in this 10-acre plot have died in the past 12 years plus another 2 percent that are dying. Extrapolating that rate would predict the loss of about 15 to 18 percent of our trees in 25 years.

This may be an aberration, since I believe we have lost a larger percentage of trees in the past three years (beginning with the drought of 2011) than we had in previous years. So if we have higher rainfall years, the rate of die-off may be lower. But then again, we could also have more drought years.

Significantly, I did not see ANY young trees or saplings with trunk diameters of even as much as a half-inch or a height of over six inches. Some short live oak and shin oak root sprouts with a half dozen leaves were seen, but the deer will take care of them this winter.

Interestingly, inside our one-acre high fence, I counted 43 mature hardwoods, and two dead blackjacks. But then I also counted 102 hardwood volunteer trees over 2 feet tall that came up because of seeds or acorns spread by birds and animals or root sprouts from mature trees—some of which would certainly become mature trees in a natural habitat as a few are already over 8 feet tall! These volunteer trees include live oaks, post oaks, blackjack oaks, hackberry, escarpment black cherry, flame-leaf sumacs and possumhaws. Clearly, young replacement hardwoods can still become mature trees when browsers are excluded!

This survey certainly doesn't constitute any kind of scientific study and the numbers I found on this one plot of land may be very different from other places in the Hill Country with other mixtures of species and other soil and environmental conditions. And, while we may hate to see the loss of any of our trees, the Hill Country will still be beautiful with fewer trees and it probably had fewer in the past than it does now anyway. But it would be nice if we had fewer deer to hasten the decline of our hardwoods.

Common Hill Country Cacti

Note: cacti and succulents are not really woody plants so they don't really belong in a section on trees and shrubs, but they are not grasses or forbs either, so I have included them here.

There are at least 150 species of cacti in Texas, and most of these are found, not surprisingly, in West Texas. All cacti are succulents (store water in juicy tissues), but not all succulents are cacti. With very few exceptions, cacti do not have leaves but have fleshy green stems. Spines can vary greatly in size, shape and color, and on prickly pears and related cacti, can be of two types, the regular substantial, larger spines and the small hair-like clusters called glochids.

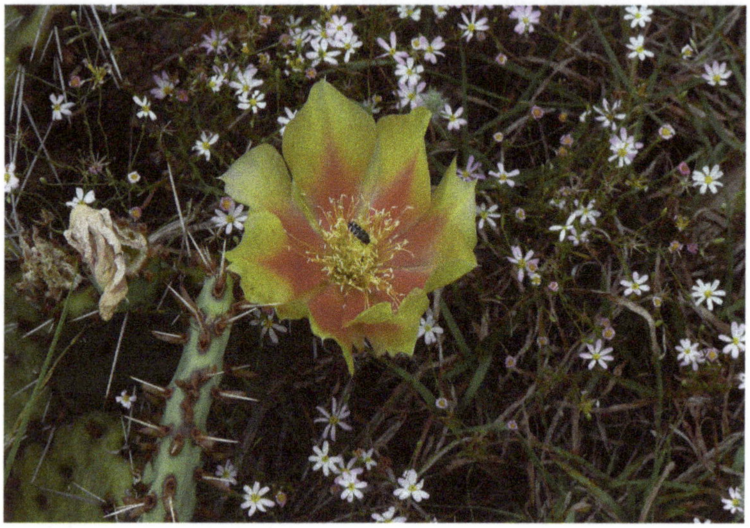

Plains prickly pear *(Opuntia macrorhiza)*

Agaves and yuccas are succulents but are not cacti.

There are at least 19 species of cacti found in some part of the Hill Country. Here are the ones I consider the most common.

The most common Hill Country cactus is the Texas prickly pear, *Opuntia engelmannii* var. *lindheimeri*. It has very large (6 to 12 inches) nearly circular pads, yellow flowers with yellow centers and reddish to purple fruits (tunas). The fruits have glochids, but not spines. Another common prickly pear is the Plains prickly pear, *Opuntia macrorhiza*, which has much smaller near-circular pads (3 to 5 inches) and the flowers are yellow with red centers.

Although very different in shape, a related cactus is Christmas cholla, or pencil cactus or tasajillo, *Cylindropuntia leptocaulis*. Instead of pads, it has pencil-thin stems and is usually multibranched with 1 to 2-inch spines. Some call it a cowboy Christmas cactus because of the red fruits arranged up and down the green stems in the late fall into winter.

The claret cup cactus, *Echinocereus coccineus*, is a cluster of several stems from 2 to 12-inches tall and 1½ to 4-inches in diameter. The surface of the stems has ridges running up and down. The blooms are a bright orange-red and the fruits ripen to a bright red also with short spines.

The strawberry pitaya or strawberry cactus, *Echinocereus enneacanthus* var. *brevispinus*, is similar in appearance to the claret cup except the individual stems are somewhat smaller than the claret cup and some of the stems appear to be lying down rather than sticking up. The blooms are pink or magenta and funnel shaped. The fruits are red.

The lace cactus, *Echinocereus reichenbachii*, is a small cylindrical cactus which is 3 to 10 inches high and 2 to 4-inches in diameter. One first notices that it is covered in white spines that are arranged in bunches along vertical rows. The spines almost obscure the stem underneath, but in spite of the number of spines, they are mostly flattened against the cactus so that one can touch it gently without getting stuck. They are frequently found in colonies. The blooms are pink to magenta.

The horse-crippler cactus, *Echinocactus texensis*, is a very low-growing, but substantial plant with very large, stiff spines. It can be difficult to find because often it only rises an inch or two above the soil, although it can be a foot in diameter. It has prominent, deep ribs. The flowers are salmon pink with lacey pedals and the fruit is scarlet red.

Texas prickly pear *(Opuntia engelmannii var. lindheimeri)*.

Another cactus I would like to talk about is not common at all, in fact it is quite uncommon. The Tobusch fishhook cactus, *Sclerocactus brevihamatus* var. *tobuschii*, is endemic to this part of the Hill Country (meaning it grows nowhere else in the world!) and is listed by both federal and state agencies as Endangered. It is found almost exclusively in Kerr and Bandera counties and some adjacent counties to the west. I have been involved with projects to count individual plants and monitor their growth characteristics in a Nature Conservancy preserve in Bandera County. This fishhook cactus is a very small cylindrical cactus with stems from 1 to 3 inches tall and usually less than 1 or 2 inches in diameter. It has greenish-yellow flowers. And yes, some of the spines are curved into a hook shape.

If you want to grow cacti, I have two pieces of advice. First, be certain the cactus can tolerate our cold winter spells, many cacti found for sale cannot. Second, make a very well-draining soil mix by adding a lot of sand and caliche (or crushed granite) to native soil and make a raised bed.

Native Succulents of the Hill Country

Hill Country Cacti were discussed above. All cacti are succulents (store water in juicy tissues), but not all succulents are cacti. With very few exceptions, cacti do not have leaves, but have fleshy green stems and spines (aka thorns). Succulents do not have spines, although some species have leaves with sharp points and/or sharp hook-like structures along the edge of the leaf.

Most experts place all of the succulents in the Hill Country in the Century-Plant family, (Agavaceae).

The most common succulent in the Hill Country is probably the Twist-leaf yucca (*Yucca rupicola*). This yucca is endemic to the Hill Country, meaning it grows natively nowhere else. It has stiff leaves that are 1 to 2-feet long and 1 to 2-inches wide. The leaves are usually slightly twisted. The flower stalk would be about 5 feet tall with large white bell-shaped flowers in the spring—that is if the deer didn't eat it first, which they usually do.

Buckley yucca (*Yucca constricta*) has 1 to 2-feet long, narrow leaves usually in a spherical cluster. The edges of the stiff leaves usually have white threads hanging from them and the points of the leaves are very sharp. The flower stalk can be 5 to 6 feet tall and it produces clusters of large bell-shaped white flowers in the spring.

The red yucca (*Hesperaloe parviflora*) is native only to the western part of the Edwards Plateau, but it is commonly grown as an ornamental throughout the Hill Country. It has 3-foot-long olive-green leaves that are frequently inrolled and have white threads hanging from them. The 5-foot pink flower stalk has small red or coral flowers that attract hummingbirds.

Texas sotol (*Dasylirion texanum*) has 3 feet or longer light green narrow leaves which have hook-like structures on the edges of the leaf that are curved toward the tip. This is very effective protection from browsing animals. Sotol produces 8-foot-tall flower stalks with small yellow flowers closely packed along the top of the stalk.

There are two similar species of nolina in the Hill Country, devil's shoestring (*Nolina lindheimeriana*) and Texas beargrass or sacahuista (*Nolina texana*). They are both characterized as having very long (2 to 4 feet) very narrow (1/4 inch) flexible leaves which arch up from the base about 2 feet and then hang down to the ground. They resemble a very large clump of grass. But they are not grasses.

Nolina lindheimeriana has flat leaves that are very finely toothed. Its flower stalk is usually about 3-feet tall with tiny cream colored flowers arranged on loose open branches in April to May.

Nolina texana has leaves that feel round with a flat side with no toothed margins. The off-white flowers are borne on a short flower stalk that does not grow up above the leaf vegetation. It blooms from March through June.

One more member of the Agavaceae family, the Spanish dagger (*Yucca treculeana*) is native only to the extreme southwest part of the Hill Country. It has very long, wide and stiff dagger-like leaves with very sharp, pointed tips. It produces a very large, heavy flower cluster with cream-colored blooms tinged with pink.

There are, of course, many more species of agaves and yuccas that are native to the Trans-Pecos region of Texas but are often seen in people's cactus gardens throughout the Hill Country.

Many species in the Agavaceae family are pollinated by a large yucca moth which is uniquely adapted to the large blooms of most species, and this symbiotic relationship is important to the survival of both the moth and the agaves.

Native Americans utilized many species of agaves and yuccas. For example, they would strip the edges with the prickles off the sotol leaves and use the soft leaves to weave baskets and mats. They dug up the large tubers or roots at the base of several species and baked them in hot rock ovens, or ground them into a flour for various uses.

Deer usually avoid the leaves of all of our native succulents, although when desperate enough, nothing may escape their browsing. The flower stalks, on the other hand, tend to be great favorites of deer, so many folks never get to see their yuccas bloom.

Nurse Plants. How Many Young Plants Survive the Deer

When you walk around a pasture or natural area, pretty soon you realize that Mother Nature places plants in what might seem to be a random arrangement. If we humans had placed all the trees and shrubs on the landscape, we would probably have put things in rows or some kind of "logical" groupings and probably some kind of spacing separating individual plants from each other. While Mother Nature's plant arrangements are certainly not anything we would think of as "logical," they are far from random. There is a reason everything is where it is, even if it is not obvious to us.

First, trees or shrubs are where they are because that is where the acorn or seed was when it germinated. I know that is obvious, but it explains a lot. The seeds, acorns or nuts of most trees and shrubs are moved around by animals, rather than, say, the wind. Yes, some trees have seeds that are light enough and have thin membranes that allow them to drift short distances in the wind, but the seeds are not carried longer distances that way.

Most all berries either fall down under the parent tree, or are eaten by a bird or other animal and then transported some distance in the animal's digestive system before being deposited elsewhere. Of course, squirrels also carry nuts and acorns around and bury them, theoretically to find them later.

But the point is that the birds and animals cause the trees and shrubs to be where they are. But not all of the seedlings planted by the birds or animals survive, because they are eaten at an early stage in their lives by grazers and browsers. Which is where nurse plants come into the picture.

Nurse plants are plants that have the ability to protect young saplings from being eaten and thus allow the young plants to grow to a stage where they can survive without protection. The most common nurse plants in this part of the Hill Country are prickly pear, especially Texas prickly pear, the large pad species (*Opuntia engelmannii* var. *lindheimeri*) and agarita (*Mahonia trifoliolata*).

It is not uncommon when walking on a ranch or along a trail in a park to see a small tree growing up inside a large prickly pear or agarita. And it may be the only place where you will find a young hardwood tree only 4-feet tall anywhere in the area. A bird or a small animal either perched on the prickly pear or agarita bush or crawled up inside and then left their droppings containing the seed.

As the first young leaves emerged, nothing could get to them to eat them and the new plant grew bigger and bigger, eventually sticking out above the nurse plant but still out of reach of browsing critters. Eventually the tree will be big enough to have sufficient leaves above browse height so that it could survive even if the prickly pear or agarita were to die.

The most common hardwood trees we see growing up inside nurse plants are hackberry, escarpment black cherry, Texas redbud, Carolina buckthorn, Spanish oak and cedar elm. Other than hanging over a steep cliff along a creek bed, this may be the only place that these deer-favorite trees can be found as youngsters.

Large cedar (Ashe juniper) trees can sometimes also serve as nurse plants. It is not uncommon, especially in parts of Bandera County to find young madrone trees growing up inside the protection of a large cedar bush which has limbs down to the ground.

Of course, the nurse plants also provide protection for small animals as well. Cottontails are particularly fond of making their nests inside large prickly pears.

Sometimes Mother Nature hasn't provided as many nurse plants as are needed, and we can step up and take over for her. We can make small, loose piles of cedar branches to accomplish the same thing, and at the same time become nurse areas for new grass or wildflowers. We can make circular cages out of tree branches or small logs to protect larger areas from the deer, or we can build wire exclosures to accomplish the same goal. This is especially successful if you find a small hardwood sapling that has not been eaten, usually in the spring, and you cage it, you will almost always have the makings of a mature hardwood.

— SECTION III —

ANIMALS

When people think about the Texas Hill Country, the things that most often come to mind are the hills and the trees, somewhat evergreen even in winter, open rangeland, clear creeks and generally beautiful scenery. But not too far from many people's minds are the abundant white-tailed deer herds. The operative word here is certainly "abundant."

I don't know of anyone who doesn't like to see and watch deer, and their numbers certainly serve to attract hunters to the Hill Country. (My last deer-hunting trip in the early 1960s was down here in the Hill Country.)

But the abundance of deer is also a problem. Anyone trying to grow almost anything around their house in the Hill Country certainly has to contend with these omnipresent browsers. And the problems they cause by eating virtually all of the hardwood tree sprouts is a major problem for the health of the Hill Country habitat.

White-tailed deer are, of course, not the only large animals one sees in the Hill Country. There are also the common livestock (cattle, sheep and goats) seen on many ranches, and a myriad of exotic ungulates brought to the Hill Country as game animals and in some cases as pets.

In addition, the Hill Country is home to a large variety of smaller animals, some quite common, some very secretive, and all very interesting to watch and enjoy. This is especially true for those of us living in the country.

Understanding something about all of these animals adds to the pleasure of living in the Hill Country and the joy of watching nature.

WHITE-TAILED DEER

I am sure everyone knows about and recognizes a white-tailed deer, even if their only experience is seeing them while driving down any Hill Country road, but perhaps some facts about them will be helpful.

Hill Country white-tailed deer (*Odocoileus virginians*) are in the Cervidae or deer family. Most Hill Country males (bucks) will weigh between 100 and 250 pounds while the females (does) will weigh between 75 and 150 pounds. They breed mainly in late October through November, have a gestation period of 6 to 7 months and, in good conditions usually have twins, single fawns in lesser conditions.

The fawns can walk within a few hours but spend most of their first few weeks curled up in thick vegetation until the doe comes to nurse them.

Bucks begin to grow antlers in late spring or summer when the antlers are covered in velvet. The antler material is bone and is shed after the rut in the winter. This distinguishes antlers from horns on cattle, sheep, goats, etc., which grow continually throughout the life of the animal and which are composed of chitin, a material similar to our fingernails.

For most of the year does form lose associations with a few other does and their fawns. They will drive away the buck fawns before the rut begins. Bucks are usually solitary in spring and summer, may form buck herds in the fall, and may associate with the does in the winter.

What Are Those Critters Eating Out There?

The Hill Country has lots of herbivores; livestock, wildlife, and exotics, that are living off the land. What exactly are they all eating? It may not be what you think. Studies some years ago out at the Kerr Wildlife Management Area west of Hunt, have pretty much answered that question. Here is what we know.

There are three broad categories of forage: browse (leaves of trees, shrubs and woody vines), forbs (broad-leaf weeds and wildflowers), and grass. White-tailed deer have plants they really like to eat and others they seldom eat. Well, all other animals have their food preferences too. Some of these preferences are based on the palatability of the plant, others on the biology of the animal. Animals with thin, flexible lips (sheep, goats, deer and most exotics) can nibble off small leaves even between thorns, where those with wide thick lips (cattle, horses) are not very good at that.

One of too-many Hill Country white-tailed deer.

It will come as a surprise to no one that cattle eat mostly grass, in fact they can survive on 100 percent grass.

Sheep, if given the opportunity to choose among all three classes of forage, will eat nearly equal amounts of all three forages, but they can be quite happy living on 80 percent grass and smaller amounts of browse and forbs.

Given their preference, goats will eat mainly browse and forbs and only a little grass, but they can do quite well on larger amounts of grass if they need to.

White-tailed deer will prefer edible forbs if available and browse if not, but will eat only very little grass. Even when deer are malnourished they are unlikely to eat more than about 15 percent grass, except in the spring when fresh green grass shoots are present. It is not that they are just picky eaters, they just can't digest much grass.

All three forage classes provide primarily carbohydrates for the animals, sugars, starches and cellulose. We humans can only digest sugars and starches. But ruminant animals have a digestive system that allows microorganisms in their four-compartment stomachs to digest cellulose, so they can obtain nutrition from foods that we could not. But some plant materials have a component of the cellulose that is very hard to digest. It is called lignin, and it is partly what makes some plant parts stiff. There is a lot of lignin in tree trunks, less in the leaves of trees and forbs, but a fair amount in grass. So grass is actually harder to digest than forbs or browse.

The reason that cattle can live on grass and deer can't has to do with the structure of their rumens. Cattle have very large, compartmentalized stomachs that allow for a long digestion time, so they can digest the more difficult-to-digest lignin and the cellulose associated with it. Deer, on the other hand, have relatively smaller, more open rumens that allows for a very short digestion time, and thus they cannot digest grass with lignin very well.

It turns out that most all of the common exotic herbivores in the Hill Country eat like sheep and goats; they can live on all three types of forage. But white-tailed deer, for all practical purposes, can survive on only two types, browse and forbs. The consequence of this is that, in competition with sheep, goats or any of the exotics, white-tailed deer are at a disadvantage. Once browse and forbs are all eaten, all of the other animals can switch to grass and survive, whereas the white-tailed deer cannot. This was dramatically demonstrated at the Kerr Wildlife Management Area where in a direct competition between white-tailed deer and sika deer, sika survived and multiplied and the white-tailed deer died out.

I have left out the fourth food source available to animals at times, mast. Mast is defined as nuts, acorns, beans, berries, etc. that make up the fruits of many range plants. Just about all animals utilize these foods when available, but the problem is that they are very seasonal, usually only available in the fall. While mast helps animals get in good condition for the winter, it is not available for most of the year.

Is There Anything Deer Won't Eat?

How many times have we all heard that question, or asked "What can I plant that the deer won't eat?" It seems like a perfectly legitimate question. But it is the wrong question, and asking it implies an assumption that is seldom, if ever, true. We ask it because we have all heard a couple of common phrases, "deer-proof" and "deer-resistant," and we assume there are plants that fall into these categories.

"Is this or that plant deer-proof or deer-resistant," we ask, as though a plant has some kind of immunity to being eaten. It doesn't. It is not up to the plant, it's the deer that decides what to eat.

We tend to anthropomorphize the issue by thinking about the kind of things we would want to avoid and assume a deer would act the same way. We usually think of things that have thorns or prickles, a bad odor, or a disgusting texture as things deer would not like to eat. But it turns out that some of the things that deer really like to eat have thorns or prickles (*e.g.* greenbrier), and some of the things they seldom eat appear to have none of the above characteristics.

We often think that it is the properties of the plant that cause a deer to eat it or to avoid it, and that will hold true wherever the plant is found. But what does and does not get eaten depends more on what else is available and how many deer there are. Deer, like us, have food preferences, things they really like to eat, things they usually eat if available, and things they usually avoid.

Given the choice between a bologna sandwich, a hamburger or a T-bone steak, most of us will go for the steak. But if there aren't any steaks left, we will be happy enough to have a hamburger. And if bologna sandwiches are all that are left, if we are hungry enough, we will likely take that. Deer do the same thing. They will almost always go after any Spanish oak (Texas red oak), kidneywood or coral honeysuckle they can reach, but will usually leave any cowpen daisy, mealy blue sage or willow baccharis alone.

A given plant in my yard might be eaten to the ground, but that same plant might go untouched in your yard if you have a lot of things that are higher up the deer food preference list. In other words, what is eaten depends on what else there is to eat.

In most areas, what is available to eat is at least somewhat determined by how many deer there are, since in areas of high deer populations most of the highly preferred plants will have been eaten to extinction. Thus in those areas the deer are probably routinely eating things on the bottom of their food preference list. And if the deer population is high enough and the area is largely browsed out, starving deer might eat almost anything.

If that sounds extreme to you, then, like most of us, you have probably never been really, really hungry. But I remember as a kid having a Sunday School teacher tell us about his experiences in a German POW camp during the war, and how they ate cockroaches!

If you think about that, you can understand why deer sometimes eat things they are "not supposed to eat," things that are "deer-resistant" or "deer-proof." Maybe we should quit using those terms.

So what can you plant that the deer won't eat? The short, accurate answer is, probably, rocks. But that isn't much help. The best answer is to plant native plants that are on the low end of the deer preference list as those plants are the least likely to be eaten, but know that if the deer are desperate, they might eat those plants too. For example, cedar is at the bottom of the deer food preference list, but in some areas examination of deer rumens reveal that over half of the contents are cedar.

If you have a fenced-in area that deer can't get to, then planting things that are the highest on the deer food preference list would be great, because those are the species that are rapidly declining in the Hill Country due to the high deer populations and you will be helping to maintain the species.

Common Hill Country Forbs Seldom Eaten by Deer or Anything Else

A forb is a non-grass-like herbaceous plant. It can be perennial, in which case it dies back to the ground or a small cluster of leaves in the winter and puts up new growth in the spring, or it can be an annual. It is thus not a woody plant (plants that put new growth on old wood). Most folks refer to forbs as wildflowers or weeds, depending on whether they like them or not.

Generally, deer prefer most trees and shrubs and avoid most grasses. Some of their very favorite foods are forbs, but there are also a number of native forbs the deer almost never eat. And in fact these same forbs are almost never eaten by any of the exotics or livestock either. The result is that these forbs are more commonly seen than many of the more famous, and more often eaten, Texas wildflowers.

Here are some of the more common forbs that fit into the seldom-eaten category.

Mealy blue sage is a 1 to 2-feet tall perennial with narrow leaves and a blue flower. It blooms in the spring and fall and is sometimes confused with bluebonnets. Plants are sometimes available from nurseries, but I would avoid the hybrid cultivar, "Henry Duelberg."

Prairie verbena is a low 2-foot diameter plant with reclining stems that turn up at the tips to show clusters of purple flowers. It is a perennial that blooms from March to October.

Mexican hat, also called Prairie coneflower, is a very common open bushy plant, usually from 1 to 3-feet tall with very narrow leaves. Flowers are at the end of branched stems and consist of a brown or tan cone-shaped center with brown and yellow ray flowers (petals) arranged around the bottom of the cone. Bloom period is spring to mid-summer.

Two-leaved senna is a 1 to 2-foot-tall perennial with very unusual-shaped leaves (think of the shape of your fingers when you make a "V" sign). It produces showy 1 inch yellow flowers from April to October.

Frostweed is the tall (3-6 feet) large-leaved plant you see growing in the shade of trees. It has greenish-white blooms in August to November. It is a nectar plant for Monarch butterflies. In the early morning after the first hard freeze you can see ribbons of white ice-like material oozing from the bottom of the stems as the stems burst open.

Snow-on-the-mountain is the forb with light green leaves with white edges, usually about 2 to 3-feet tall branching near the top candelabra-style. It has small whitish flowers in clusters at the end of each branch. It has a white milky sap that should be avoided; if you get it on your hands, wash them immediately. Do not touch your face with your hand as the sap can be extremely painful to the eyes.

Cowpen daisy is an annual that reseeds itself quite well. It grows from 1 to 3-feet tall and has gray-green-appearing leaves and 2-inch yellow daisy-like flowers from April to November. And yes, it will grow untouched in a cow pen.

Silver-leaf nightshade is a perennial that grows from 1 to 2-feet tall with silvery-green leaves and violet to purple 1-inch petals with yellow centers. Each flower produces a ½-inch yellow berry. This flower is in the same genus as western horse-nettle and buffalo bur, but it has very few prickles.

Zexmenia is a bushy perennial between 1 and 2-feet in height and diameter. The leaves and stems are covered with stiff hairs, and each stem produces a yellow-orange flower at the tip, throughout the summer. A very hardy, drought-tolerant plant.

Queen's delight is a perennial that grows to a roundish shape a foot or so tall with very narrow linear leaves. It has rather inconspicuous greenish-yellow blooms in spring and summer.

There are many other seldom eaten forbs in the Hill Country, but these are probably the most common. Buffalo bur and various thistles are common in newly disturbed soil, but are usually replaced in time with grasses and other forbs.

Some Other Plants That MIGHT Not Be Eaten by Deer

With the caveat that anything I include here may indeed be eaten in your yard, I believe these plants are less likely to be eaten in most areas.

For shrubs, cenizo, evergreen sumac, Texas mountain laurel, and Mexican silktassel (all evergreen shrubs), are probably safe to plant, but in higher population areas, they may be browsed. Shrubs probably safe in low-deer populations would include agarita, autumn sage (*Saliva greggii*), copper canyon daisy, damianita, flame acanthus, skeleton-leaf goldeneye, Texas lantana (native, not "new gold"), Texas persimmon and yellow buckeye.

Native cacti and succulents are not usually bothered by deer. Native prickly pear are safe from deer as are the native claret cup, strawberry cactus and lace cactus. Most yuccas and agaves are unlikely to be eaten, although the flower stalk that many of them put up in the spring seems to be a favorite treat for deer. Two native succulents, beargrass (*Nolina texana*) and devil's shoestring (*Nolina lindheimeriana*) are not eaten but again their flower stalks may be.

I think it is best to assume that any native hardwood tree will eventually be eaten by deer. These animals obviously prefer some trees to others, but in the 5 to 10 years between the time when you buy a tree in a small pot and it grows to a height such that the deer can't reach most of the leaves, the deer will almost certainly at last nibble on it occasionally. So if you are planting a tree that is not in a high-fenced yard, it will need to be caged for several years.

If you find a small root-sprout or sapling of any native hardwood before the deer find it, you will likely have very good luck growing it to maturity if you cage it before the deer find it. "Volunteer" plants that come up on their own frequently have a higher probability of surviving (if not eaten) because they are already established in that spot and may have the advantage of an extensive root system to draw from.

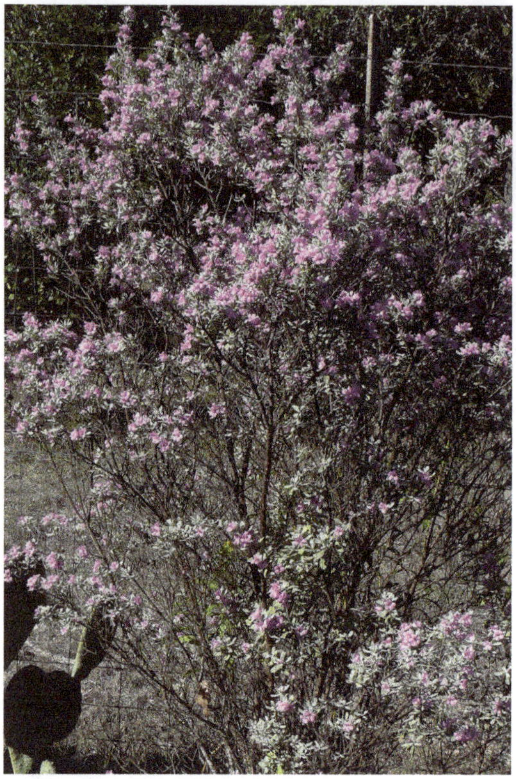

Cenizo several days after a good rain.

Grasses, are almost never eaten by white-tailed deer to any significant extent, with the exception of very tender shoots such as on annual ryegrass. So planting some of the larger native grasses such as big bluestem, little bluestem, switchgrass or yellow indiangrass (the "Big Four" of the tall grass prairie), plus Lindheimer muhly or other mulhys, as ornamentals is completely safe. Also, lower growing grasses that can be attractive include Inland seaoats and lawn grasses like buffalograss, curly mesquite and blue grama.

It is important to note that not all failures to grow new plants can be blamed on deer. Humans with weed-eaters, lawnmowers, herbicides, or fertilizer have been known to do in a lot of new plantings.

It is also important to emphasize that ALL newly-planted plants need to be watered until they are well established, meaning that their roots have grown out into the native soil and have achieved a large enough root mass to support the top growth even in a drought. So, it is important to keep the ground around the plant moist for the first year and don't let a little 0.1-inch of rain fool you into thinking that light shower did anything for the plant.

Please note that all of the above is offered as my best advice, but certainly without any guarantees that some of the things I suggested won't be at least nibbled on.

Deer Hunting in the Hill Country

People's views of hunting seem to run the gamut from strongly opposed to strong defenders and everywhere in between. Maybe I can put some things into perspective.

I grew up in a hunting family and hunted a lot as a kid, but I haven't hunted in many years. I support deer hunting in Texas as a very important activity, and hunting in general, with some reservations.

The Hill Country has seen an increase in the quality and quantity of deer habitat in the last 150+ years, primarily caused by man. As settlement began in the early 1800s and livestock were grazed continually on the land and wildfires were reduced, woody plants (which provide browse for deer) began to increase making for a better deer habitat. Man also killed all of the large predators to protect his livestock, but the deer benefited as well, and ranchers providing watering places for livestock also helped improve the deer habitat.

Even with all of the above, the deer population was fairly low in the early 1900s, but began to increase after the 1930s when restrictions on deer hunting were first introduced. Then in the 1960s the screw worm fly was eradicated from Texas, the last natural predator of the white-tailed deer, and the population increased dramatically from the 1960s through the 1990s.

Today the deer population in the Hill Country is way above the carrying capacity, meaning they are eating more than the habitat can replace every year. The result is that the deer are malnourished in many places and the habitat is being severely degraded. The excessive deer population is preventing any replacement hardwood trees and shrubs from becoming mature in much of the Hill Country. The severe browseline on all vegetation being eliminated from about five feet down on many properties means the natural habitat of many native birds and animals has been destroyed.

With no natural predators of significance, the only control on the deer population is the food supply, which is inadequate even where folks are feeding them. Hunters are the only other control, (imperfect and limited as it is) that we have on the deer population. Well, there is also vehicles killing deer on the roads.

The problem is that hunting is not controlling the deer population to a healthy level. Not enough deer are being taken. As the population of Texas continues to increase, most of the increased numbers of people are in the cities, and the percentage of people that are hunters is declining. Some advocate extending the season or the bag limit as a way to have more deer harvested. But a hunting license already gives the hunter the right to take 5 deer, but the average hunter takes only about 1 deer per year, and studies show that extending the season doesn't increase the number of deer taken significantly.

It has been legal to take does for a number of years now, and that has helped somewhat, because taking does has a much greater impact on the population than killing just bucks. If every hunter would take an extra deer, preferably a doe, every year, it might begin to make a measurable difference in the population. Some hunters limit the number of deer they take because they don't want any more meat, but field dressed carcasses can be donated to Hunters for the Hungry or various church charities.

There is a new trend among hunters that may be limiting the number of deer they take, but which I very much applaud. For many hunters these days, the activity is not just a "man's thing," but a family thing. More and more hunters are bringing their families to their deer leases and "camping out" or staying in a hunting cabin and making it a sort of nature outing or vacation for the whole family. It may be the best experience some of their children ever have in being in the country with nature and away from their electronic devices, even if the time spent actually hunting is reduced.

These outings are fighting "Nature Deficit Disorder." It may not help with the deer population, but anything that introduces more people to the country and natural areas and nature in general is a good thing.

A Plea to Hunters: Take More Deer

All landowners and most everyone else in the Hill Country know that the deer population around here is very high. What might not be obvious to everyone is the damage they cause.

High deer populations obviously cause more collisions with vehicles than would be the case if the population were lower, and the high populations also cause the deer to venture into people's yards in search of food and thus cause lots of damage to our prized landscape plants.

I have previously discussed the fact that because of the excessive numbers of deer, almost none of the normal replacement seedlings and saplings of our native hardwoods are surviving to become mature trees. If you look around most any Hill Country property, you will see numerous mature trees with trunks. But you won't find hardly any 1 or 2 or 5-year-old trees. What is going to happen when the older trees die of drought, oak wilt, hypoxylon, lightning or just old age? The answer is, we won't have any. Rufus Stephens, a wildlife biologist for the Texas Parks and Wildlife Dept. in Kerrville, described the situation as a "slow train wreck" in a recent talk.

Some hunters may be under the impression that harvesting does will reduce the deer population and thus reduce the number of "trophy bucks," but in fact, reducing the population will allow the herd to become better nourished and that will contribute to better "quality" bucks. Harvesting a doe has a greater effect on the future population by preventing her future offspring and their offspring. Some states have begun to require hunters to take one or two does before they are allowed to take that "trophy buck." There is certainly an element of the hunting culture that tends to make some hunters avoid does, and for other hunters, the lack of freezer space at home may be a factor. But unwanted deer can always be donated to Hunters for the Hungry or other charitable organizations.

So, for the sake of the health of the Hill Country ecosystem, for the future of our beloved oaks, and for the health of the deer herd, we need the help of all of you hunters. As Rufus Stephens says "Please, take more does!"

The Natural Food Web: All Things Are Interconnected

Most of us learned about our nutritional food pyramid in school, where we were advised to eat lots of the bottom layer (grains, cereals), slightly less fruits and vegetables, much less meat and fish and only a little of the top of the pyramid, sweets. The food pyramid has recently been replaced with something called the "food plate" which shows what we should be eating in a kind of a pie chart (no pun intended) superimposed on a plate.

In biology, the idea of a food pyramid has long been taught as having at its base plants, and above that the herbivores which eat the plants, followed by the carnivores, which eat the herbivores. This is now considered much too simplified and it has also been replaced by what is called the food web.

With the food pyramid, it was easy to think of plants as producers (making food from carbon dioxide in the air, water and nutrients from the soil, and energy from the sun) primary consumers, that is animals which eat the plants, and secondary consumers, which are animals that eat the primary consumers. But the natural world is very much more complex even than that. The food web, depicted by drawings containing many arrows connecting many different producers and consumers, is more accurate.

Think of it this way. In a typical Hill Country savanna, there are many different kinds of plants, which are eaten by many different kinds of herbivores. Rabbits may eat the grass, songbirds and caterpillars may eat the forbs, and squirrels and turkeys may eat the acorns of the oak trees. Deer may eat the forbs as well as the leaves of the oak trees, grasshoppers may eat both grass and forbs, various insects may eat the leaves of the forbs as well as the trees.

Then, hawks may eat rabbits, squirrels and songbirds, as may foxes and coyotes. Lizards and praying mantis' may eat the caterpillars, grasshoppers and other insects.

So numerous herbivores may eat every kind of plant and numerous carnivores may eat every herbivore. But it is even more complicated than that. There are other categories of consumers and producers. Many animals are omnivorous, like ourselves, and eat both plants and animals, including raccoons, skunks, opossums, armadillos, foxes and coyotes, so they can be classified as both primary and secondary consumers. Then there are animals (including mammals, birds and insects) that eat carrion, animals that feed on animal excrement and bacteria, fungi, and insects that decompose dead plant and animal material, as well as a whole world of soil organisms that are essential in recycling nutrients back into living plants.

If one were to try to depict all of the interactions, or put another way, all of the paths of energy that flow through an ecosystem, it would be much too complex to represent on a single page diagram. And in fact there is more than one food web. There are also food webs based solely on all of the organisms in the soil, other food webs based on aquatic systems which include plants, fish, amphibians and insects, and various other special food webs.

At each stage in a food web, when food and energy moves from one organism to another, energy is lost as heat. What this means is that it takes many times as much biomass of a primary producer (plants) to produce one pound of a primary consumer. And in turn, it takes many pounds of a primary consumer, eaten by a secondary consumer, to make a pound of secondary consumer. This loss of energy at each stage of the transfer is why we could feed an estimated ten times as many people if we all ate corn instead of feeding the corn to cows and then eating the cows.

The complexity of this process is in many respects why a diverse ecosystem is fundamentally a healthy, stable system. The more different plants that grow, the more different species of consumers there are, the greater the resiliency of the system to withstand upsets, such as a disease, which greatly reduces the population of some plant species, or a drought that affects different species differently, or the introduction of an exotic species which disrupts the natural food web. All of these kinds of upsets can best be tolerated by a healthy diverse ecosystem with all of its complex food-web interactions.

All things are interconnected.

Animals and Their Food Choices

When we want something to eat, our available choices are many. We can pick one of a long list of restaurants and other prepared-food places, or we can go to the grocery store and chose from an unimaginable assortment of things to eat. Furthermore, most of these choices are available to us 365 days a year. And most of us have lived with these conditions for so long that we don't even think about how truly incredible that is.

Our ancestors, and the Native Americans before them, certainly didn't have it this easy. And neither do all of the native animals that live around us today.

We are so accustomed to having such a large choice of things to eat, that we really only eat those things that we really like—our favorite foods. Animals, on the other hand, live in a totally different world. I was reminded of this recently when I looked at a display at the recent Hill Country Land-Use Expo prepared by the local Texas Parks and Wildlife biologists. They laid out cuttings of probably 60 or more native plants on three different tables. One table was for plants that deer really like to eat, another for plants they will eat, but are not favorites, and a third for plants that they only eat when very hungry.

I was already well aware of this deer food-preference ranking, but seeing samples laid out like that revealed something very striking. On most properties in the Hill Country, certainly most that have a distinct browseline, one would be hard pressed to find any of the favorite food category plants below the browseline, and maybe not many of the intermediate category of foods either. Deer, in overpopulated areas, almost never get to have any of their favorite foods.

And it gets worse. Most of the favorite deer foods are deciduous plant leaves, so from December until at least March, none of these foods are available anywhere. And in times of drought, the amount of these foods is greatly reduced even in the spring and summer. So even in areas where the animal population is not really excessive, they still have to go without their favorite foods much of the time.

When humans think of our favorite foods, we may think a little about the nutritional aspects, but most of us think about taste. It turns out that most of the deer favorite foods are in fact actually nutritionally good for them, and many of their least favorite foods are not really very helpful in terms of nutrition.

Most of the above could also be said about all herbivores, and to some extent, omnivores as well. The bottom line is that most of the animal world lives not on a short list of favorite foods, but on what is available, whether they like it or whether it is nutritious or not. And the same can pretty much be said about predators as well.

Raccoons and skunks will eat whatever they happen to find, whether it is the dog food you left on the porch, or a beetle they happen to find, or a crawfish in the creek, or a dead squirrel. The mockingbird will exist and feed its young on a collection of whatever insects happen to be available at the moment, and when insects are scarce in the winter, berries will have to do. The praying mantis can't be too picky, sitting around waiting for something tasty to eat, he has to grab anything that happens to come along.

If animals can't find enough food for good health, they may be out in the daylight taking risks in areas with high human populations just trying to survive, or just to be able to feed their young.

Herbivore populations will rise and fall depending on the available vegetative forage which of course is determined by both rainfall and the competition from livestock. Predator populations rise and fall with the herbivore populations, although with a short time lag.

So when you see or hear the term "deer-resistant" or "deer-proof," be very skeptical. Deer eat what is available, and if the only available forage is what someone calls "deer resistant," then that is what they will eat. And the same goes for most other animals as well.

The more we understand what the lives of our wild neighbors are like, the more we have to admire them.

FERAL ANIMALS

Exotic Ungulates in the Hill Country

In the 17th century, Spaniards introduced a number of exotic animals to what is present-day south Texas, including cattle, horses, sheep, goats and pigs. None of these animals were native to the Western hemisphere. When the settlers of northern European ancestry began moving into the Hill Country in the early to mid-1800s, they brought more of these animals with them, all things we now refer to as livestock. An exotic animal is one that is not native to the region or even to adjacent regions.

Beginning in the 1930s, and continuing today, many species of exotic ungulates have been introduced throughout the US, but with the highest populations in the Edwards Plateau. My dictionary defines an ungulate as "a hoofed, typically herbivorous, quadruped mammal." Think mostly cattle, antelope, deer, sheep and goats.

The most common such exotics include axis, fallow and sika deer, blackbuck antelope and aoudad sheep. But there are as many as 200 species of exotic animals in Texas, mostly native to Asia or Africa. It is estimated that there are at least 400,000 individual exotic animals confined to Texas ranches, and maybe a fourth or a fifth that many more that are free-ranging, and these numbers don't include feral hogs or cats.

There is a fundamental difference between the exotics brought to this county by settlers as livestock, and these more recent arrivals of exotic ungulates. The former were readily domesticated, and could be easily herded, handled, moved, kept inside low ranch fences, and their numbers controlled. And, they provided food, fiber and milk for the settlers, as they do for all of us today.

On the other hand, these newer exotic arrivals are not domesticated, or in most cases domesticatable. They are wild, hard to herd or handle, and most of them can jump regular low ranch fences. The purpose for which they were brought here was not to provide food or fiber, but primarily to be hunted as trophy animals. (Some small numbers are currently being kept as pets, and in a few cases of endangered species, raised to protect the species).

In Texas, native game animals (white-tailed deer, pronghorn, quail, turkey, etc.) are considered property of the state, wherever they exist, and the state therefore regulates the where, when, how and how many can be taken by hunters. Exotic animals, on the other hand, are not property of the state and are in fact considered livestock and the property of the landowner.

Most exotic ungulates eat like goats, meaning they can thrive on browse (woody plant leaves), forbs (broadleaf herbaceous plants) or grass, and therefore they compete with our usual livestock species as well as with white-tailed deer for food. This is particularly troublesome for our white-tailed deer since they cannot survive on a diet of only grass.

This was demonstrated conclusively at Kerr Wildlife Management Area when an equal number of sika deer and white-tailed deer were placed in a high-fenced pasture and left there. After a few years the white-tailed deer had all died out, but the sika population had increased dramatically. In the beginning both species ate a lot of browse, but when all of the browse was eaten, as well as the forbs, the sika did fine living on grass, but the white-tailed deer couldn't survive.

So the existence of these exotics means they are in competition with both our native wildlife and, if livestock are on the same property, with livestock as well. It is essential, therefore, that the numbers of all three types of animals, livestock, native white-tailed deer, and exotics be controlled to within the carrying capacity of the land, or the health and productivity of the land and the animals will decline.

The most serious problem is that not all exotics have been/are being confined to their owner's property, but have become feral (free-ranging) and are therefore damaging properties throughout the Hill Country. We have seen that controlling white-tailed deer numbers is difficult because hunting is not a very efficient or effective population control method, and we are now seeing the same problem with exotics.

Exotic Animals and the Problems They Cause

When I use the term "exotic animals" most people are probably thinking about all of the exotic ungulates that one sees on Hill Country ranches, the sika, fallow, axis, aoudad, blackbucks, and maybe another 200 species of African and Asian origin. These animals are certainly the largest, most obvious examples. Once these ungulates are on a ranch, they are not considered to be "wildlife," but are "livestock" and the property of the ranch owner, just like all other livestock.

So adding yet another species, say an axis deer, to the mix of livestock does not, in theory, change the conditions on the ranch. That is: IF they are not stocked beyond the carrying capacity for grazers and browsers, IF the ranches were devoid of native white-tailed deer, and IF the exotics did not escape to become feral. But these are big "Ifs," especially in the case of the animals escaping ranches and becoming feral.

But wherever these ungulates compete with our white-tailed deer for forage, with our livestock for grazing, or come onto other people's properties and overbrowse or overgraze these properties, then we have a problem.

And if instead of some of the exotic ungulates, it is feral hogs that come onto your property, destroying riparian areas, crops, lawns, gardens, fences, and just about anything else they want, then the problem of these feral animals is even a greater problem.

And then of course, there are the millions of feral cats that prey on our songbirds and spread diseases such as rabies.

The major problems with all of these animals is that they represent new species added to the ecosystem, which disrupts the long-standing balance of predator-prey and consumer-producer relationships in existence for thousands of years before humans arrived here. And those species that become feral, or free-ranging, and thus are not in the control of humans, are by far the worst offenders.

When the movements, actions and populations of feral animals are uncontrolled, and no natural limit on their population exists, other than depletion of their food source, real damage to the ecosystem occurs. Sometimes, I think it is easier to see the damage caused by invasive exotic plants, as when a tree becomes covered with kudzu, or a field becomes covered with thistles, or a creek becomes choked with *Arundo donax*, than to see the effects of feral animals on the landscape.

And of course, the exotic mammals mentioned above are not by any means the only types of exotic species that are causing us problems. Here are a few of the others: Africanized honeybees, apple snail, Asian tiger mosquito, Asian carp, Asian clam, brown tree snake, English sparrows, Eurasian collared dove, European starlings, fire ants, Formosan termite, German cockroach, house mouse, Norway rat, nutria, and zebra mussel.

The environmental damage caused by the introduction, accidental or intentional, of exotic animal species is considerable, and, when exotic plants are included in the list, exotic species introduction is the second leading cause of species extinction worldwide. (Second only to habitat destruction for "development.")

And it is not just the environmental damage that these exotic species cause, there is also a huge monetary cost, both governmental and individual, to combating, controlling and attempting to eliminate these invasive species. The U.S. Fish and Wildlife Dept. estimates the costs to be $120 billion PER YEAR.

It would of course have been much better and cheaper to have been able to prevent the introduction of these exotic species in the first place, but in the past we didn't know which of the introduced species would become feral and/or invasive, and we still cannot always correctly predict which species will and which will not become a problem. And it is only after-the-fact that we have laws to prevent the importation of known invasive species.

And many species were accidentally introduced, or actually smuggled into the country.

So when it comes right down to it, about the best we can do is to try to identify problem species as early as possible and to take action to control and/or eliminate the problem when it is in its early stages. And we can try to educate people to not buy, introduce, or allow to propagate, any exotic species on their property.

Feral Pigs: A Growing Problem in Texas

Back in the 16th, 17th, and 18th centuries, it was common for sailing ships from Europe to bring along some domesticated pigs (or hogs if you prefer), both for food along the voyage as well as for food at their destination if, as was common, they had to stay some places for months until trade winds became favorable.

So it is not surprising that when Spanish explorers and settlers came to South Texas during this period, they brought pigs with them as well as horses, cattle, sheep and goats. During this earliest period of Texas settlement, animals were allowed to roam free until people needed meat and hunted them down. Thus began the first feral exotic animals in Texas.

While the other animals (cattle, sheep, goats) were also allowed to roam freely to graze, they could be rounded up or herded and moved and were therefore more "domesticated" and today we don't have any significant number of these other species as free-ranging feral animals.

Pigs, however are different. They are able to survive under more diverse and adverse conditions. They multiply faster than the other animals listed above; they are omnivores instead of strict herbivores and can eat almost anything. They are better able to survive injury and disease, and once they revert to the wild, they can be very wary of man. All of this has made the feral pig a very successful invasive animal.

Pigs (*Sus scrofa*) are in the Suidae family and differ from the other even-toed ungulates (cattle, sheep, goats and deer) in that they have crushing cheek teeth, upper incisors, and a simple stomach (thus they are not ruminants). By the way, the javelina or collared peccary (*Pecari tajacu*) is in the Tayassuidae family and is in fact not a pig.

The descendants of the escaped pigs of the early Spanish settlers, plus escaped domestic pigs from the eastern U.S. and a few wild boars from Europe make up the feral pigs of Texas today. The range of feral pigs has gradually expanded from the south and east to the north and west, so that today they are known in virtually every Texas county. It is estimated that there are 2 million feral pigs in Texas, which is about half of the total population in the U.S.

Most adult boars weigh about 130 pounds, with sows weighing a little less, although larger individuals are seen. They are extremely good at reproduction. While it is an exaggeration, it is often said that feral pigs are born pregnant. They can breed as early as 6 months and produce 2 litters every 12-18 months of 4 to 8 piglets each. They usually travel in groups of a few sows and their piglets of various ages. Boars are solitary much of the time.

Part of the problem with feral pigs is the same kind of problem presented by any feral exotic animal, from fire ants to nutria to axis and fallow deer and blackbuck antelope. They represent a rapid introduction of a non-native animal into a native habitat which introduces new competitors for food and shelter, new predators for native prey, and new consumers for native vegetation. In the case of feral pigs, since all of the large predators have been eliminated or nearly so, there is no natural predator capable of significantly controlling the population.

Feral hogs taking advantage of food intended for deer.

Feral pigs can be very destructive to many crops as well as fences and other man-made facilities. They can disrupt the soil along riparian areas leading to enhanced erosion. Feral pigs are a serious threat to ground-nesting birds and small animals. They can also consume large quantities of feed landowners put out for livestock and deer. They have poor eyesight, but excellent senses of smell and hearing. They generally shy away from humans, but if cornered they can be dangerous.

Feral pigs also may harbor a number of serious diseases which can be transmitted to livestock, wildlife and humans. A partial list includes anthrax, brucellosis, campylobacter, leptospirosis, plague and salmonellosis, plus a number of viruses as well. So having them around or handling them or their meat can be hazardous.

Since there are no natural enemies, as of now the only limitation on their number appears to be landowners trapping and/or killing them. Feral pigs can be hunted any time of the year, day or night, but a hunting license is required.

It should be noted that many people hunt them for the meat, which I hear is quite tasty, but you need to know what you are doing.

SMALL HILL COUNTRY ANIMALS

Understanding Our Furry Friends and Neighbors

All of us who live in the country or the suburbs, or even sometimes in town, encounter members of our native wildlife community at least occasionally. But how much do we really know about our furry friends? I would guess that raccoons and skunks are among the most populous of our small native mammals, so I will start with them.

Northern Raccoon (*Procyon lotor*): Raccoons are certainly one of the most visible native animals not only in the Hill Country but throughout most all of Texas and the US for that matter. This is probably partly because they are so distinctive and easily recognized, partly because they have learned how to live in close proximity to us, and partly just because of their numbers. They are nocturnal, but are commonly seen around dusk and dawn, or, if disturbed from their sleeping place, even during the day

Most adult raccoons have a body length of about 2 feet and weigh between 10 and 25 pounds. They are omnivorous, with berries, acorns and nuts making up around half of their diet, and insects, especially grasshoppers also being a large part of their diet. But they also eat reptiles, amphibians, small mammals, baby birds and bird eggs. Texas persimmons and prickly pear tunas are favorite foods in the Hill Country.

They den just about anywhere that offers protection, hollow trees or logs, underground dens, rock crevices, under barns, sheds or other man-made structures away from much human activity. Females bear 3-6 young in the spring and will use the same den until the young are about 2 months old, after which the family group may wander and sleep in different sites every day.

They readily climb trees either to escape predators or in search of food. They can climb down a tree either head first, like a squirrel, or rear first, like a bear. They are also fond of creeks, streams and lakes where they may find crawfish or other invertebrates. They do not hibernate in the Hill Country, but may stay holed up in a den for days during really cold spells. The average raccoon in the wild lives about 3 to 5 years or less.

The other two members of the raccoon family (*Procyonidae*) are ringtails, also native to the Hill Country, and the white-nosed coati, native to south Texas.

There are 5 species of skunks in Texas, 4 of which can be found in the Hill Country. By far the most common is the striped skunk (*Mephitis mephitis*), followed by the hog-nosed skunk (*Conepatus leuconotus*) and the less-common spotted skunks; western spotted skunks (*Spilogale gracilis*) and the eastern spotted skunk (*Spilogale putoris*). Everyone knows what a striped skunk looks like. The hog-nosed skunk has a white back, not striped, a white tail, a long nose but no white mark between their eyes, and very long front claws. Spotted skunks are, as you might have guessed, spotted.

Skunks are omnivorous, their favorite foods being insects, particularly grasshoppers, beetles and crickets. They also dig for grubs and worms. They won't pass up any opportunity to take bird eggs or small birds, and they love fruits, berries and nuts. The hog-nosed skunk will plow through the ground looking for grubs and worms, which is why it is sometimes called the "rooter skunk."

Striped skunks breed in late winter to early spring and have 4-7 young in May or June. The young have striped skin, are blind at birth, and develop musk before they are two weeks old.

Skunks are not generally that fearful of humans, or predators in general. They can usually be quietly approached to within 10 or 15 ft. Presumably this apparent tameness is because their defense isn't to flee but to spray. They usually, but not always, will warn you by stamping their front feet and clicking their teeth. But if they raise up on their front feet, run! They can usually spray multiple times if they need to.

Skunks will den in any available hollow log, crevice, or other shelter, including old armadillo burrows or other abandoned small animal burrows. They are largely nocturnal, but being out in the daytime is not that uncommon. They do not hibernate, but will sleep through winter cold spells.

Two Common, but Unusual, Hill Country Mammals

Two of the more unusual Hill Country mammals are armadillos and opossums.

The Nine-Banded Armadillo (*Dasypus novemcinctus*) certainly needs no description from me; everyone easily recognizes these little critters. They are the only North American animal with heavy bony plates (large shields over shoulders and rump and nine bands in between). They have four toes in front and five in back, all with very large strong claws for digging. On average they are about 18" long and weigh about 12-15 pounds.

The armadillo's main diet is insects and invertebrates which they usually find by sniffing and digging, but they will take advantage of carrion if they find it, as well as ground nesting bird's eggs. In summer they are most active at night, but in winter they may be more active during the day.

Armadillo drinking.

Their reproductive process is unusual; they mate in midsummer, but implantation does not occur until October or November and the young are born in March. The other unusual aspect of their reproduction is that usually four identical quadruplets are born, fully formed, eyes open, able to walk.

While armadillos can inflate their bodies to float on water and swim, they can also decide to sink and walk across the bottom of streams and ponds.

During the last century, armadillos expanded their range from South Texas east to Louisiana and north throughout most of the rest of Texas, except for extreme West Texas. Their range is limited by climate (they can't survive long freezing spells), availability of soft dirt for digging out food, and the need to drink water every day. Their numbers are actually declining in recent years for reasons that are somewhat uncertain, but may be partly due to people taking them to make articles from the shells and partly due to the increase in feral hogs which prey on their young. The armadillo is the official Texas state small mammal.

The Virginia Opossum (*Didelphis virginiana*) is another common Hill Country mammal with unusual characteristics. They are the only North American marsupial (raise their young in a pouch like a kangaroo). Their tail is prehensile (can grip things like a monkey) and they have opposable thumbs on their hind feet, both of which allow them to climb trees. All of the possums I have seen in this area have been the grayish phase, but there is a dark phase that is nearly black, which is more common in South Texas. Opossums inhabit all of the state except the driest parts of West Texas.

Opossum on the run.

Possums are about the size of a house cat, with a whitish face, black ears, pink toes and a bare, scaly tail. They are nocturnal, but will venture out in daylight during the winter. They are more common in wooded areas, particularly along riparian areas, than on open grasslands.

The young are born after only about 2 weeks' gestation and move to the mother's pouch where they attach themselves to a nipple. At this point the young are about the size of honey bees and a half dozen can fit in a teaspoon. The mother can accommodate up to 13 babies in her pouch, but sometimes she bears more than that so some do not survive. The young remain in the pouch for up to two months. After that, the young may cling to the mother's back as she moves around until they are somewhat older.

Opossums are believed to be among the oldest, most primitive mammals in the New World and are believed to have been mostly unchanged for 50 million years. They have 50 peg-like teeth (the most of any mammal) and their skull has a bony ridge along the top somewhat similar to some dinosaurs.

Opossums will eat just about anything they can find: insects, seeds, berries, fruit, bird eggs, fish, frogs, small mammals and carrion. They are particularly fond of sunflower seeds and even thistle seeds that people put out to feed birds.

They can be aggressive in their defense if threatened, but if they think this tactic won't work, they can "play possum" in which they roll over and "play dead" with their eyes closed and their mouth open with their tongue hanging out.

Two Hill Country Residents that are as Smart as Foxes

There are three species of foxes in Texas. The small swift or kit fox (*Vulpes velox*) is an uncommon resident of the Panhandle and the Trans-Pecos. The two species that inhabit the Hill Country are the gray fox and the red fox. All foxes belong to the canine (Canidae) family.

The native gray fox (*Urocyon cinereoargenteus*) is the most common Hill Country fox. It is grayish on the back and sides and reddish on the nape, shoulders, chest and legs. It has a large bushy tail with a black stripe along the top and a black tip. Note that a gray fox has a lot of reddish coloration which has caused some folks to misidentify it—the black tail tip may be the best identifying mark. Gray foxes are about 2 feet long, not counting the tail, about a foot high at the shoulder and weigh on average about 10 pounds. Sometimes when people only get a glimpse of an animal, they have difficulty telling the difference between a gray fox and a coyote, the latter of which is roughly twice the size of the fox.

A Gray Fox in the Hill Country.

Gray foxes range throughout the state and inhabit most habitats, especially edges where woodlands meet more open areas. Most are believed to live less than 5 years in the wild. They den almost any place they can find, including hollow trees. They don't generally dig a den, but may enlarge a den of a smaller animal.

They are omnivorous, preferring mice, moles and rabbits, but also eat small birds, berries, fruit, nuts, fish, insects, carrion, and even sunflower seeds. They are most active at night, but may be out in the early morning or late afternoon.

Pairs appear to be monogamous, and may mate for life. Breeding takes place in winter with the young, called kits, born helpless and blind with black fur in April or May. Both parents are involved in feeding the young.

A most unusual trait of gray foxes is that they can climb trees! Unlike almost all other canines, they can rotate their forearms in a way that allows them to grasp the sides of a tree trunk and have been seen as high as 20 feet off the ground. I was once on a trail ride and noticed a fox avoid the lead horse and climb up a small live oak about 15 feet tall. As I got even with the tree, I stopped and searched for the fox, which I know didn't come down from that tree, but I could never see the little critter.

The red fox (*Vulpes vulpes*) is much less common in the Hill Country than the gray fox. It is not actually a native of Texas. It was introduced into East Texas in 1895 by people who liked to go fox hunting with dogs and horses like they do in England. But when they tried to hunt the gray fox, they found that it would just climb a tree and stay there so there wasn't much of a chase. Red foxes are now found over most of the state, but in my experience are much less common than gray foxes in the Hill Country.

The red fox may be slightly larger than the gray fox, with longer legs and may weigh a little more. There is more variation in color among individual red foxes than gray foxes. Red foxes also have distinctly different winter and summer coats, but they tend to be more reddish on the sides and back with legs nearly black and a white tip on their tail.

Their favorite habitat is one of diverse vegetation with a mixture of trees, shrubs and grass. Their den may be a hollow log or under a rock, but they may dig a den and leave a mound of dirt in front of the den, which they then mark with scat. The food habits and the reproduction characteristics of the red fox are very similar to those of the gray fox. They sometimes emit high-pitched barks or yelps.

The red fox is the most widely distributed canid in the world, ranging across North America, Europe, Asia and North Africa.

The average life expectancy of a kit (baby fox) in the wild is less than a year. The main predators of foxes are humans and domestic dogs. The main potential threat to their survival as a species is indiscriminate predator control practices.

A Look at Our Native Hill Country Squirrels

Our local rock squirrel.

There are ten species of squirrels in Texas, with three species listed as residents of the Hill Country. Of the ten species, three are classified as tree squirrels and seven are classified as ground squirrels, which also includes chipmunks and the black-tailed prairie dog. The latter was once here but has long since been extirpated.

Our three Hill Country squirrels include two ground squirrels, the Mexican ground squirrel *(Spermophilus mexicanus)* and the rock squirrel *(Spermophilus variegatus)* and one tree squirrel, the eastern fox squirrel *(Sciurus niger)*. The other ground squirrels primarily inhabit Western Texas, while the other two tree squirrels, the Eastern gray squirrel *(Sciurus carolinensis)* and the southern flying squirrel *(Glaucomys volans)* dwell in East Texas. All of these critters are in the order Rodentia and the family Sciuridae.

The Mexican ground squirrel is a small chipmunk-like animal with nine rows of square white spots along its back. I know they are supposed to live in Central Texas, but I have never seen one anywhere east of Junction, so I won't discuss them further.

By far the most common squirrel in the Hill Country is the eastern fox squirrel, the one we all see almost everywhere. Its body is about a foot long and its tail is almost the same, and they weigh from 1 to 2 pounds. Its back is gray, but its belly, chest and the sides of its legs are rusty orange, and its tail may be a mixture of gray and orange. There is a rare black morph, but I have never seen one here.

Fox squirrels live from 2 to 5 years in the wild. If available, they prefer to nest and den in hollow trees, and in the winter may have communal dens. If no suitable hollow trees are around, they may build nests of twigs and leaves, especially in summer, which can be up to about 2 feet in diameter.

They sometimes have two litters in a year, one in March or April and another in August or September. They usually have two to four young per litter. The young leave their mother and are on their own in about three months.

Fox squirrels are largely vegetarian, their main food being nuts, acorns, buds, seeds and green shoots, but have been known to also take birds eggs and insects. We have all watched squirrels burying acorns, especially in the fall when more acorns are falling than they can eat. I have heard many people wonder whether they ever find the nuts or acorns they bury—the experts claim they find them by smell, not by remembering where they buried them.

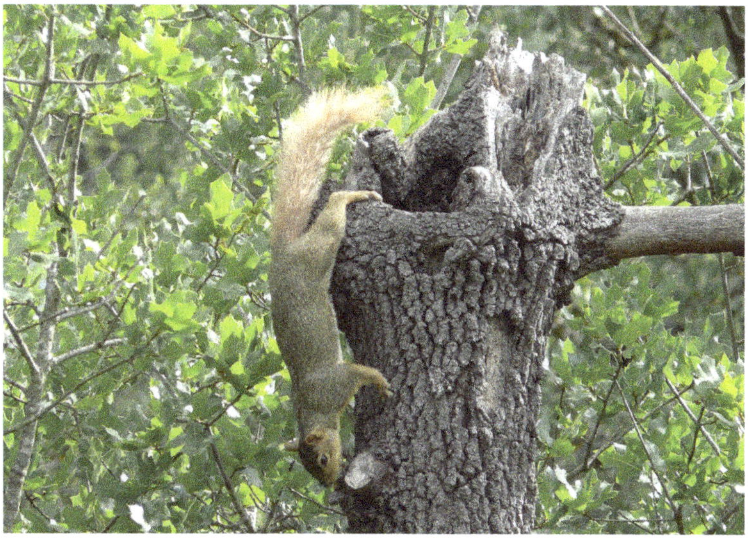
An Eastern fox squirrel hanging our in the authors "squirrel tree".

Fox squirrels, like most of their relatives, are diurnal, meaning they are active during the day, but unlike many animals they don't usually become active until a few hours after sunrise—they may be the only animals that sleep later than I do!

I consider our fox squirrels the most entertaining animals to watch. They are extremely agile and flexible. Have you ever watched one walk a telephone line to cross a road? They can climb a tree 30 times their body length in a matter of a couple of seconds! They are also capable of complex problem solving whenever we humans put out bird food where we think they can't get to it.

The rock squirrel is a ground squirrel, but one capable of climbing trees almost as well as the fox squirrel. They are larger than most other ground squirrels, almost as large as the fox squirrel. All the ones I have seen in Kerr and Gillespie counties have a head and the front part of their body very dark gray or black, with the hind part of the body lighter colored and somewhat mottled. In other areas they may have different markings.

They like rocky areas and den in a burrow they dig, usually under a rock. Rock squirrels typically have 3-9 young, once a year. They are omnivorous, eating green plants, seeds, nuts, fruit, insects, and bird eggs. They hibernate in this area for the coldest months.

I have observed one scavenging sunflower seeds from under our bird feeder and filling his cheek pouches, then coming up on the porch and eating his collection, then repeating this several times. When it is really hot out and the concrete porch floor is cool, he will sometimes lay out spread-eagle to cool off.

Cottontails and Jackrabbits, It Wouldn't Be Texas Without Them

Two of my favorite animals are cottontails and jackrabbits. As a kid in West Texas, I could always find at least one or the other in a five-minute walk into the pasture. They are nowhere near that populous now.

Cottontails are rabbits, but despite the name, jackrabbits are not. Jackrabbits are hares. Rabbits are born naked, blind and almost helpless. Hares are born fully furred, eyes open and able to hop. Neither rabbits nor hares are rodents, they belong to the order Lagomorpha and the family Leporidae.

Three of the four species of rabbits in Texas have ranges that overlap in our part of the Hill Country, the swamp rabbit *(Sylvilagus aquaticus)*, the desert cottontail *(Sylvilagus audubonii)*, and the eastern cottontail *(Sylvilagus floridanus)*.

The swamp rabbit is slightly larger than the other two with slightly longer ears. As the name suggests, it mainly inhabits areas along rivers and creeks or marshes. It very seldom ventures out in the daytime, unless flushed from its bed. All rabbits can swim, but this one is the only one to do so on its own without being chased. Its main range is the eastern part of the Hill Country and further east.

An Eastern cottontail foraging in the waining hours of sunlight.

The desert cottontail has very slightly longer ears, relative to its foot length, than the eastern cottontail, a difference too slight to tell by simply watching the animal. Its main range is the western Hill Country and further west.

Since telling the difference among these three in the field is very difficult, and since the most widespread rabbit in Texas is the eastern cottontail, it is the only rabbit I will discuss further. The biology of all three rabbit species is very similar.

The eastern cottontail is about 15-18 inches long and weighs from 2 to 4 pounds. It lives from 1 to 3 years in the wild, although the average newborn lives less than a year.

They are strictly herbivores, eating grass and other green plants from spring to fall and twigs and bark and other woody plants in winter. They are active at night, but also during the morning and evening, especially in winter.

They can have as many as 3 to 4 litters a year, usually of 3 to 6 young. The mother makes a nest of leaves, lined with her chest fur and covered with other plant material. Usually, the mother only comes to the nest near dawn and dusk to nurse the young, otherwise she will not be at the nest. Unfortunately, many people find a nest and conclude that the mother "abandoned" it so they take the young to raise, usually with poor results. Once the young open their eyes and

A Black-tailed jackrabbit poised to run if necessary.

move about outside the nest, they are on their own. A four or five-month old rabbit is pretty much indistinguishable from an adult.

Cottontails are generally silent, but if attacked can emit a very loud piercing scream.

We have at times had a single cottontail living in or near our yard. On some occasions, it would approach us as if it were a pet, and if tossed a handful of sunflower seeds, it would gladly eat them, even with nice green grass all round.

The black-tailed jackrabbit *(Lepus californicus)* inhabits almost all of Texas except for the extreme southeast corner. They are 18 to 24 inches long and weigh from 4 to 8 pounds. They have been known to leap as far as 20 feet and to run up to 45 miles an hour for short distances.

They eat mostly green plants, including many row crops, but will resort to twigs and bark in the winter. I have seen jackrabbits digging for shallow grass roots in the winter. Jackrabbits, like the cottontails, re-ingest soft fecal pellets to gain more nutrition from their food.

Jackrabbits usually have from two to six litters a year of one to six young. The nest is a minimal scrape in the dirt with some grass and fur added. The young are eating plants within two weeks and are weaned and completely on their own within four. Like the rabbits, the mother only comes back to the nest or to individual young for a few brief visits a day.

Three More Native Hill Country Small Mammals: Two Big Rats and a Pseudo-Cat

These three Hill Country mammals are very different in most of their characteristics. Two big rats, one climbs and eats trees, one lives in or near the water, and a cat-like animal that isn't a cat.

The North American porcupine *(Erethizon dorsatum)* is in the order Rodentia. At up to 25 pounds, they are the second largest rodent in our area; only the beaver is larger. They are slow-moving animals with small heads, eyes and ears and an array of quills on the rump and large tail. Although they appear to be somewhat clumsy, they are actually very good climbers.

The porcupine is an herbivore whose diet varies with seasons, being mostly herbaceous ground vegetation in the summer, mostly inner tree bark and twigs in the fall, totally inner tree bark in the winter, and then significant amounts of ground vegetation in the spring. I had one eat a whole row of romaine lettuce one year!

The young are born with eyes and ears open and teeth erupted, and with quills! The newborn's quills are soft, but harden quickly. They nurse for only a month and are on their own within 6 months.

In their relaxed, unthreatened state their quills lie down along their back and tail, but upon being startled or threatened, they can raise them in an instant to point up and protect the animal. They can swing their tails and drive the quills into an attacker. The quills have barbs on the end making removal very painful.

Porcupines only occupied a few mountainous areas in the Trans-Pecos region in the late 1800s, but have since expanded their range, possibly because of increased tree density, into most of the western half of the state.

The American beaver *(Castor canadensis)* is a large (up to 50 pounds) aquatic animal with a large flat tail. It is an herbivore that feeds mostly on soft inner tree bark (especially willows and cottonwoods), aquatic vegetation and green leaves. While we have all seen films of beavers building dams across small streams, in our part of the country, they usually dig out a den along a creek or river bank.

They have only one litter per year of 3 or 4 young, called kits. The kits are born with hair, eyes open, teeth visible and weigh about a pound.

Beavers were extensively trapped for their fur in the early 1800s and were quite rare in many areas by 1850, but after strict harvest regulations and some restocking, their numbers have returned to normal.

Animals that may be mistaken for beavers are the introduced nutria, which is generally smaller and with a naked round tail instead of a flat tail, and muskrats, which are much smaller and not generally found in the Hill Country. One tell-tale sign of a beaver is a tree stump near the water where the cut is pointed like a pencil.

The ringtail *(Bassariscus astutus)* is a small cat-like animal with big eyes with white rings around them, large ears and a very long black and white striped tail. It is sometimes referred to as a "ringtail cat," but in fact it is not a cat, but is in the same family (Procyonidae) as raccoons and coatis.

Ringtails are about the size of a large squirrel, and they climb trees as well as squirrels, including descending head first. They can move very fast and jump from tree to tree like a squirrel. They are omnivores, eating just about any small animal, fruit, green leaves, crayfish and insects. Years ago, miners caught them and put them in mines to catch rats and mice, and they were called miner's cats. They are strictly nocturnal and thus almost never seen in the daylight, so many folks never know they are there.

They sometimes have at least temporary "home ranges" which can be large for such a small animal and they tend to use the same "latrine" area for their droppings repeatedly, which is one sign that one or more may be near.

They can make a den in a hollow tree, in rock crevices, or dig one underground. They have one litter of 2 to 4 young a year.

Hill Country Venomous Snakes: Feared, Maligned and Misunderstood

I don't think there is anything in the natural world that is feared, maligned or misunderstood more than snakes. I know there is nothing else about which there are so many myths that are so widely believed. Here are the facts about the Hill Country venomous snakes.

The best numbers I could find show that in a recent year there were about 7000 snake bites in the whole US. Of those, only 4 people died. We don't know how many of those were bites from pets or snakes kept in zoos and the like, but it could be a lot. Also, there is no record of how many of the bites did not involve venom; approximately half of all snake bites do not have venom injected. So your odds of being bitten by a wild native venomous snake are clearly not zero, but they are very low. And your odds of dying from a snake bite are very nearly zero. You have lots more things to worry about.

Fifty percent of all snake bites are to 18-28 year-olds, 90 percent of those to males, nearly always to the hands or feet.

There are 105 species of snakes in Texas, of which 26 are common in the Edwards Plateau and another 16 are uncommon or rare. Of the snakes found in the Edwards Plateau, 3 common ones, the coral snake, the broad-banded copperhead and the western diamondback rattlesnake are venomous. The western cottonmouth, also venomous, is regarded as uncommon or rare. These four make up a very small percentage of Hill Country snakes.

In 15 years of tromping around many miles of pasture on many different properties in the Hill Country, I have personally encountered only one venomous snake, a rattlesnake, not counting a visit to a friend's rattlesnake den in Lampasas Co. Rattlesnakes are certainly the most commonly encountered poisonous snake in this area, and I do have a friend who was bitten and know of several folks whose dogs have been bitten. Once you have heard the sound of a rattlesnake, you never forget it, but having missed stepping on one by about 4 inches out in Big Bend, I noted that it never rattled.

Copperheads are described as generally uncommon, but locally common. Where they occur, they can be common, but most of the Hill Country will not have any copperheads. Apparently, they do not range widely or scatter far from their birthplace. I read that there is no record of anyone ever dying from a copperhead bite.

Coral snakes have bands around their bodies in three colors, red, yellow and black, with the yellow bands between the black and red bands. They are small, non-aggressive snakes with short fangs that cannot penetrate a leather shoe. Only about 1 percent of all snake bites are from coral snakes, and virtually all of them are from someone touching the snake. They tend to spend most of their time either in underground burrows or in thick leaf litter.

It is unlikely that you have ever seen a water moccasin (cottonmouth) in the Hill Country. If they are in this area, they are very rare. Most people seem to assume that if they see a snake in the water it is a water moccasin, but in fact it is almost certainly either a blotched water snake or a diamondback water snake, both of which are common in this area and are totally harmless. When a moccasin swims, its whole body floats on the surface. Other snakes swim with their head out of the water but the rest of the body somewhat submerged. Nearly all snakes have white mouths, so that is no indication that it is a cottonmouth.

If you are bitten by a snake, first try not to panic. It may be painful, but it won't be fatal. Get to a hospital as soon as safely possible. Don't worry about catching or killing the snake. If it is a coral snake, you will have noticed the bright colors, if it is anything else, it doesn't matter what it was because the treatments are the same. DO NOT put on a tourniquet, DO NOT cut open the fang marks and suck out the blood, and do not put ice on the area. If possible, keep the bite area at the same level as your heart.

Harmless Hill Country Snakes

Priscilla opened the back door and said "You want to see my snake?" Grabbing my camera as I usually do whenever she says something like that, I followed her back outside, expecting her to lead me to where she had once again found our resident 5 foot long western coachwhip. Instead, as soon as I was outside she showed me the prettiest little baby eastern blackneck garter snake she was holding. It was at most about 9 inches long and no more than about a quarter of an inch in diameter with the brightest yellow, orange and black markings.

After I took pictures she let it go where she had found it under the blackjack tree. A short while later, she came back in and reported she had found it, or another one like it, some distance away in one of the many nursery pots she is tending on the other side of the garage. I went out to look and soon saw a second one and then a third, all within a foot or two of each other.

These were all obviously newborns (these garter snakes are live-bearers). My mind immediately went back to a little over two years earlier when I found two eastern blackneck garter snakes mating out in the RV barn, and then just a few months ago when I had again seen the male (or one like it—males are much smaller than the females) in nearly the same place in the barn.

Seeing the three brightly-colored little guys in one place also made me think about the coachwhip and worry about their safety. Most recently the coachwhip was spotted in the blackjack being scolded by the pair of cardinals after two of their three fledglings had flown into the blackjack.

While we hadn't seen the Texas rat snake for a while, I knew these little ones wouldn't be much more than a snack for him. After all, he seemed to have no trouble with the two turkey eggs we saw him make off with in a previous year.

The above-mentioned eastern blackneck garter snake *(Thamnophis cyrtopsis ocellatus)* is one of several garter snakes in Texas. They and the several ribbon snakes all have brightly colored stripes running the length of their body. There are no venomous snakes in Texas that have that kind of coloration.

The silvery-tan western coachwhip *(Masticophis flagellum testaceus)* may be the fastest snake in Texas and it is active during the daytime, so it is easily seen. But if it wants to hide, it climbs into a shrub and disappears among the branches. Sometimes it will crawl some distance away, then raise its head up to get a better look at you.

The Texas rat snake, also called a "chicken snake" *(Elaphe obsoleta lindheimerii)* may be one of the most common snakes in our area. They are large (usually 5-6 feet) heavy-bodied animals with dark brown blotches on a lighter background. They are equally at home in trees or on the ground.

Of the other common snakes in our area, my absolute favorite, mainly for its color, is the rough green snake. It is a uniform medium-green color, usually about 2 feet long and about as big around as your finger. Its color blends in well with green leaves so it is camouflaged while in shrubs, which is where I have found most of the ones I have seen.

In terms of water snakes, the only common water snakes in the Hill Country are the blotched water snake and the diamondback water snake. Both have relatively dark bodies and are usually between 2 and 3 feet long. While they spend most of their time near water bodies, in dry times they may be seen far removed from water.

The eastern hognose snake is certainly the greatest actor among the snakes. If threatened, the first thing it will do is to inflate its neck and upper body to appear much larger and somewhat more rattlesnake-shaped, and to also vibrate its tail, which if done in dry leaves, sounds a lot like a rattlesnake. It may also hiss and make fake strikes. If all else fails, it may play dead by rolling over on its back and letting its tongue hang out. If you turn it over, it may flop back upside down again.

Please note that all of the snakes mentioned here are harmless and non-venomous, but important constituents of our native habitat.

Hill Country Wild Turkeys

Three gobblers display for two hens in the background.

There are three subspecies of wild turkey in Texas—the eastern turkey *(Meleagris gallopovo silvestris)*, Merriam's Turkey *(Meleagris gallopovo merriami)* and the Rio Grande turkey *(Meleagris gallopovo intermedia)*. The eastern turkey is found in roughly the eastern ¼ of the state, the Merriam's turkey in only the higher elevations of the Trans-Pecos region, and the Rio Grande turkey is found in a large fraction of the central part of the state from the coast to the pan handle.

The Rio Grande turkey is the only one found in the Hill Country or the

Edwards Plateau. The visual differences in the three subspecies are fairly slight, the eastern being slightly darker in color and the Merriman's having whitish tail tips, compared to the Rio Grande. The gobbler or toms (males) of the Merriman's are the heaviest, up to 26 pounds, the eastern next, between 19 and 21 pounds and the Rio Grande average between 16 and 18 pounds. The hens (females) of each species are considerably smaller than the males.

Gobblers have a tuft of hair-like feathers hanging down from their breast called a "beard," but about 15 percent of hens have that also. Gobblers have a fleshy growth on top of their head called a "snood" that hangs down on the side of their face. The snood will elongate and become bright red when in the presence of a hen. Gobblers also have roundish red fleshy growths on their necks called "caruncles." Hens have very much smaller, less colored snoods and caruncles than gobblers.

Mating season in central Texas starts in late February or early March. Males display when anywhere in the presence of hens or just to compete with other males. They do not have a territory to defend and will mate with as many hens as they can. Gobblers do not take any role in nest building or rearing the young.

Hens preferred nest sites are among tall grass or short shrubs as cover for the nest and eggs. They also prefer water not to be too far away from the nest. Hens can lay up to as many as a dozen eggs over a two-week period—hatching occurs after about 28 days of incubation. Nest predation is a major factor in limiting the number of young (poults) produced.

Turkeys are in the order Galliformes, along with quail, grouse, pheasants, and chickens. They are characterized as having strong beaks and feet, scratching for their food, and having the young being able to walk and feed themselves within hours of hatching. Poults develop flight feathers and can fly to a roost within two weeks of hatching. Typically, a hen may hatch 8 to 10 poults but only two or three may survive through the summer.

Turkeys are usually seen in loose flocks, sometimes only a few individuals and at other times with as many as 30 or 40 birds slowly "grazing" through the pasture. We frequently see individual hens or small flocks of hens fly into our yard to scratch under the bird feeders for spilled sunflower seeds and/or to drink from the recirculating "creek" we have in the back yard. They also just amble throughout the yard eating whatever grass or forb leaves they see that they like and searching for grasshoppers and other insects.

On two occasions we have had hens nest in tall grass under a tree in the front yard, which meant they had to fly over the fence every day to lay their eggs and then fly back over the fence to feed when incubating. The attraction was probably better cover inside the fence than in the overgrazed pasture outside.

Unfortunately, neither nesting hen was successful. The first had laid 8 to 10 eggs but then we saw a Texas rat snake with two eggs in its body crawling away one day and eventually all the eggs disappeared. The second nesting attempt was two or three years later in a similar spot. Egg laying was occurring but when only a few had been laid we found a bunch of tail feathers near the nest and no eggs one day. Shortly after that we saw a hen with no tail feathers, but otherwise apparently OK. Shortly after that, we saw a raccoon with a definite limp. You can write your own story about what may have happened.

It is obvious that ground nesting birds of all kinds need to attempt to raise large broods in order to have enough survive to maintain the population.

Coyotes: Rural and Urban

A recent edition of *Texas Wildlife* magazine contained two articles about coyotes that I found fascinating and informative. Here are, briefly, some of the things discussed in these articles.

First, some basic facts: Coyotes are about the size of a medium-sized dog, about 18 to 24-inches high at the shoulder and 3-feet long. They weigh between 25 and 40 pounds. They are mostly, but not strictly, nocturnal. They are true omnivores, eating small mammals, reptiles, amphibians, birds and bird eggs, insects, fruit (including melons and prickly pear tunas) and carrion. Coyotes mate for life. Pups are usually born in April or May.

Wildlife biologist Steve Jester describes the wide fluctuation in coyote population numbers throughout the year, from a low of about 270,000 in the state in March, before pups are born, to a high of about twice that number just after the pups are born. This indicates a high mortality of the young, although once a pup reaches maturity, its lifespan can be as much as 10 to 15 years.

Interestingly, estimates of population densities in Texas indicate that the Hill Country has the lowest population with only about 0.5 coyotes per square mile compared with 6 coyotes per square mile in South Texas.

In an article by Colleen Schreiber, reprinted from *Livestock Weekly*, the work of Professor Stanley Gerht was described. This was a long term study of urban coyotes in Chicago that involved radio- and GPS-collars, DNA, and food studies of about 700 coyotes. The Chicago metro area has about nine million people and an estimated 7000 to 8000 coyotes. The people have been there much longer than the coyotes, so it is not that the people moved into the coyote's habitat, but that the coyotes moved into Chicago.

This work tells the story of a teenage male that was collared when he was living with his parents. He later dispersed and became part of a pack that established an adjacent territory, then he became the alpha male and helped raise six litters. He was hit by a car 11 years after being first collared.

A female coyote collared in 2000 spent her entire life within about 5 miles of O'Hare Airport, raised seven litters averaging eight pups each and died of natural causes. Her mate was with her the whole time and is still in the area.

The study found that urban coyotes are more strictly nocturnal, have larger litters and a longer lifespan than rural coyotes. Pup survival is 61 percent in Chicago compared to 13 percent in rural Illinois. Vehicles are the main cause of death in the city while hunting or shooting is the main cause in rural areas. There is even a video of a coyote looking both ways before crossing a road!

Rodents and/or rabbits are a main source of food for the urban coyotes. Deer (mostly carcasses, not kills) are also a significant portion of the diet. Fruits of all kinds also make up an important part of their diet. Surprisingly, domestic house cats (or feral cats) and human garbage make up only 1 and 2 percent respectively of urban coyote diets.

During a 16 year period, only 17 cases of attacks on dogs were reported, and most of these were in February, the beginning of the breeding season. There have been no reports of coyotes attacking people.

Chicago has a program to remove problem coyotes from an area, and less than 5 percent of the collared or marked coyotes were ever labeled as "nuisance" animals.

The bottom line seems to be that coyotes can simply learn to live in urban areas without much conflict with people, even in areas where we would conclude there is no suitable habitat for them.

Given the lifespan, the litter size and the small territories many of these urban animals live in, their vision of a good habitat must be different than our vision. Likewise, who would have thought that South Texas would have over 10 times the coyote population of the Hill Country? Are more coyotes being hunted or trapped or shot as predators in the Hill Country to cause this difference? Are there that many more food sources in South Texas?

This just seems to me to be one more example of us humans not understanding Nature very well. Who would have thought 7000 coyotes would choose to live in Chicago? I wouldn't.

The Blackjack Oak and the Squirrel Family

When we built our house, we had a lone blackjack oak growing at the south end of our house in a small clearing between several post oaks and a couple of small cedars. We soon noticed it was showing signs of hypoxylon with the bark sloughing off the upper branches. Then one night the entire top broke off in a windstorm about 12 feet up the one-foot diameter trunk.

This left the tree with only one very small branch about half way up. It was obvious that the top of the tree was hollow. Many folks would have cut it down. But we are much more into letting Nature take its course, so we let it stand so if it died it could harbor insects that would make the woodpeckers happy.

Well, it didn't die. The lone small branch, now having at its disposal the large root system of a much larger tree began vigorous new growth which in a couple of years totally encircled the trunk with new branches. We did water it a bit occasionally.

Hollows in trees are not often overlooked by our native cavity nesting birds or by our resident eastern fox squirrels. So for the last two or three years, a momma squirrel has found the Blackjack much to her liking (No, I really don't know if it is the same momma squirrel, and given their lifespan, it probably is not).

This year, we watched a bit more carefully and were entertained by the antics of this year's brood. We had seen momma a few times earlier, but in mid-March we first saw the babies—triplets.

At first the little ones would just come up to the top of their cavity and look over the edge to view the world they had so recently entered. Then they would crawl out on the dead limb at the top. Then they would timidly crawl down the trunk a few feet only to quickly return to the safety of their hollow tree.

As they became ever more agile, they would crawl over each other, jump short distances and race up and down the trunk, but never quite reaching the ground. Then they learned to climb through the branches and go out onto the smaller limbs. Occasionally, early in the morning, I would see one hang from his back feet and stretch his body and his forearms as far out as possible as if it felt good after a night curled up with his siblings.

Eventually, as the tree was budding and leafing out, we could see them tasting a few of the buds, and they even explored the grape vine that was growing up the trunk.

Finally, in less than a month, the triplets had learned to jump from the branches of the Blackjack to the small cedar and from there to climb onto the top of the wire fence, balancing on the wire by flipping their tail from one side to another. And in a couple of more weeks they appeared to be on their own, mostly going their separate ways. But at least once recently all three came together and piled on top of a small bird house attached to a fence post.

It is amazing, if you just let Nature do its thing, how much you can learn and how much fun it is to watch.

We Humans Make Life Tough for Wildlife

As just one species in the complex web of life on this planet, we can't claim to have been very good neighbors or friends to all the other animals and the plants on the Earth. In fact, we can be viewed as being the most destructive bullies around.

We have cut down forests, plowed up the prairies, paved over vast stretches of the land, set forest fires and grass fires, and killed off many species to feed and clothe ourselves, as well as some species just because we could. It would be easy to say that most of the worst of this wanton destruction took place many years ago, and that we wouldn't do all of that any more, but that would not be true. Habitat destruction was and still is the number one cause of species extinction worldwide.

In a 25 year period ending in 2007, the United States lost an amount of farms, ranches, prairies, forests, and wetlands equal in area to the size of Indiana to "development" (suburbs, shopping centers, roads and parking lots)! I suspect that the size of the native habitat loss might have surprised you, but not the fact that it is still occurring. We continue to have to make more room for the increasing population of humans: the population of Texas is predicted to double in the next few decades!

Hopefully, future "development" will eventually become less wasteful of energy, water and land and more environmentally friendly—we do know how to do it.

But there are a lot of other ways where human activity negatively impacts wildlife and native habitat. Mining and pollution of air and water are two such activities.

Strip mining of coal and most all other minerals can be highly destructive to native habitat both in terms of all of the vegetation stripped off the land, but also in terms of subsequent erosion and waste-water that pollutes local streams, lakes and rivers. Underground mining creates somewhat less pollution, but often still produces large amounts of waste.

Oil drilling, production and transportation leads to creation of waste ponds and spills that have led to the destruction of much wildlife, both marine and land-based, as well as contamination of both surface and groundwater.

Burning of fossil fuels not only produces polluted air that affects humans and wildlife alike, but it also pollutes cooling water as well as process water.

No form of energy is free of environmental problems. From mining operations for coal and minerals used in nuclear power and photovoltaic cells for solar panels, to the disposal of waste products, to the alteration and/or destruction of habitat to make room for all of the associated energy related activities, to the vast use of scarce water resources, all forms of wildlife are, at best, a minor consideration. Even electricity-generating windmills kill birds and bats!

It is easy to point the finger at industry, and it deserves a lot of blame, but we are the ultimate consumers of all this industrial production, and thus responsible for its pollution, and habitat destruction. And that doesn't count the many things we do that directly endanger wildlife. Just count the carcasses along the roadsides to see the effects that modern man's inventions have on wildlife that didn't evolve to evade anything moving at 70 miles an hour. And then of course, there are the many birds that succumb to all of our collective picture windows.

Finally, we have to add the destruction of wildlife caused by our domestic dogs and cats, which, because of their genes and their huge numbers, take a heavy toll on birds and small animals every year.

Now, much of the wildlife destruction I have just described is the result of unintended consequences of our modern way of life, and I don't think anyone would want to go back to living in the 1800s. But certainly, many of our human activities could perhaps be altered to cause less destruction if the impact on wildlife were considered.

Life would be easier for wildlife if we humans thought more about them and their habitats and tried to avoid causing any more problems and destruction than necessary.

What Our Common Native Animals Eat

Animals can be divided into categories based on what they eat. Herbivores eat only plant material. Carnivores eat only other animals. Omnivores eat both plant material and other animals.

Among our native mammals, only bobcats and mountain lions are true carnivores, and they are not very common in the Hill Country. Foxes and coyotes are in the Order Carnivora, but their diet is truly that of an omnivore, as are the diets of raccoons, opossums, skunks, armadillos, and squirrels. True herbivores include rabbits, hares, deer and porcupines.

Specifically, here are the most common diets of our common mammals:

Gray Fox: omnivore; small mammals such as mice, rabbits and hares, also birds, berries, persimmons, nuts, fish, and carrion.

Coyote: omnivore; small mammals, reptiles, amphibians, birds, bird eggs, insects, fruit, persimmons, carrion.

Raccoon: omnivore; crayfish, fish, reptiles, amphibians, nuts, fruit, small mammals, baby birds, bird eggs, insects.

Opossum: omnivore: insects, berries, fruit, bird eggs, fish, reptiles, amphibians, small animals, carrion, worms.

Ringtail: omnivore; reptiles, amphibians, nuts, fruit, leaves, bird eggs, insects, small animals.

Striped Skunk: omnivore; insects, small animals, earthworms, grubs, bird eggs, amphibians, fruit, berries, nuts, seeds, reptiles.

Armadillo: omnivore; mainly insects, also carrion of small animals.

Porcupine: herbivore; soft bark, green plants, tree leaves, leaf buds.

Cottontails: herbivore; grass, other green plants, twigs, bark, and other woody plants in winter.

Jackrabbit: herbivore; green plants in summer, twigs, bark, leaf-buds, dried grasses and berries in winter. I have seen them digging for grass roots as well.

Rock squirrel: omnivore; green plants, seeds, insects, fruit, nuts, bird eggs, baby mice, carrion.

Fox squirrel: omnivore; acorns, nuts, seeds, fruit, mushrooms, bird eggs, baby birds, mice, insects, carrion.

White-tailed deer: herbivore; browse (woody plant leaves including trees, shrubs and vines), forbs (weeds and wildflowers), a small amount of fresh tender grass. In winter, acorns and nuts, twigs and buds and especially live oak leaves.

Our non-mammal critters have interesting food habits also. Lizards, snakes, frogs and toads are all carnivores. Lizards eat almost entirely insects (only live insects at that). Frogs and toads will eat just about anything that moves and will fit in their mouths, including smaller frogs, but again they will not usually eat anything unless it is alive.

Snakes have the ability to unhinge their jaws and so can swallow prey that are significantly larger than their own bodies. Prey can include anything from rats and mice to lizards, frogs, toads, birds and eggs, and smaller snakes. Smaller snakes eat mostly insects, worms and other invertebrates they find in the soil and leaf litter.

Most songbird species fall into the category of insect eaters, which also eat berries and fruit, especially in the winter, or seed eaters which also eat insects, especially feeding insects to their young. Wading birds eat mainly fish, frogs, toads, and crustaceans. Some ducks eat mainly vegetation, some eat fish.

Raptors (hawks, owls and eagles) are carnivores and eat either birds, small mammals or fish.

Scavengers such as vultures, crows and ravens eat mostly carrion, but are also adept at finding human garbage.

All of the above diets are the common textbook lists given for these animals, edited somewhat for Hill Country conditions. This does not mean that any of the critters above won't also take advantage of things humans put out, including pet food, deer food, and bird food. With the exception of feeding birds, most all wildlife specialists advise against putting out food for the other animals, especially on a regular basis.

It is important to note that just about everything listed above is also the potential prey for something else, so while they are all out looking for food most of the time, they also have to keep an eye out for potential predators. Only the top predators don't have to worry about being prey, although they do have to worry about humans and their machines.

Which Native Animals Could Cause You the Most Harm?

This topic came to me in a recent article in Texas Wildlife by Todd Steele about the various dangers we might encounter outdoors. I didn't take a poll, but I bet the majority of people would answer the above question that they are most afraid of snakes.

I have not been able to find any actual data on numbers of snake bites in Texas, but I did find that nationwide; only 0.06 percent of all snakebites in the U.S. are fatal. So while human deaths from snake bites are rare, they can be very painful and some folks have long-lasting effects from the venom. And, anti-venom treatments can be very expensive.

Interestingly, fifty percent of all snake bites are to 18-28 year-olds, 90 percent of those to males, nearly always to the hands or feet. Steele points out that "A large percentage of snakebites come from people trying to dispatch one." I suspect those two facts are related.

While not so much a danger here in the Hill Country, Steele notes that alligators are another reptile that one needs to be cautious about. Down along the coast, fishermen need to be wary of several things in addition to alligators. Stepping on a stingray while wade-fishing can be very painful, and a couple of saltwater catfish also have toxic fins to avoid. In the last 100 years, only two fatal shark attacks have occurred in Texas.

Africanized bees can be extremely aggressive and will pursue trespassers up to a ¼ mile, so you certainly want to avoid any hive you don't know to be safe. Most of us have experienced red imported fire ants, and while not the danger that the Africanized bees can present, they can certainly be unpleasant and some people may have an allergic reaction to them. (Neither of these are native, of course.)

Staying with insects, scorpions, and brown recluse and black widow spiders can certainly render painful bites or stings, and these critters can be found in and around human habitation so the chance of people encountering them is greater around homes than out "in nature." Brown recluse spider bites are not necessarily painful at first, but can lead to very severe tissue damage in a few days if not promptly treated.

The number of feral hogs is growing fast in Texas, (currently estimated at about 2.6 million) and may eclipse the number of white-tailed deer (around 4 million) in a few years. I don't know for sure if there have been any cases of hogs attacking humans in Texas—they would much rather run away than to attack. But the boars have really impressive sharp tusks and will certainly attack if threatened—something many dogs have discovered. Sows with piglets can certainly be ferocious as well.

The apex predator in Texas is, of course, the mountain lion. There is no doubt that mountain lions are capable of attacking and even killing a human, and whenever such an event occurs, it certainly makes the news and thus causes many people to fear them. But in fact, in the last 35 years there have been only four attacks by mountain lions on humans in Texas, according to the Texas Parks and Wildlife Department. There have been no fatalities from attacks in Texas. If you come upon a mountain lion while on foot, do not run like a prey animal. Instead, try to look as large as possible, wave your arms, make noise and fight back.

So what is the native animal that poses the greatest danger to humans in Texas? That would have to be the white-tailed deer. I know. Those gentle creatures with the big brown eyes that like to chew on your flowers seem so harmless. But there are four million of them in Texas, and they are jumping fences and crossing roads and in 2013, nearly 6000 Texans collided with a deer while driving. And we don't know how many accidents they caused by drivers trying to avoid hitting them. Insurance statistics show that one out of every 333 Texas drivers will hit one. In 2013, eleven of those collisions were fatal. Nationwide, 1.25 million collisions occur every year resulting in 150 deaths and 10,000 injuries and a cost of about 4 billion dollars.

So if you are headed out camping or hunting or fishing or to hike in the woods, be especially careful on the drive out there.

ANIMAL BIOLOGY

Animal Behavior Studies: Fascinating Stories of How Animals "Think" and Act

Dr. Kent Rylander, retired Texas Tech Professor, author of the book, "The Behavior of Texas Birds," and a friend of mine, tells a fascinating story about a classic experiment in animal behavior. The researchers removed an egg from under a sitting goose and placed it next to the nest. The goose got up, extended her neck so that she could reach over the egg with her bill, and then pulled her neck back, pulling the egg back toward the nest. This motion was repeated until the egg was back in the nest.

But then the researchers noted that if the egg rolled away from the goose and down a hill, the goose continued the motions of raking the egg back into the nest without the egg even being there. So once the motion of retrieving the egg was begun, it continued even though it wasn't accomplishing anything. They then discovered that if they placed other smooth round objects near the nest, (including a volleyball!), that the goose would retrieve those also.

The conclusions from this work are that the egg retrieval is an instinctive or innate behavior triggered by the sight of an egg outside the nest. They also found that this behavior only applied to adult, female geese on a nest and was not observed in any other setting. Any egg-like object next to a nest triggered in the female goose a set of actions that were neither "learned" nor necessarily even "logical," but were clearly inherited. (The female goose never saw her mother do this.)

There are numerous other examples of animals displaying actions that are triggered by some specific event or occurrence in the environment. Here are a few other examples:

Male stickleback fish have a red belly, and they are aggressive in defending their territory, chasing all other male sticklebacks away. When researchers made a model of a male stickleback without the red belly and placed it in the territory of other males, it was ignored, but when they made many other models that didn't look anything like a stickleback, or even a fish for that matter, but which had red lower parts, all of those models were attacked.

Similarly, a male robin will attack a bundle of feathers with a red middle even though it doesn't even look like a bird, but a stuffed juvenile robin without the red breast will be ignored. In both of these cases, it is the red color that triggers the response, not the similarity in form, shape or size.

This raises another question. Can learning override this innate response to certain triggers? "Learning," in this case is defined as the modification of behavior with experience. The answer appears to be yes, at least in certain cases.

Gull chicks, just hatched "know" to crouch and freeze whenever they hear an adult gull sound an alarm call. These same chicks, when first hatched, also display the crouching response to almost any moving objects above them, which is essential for avoiding predators.

In time, however, the chicks "learn" that certain bird shapes they see flying above them are harmless and they cease responding when, for instance, a duck or a songbird flies overhead. But they still respond when the shape they see above belongs to a predator. It turns out that most predators show a shorter head and neck profile than most other birds, and so it is only the "predator" shapes that trigger a response.

But it is more complicated than that even. Researchers fashioned a "bird shape" to fly above the chicks that had a shape which, when flown above the chicks in one orientation appeared to have a short head and a long tail (like raptors), and it triggered the crouch response. But when the same shape was flown over the chicks in the other orientation, it appeared to have a long neck and a short tail (like ducks), and the chicks ignored it! By the way, turkey and pheasant chicks respond the same way.

So the next time you see a young squirrel burying an acorn, ask yourself, is this a response to some trigger like the length of the days or the presence of acorns, or did he learn this from his mother? He wasn't born when his mother buried her last acorn in the fall. Did he learn it from other squirrels?

Nature, like most of life, offers more questions than answers.

Animal Behavior: The More You Know, the More Amazing It Is

The scientific study of animal behavior is called Ethology. Much of Ethology is concerned with understanding what is instinctive behavior and what is learned behavior. Instinctive behavior, sometimes called innate behavior, is inherited and not based on any prior experience. Exactly how instinct is transmitted from one generation to the next is not fully understood, but the fact that it exists and the resulting observable actions are what I find really fascinating. Here are some examples.

Consider this: A sea turtle crawls up on a beach, digs a hole in the sand, lays eggs and then goes back to the sea and swims off, not to return for at least another year. Every female sea turtle of that species that was originally hatched on that beach does the same thing at the same time of year at the same place. And they have been doing it for centuries! How do they know to do this? They didn't see their mother do it. They are solitary animals, so they didn't just "follow the leader" to do it.

Here is another example. A baby bird hatches, momma and daddy feed it, it grows up, starts to fly and feed itself. Then next year it goes through a mating ritual, chooses a mate, builds a nest, lays eggs and incubates them, all actions that the bird had never observed before. And this happens SUCCESSFULLY over and over for hundreds or thousands of generations and millions of individual birds of that species.

Bird migration has always been fascinating to people because it is difficult to comprehend such a small animal being physically able to fly such long distances, in some cases without stopping. But aside from the physical feat, how do they manage to know where they should be going and how to get there? For the species to survive, it is important that they get to the correct winter and summer ranges in order to have the proper food supply and/or nesting grounds. To make it more amazing, for some species, the juvenile birds do not migrate with the adults!

I have been watching a large yellow garden spider living just outside our window where I can observe it closely. Every so often she eats her web and then rebuilds it. Watching her reconstruct the web by walking around the circumference and sticking the silk to the radial spokes shows what appears to be a concept of geometry and engineering. Whatever it is, it is clearly instinctive, because she never saw her mother do this. In fact, she never saw her mother, period.

Embryonic-sized opossum babies know to crawl through their mother's hair to reach her pouch, or else they will shortly die. Most reptiles never see their parents and receive no help from them in finding food, avoiding predators, etc.

All of the above are probably instinctual, whether we understand exactly how that works or not. But animals do some pretty amazing things that are clearly learned activities also. Many animals appear to have a memory of the location of various things in their home range, certainly at least where water, reliable food sources, nests and dens, etc. are located. They also learn from their own experience; if you have ever watched a squirrel figure out the logistics required to get to a particular bird feeder, you know that once they have done it successfully, they remember exactly every step necessary to get to it again.

I don't know if it is instinctual or learned, but I have always been fascinated by the ability of some prey animals to be able to recognize at some distance the difference between a predator and a prey animal. White-tailed deer pay little attention to any squirrel, rabbit, turkey, goat, sheep or any of the exotic ungulates. Even cattle, which are many times their size, don't really upset deer, although the deer do usually give cattle their space. But yet the smallest dog, cat or fox, all clearly too small to be a threat, can cause the white flag to go up and the deer to flee. Most predators have both eyes in the front of their head while most prey animals have their eyes on the sides...do the deer know this? If so, how do they know?

The more I know about the natural world, the more wondrous it seems.

Predators and Prey: A Complicated, Often Misunderstood Relationship

Last month, I was watching a herd of deer gathered around a feeding station where feed had apparently just been dispersed (a practice I don't recommend). Then all of a sudden, the entire herd bounded off in one direction, tail flags up, clearly having been spooked by something. Then a few seconds later I saw a lone coyote trotting up from the opposite direction. He had obviously lost the element of surprise and decided not to try a, probably futile, pursuit. He sniffed around the feeding area for a short time and finally trotted off in a different direction.

This event got me to thinking about the relationship between predators and prey, how complicated it is and how it is often misunderstood. The word "predator" usually conjures up thoughts of large predators, wolves, bears, cougars, lions, etc., but most predators are much smaller, and are interested in correspondingly small prey.

Quail, for instance, have to worry about many different predators, including hawks, most all of the small omnivorous mammals, snakes (mainly after eggs and chicks), and even non-native predators such as feral cats and hogs. Songbirds have to worry about hawks, snakes, ringtails, feral cats, and, occasionally other birds as well. Small mammals such as rats, mice, rabbits and hares are a favorite food of nearly all predators including hawks, owls, coyotes, foxes and snakes.

Insect eaters are predators as well, and these include flycatchers such as mockingbirds and phoebes, frogs, toads, and lizards, and mammals such as skunks, armadillos, bats, shrews, mice and rats. Herons and egrets prey on small fish, crawfish, frogs and snakes. Ospreys take fish, as do some water fowl.

The point is that there are lots of animals that are predatory on other animals for at least some of their food, and there are lots of animals that are potential prey for numerous predators.

We humans tend to take sides in these predator-prey encounters, especially when we watch lions chasing an antelope on TV and, consciously or unconsciously, begin rooting for the antelope. Even though, biologically, we humans are also predators, we tend to think prey animals are more to be protected than predators. But from the standpoint of a healthy ecosystem, both types of species are important.

When European settlers began moving into Texas, most of them brought with them domestic livestock; cattle, sheep, goats, pigs and chickens. All of these exotic animals were slower and easier prey for the resident predators than most of the native prey animals. But the domestic animals were very important to the very survival of the settlers, so they shot just about all predators on sight.

Thus began the elimination of our larger native predators. The last bear and wolf were killed in Kerr County a little over a hundred years ago. Not all of the killing of predators was done by people protecting their livestock. Many hunters have also contributed to the reduction in predator numbers in the belief that fewer predators means more prey game animals (quail, dove, ducks, deer).

This belief, however, fails to take into account that prior to settlement, there were much greater numbers of all predators, especially large ones, coexisting with sizeable numbers of large prey animals (deer, elk, antelope, bison). The elimination of large predators is generally given as the main reason for the increase in white-tailed deer throughout the state. However, the last major predator of deer, the screwworm fly, was eliminated by the USDA, not by hunters.

We are now left with the situation of almost no natural predators of white-tailed deer, and the overpopulation of deer to the point of destroying the native habitat for themselves and other wildlife. We are clearly not going to try to return the wolf to the Hill Country, but we should recognize the fact that predators play a useful, important part in maintaining a healthy ecosystem and the prey animals are not necessarily more important or more deserving of protection than predators.

An ideal, healthy, sustainable, ecosystem would have predators and prey in such numbers that the predators would not take more prey animals than could be replaced in the next year and the prey (herbivores) would not take more forage than the vegetation could replace in the next year. Under these conditions the "balance of nature" could be maintained long term. We haven't yet figured out how to attain such an ecosystem without the natural predators.

Animal Society is Varied, Complex and Mysterious

Most of us are fascinated by watching animal behavior, especially their interactions with their own species. It is these intra-species interactions and associations that we call, anthropomorphically, "animal societies."

To start with the basics, some animals are loners and some like to be part of a group. Some groups are small and some are huge. Some are temporary and some are life-long. We have special words for groups of animals like flocks, schools, herds, prides, packs, pairs, families, etc.

Even if we limit our discussion to mammal behavior, there is still a wide variation in types of social interaction.

Probably the most common type of association among mammals is a family group including the mother and her offspring. The male may or may not be present during and after the birth. For many species, the male and female come together to mate and thereafter part ways, leaving the female to raise the young by herself. For other species, such as coyotes and foxes, they mate for life and the male usually helps to raise the young.

A nearly-mature non-native Blackbuck antelope.

For most species in which the male is not involved with raising the young, the males are mostly solitary, such as mountain lions and other felines and bears, but also deer, raccoons and skunks. At times, non-breeding adults of some species such as coyotes will form loose associations or temporary packs.

Many of the larger prey species that evolved to have to evade large predators form herds, usually made up of males, females and young. Being only one individual in a large group of your species gives you a much better chance of evading a predator. Our white-tailed deer certainly fall into that category, although our deer do not form the really large herds like some of the African herbivores. I have, however, heard from several folks that have observed herds of feral exotic axis deer in excess of 50 animals.

Our white-tailed deer appear to form rather fluid herds usually made up of mostly does and fawns or yearlings, probably many of which are related. But it doesn't appear that any of these small herds are fixed in numbers, but instead one sees fewer deer at times and more at other times, sometimes bucks are included and sometimes they are not. Sometimes small groups of bucks are seen.

We know that during the rut in the fall bucks will spar with each other for dominance to breed the does in the area and that about that same time the females appear to drive off their male fawns. But because of the loose associations, white-tail bucks don't seem to have the harems that are seen with elk, for instance, in which the dominant buck continues to drive off all other bucks and mates with all of the females in his "harem." But we know from genetic studies that the dominant white-tailed buck is not the one breeding all of the does in his area.

One of the common exotic ungulates in the Hill Country is the blackbuck antelope. They have a different type of social structure. The mature bucks establish a territory which they defend against all other bucks and which they mark with urine and droppings. The does roam around in herds and whenever the doe herd moves into a buck's territory, mating can occur with any does in season. Immature bucks form "bachelor herds" but try to stay away from dominant bucks' territories.

In order for a buck to be able to maintain his territory, he has to fight off any other bucks, and will do so until he himself is defeated. Interestingly, I have seen on two different occasions a dominant buck chase an old, crippled buck out of his territory even though the likelihood that the latter would be any competition was very low.

In the bird world, many species of males go to great lengths to attract mates. In some species, both sexes build the nest, in others only one sex does this. In most species, the male helps to feed the young. Quite a few species of birds mate for life such as eagles, geese and swans, even though they may also be part of a larger flock at certain times of the year.

Recently, on the Texas coast, I observed two apparently male turtles in some kind of circling maneuver before they both attempted to mate with a female.

Animal societies are as varied as the animals themselves.

Wildlife Have to Survive All Year

On the morning after a recent snowfall, I spent some time looking out the windows watching the birds and the squirrels and the deer. It occurred to me that the lives of wildlife are a lot more difficult than we usually think about. All of our wildlife friends have to survive the worst weather conditions in all seasons.

Wildlife have to survive not only during times of good weather and abundant food, but they also have to survive in times of the worst weather and little or no food. And they have to dodge their enemies not just most of the time, or even 99 percent of the time, but 100 percent of the time. And they have to do this not only as adults but as babies and juveniles as well.

Animals that eat vegetation have to survive not just during growing seasons in good rainfall years, but in seasons of no growth and droughts. Insect eaters likewise can't survive only on insects during times of insect abundance, but they have to survive times when insect populations are low or non-existent. Seed eaters have to find food all year long, not just in the summer and fall when most plants produce seeds.

Good habitat for wildlife must provide all the essential elements wildlife need, food, water, shelter, and a place to raise their young year round. Or, as Leopold said, wildlife cannot live in habitat that provides "only kitchens or only bedrooms," anymore that we could.

Some birds solve the problem of there being no winter food in one area by migrating to areas that do provide the essentials of life. But not all birds migrate. The only local mammals that migrate are bats, and even those bats that do not migrate south in the winter hibernate. So everything else has to survive winters by continuing to find food, even in inclement weather. Many animals such as skunks and raccoons will sleep through very cold spells in a den. Armadillos are sometimes killed by long cold spells.

Of course we don't often have enough snow to be any kind of factor for wildlife, at least for very long, but I did notice a couple of things this morning before the snow melted. The one or two inches of snow on the platform bird-feeder prevented our local cardinals, titmice, chickadees and house finches from getting any sunflower seeds. The second thing is that the birds and squirrels were a lot more visible to predators against the snow than they usually are against the grass or tree branches.

I am always in awe of birds being able to survive long cold winter nights. When you think of a bird that is only 2 inches tall and weighs only an ounce or les, maintaining its body temperature over a cold windy night, that is remarkable.

And it is not just cold weather that challenges wildlife. Summer droughts may dry up water holes and reduce the amount of vegetation, which reduces seed production as well as insect production, all affecting bird survival.

What may not be obvious to us is that in times of severe weather or reduced food sources, populations of various species decline. In times of abundant vegetation, herbivore populations tend to increase, followed by the populations of predators. And the reverse is also true; when prey species decline in numbers, predator numbers will fall as well.

Each species in each habitat likely has a limiting factor that determines the limits of their population. It may be winter feed, or water, or cover from predators, or lack of suitable areas to raise their young, but something determines the population of that species in that habitat. For quail, for instance, a habitat without areas of bare ground between clumps of grass will limit the ability of their newly-hatched chicks (only about 2 inches tall) from moving about and finding seeds and insects. For squirrels, long open distances between trees where they are more vulnerable to predators will limit their population.

We probably don't know enough to always know what this or that species needs most, or what is most limiting their numbers, which is why we need to work to provide the most diverse healthy habitat possible for all critters.

The Amazing Monarch Butterfly

I have always been amazed that tiny hummingbirds are capable of migrating across the Gulf of Mexico and down into South America and back every year. They are so small (the average ruby-throat only weighs 3 grams, a little over a tenth of an ounce, and they have to beat their wings so fast.

But there is one animal that has an even more amazing life story; the Monarch butterfly. This is what makes it so amazing.

A monarch butterfly on a Texas milkweed.

We begin sometime around the first of April, give or take a couple of weeks depending on the weather, when the butterflies begin to arrive in the Hill Country. The monarchs have left their wintering ground in Mexico, probably mated there, or maybe as they arrive here, and the females are looking for some milkweed plants on which to lay their eggs. The most common native milkweeds in this area are the antelope horns (*Asclepias asperula*), Texas or white milkweed (A. texana), and hierba de zizotes (*A. oenotheroides*). None of these plants are all that common, although they are certainly not rare either.

The eggs hatch in 3 to 6 days into what is called the first instar, or first of 5 successive larvas or caterpillars, each bigger than the previous one. The bigger ones have black, yellow and white bands around their bodies and a pair of antennae near each end. The final instar, after gorging on the milkweed, forms a chrysalis or pupae, and seven to ten days later the adult butterfly emerges. The total time from egg laying to the new adult takes about 5 weeks.

This adult then begins a migration northward, with stops along the way for nectar, to mate, lay its own eggs, and die, and a new generation is born. This process of creating new generations of monarchs continues into the summer all the way up into the northern U.S. and southern Canada.

But then something really interesting happens. In late summer or early fall, the generation of monarchs that hatch at that time do not mate and lay eggs just then. Instead, they go into what is called "reproductive diapause," and do not breed. They then begin the long migration south and southwest, thousands of miles over areas they have never seen to a small wintering ground in the mountains of Mexico where they have never been! In fact, none of the last several generations have ever been there either!

They tend to wait for favorable north winds to help them along and stop to nectar when the winds are not favorable. A large fraction of all monarchs cross the Red River and travel through central Texas, some from Minnesota, some from New England, arriving sometime in early October. Some butterflies arrive from the east along the Texas coast and travel along the coast to Mexico.

Their migration takes them to the Sierra Madre Oriental Mountains in Mexico, then south and then west to the very small area in central Mexico where the vast majority of all monarchs in North America overwinter hanging from fir trees. Then, those butterflies that survive the winter, as well as having survived predators, disease, automobiles and insecticides, many fewer in numbers now, begin the migration back north in the spring. And here in the Hill Country they lay their eggs about eight months after they emerged from their pupae in the north.

Somehow, the genes in the DNA of monarchs, along with whatever serves as their "brain" or nervous system is programmed to cause the butterflies to migrate north in the spring with adults dying and creating new generations along the way. But then to sense shortening days and/or cooler temperatures and to cause a new generation to be born that, instead of living only a few weeks, lives for eight months. And in those months, it migrates thousands of miles, winters hanging in a fir tree and then flies back to Texas in the spring to start the cycle all over again.

Because of man's converting native pastures containing milkweeds into farms, heavy use of insecticides, air pollution, plus the logging of their wintering grounds, the populations of monarchs have declined over the decades, and it continues to fluctuate because of weather conditions. But in spite of all of these problems, these amazing little insects persevere and survive and give us something beautiful and inspirational to look at twice a year.

Of Bees and Butterflies and Other Sad Tales

Our native and even non-native bee and butterfly populations are seriously threatened from several sources, mostly, but not totally, man-made. Here are their stories.

First, some facts about bees. When the word "bee" is used, most people think of the kind that live in large colonies or hives, mostly provided by man. The bees that occupy these hives are not native bees, but species imported from Europe by early settlers. The settlers brought the bees to provide them with honey, but what they didn't know is that they were lucky to have done so, because many of the fruits and vegetables they also brought with them needed that species of bees to pollinate these European plants.

In the 1950s, African bees imported into South America began to mate with European honey bees, thus producing the "Africanized honey bee."

But of the 700 species of bees known in Texas, nearly all are native and include several types of bees, including bumble bees, carpenter bees, leaf-cutter bees, mason bees, mining bees and sweat bees. With the exception of bumble bees, virtually all of the other bee species are solitary bees rather than the colony-forming honey bees. Bumble bees form much smaller colonies than honey bees.

You have probably heard of the problems with the European honey bees suffering from a disease or syndrome called "colony collapse disorder" in which whole hives of bees simply disappear. A lot of work has been and is being done to try to understand the problem and find a solution. Possible causes include parasites, disease, pesticides and stress from hive movement, or possibly a combination of factors (commercial operators move large numbers of hives from one area to another to pollinate specific crops at specific times).

Increasing use of pesticides as well as native areas being cleared for farming have also greatly affected the native bee populations.

I wrote above about the amazing Monarch butterfly and its migration from the mountains in Mexico through Texas and the Midwest to the Northeast and back each year.

In Mexico in the winter, all of these migrating Monarchs cling close together in huge masses on pine and fir trees in a single area. Over the years the area covered by Monarchs has been recorded. In 1995, they covered 44.5 acres. Last year they were down to about 3 acres, and in 2013-2014, down to only 1.65 acres!

The causes for this precipitous decline are believed to be several. First, there was illegal logging in the Mexico mountains where the butterflies wintered, but that problem appears to have been largely stopped. Then there is the increase in the amount of non-farmland converted into farmland and thus the loss of native habitat.

But it is believed that the main cause of the decline in the Monarch numbers is the greatly increased use of genetically modified (GM) corn and soybeans. "Roundup Ready Corn," a genetically modified corn that is resistant to the herbicide "Roundup," has allowed farmers to greatly increase the use of the herbicide, which in turn has killed the native milkweed plants (at least 80 percent by some measurements) that monarchs need to lay their eggs and for the larva to eat.

In addition, some GM corn also has inserted into its genes the pesticide Bt, which becomes part of the pollen of the corn which blows off the fields onto native areas, coating milkweed plants. There is some concern that this is killing butterfly larva also.

So, the cause of colony collapse of hive-bees may or may not be man-made, we just don't know yet. But the increased use of insecticides of all kinds by farmers and homeowners alike is certainly affecting the number of these other important pollinator bees.

The drastic drop in monarch populations is almost certainly caused by humans. We don't yet know the full extent of the GM crop effects on other pollinators, because we don't have as good a measure of their numbers as we do for Monarchs.

When is a Bug Not an Insect?

An insect is usually described as an arthropod that has an exoskeleton, three body segments (head, thorax, abdomen), the head usually has antennae, mouthparts, and compound eyes and the thorax has three pairs of legs.

Non-insect arthropods include those with 1, 2 or multiple body segments, but never 3; they may have 8, 10 or more legs, but never 6; they have no wings and simple but not compound eyes. So when is a bug not an insect? When it is a scorpion, a spider, a tick or mite, a sowbug or pillbug, a centipede or millipede or a harvestman.

Scorpions have 4 pairs of legs plus pincers and long tail. Spiders have two body segments (cephalothorax and abdomen), are wingless, have 4 pairs of legs, and no antennae. Ticks and Mites have a single body segment, 8 legs, wingless, piercing-sucking mouthparts and no antennae. Sowbugs and pillbugs have 7 pairs of legs. Centipedes and millipedes have many body segments and centipedes have one pair of legs attached to each segment and millipedes have two pairs of legs attached to each body segment.

Harvestmen certainly look like spiders, but they have only one body segment with 8 legs and 2 eyes. Most of us grew up calling them daddy-long-legs. They are in a separate Order, the *Opiliones*. There are lots of different families of harvestmen worldwide. In Texas there are 18 different species, all in the *Phalangiidae* family.

There is a common myth that harvestmen are highly poisonous but have too small a mouth to bite humans. They do secrete a smelly fluid which may be the basis of this myth, but it is quite harmless, as are the harvestmen themselves.

In contrast to spiders, which have piercing-sucking mouthparts and only ingest liquids, harvestmen can ingest small bits of solid. They are omnivorous and eat mainly small insects, bits of plant debris, dead organisms and bird dung.

During the summer in the daytime, we can always find from one to 3 or 4 different aggregations of harvestmen clustered together on the rock walls underneath our porches or under the eaves in protected areas. They don't use the exact spot every day, so how they find each other to congregate is a mystery. If disturbed, sometimes they will bob up and down, presumably to look even larger and to discourage potential predators.

If one loses a limb, the limb will twitch, apparently to confuse any predator while the healthy 7-legged harvestman escapes. They can be observed "cleaning their legs" by alternatively pulling each leg through their mouth part. These are fascinating, fragile-looking creatures that have survived for at least 400 million years according to amber fossil records.

Everyone might be interested to know that chiggers are really mites. It is the larval stage that attaches to your legs when walking through grass and they crawl to some protected area in your socks or other clothing and attach to your skin where they feed for a day or two, then fall off. After that you may begin to experience itching and a reddish welt. This larva is only 1/150th of an inch long, which is why you never see them.

Ants, wasps, scorpions and spiders may be critters to avoid getting too close to, but the majority of arthropods have some beneficial quality such as pollination of desirable plants or control of other insect populations, or, in the case of many insects, they are just beautiful or interesting to watch. It is also important to remember that bugs are at the base of the food chain and are necessary food for birds, reptiles and other small omnivores and therefore are important for the higher carnivores as well.

So just because it is a "bug" doesn't mean it is bad. Natural populations of native insects are part of a healthy native habitat and therefore we should not try to eliminate all "bugs." We try to never use any insecticide outside (with the exception of an occasional wasp nest by the back door or fire ants in the electrical box). We have never lost a native plant to insect damage—remember that all native plants survived alongside all of our native insects for thousands of years before we and our chemicals came on the scene.

— SECTION IV —

RAIN AND WATER

You can't live in the Hill Country very long and not become acutely aware of the current state of rain or drought we are in and the fact that whether it is a wet period or a dry period, tomorrow may be either the beginning of the next drought or the next flood.

Everything about rainfall, how much and when, how much we capture on the land and how much runs off, how we can improve water capture or harvest rainwater, how we can survive the drought, become of interest to every Hill Country resident.

City residents as well as those of us in the country also have to be concerned about the reliability of our domestic water supply. Those of us who lived here during the drought of 2011 will not soon forget how the uncertainty of our water supply was brought home during that time.

An understanding of the hydrologic cycle, of aquifers, and of how much water we have and who gets it is something every Hill Country resident needs to know.

DROUGHT

Note: The first several essays were all written, in the sequence presented, during the drought of 2011. From the beginning of October in 2010 until September 26th in 2011 at our house in Gillespie Co. north of Kerrville, we received only 5.9 inches of rain. For all of 2011, we received only 13.5 inches. These essays are included here to give readers a sense of how I viewed the drought as it was occurring.

Is it a Drought Yet?

As this is being written, on April 24, 2011, at our house we have received very slightly over 3 inches of rain in the past 7 months! In a season when most plants need to use the most water to fill out new leaves and put on new growth, the ground is bone dry.

Ever since this area was settled by people from Europe and the eastern US, all people accustomed to areas of higher rainfall, it has been popular to view droughts as abnormal, unusual events and periods of average or higher rainfall as "normal." In fact, droughts are as common as periods of heavy rainfall. The oft quoted description of our climate being one of drought, punctuated by periods of floods, has some validity.

So, if this is the way it is, we should all accept it and learn to live with the droughts as well as the floods. The solutions are, obviously, to use less (conserve) and capture more water.

As a kid growing up in the drought of the '50's, in a part of Texas that "normally" gets about 15 inches of rain a year, I learned to waste little and do with less. I remember an incident I witnessed soon after I went away to college in the Midwest. I was in the men's room when someone came in, threw a cigarette into the toilet, flushed it, and walked out. I remember being literally shocked that someone would waste water like that.

There are things we can do inside and things we can do outside to conserve water. Some of these are easy and can be done right away, some are more complicated and are more long-term actions.

Inside, I am sure everyone has seen the list of things to do to conserve water; turn off the water when brushing your teeth, only run dishwashers and clothes washers when you have a full load, use a low-flow shower head and take "Navy" showers, etc. I know that some people catch water in basins or buckets from the sink or shower when they are waiting for the water to get hot and use it to water their plants. These are all small things, but small things add up if enough people do them often enough.

Longer term, whenever it is time to replace a dishwasher, clothes washer or toilet, replacing them with high-efficiency, low water-use appliances saves a lot of water.

Outside, there are lots of things we can do, and as much as 40 percent of all water use is for landscape use. For established plants, it is almost always better to water deeply but less often than to water lightly frequently. Sprinklers of all kinds are substantial water wasters because of evaporation of the small droplets and, on windy days, some water simply blows away. Drip irrigation for flower beds, shrubs and trees is much more efficient than other methods, and, once installed, requires very little effort.

Mulching all bare ground areas in flower beds and around trees and shrubs helps keep the soil cool, thus reducing evaporation and keeping the microorganisms in the soil healthy. Too much mulch, however, can capture too much of a light rain or sprinkled water so that the water never gets to the mineral soil where the roots are. An inch or two of mulch is probably the optimum amount.

In really dry times when lawn grasses essentially quit growing or even become dormant, stop mowing! Mowing too frequently and too short is very hard on the grass in hot dry weather and trying to keep it green under those conditions wastes even more water. When you do mow, set the mower at the highest setting you can, as taller grass shades the soil and reduces evaporation. Mow only when it really needs it, not just because it is Saturday.

Reducing car washing and other non-essential uses of water, at least in times of droughts, is certainly an easy thing to do.

Longer term, you can save water by reducing the size of your lawn (non-native lawn grasses are the largest water hogs in landscapes) and by replacing non-native water-loving plants with native plants. Harvesting rainwater for landscape use is an excellent thing to do, whether it is just a few rain barrels under some gutter downspouts or larger, more elaborate systems.

Is It a Drought Yet? Part 2

Previously I discussed some things we can all do to conserve water. Now, I want to discuss in a more general way some aspects of living in a semi-arid region. We humans are, I believe, fundamentally optimistic. So it is natural for us to look at periods of rainfall as normal, the way things should and will continue to be, while we view dry periods as abnormal times to be survived until "normal" times return. In fact, both periods are normal and to be expected.

If we can accept the above as fact, then we can get ourselves into a mind-set that expects both wet and dry periods and we can more easily adjust our lives and activities to accommodate both.

While water restrictions and/or reduced water availability are an inconvenience for those of us who have landscapes to maintain, consider the ranchers in the area. For them it is more than an inconvenience, it impacts their livelihood. Buying feed and/or reducing stocking rates, the normal responses to dry times, can be costly, and the overall condition and productivity of the land decreases as well. Likewise, wildlife, especially the overpopulated deer, will have less to eat in dry times.

During dry times, vegetation dies or becomes dormant, or dries out so that the moisture level is low and thus the fuel value is high. Under these conditions, everything burns much more vigorously and dry winds cause flames to spread at an alarming rate. This is just one consequence of living in a semi-arid region, and why we need to prepare ourselves and our homes for it.

One thing to keep in mind in times like these, is that drought has happened before, lots of times. Most all of us are relatively new to the Hill Country. But the native trees and shrubs and forbs and grasses have been here for eons. And they have survived all this time with periodic fires, buffalo herds, Indian wars, European settlements, cattle drives, the dust bowl and the drought of the 50s. If our native plants have survived all of that, they will, for the most part, survive whatever is happening to us now.

Large mature native trees have seen several periods of drought in their lifetimes. In severe cases, if things get worse, some might defoliate, but will likely leaf out again when the rains return, or next spring. Grasses easily go dormant in times of drought, but green up after significant rain. Grass and wildflower seeds can survive many years of waiting for the right conditions to germinate, so in most cases they will return without any help from us.

Newly planted trees or shrubs are at the greatest risk of dying in times of hot, dry weather, mainly because their roots are still confined to the dirt that was in the pot they came in and have not yet spread out into a larger area. This is why the preferred time to plant these woodies is the fall because they have more time to develop larger root systems before hot weather returns. So pay particular attention to any newly planted trees and shrubs, and make sure the root ball stays moist for at least the first year after planting. As planted trees grow, however, the area that most needs to be watered is under the dripline of the tree, not around the trunk.

Another thing to think about is the wildlife around your place. Their usual source of water may have dried up in the drought, so you might want to provide extra sources of water for birds and other wildlife during these dry times.

The point of all of this is that, we should consider as a role model the prudent rancher who stocks his ranch not for the best of times, but for average times, knowing that droughts will come. We should design our landscapes and maintain our homes with the thought that there will be times of little rainfall, and possibly water restrictions or well problems, so we need to be prepared for those times.

In other words, don't plant your garden expecting good rainfall, because you will be disappointed sometime in the future. Design your landscape assuming it will be dry at times, and you will be better able to survive the next drought.

How the Drought Is Affecting Our Native Wildlife

It is August 11, 2011. I suspect everybody is getting really fed-up with this drought, and trying to keep our most-prized plants alive is making a lot of us really cranky. And it is much worse for our farmers and ranchers trying to make a living. But the drought is certainly causing problems for our native wildlife too. Here is what I think is going on with the wildlife.

The effects of the drought start with the smallest creatures. Many insects whose larval stage spends the winter underground might not have emerged as adults this year because the ground was so hard and dry. Many insects may have become desiccated in the egg or larval stage and never made it to the adult stage. It seems to me that there are significantly fewer spiders, butterflies and moths this year than usual.

A lower insect population has huge ramifications for all of the animals that depend on insects for food, and that includes birds, lizards, frogs and toads, and even many of our small mammals, especially bats, skunks, raccoons and armadillos. Even seed-eating birds need insects to feed their young, as do hummingbirds. A reduced insect population means that many songbirds will raise fewer offspring, and many species that usually raise two broods a year may only have one brood this year.

Songbirds that usually feed on grass and forb seeds will find the pickings pretty slim this year, which may make them more dependent on backyard feeders.

Lack of water in places where it can usually be found also directly impacts the populations of insects that need water for one of their life stages. Reduced amounts of standing water also affect frogs, turtles, crawfish, and many species of small fish. Their reduced populations mean less food for the higher animals that usually feed on them.

Fewer young birds and lower populations of songbirds in general mean less food for all of their predators, such as many small mammals, hawks and snakes.

Most all of our small mammals; raccoons, skunks, possums, armadillos, rabbits, rats and mice will likely have a much harder time finding food. The result is likely to be that they will become more desperate and range wider in their daily search and thus are more likely to come into people's yards where there may be sources of green plants or other food. It is also likely that they will be out more often in the daylight hours when they can't find enough food at night.

All of these animal's populations will eventually be impacted as they are able to raise fewer young and also are more likely to be killed as they are more active and come into contact with people more frequently.

The populations of rabbits and hares, as well as rats and mice are known to fluctuate widely from time to time because of various environmental conditions. What is also known is that once the population of these prey animals declines significantly, a decline of all of the predator populations follows, usually a year or two later. So we may see a decline later in the population of hawks, owls, foxes and coyotes. Animals that eat carrion will do alright for a while, but as the populations of all animals decrease, they will eventually be affected also.

The white-tailed deer are doubly stressed by the extreme heat and drought. We had such a good year early in 2010, with abundant rainfall into September, that both the bucks and does were in good condition during the last breeding season, so many does carried twins or triplets into the spring. They are now being stressed trying to raise more fawns than the current pasture conditions will allow and having to travel farther for water. The general overpopulation of white-tailed deer and their having to compete with livestock and exotic ungulates makes their plight even more serious.

Both deer and livestock are susceptible to heat stress in these conditions and may be seen breathing with open mouths.

How significant all of the above effects may be will obviously depend on how long and how severe this drought turns out to be. We know that it is certainly one of the worst droughts on record, so we really don't have much experience with these kinds of conditions, nor do our wildlife.

What is the Drought Doing to Our Native Trees and Grasses?

It is the first of September, 2011. Let's think about what this drought is doing to our native grasses, forbs and woody plants. What happens to the vegetation, in a very large part, determines what will happen to our wildlife, and for that matter our livestock. Without vegetation, we wouldn't have any wildlife.

At this point it is probably safe to say that there have been longer droughts in the past, but quite possibly none as severe as this one. As of now, over the last 11 months, we have had a little less than 6 inches of rain at our house.

To the casual observer driving along looking at the scenery, it may not be apparent, but many of our trees are showing signs of stress. Live oaks are the most common hardwood tree in the Hill Country. This past March and April, when the live oaks were undergoing leaf exchange (dropping last year's leaves and growing new ones), we were already in a serious drought, so the oaks didn't have as much water available in the soil as was needed to produce a normal amount and size of new leaves. Water is required not only to transport nutrients from the roots to the leaves, but also as a raw material for the process of photosynthesis to make new leaves.

So the net result is that many live oaks have a thinner canopy, fewer leaves and smaller leaves, than they would in normal years. It is unlikely that even were we to get a big rain tomorrow that the trees would grow any more leaves this year. Presumably, if we get rain before next spring, next year's growth will be back to normal.

There are individual blackjack, post and Spanish oaks, as well as other kinds of hardwoods, that have either lost leaves or the leaves have turned brown (blackjacks seem to be suffering the most). It is certainly too early to declare the trees dead. Assuming rain before next spring, they may very well leaf out again.

But it is also true that all of our large native trees are being stressed by these conditions, and this stress can make the trees more susceptible to diseases, such as Hypoxylon, that could kill them in the next few years. So even if trees appear to have survived the drought, they may succumb to the stress in years to come.

What can you do to help? If watering is an option, soaker hoses or drip hoses around the dripline are the most effective, and if the ground under the dripline is not covered with leaves or grass, then putting an inch or two of mulch down will also help. Water mature trees until the ground is wet 6 to 8 inches down (when you can push a 6 to 8-inch screwdriver blade all the way into the ground), every 3 to 6 weeks at least until winter. Please observe water restriction rules.

All the native grasses have long since gone dormant, and some grass plants may have died. Most areas of native grasses have an abundance of grass seed already in the soil waiting for favorable conditions. So when rains do come, most of the grasses will recover either from breaking dormancy or from regrowth from seed. Obviously, the longer the drought continues, the more time it may take to recover.

The drought is forcing some ranchers to keep animals on worn-out pastures too long, causing excessive degradation which may take years to recover. Long term, removing the animals would be best. One problem is in areas where animals congregate, the hoof action of the animals will grind up the grass leaves to the point of laying the ground bare.

Where there is bare ground, the temperature of the soil is 20 to 30 degrees hotter than soil that is shaded by leaf litter or vegetation. This hotter temperature not only destroys the bacteria and other microorganisms that are essential to healthy soil, but also bakes the last traces of moisture out of the ground. Wherever this happens, the feeder roots of any vegetation will likely be destroyed.

Another thing that happens when grass isn't growing is that animal trails become bare ground trails that can then become the beginning of erosion when rains do come.

There are probably viable seeds for many forbs still in the ground, and in time, with rain, they will recover too.

More Drought Talk

October 13, 2011. Well, I have already written several drought essays in the past few months, but it seems to be about the only, or at least the most frequently, discussed topic wherever I go these days, so here is my current assessment.

Some folks have received a few good rains in the past few weeks while others have suffered the sight of rain clouds passing them by. Such is the nature of Texas thunderstorms. When I was a kid in West Texas, where you could see for miles and miles, it seemed like we saw dozens of rain clouds on the horizon for every one that actually came over us.

Some of you who have received a couple of inches or more may be feeling like the drought is over. I am sorry to say, however, that it's not, not by a long shot. If you got an inch or two or more in the last few weeks, it may certainly have helped save your trees, at least for a while, and it might have even greened up your lawn or pasture grasses. But the soil moisture deficit and plant moisture levels are still a long way from "normal" and there is still a lot of bare ground out there soaking up the sun's rays and cooking the water out of the soil. Springs, seeps and creeks are nowhere near normal flow levels and we don't even know the full extent of the aquifer deficits.

I attended the Gillespie County Land-Use Expo in Fredericksburg a few weeks ago where the drought was very much on everyone's mind. I listened to several speakers and talked to a number of experts I know on land management issues concerning our drought conditions. Here is a summary of what I heard.

The experts seem to all agree that stocking rates should have already been drastically reduced as most all of any useful forage is already gone and continued grazing is severely damaging the range. Yes, it will probably cost more to replace animals when the drought is over, but leaving them on the range now is damaging the ability of the grasses to recover and prolonging how long it will take to recover. It was stated by more than one expert that it may well take two years or more after normal rains return for forage amounts to recover.

David Oehler, Gillespie County Chief Appraiser, told ranchers to not worry about maintaining their Agriculture Tax Valuation, that he was willing to work with ranchers in these extraordinary times. Appraisers in other counties might well do the same.

Some people have trees that have either lost all of their leaves or had all of their leaves turn brown and crispy. No one can say for sure if that means the trees are/will be dead next year. If you can find next year's buds having already formed on the tips of the limbs, the chances of the tree re-leafing next spring are probably better than if it did not form buds. But if you don't find the buds, don't worry, you might just not know what to look for.

I have seen cypress trees planted too far from reliable water lose their needles and then green up again next year. So don't give up on anything just yet. But don't forget to try to keep the ground somewhat moist by watering every few weeks even through the winter if we don't get rains. You want to keep the roots healthy even in the winter.

This winter might be a good time to begin to rethink our ideas about landscaping. Even if it starts raining next week and does so all winter and spring, it doesn't make sense to assume things are going back to "normal" and put in an all-new St Augustine lawn. With either a constant, or, more likely, diminishing supply of water and an increasing number of people wanting it, we need to begin a mind-set that says water, especially for landscaping, will be limited at least at times, maybe for long times. We need to put the dream of a Houston or Dallas suburban green lawn out of our minds.

Lessons Learned from the Dust Bowl

PBS recently aired a two-part, four-hour documentary film by Ken Burns on the Dust Bowl. The Dust Bowl was over before I was born, but what I had never thought about until I watched the film was how close I was, in both time and distance to the southern end of the most affected counties in Texas. And watching the film and listening to the tales of the survivors brought back a lot of childhood memories from the late 1940s and early 1950s.

The causes of the Dust Bowl appear to be of two types; a period of severe drought, high temperatures and high winds, and the agricultural practices of the farmers of the plains. The worst of the Dust Bowl occurred from the Texas panhandle and northeastern New Mexico north to Nebraska, all of which had originally been the most prolific open grassland in the country with 6-foot high grasses. Periods of severe drought and high winds had occurred from time to time before, but the huge dust storms seen in the 1930s were never generated. The reason was that the tough native grasses held the soil and protected it from the wind.

But the settlers of the plains in the first quarter of the 20th century changed the environment, first by overgrazing the prairie and exposing the soil, then by plowing under the native grasses and planting wheat. The latter was so profitable during the first World War and into the late 1920s that the settlers plowed up more of the land than they actually needed to make a living. Farmers in the region were not even affected, at first, by the Depression because heavy rains made bumper crops of wheat.

But once the drought came and the crops failed and the land was left completely bare, an inch of topsoil that took a thousand or more years for Nature to build was lost in a single storm. Some of the soil piled up against houses so deep that people had to crawl out of windows to get out of their houses. Most of the soil was deposited all over the eastern U.S., or down into the Gulf.

The drought finally broke in 1939, and the new Soil Conservation Service (now the Natural Resources Conservation Service) developed new farming techniques such as contour plowing, crop rotation and new plows that left the stubble on the surface to protect the soil and add organic matter to the soil, leaving less land bare each year. Instituting these improved practices were supposed to prevent another Dust Bowl.

I grew up in an oil camp in Gaines Co. between Lubbock and Midland, about 50 miles from the southern tip of the Dust Bowl area. As a kid around 1949-1951, I remember watching bulldozers pulling huge 3 foot disks across the short grass/mesquite pastures around the camp and turning it into farmland. This coincided with the beginning of the "drought of the 50s." I remember what we called sand storms so dense that I couldn't see the neighbor's house 50 feet away and the sand blowing under the doors and windows and piling up on the window sills. I remember paint being abraded off of cars and windshields being sandblasted so that headlights at night would almost blind you.

But the 1950s was no Dust Bowl, for two main reasons. First, farmers planted different crops and used the better plowing techniques, but mainly, because the Ogallala aquifer underneath much of the Panhandle and extending all the way to Nebraska provided irrigation for the crops. I worked for a farmer near our camp growing cotton and sorghum throughout most of the "drought of the 50s" and he made a good living.

The lessons to be learned from all of this are: (1) Mankind is perfectly capable of causing huge climatic changes and destroying his environment. (2) Mankind is also capable of learning from his mistakes, changing his ways, and causing less environmental damage. But there is one big concern about the future. The Ogallala aquifer is not like the Edwards, which replenishes with a few heavy rains. The water in the Ogallala has been there for thousands of years and is finite. What will happen to all that area when (not if, but when) the Ogallala runs dry? Food for thought.

Eighty Years After the Dust Bowl: Have We Learned Enough?

I am writing this while on vacation in the Texas Panhandle on April 26, 2015—just 12 days after the 80th anniversary of Black Sunday, the day usually given for the worst day ever, during the Dust Bowl years. And I am just on the edge of the southern-most part of the area of the most extreme devastation.

What made these facts more meaningful was I had brought with me as some of my reading material a document published by Ricky Linex, a USDA, Natural Resources Conservation Service agent from Weatherford. The 18-page document, published on the 80th anniversary of Black Sunday, was all about the Dust Bowl, including long interviews with a couple of people who lived through and survived those times in the Texas Panhandle.

I grew up hearing stories about the Dust Bowl, and I have read Timothy Egan's book, "The Worst Hard Time," so I was not unfamiliar with what happened back then. But the coincidence of being in the region near the anniversary date of the worst day, and reading some of the accounts in Linex's newsletter, somehow made it all more real for me.

I suspect if asked "What was the cause of the Dust Bowl?" most folks would respond that the drought caused it. And that would be largely correct, but certainly incomplete. People, or rather the management practices of the landowners in the area, contributed a lot toward the soil erosion and blowing sand during those times. And in fact, it could also be said that government policies contributed to the problem as well.

The government offered generous grants of land to people to settle and "prove" the land to be productive and profitable. This encouraged way too many people to settle the region and to either plow up good grassland to convert it into marginal farmland, or to overgraze the land trying to produce too many animals on too little land. These facts, combined with what we now know to be the poor land conservation practices of the time, all contributed to the Dust Bowl.

The land had seen droughts before, but when the soil was covered by thick stands of native grasses, the grass held the soil in place as well as captured and held rainwater. So previous droughts did not result in unprecedented soil erosion and blowing sand which killed what little crops then existed and made life miserable for the new settlers.

Growing up less than 200 miles from the Dust Bowl and 15+ years later, I remember sand storms, but by comparison, we didn't have it so bad—we didn't have to string a rope from the house to the barn to find the way there during the worst storms, and we didn't have to feed tumbleweeds to the animals. Or eat tumbleweeds ourselves either! Some people really did!

But what came out of the experience of the 1930's was the establishment of the USDA Soil Conservation Service—SCS (now known as the Natural Resources Conservation Service—NRCS). The scientists at the SCS began educating farmers and ranchers about better techniques including rotational grazing, better crop selection, crop rotation, contour plowing, using different plows that left more stubble on the ground, and a host of other practices that have since greatly improved the conservation of soil and the productivity of the land. And of course, the advent of irrigation has made a tremendous change in the productivity and conservation of the region.

But it turns out that nothing is perfect. Our time on vacation in the Panhandle happened to be a time just after and during a week of very heavy rain. Driving around the area after this we saw many examples of farmland having been washed away, onto the roads in some cases, and many clean, stubble-less fields exposed to the elements of wind and water.

"Man—despite his artistic pretensions, his sophistication, and his many accomplishments—owes his existence to a six-inch layer of topsoil, and the fact that it rains"—Author unknown.

RAIN

Raindrops—Why Their Fate Matters to Us All

Think of a raindrop as a football, more specifically a football in a forward pass. If the raindrop falling from the sky hits the leaves of a plant and stays there, eventually evaporating back into the air, that is the equivalent of an incomplete pass because the football never reached its intended receiver, the ground.

But if the raindrop makes it all the way to the ground, two things can happen. It can be intercepted and run off the land. Or, it can reach the ground and soak in, a completed pass. If you own land, or if you drink water, you want that completed pass; you want the raindrop to soak into the ground.

Once the raindrop has soaked into the ground, there are still several things that can happen. It can evaporate back into the air. It can be taken up by the roots of plants and used either in photosynthesis (thus becoming part of the plant) or in transpiration (evaporating from the leaves back into the air). The raindrop could infiltrate deeper into the ground, moving slowly downhill where it eventually comes out in seeps or springs that feed our creeks and rivers, or possibly joining a deep aquifer becoming part of our groundwater supply.

How many of the raindrops fall on vegetation and evaporate back off depends on the size, type and abundance of the plants. Bigger plants and plants with high leaf surface areas will naturally catch and hold more raindrops than smaller plants. So, yes, cedar bushes (Ashe juniper) catch and hold more water than grasses, how much more depends both on how big the cedar is and also how heavy the rainfall. In light rains, the cedar catches a lot of the rainfall, in heavy rains, it catches only a small percentage (once the leaves are completely wet, all subsequent rainfall falls to the ground).

How many of the raindrops run off depends on the type of soil, the slope, and the vegetation. Native bunch grasses form the most porous, sponge-like soil of all other vegetation, and they also slow down the runoff, so less water runs off from a landscape with good, healthy native grasses. Slowing the flow of water greatly reduces erosion, some of which is caused by raindrops hitting bare ground and dislodging the soil.

Once soaked into the ground, the fate of the raindrop depends on the type of vegetation, the condition of the soil, the temperature, and whether or not it is an active growing season; the more active the plant growth, the more water will be taken up by the roots. Once beyond the root zone, the fate of the raindrop depends mainly on the type of soil and the underlying geological formations, whether it is conducive to local springs and seeps or whether the path to the underground aquifer is porous or fractured or not.

So a lot of different things can happen to our raindrop. If you own the land, you want the raindrop to soak into the ground to nourish the vegetation and possibly also to feed any seeps and springs. If you live in the city, you still want the same thing. If all the raindrops run off without soaking into the ground, there will be possible floods, silting of reservoirs, and the water will run down the river and into the gulf before your water company can capture any of it for your use. (Yes, of course we need fresh water flowing into the estuaries of the gulf, but a slow constant flow is preferable to a storm flood). When water soaks into the ground, it is acting like an underground reservoir, releasing water slowly and steadily, providing the base flow of the river.

How the land is managed determines a lot about how all of this works. A property where the cedar has been well managed, (leaving cedar on steep slopes to prevent erosion and removing much, but not all, of the remaining bushes), and where grazing has also been controlled (to prevent overgrazing and to establish a good stand of native grasses) will capture a greater portion of our natural rainfall and allow it to soak into the ground than a property that is less-well managed.

So we all have a stake in how land is managed, and a moral obligation to manage ours well. We also have an obligation to conserve our precious raindrops, it's all we have and all we ever will.

"It's Not How Much Rain You Get, But How Much You Keep"

A collection of leaf litter showing how the water ran off about 10 acres of gently sloping land in a single hard rain.

When two Texans greet each other, especially when they haven't talked since the last rain, the conversation usually begins with, "Hi. How are you? How much rain did you get?" We all have rain gauges, many of us keep records of rainfall, it's just part of being a landowner in semi-arid country. But asking how much rain did you get is not the most important question, what's important is how much did you keep?

I was reminded of the old quote above recently when I read a 1960 article by Clarence Rechenthin, an agent with the Soil Conservation Service (now called the Natural Resources Conservation Service), entitled "How Much of It Soaks in?" The point was brought home even more vividly last week when we received over 4 inches of rain in about 4 hours as we watched huge volumes of water running out of the pasture into our yard, around the house and down the hill, while our rainwater tanks were overflowing.

We clearly did not have 4 inches of rain soaking into the ground around our house. We don't really know how much ran off, but it was certainly a significant fraction of how much fell that night. And we live on what by Hill Country standards would be considered a fairly level property.

Of course, what ran off our land flowed to a little wet-weather draw behind our house, which in turn flows into a creek and helps to fill up several small ponds on the creek. Eventually the water makes its way to the Pedernales river, then into Lake Travis and finally into the Gulf. Unfortunately, it will be taking some of our soil with it and silting up the lakes.

If more of the rain had soaked into the soil, then the moisture level of the soil would have been higher and available to the trees, grasses and other vegetation for a longer time. Some of the water in the soil would have seeped slowly downhill through the soil to come out as seeps or springs which contribute to the base flow of the creek. Having higher base flows makes more water available than when it is lost during storm flows. Also some of the water may have seeped down into deep underground aquifers to replenish that critical resource.

We have of course had big thunderstorms in the past and have seen water run off the land, but the amount of runoff seemed greater last week. That was not unexpected because we have more bare ground now than in the past due to last year's drought and lack of grass growth. Water soaks into the soil under bare ground much more slowly than under native grasses, so until we regain the grass cover we had before last year, we can expect greater amounts of our major rainstorms to run off instead of soaking in.

And, because of the increased amount of bare ground, we undoubtedly lost more soil with the runoff than we would have in normal times.

It is easy to see the evidence of water running off by simply walking around and noticing places where litter dams were formed in which the flowing water picked up leaf litter and carried it floating, downhill, even if on a very gentle slope, until something caught the debris and caused it to build up in small piles.

Areas that had the greatest amount of grass cover before the drought of last year still have more ground cover than areas where the grass had been grazed too short. Consequently, areas that started with a lot of grass would have had less runoff and erosion after a big storm than places that started with little grass. This is just another way of saying that well-managed ranges are better able to survive droughts and to capture and hold more water than less-well managed properties.

The quality and quantity of water available to everyone is determined by the condition of the land on which the raindrops fall.

And Then the Rains Came!

After a very hot, dry summer the native vegetation was in pretty sad shape in early September. Many trees were showing signs of stress, either dropping leaves or wilting. Most grass had long since gone dormant brown, and many wildflowers had either died or were in an extremely wilted or browned out condition. It was not like we hadn't seen this before, in fact it is getting to be somewhat common, but nonetheless, it is painful to watch.

And then the rains came!

Gayfeather, or Liatris, after the rain.

At our house, we had almost three inches in one day in early September! We were seeing changes in less than 24 hours and on the second day major differences were noticed. The shrubs that were showing obvious signs of wilting before were now looking bright and healthy. The buffalograss went from brown to green overnight.

Two or three days after the rain I took a walk around the pasture, looking at the changes the rain brought. There was green grass to be seen in many places, but it was mostly under trees that the greenery was most notable. One could see green circles under trees and brown or gray grass outside of those circles. As the days went on and we got a few more showers, more of the grass in the open areas began showing new growth. In some cases, green growth could be seen even among the dead gray leaves of some bunchgrasses.

Why this pattern of grass greening up? The greener grass under trees can be explained as follows. The shade provided by the trees kept the soil under them cooler and thus reduced the amount of evaporation of water from the soil. This is in spite of the amount of water the trees were taking up. The cooler, wetter soil conditions under the trees allowed the grass there to be less affected by the hot dry days and, even though it had gone dormant, it was in better condition than the grass in open areas. So it was in better condition to respond to the rain.

In the open areas, much of the grass had turned from brown to gray, an indication that the leaves at least, if not the whole plant, were no longer just dormant, but dead. In general, grass that has turned brown is assumed to be dormant, but grass with gray leaves either means that those leaves are dead and will not green up again or possibly that the whole grass plant is dead. If a grass plant with gray leaves is easy to pull up, it is probably dead, if not, the growing points near the ground and the roots may still be alive. Obviously some of the grass plants in the pasture were not totally dead as they began to show new growth in a few days, but still much less vigorous than the grass under the trees.

A number of wildflowers and perennials that hadn't had a bloom on them in a long time suddenly burst into bloom. A partial list includes rose pavonia, zexmenia, various salvias, gayfeather, Lindheimer senna, bush sunflower, mealy blue sage, straggler daisy, cowpen daisy, Greggs mist flower, fall obedient plant, passion vine, and lantana.

While the trees were obviously helped a lot by the good rain and seem to have stopped dropping their leaves, they were undoubtedly stressed during the summer and this could lead to the loss of some trees in the next year or two.

The important lesson here is that native vegetation, having evolved to be here with our frequent dry spells as well as our wet spells, is extremely resilient and can usually bounce back from all sorts of extreme conditions. The fact that the native grasses have quickly begun to put up seed heads and reproduce so the species will prevail even if the individual plants do not demonstrates why these plants have survived here for so long. That the forbs have begun to flower shows the tenacity of these plants to produce seeds and reproduce even under less than ideal conditions as well.

Not every species will do well all the time, some will do better under the conditions of one year and others may do better under different conditions another year, but as long as we protect the diversity of native species, they will be with us for a long time.

Nature's Response to Rains and a Change of Seasons

I take a walk around our yard and the adjoining pasture often just to look at nature. On one such walk recently, after the good rains in early September and the middle of October, I made a number of observations. Here are some of them.

A lot of vegetation responded very nicely to the new rains. A bois d'arc tree planted about 8 years ago struggled through the summer in spite of our watering it occasionally, but is now quite healthy looking. Likewise, a 10-year-old chinquapin oak lost a lot of its leaves, but after the rains it has produced quite a few new leaves and it has healthy-looking buds for next year. Also a post oak which had largely defoliated by late August has actually re-flowered again—I didn't even know that was possible!

The acorn crop around our place doesn't look very good this year—lots of acorns, but all very small—they needed more rain in the spring and summer to fully mature. It does appear to be a very good year for juniper berries, however. Unfortunately for many allergy sufferers, it looks like we might be seeing very high pollen counts in a few weeks as well.

I found a snake skin while walking around. Given the size (about 5 to 6 feet long) and the kinds of snakes we most often see around the house; my guess is that it was probably a Texas rat snake or a Western coachwhip.

Butterflies seem to be most active on warm fall days, especially after a rain, and this year is no exception. Unfortunately, the monarch population is way down this year, so seeing one is an even bigger treat than usual.

As a grass lover, fall is always a good time for me as it is when more species of grasses put up a seed head and show themselves off than any other time. This year, with the early September rain, the fall grass crop is even better than usual.

In just a short walk, in addition to the ubiquitous, invasive KR bluestem, I saw plains lovegrass and meadow dropseed in profusion, with lesser amounts of Hall panicum, cane bluestem, Texas grama, sideoats grama, and an occasional Nealley grama and windmillgrass.

Unfortunately, I also encountered oldfield threeawn, as near to worthless as a grass can be. I always say that any native plant has some benefit to the habitat, holding the soil if nothing else. But this annual grass produces almost no forage and it does make lots of seeds with sharp-pointed barbs which can stick into an animal's mouth and nose and catch in their fur or wool to make for a real nuisance.

Mealy blue sage responding to fall rains.

I also encountered a colony of mealy blue sage in full bloom. This flower usually blooms in the spring and early summer, but the fall rains really invigorated this patch this year. Along with cowpen daisy, another wildflower which nothing eats, these two really brighten the fall landscape even in a grazed pasture.

And finally, even though I have walked these few acres dozens of times a year for the past dozen plus years, on this particular walk, I discovered a mammillaria cactus I had not noticed before.

One of the things I like best about natural habitats is that they are ever-changing, either because of the changing seasons or recent rains, or because of new plants emerging and old plants dying. Just observing these changes is part of what makes Nature so interesting and never boring.

RIPARIAN AREAS

Twenty years or so ago you would be hard pressed to even find the word "riparian" in lay media. But we have now become aware of the importance of riparian areas and the proper management thereof as well as how we have largely been mistreating these vital areas for many years. Human tendency in the past has been to do just about everything wrong in terms of managing our creeks and rivers and the land adjacent to them.

And to complicate things further, how riparian areas are managed has become intertwined with issues having to do with our water supply and how it is allocated. Hopefully, those who have riparian areas on their property will learn the new science about these areas and manage these areas properly.

Riparian Areas: Sensitive, Fragile, Beautiful, and Vital, But Often Abused

A very healthy-looking small stream in the Hill Country.

Riparian areas or riparian zones are defined as the land area along the edge of the water up to and including the flood zone. And in this context, the flood zone includes that area that generally floods every year or two, but not up as high as the "100-year flood plain."

The condition of the riparian areas is vitally important to all wildlife, as well as the quality and quantity of water for our own use. Life as we know it depends on healthy riparian ecosystems.

So what constitutes a healthy riparian area, as opposed to one that is unhealthy? The simple answer is vegetation. A healthy riparian area will contain an abundance of several types of vegetation ranging from small sedges and grasses along the water's edge to larger grasses and shrubs and finally deeply-rooted large trees.

The important functions of this vegetation are to hold the soil in place, even during a flood, to reduce erosion, to catch and hold sediment washing down from upstream, and to maintain the soil in a healthy, porous condition allowing for deep infiltration of water into the water table which maintains the base flow of the stream.

Other functions of this vegetation are to shade the stream thus keeping the water temperature at healthy levels for fish and other aquatic species, to provide habitat for numerous birds, butterflies, dragonflies, and larger animals and forage for grazers and browsers.

Riparian vegetation is generally classified as "colonizers" or "stabilizers." The former are generally small plants that can become established in damaged areas and grow roots quickly to help hold the soil in place until stabilizer plants which are better able to hold the soil permanently can get established.

Stabilizer herbaceous plants include larger sedges such as Emory sedge and sawgrass, large grasses such as switchgrass, eastern gamagrass, Lindheimer muhly, and bushy bluestem, and forbs such as American water-willow. Woody stabilizer plants include buttonbush, bald cypress, black willow, baccharis and sycamore.

While all of these species have different abilities to stabilize the soil, it has been shown that combinations of several different types together provide far more stability than any one species alone. Think of the root systems of these stabilizers as the "rebar" holding together the riparian soil.

The porous riparian soil holds huge quantities of water which is what provides much of the base flow to the creek in dry times, so the condition of this soil is critical to stream flow. Soil that is stripped of its vegetation by mowing or grazing or that is compacted by animals or vehicles will contain much less moisture.

Unfortunately, we humans believe that we should be able to sit on our porches above the creek and look down and see the water, or to have a large mowed lawn next to the water's edge where we can sit and fish or swim or just enjoy the bubbling brook. Or we have cattle and the creek is their only water source so they spend a lot of time along the banks. While these activities may be logical and just part of our human nature, they are counterproductive to a healthy riparian ecosystem.

Healthy riparian areas usually have the densest vegetation, from big trees to an abundance of shrubs, forbs and grasses. Put simply, you can't see the water from a distance in most healthy riparian areas of small streams, because it is obscured by vegetation. If that vegetation has been removed, either by humans or their animals, that stretch of the stream is no longer healthy and will be subject to greater erosion in the future.

Other than areas where native vegetation has been removed, the next greatest threat to a healthy riparian ecosystem is invasive exotic plants which crowd out mixtures of native species and replace them with a monoculture of exotic plants. The two most common are giant reed (*Arundo donax*) which can grow 20 feet tall and crowd out everything else and is common along the Guadalupe and its feeder creeks, and Salt cedar (*Tamarisk ramosissima*) which is more common in our western rivers. Other problem exotics are Chinese tallow, Chinaberry and vitex.

If you are fortunate enough to have property on a creek, I urge you to call the Nueces River Authority at 800-278-6810 and ask for a copy of the booklet "Your Remarkable Riparian." You will be glad you did.

"It Ain't What We Don't Know That Pains Us So"

Years ago, a rather philosophical colleague of mine would stop by my office occasionally and we would talk about our work and usually solve one or two of the world's problems as well. One of his favorite sayings, that seemed to apply in a lot of situations, was:

"It ain't what we don't know
That pains us so
But the things we know
That just ain't so."

I think about this saying often because it seems to apply to a lot of situations having to do with land management and the way we humans interact with native habitat. And I can think of no issue where that saying is more appropriate than in the area of riparian area management. We humans tend to do the very worst job of land management when it comes to riparian areas. Riparian areas are the most important part of the land and the areas that are the most easily, and most often, abused.

I recently attended a day-long symposium on riparian and stream ecosystems in which one of the speakers presented a list of "myths and misperceptions" about creeks and rivers. The list included the ideas that floods, droughts, and vertical banks are all bad, that removal of trees will result in greater streamflow, that rivers should be wide and straight, that large downed logs should be removed, and that humans have to "fix" damaged creeks.

A lot of these misperceptions are based on a lack of understanding, or misunderstanding, of the physics or mechanics of water flowing in a stream and picking up and depositing sediment and the storage of water in the banks of the floodplain.

To begin with, water doesn't flow in a straight line path down a creek or river, but rather a corkscrew pattern with the flow rate being faster at the surface and slower on the bottom. This causes the path of rivers to not be straight but to be winding, everything else being equal. Winding rivers flow slower and thus have less energy to carry sediment and cause erosion. Flow around a bend is fastest on the outside and this is where most bank erosion occurs and slowest on the inside, which is where most sediment is deposited.

Rivers and creeks with deeper channels and wider flood plains have more riparian sponge soil along the sides to hold more water to maintain the base flow between rain events. Conversely, rivers and creeks with wide, shallow channels and very little riparian sponge along the sides have little capacity to maintain a base flow between rain events. The way to build more flood plain area is to trap sediment, especially during flood events, and the way to do that is to have healthy diverse vegetation along the riparian area. Anything else that slows down the water flow, such as downed logs, helps to trap sediment because the slower the water moves, the less energy it has to keep sediment suspended and the more sediment will drop out.

If you have a riparian area on your property, you want to be trapping sediment from your upstream neighbors, not seeing your soil eroded and deposited on your downstream neighbors' property.

Storm Damage Along Your Creek? Don't Rush to Clean Up Too Much

While most of us in the Hill Country were spared the devastating flood damage experienced by some of the folks in Blanco and Comal counties in 2015, the recent rains have certainly changed the look of a lot of creeks and rivers in our area. Some folks have experienced erosion of banks, some have seen deposition of alluvial soil, some have lost trees and other vegetation and many have accumulated debris ranging from leaf litter to large tree trunks.

While the changes that have occurred in most places are really just part of the natural functioning of riparian areas, many landowners consider these changes to be "damage," and our minds automatically react to damage with ideas of how to "repair" the damage that the flood "caused."

Unfortunately, the ideal picture many folks have in mind about how a riparian area should look is something that resembles a city park or a golf course, with closely mown grass and a few scattered trees. This leads to the idea after the flood that the area needs to be "cleaned up."

In fact, the experts agree that this is just the opposite of what a healthy, functioning riparian area should look like. Healthy riparian areas should have abundant vegetation of all types from the water's edge out into the flood plain, including sedges, rushes, grasses, shrubs and large trees.

Another misconception about riparian areas is that everything should be done to "speed up" the flow of water, a view that seems to be particularly common in cities. But doing so just passes flood problems downstream and in speeding up the flow of water, what is really happening is increasing the energy of the flowing water which leads to more severe erosion. We really need to slow down the flow of water to reduce the energy to reduce erosion and to allow the water to soak into the porous soil in the floodplain. And what slows down the flow of water and dissipates the energy and reduces erosion? Vegetation, both alive and dead.

If you had erosion during the flood, it may have been because you didn't have enough vegetation to slow down the water and hold the soil in place (or the flow was not slowed enough upstream). If you had deposition of alluvial soil coming from upstream, that deposition is building up the floodplain and increasing the riparian sponge which stores the water along the creek or river providing for the base flow between rain events. If you have had an accumulation of organic debris (leaves, limbs, tree trunks), that material will help to slow down the water during the next flood and help to trap sediment. It also adds organic matter to the soil making it more fertile.

I am certainly not in a position to tell every landowner of a riparian area exactly what they should do with their property. What I am suggesting is that every landowner educate themselves about the functioning of their riparian area before embarking on any "cleanup" work. (Kind of like the old carpenter's rule, "measure twice, cut once")

Most of the experts I know are more likely to recommend leaving the area alone rather than to embark on a massive cleanup. Employing heavy machinery in a riparian area almost always makes things worse rather than better. Mother Nature will eventually "repair" the "damage," but she doesn't necessarily do so on a time scale that humans like. And the results will be what Mother Nature thinks is best.

My advice to landowners with flood damage is to get expert opinions from government agencies such as the Natural Resources Conservation Service or the Texas Parks and Wildlife Department. Importantly, their advice is not influenced by any financial considerations as to whether you do or do not take their advice.

WATER

As a naturalist, there is one topic that I can count on being able to get the attention of even the most nature-apathetic person in the Hill Country—Water! Everyone thinks about it, everyone worries about it, everyone has an opinion about it, some very informed, some not so much. I have never seen any survey data on the subject, but I suspect most big-city dwellers have a very different view of water and its future supply than the average Hill Country resident.

I don't expect that the following essays will necessarily change anyone's mind about how they feel about water, but I hope to raise the main issues in a way that improves some folks understanding of the issues.

Water: Where it is, Where it Comes From, Where it Goes

The water cycle, or hydrologic cycle, is a depiction or description of where water is on the planet, how it moves from one place to another and the factors that influence these movements. To begin with, a couple of astonishing facts.

First, the amount of water on the planet is essentially constant. In spite of how it may seem to us during droughts or floods, no water is actually being destroyed and none is being created. Secondly, of all the water on Earth, only 2.75 percent of it is fresh water! And this is distributed as follows; 2.05 percent is frozen in ice sheets at the poles and in glaciers, 0.68 percent is ground water in aquifers, and only 0.011 percent is in surface water in lakes and rivers. And most surface water is confined to two places, the Great Lakes and a large lake in Russia. So percentage wise, that doesn't leave much for the rest of us.

Taking a look at the big picture of the water cycle first, the sun provides the energy necessary to evaporate water from the oceans, and as the water evaporates, it leaves behind the salt in the ocean and becomes fresh water. As the water rises in the atmosphere, it cools and condenses into tiny droplets to form clouds. The clouds can be carried by winds, which are also fueled by energy from the sun, until conditions are right for precipitation in the form of rain, hail or snow.

As the rain hits the land, it either runs off the surface downhill into a stream or river, or it soaks into the soil. From there the water either seeps underground into deep aquifers or flows in shallow aquifers downhill toward the river valleys providing the base flow of the river as the water runs back into the ocean. If the precipitation is in the form of snow, it will stay where it falls until it either melts or, to a smaller extent, sublimes back into the atmosphere.

Some of these processes take only a few days, some can take thousands of years. If the rain occurs over the ocean, then the water is returned to the ocean in a matter of days. If it falls over land as rain, it may take several months to flow downhill in streams and rivers to get back to the ocean. If it falls as snow in the higher mountains, it may take even longer. If it falls over the Arctic or Antarctic, it may take thousands of years before it returns to the sea. Some ice on Antarctica has been dated as 800,000 years old!

There are a few other aspects of the water cycle. When water soaks into the ground, some of it can evaporate back into the atmosphere directly from the ground. If the water is instead taken up by a plant, one of two things can happen. If the water taken up by the plant is used in photosynthesis to produce carbohydrates (starches, sugars, cellulose) then some water is actually used in that chemical reaction and becomes part of the carbohydrate molecules. Much of the water taken up by a plant, however, is not used in photosynthesis, but is re-evaporated from the leaves of the plant in a process called evapotranspiration. This transport of water from the roots to the leaves helps bring minerals from the roots up to the leaves.

The water that was used in the chemical reaction to make plant tissues is released again as water when the plant material decomposes or is burned or eaten.

Obviously all of these processes take place without any help from us humans, and in fact have been taking place long before there were humans. So you might ask, what does this all have to do with us? Well, if we own land, we can have an effect on how the water cycle works on our property. We want the rain that falls from the sky to reach the ground and to soak into the ground, not run off. And we want any water not used by the plants to replenish the local aquifers as well as the deep aquifers where our water wells are.

We can accomplish this by managing for healthy native grasses that increase infiltration into the soil, prevent runoff and reduce evaporation from the soil.

Understanding Aquifers: What They Are and What They Are Not

First, a disclaimer. I am not trained in geology, hydrology or any related field. I am certainly not an "expert" in these fields, so what I say below is likely to be an oversimplification. But I know many people are interested in our aquifers and may also have some misconceptions about them. Hopefully, I can shed some light on the subject.

First, I think a very common misconception is that an aquifer is a large underground "lake" or an underground cavern filled with water. Another common misconception is that the water in an aquifer is separate from and/or different from the water in our creeks, rivers and lakes.

My dictionary defines an aquifer as "a water-bearing stratum of permeable rock, sand or gravel." I think the best way to envision an aquifer is to think about filling a water glass to the top with sand, so that the glass is "full" of sand. But you can still pour some water into the glass, slowly, and you won't displace the sand. You can see the level of the water in the glass, and you will eventually fill it up with water also. Even though the sand had "filled" the glass, there was still room to add water to the glass—the water was simply filling the spaces between the sand grains; the spaces usually referred to as "pores."

Some aquifers are actually strata of unconsolidated sand or gravel, although many, if not most, are in fact rock. Sandstone rock is, in its simplest form, just sand grains stuck together to form a rock. Many other types of rock, including limestone, which would look to us to be a "solid" rock, do indeed have pores that can hold water.

In order to be a significant aquifer, the formation has to have three important properties: sufficient pores to hold a useful amount of water, the pores have to be connected together enough to allow for the flow of water (something that is referred to a "permeability"), and the formation has to be above a layer of rock that is not permeable.

If the pore space is too small, referred to as a low-porosity formation, then it can't hold enough water to be useful to humans. If the permeability of the formation is so low that water will not flow from the rock into a well-bore, then it can't support a useful water-well. (In the oil field, low permeability formations are made useful by fracking.) Finally, if there is no low-permeability formation below the strata in question, then water will not accumulate in that strata but will simply seep deeper underground—something has to "confine" the water in a permeable formation to keep it in place.

Those of us who live in the San Antonio TV coverage area are accustomed to hearing about the Edwards aquifer and its state of recharge or depletion. The Edwards is an unusual aquifer in that it actually has places where the water resides simply in pools or large cracks and holes in the limestone, and in addition, there are places on the surface where, during heavy rainstorm events, rainwater can actually flow directly from the surface down into the aquifer. These characteristics make the Edwards unusually easy to be recharged by rainstorm events and for the water to easily flow through the highly permeable formation. But even the Edwards is not a giant cavern full of water covering many miles.

In our area, underneath the Edwards in many places lies one or more aquifers often referred to as the Trinity. These aquifers are much slower to display any recharge reaction to a rainstorm event. Like many other aquifers around the country, exactly where and how they are recharged is not as clear, but it probably involves either water seeping into the ground and down through many layers of soil and rock, or possibly in places where the formation is close to the surface, it is recharged from creeks or streams.

Water from both the Edwards and the other aquifers may in places provide the springs that feed our creeks and rivers, and in other places water from the creeks and rivers may help recharge the aquifers. And we don't always know where all of those places are. It is all the same water, it just resides in different places at different times and in time it will all flow downhill to the ocean, evaporate and start the process all over again.

The Ogallala Aquifer. Lessons for Us All?

A recent long, detailed, article in the National Geographic brought back memories. It was entitled, "To the Last Drop" with the subtitle, "The Ogallala aquifer turned the U.S. Midwest into the nation's breadbasket. What happens when the water runs out?"

I grew up between Lubbock and Midland on the southern edge of the Ogallala aquifer. When I was 10 years old, I started to work for the cotton farmer who had a farm next to the oil camp where we lived. My first job was to set syphon tubes to syphon water from an open ditch into the rows of cotton (My hands were almost too small to do that!) A year or two later the farmer bought aluminum pipe with sprinklers that we could move, one joint at a time, to water the cotton.

The water for all of that irrigation came from wells drilled into the Ogallala aquifer. They were what I considered at the time to be huge wells, 6 inch pipes full of water coming out of the ground, powered by old car engines running on propane.

All of the 6 years I worked for that farmer was during the "drought of the 50s," but that cotton got all the water it needed. Granted, I was just a kid, but I don't remember a lot of talk and worry about the drought back then—we had all this water just underground.

The Ogallala spans most all of the Texas panhandle north of Odessa all the way north through Nebraska. For much of the panhandle and all the way into Kansas, the aquifer is severely depleted and is becoming more so every year, including the spot where I worked on that farm. In those areas, the Ogallala is not being recharged to any significant extent—the water they are mining has been there since the last ice age about 15,000 years ago! Much of the aquifer in Nebraska is being recharged.

In the area surrounding Lubbock, 73,000 wells are in use. Some are so weak that no single well can feed the big center-pivot sprinkler systems now in use, so multiple wells feed one sprinkler system. (The record is 21 wells for one system!).

Ground water in Kansas and Nebraska belongs to the state and the state issues water rights to property owners, but many of those areas have more water rights granted than exist in the ground. In Texas, landowners can pump as much water as they want from under their land.

In a book on the history of the aquifer, *Ogallala Blue* by William Ashworth, he argues that it is not cotton or corn or dairies that are to blame for the decline of the aquifer, but rather cotton and corn and dairies and alfalfa and millet and beef cattle and lawn sprinklers that are to blame.

It takes about 460 gallons of water to raise and process the beef for one, quarter-pound hamburger!

Down here in the Hill Country we don't have the Ogallala aquifer, but rather the Edwards and/or Trinity. While the Edwards down in the vicinity of San Antonio demonstratively recharges in large rains, the rest of the Hill Country aquifers recharge much more slowly. We, of course, don't have the truly large scale irrigated farms of the High Plains, where the green circles of center-pivot farms can be seen from space. We do certainly have some of the same type of irrigated farms seen in the panhandle, but they just are not nearly as numerous or as large as those over the Ogallala. Which is good, because our aquifers are nowhere as massive as the Ogallala once was.

But the folks that live in the areas where the Ogallala is severely depleted are looking at a future that is highly uncertain and for which there are no solutions in sight. We are not facing that kind of problem in the Hill Country. Yet. But it should be a wake-up call for all of us that we live in this area of finite water supply as well as increasing population projections, and that there are potential problems on the horizon.

Everyone; farmers, ranchers, country or city dwellers, needs to be aware of the issues and pay attention to any and all proposals for dealing with this problem. And we should remember H.L. Menken's admonition, "For every complex problem, there is a solution that is simple, neat and wrong."

Water, Our Most Precious Resource. What We Have is All We Will Ever Have.

Will Rogers once remarked about land, "They ain't making any more of it." Well, he could have said the same thing about water, and been equally correct. The amount of water on the planet is fixed and has been for millions of years. Ninety-seven percent of all water is salt water, over 2 percent is locked up as ice, leaving less than 1 percent as fresh, liquid water.

Recently, a San Antonio TV weatherman exclaimed, after they had some good rains that raised the aquifer level a little, that "we might be able to get out of stage 1 water restrictions." The excitement in his voice was probably shared by many of his listeners, but it reveals an attitude that is inconsistent with the situation we are in. The idea that once restrictions are lifted, we can "use all the water we want," may be widely held, but it is simply not supported by the facts.

There are still individuals and corporations using as much water as they can to make as much money as possible before all the wells are dry. It is legal for them to do so. But is it right?

Think of it this way. You are an astronaut on a trip to Mars with 5 others. Because of space and weight limitations, there are a limited number of food packets on board for all of you for the whole trip. You discover that one of your colleagues has been sneaking extra meals, depriving the rest of you of your fair share. How would you feel about that?

I have heard people say, about our future water situation, "Well, they will figure something out," thinking it is analogous to our future energy situation. But it is not the same thing. We continue to receive many times more energy from the sun every day than we can possibly use, so it is theoretically possible for new technologies to be developed to provide us with energy well into the future. But we don't, and won't, get any more water, the Earth has all it will ever have.

Yes, it is possible to desalinate salt water, making fresh water from sea water, but this process requires huge amounts of energy. More electric power plants create their own problems. Current power plants using coal, oil, natural gas or nuclear fuel require very large amounts of water. Can society absorb these costs? Certainly not for agricultural use. People are already complaining about comparatively small increases in the price of water.

These are obviously extremely complicated issues which will be with us for the foreseeable future. I mention them here only to make the point that we should not assume that "They will figure something out." We should instead take the attitude that our water supply is finite, that its replenishment is uncertain, and that using more than we each absolutely need is wrong. But of course, what one person considers an essential use, another may see as wasteful. It is going to take some time for us to sort out how to resolve these kinds of issues.

Most things that are in limited supply are apportioned out according to who can afford the price. Society thinks it is OK for those with more money to consume more, have more expensive cars, houses, clothes, etc. But water is essential to all life, biologically, and our society is structured on the principle that everyone is entitled to a certain amount of water. Should we ration water on the ability to pay? I hope not.

In the meantime, we all need to make water use such a part of our lives that we think about conservation whatever we do inside or outside of our homes. Water-efficient appliances inside, water-efficient landscapes and drip irrigation outside, and rainwater catchment should all be considered.

"Saving The Water and The Soil Must Start Where the First Raindrop Falls"

Lyndon Johnson said that back in 1947. He was right back then, and it is still true today. And where does the first raindrop fall? On the land. And in the Hill Country, the land generally means rangeland.

So, as discussed before, what is on the land, or what is not on the land, and its condition makes all the difference in the quantity and quality of the water available to us all.

In an experiment under the conditions of a very heavy rainstorm, 24 percent of the rain falling on native bunchgrass pasture ran off carrying about 175 pounds of soil per acre with it. In a similar experiment, when the rain fell on bare ground, 75 percent ran off carrying almost 5,000 pounds of soil per acre!

Erosion is the worst thing that can happen to our rangeland because less soil means the land can grow less vegetation. Soil cannot be replaced in our lifetimes. Clearly, from the standpoint of keeping the rainwater on the land where it can soak in, native bunchgrasses are desirable. Any vegetation, dead or alive, however, is better than bare ground.

But too much vegetation can be detrimental also. In areas with large, dense juniper (cedar), these trees intercept significant amounts of light rains and smaller amounts of moderate rains. The water caught on the leaves then evaporates back into the atmosphere. So growing good stands of native grasses and managing cedar cover can be somewhat beneficial to capturing rainfall as well as maintaining good habitat for livestock and wildlife. But the overall effect of cedar is probably not as great as some people believe.

Rangeland management has evolved over the years from concentrating on maximizing the number of livestock that could be raised (1800s though early 1900s), to gradually being concerned about growing more forage (mid to late 1900s) to improving the habitat for both livestock and wildlife (currently). These latter management practices allow ranchers to have multi-use rangeland which not only allows for livestock production, but also for wildlife habitat. This can lead to extra income from hunting, bird watching, photography, hiking, and other uses by the general public.

Many have heard the story of the Bamberger Ranch Preserve which had no surface water and no working wells when David Bamberger bought the property. But now that good management practices have been in place for some time, Bamberger not only has springs now and a beautiful lake and several creeks, but the excess water captured on his ranch now flows into the Colorado River and the folks in Austin have water they didn't have before, at no cost to them.

Fortunately, the same management practices that work to improve the habitat for multiple uses also provide the best conditions for optimal water capture. And for those of us in the semi-arid Hill Country, the latter may become even more important in the future. I was surprised recently when I read in a range management textbook, published in 1995, the following statement, "We believe that in the near future range management practices will be geared primarily toward water production rather than forage production…" (Holechek, Pieper and Herbel, "Range Management. Principles and Practices.") That prediction may be pre-mature, but it underscores the importance of good land management to our water. Just as Lyndon Johnson said.

Saving Water and Work at The Same Time

As much as 60 percent of municipal water demand in the summer is for outside use—watering lawns, landscape plants, washing cars, etc. A large part of this use is unnecessary and wasteful. We are reminded of the need to conserve water as the cities and towns begin to issue water restrictions. Here are some ideas that will not only save water, but will also save you some work.

Driving around town lately, I have noticed people mowing lawns that have largely gone dormant due to the hot, dry conditions. And I ask myself, if the grass has pretty much quit growing, why mow it? I think some of this is just habit, part of the weekly routine. But it is also counterproductive. Mowing frequently, and especially with the mower set to cut the grass short is harder on the grass and leads to the rapid loss of soil moisture.

Mowing less frequently, and especially with the mower set at a high setting, allows the grass to grow a little longer. Longer grass shades the ground more, keeping it very much cooler (20-30 degrees) and thus reducing evaporation. This means taller grass needs less water, and it requires less work on your part as well. Never cut more than a third of the grass during mowing, as doing so weakens the grass plant, including the roots. Also, allowing the grass clippings to accumulate, at least up to a point, also adds to the shading/insulating effect, keeping the ground even cooler.

If you happen to be at the stage of putting in a lawn, the most water-saving things you can do are to keep the size of the lawn to a minimum and to choose the most water-saving grass species. Buffalograss requires much less water than does bermudagrass, which in turn requires much less water than the water-hog, St. Augustine. The latter two are non-native and require fertilizer, whereas buffalograss does not.

Generally, watering is best done early in the morning.

Many of us who live in the country and thus don't have to worry about what the neighbors will say, have "lawns" of mixtures of native grasses, *i.e.* whatever native grasses happen to grow there. These "lawns" usually get mowed only once or twice a year, maybe 3" high, and in many cases, don't get watered at all!

Another water-saving idea is to use mulch on flower beds, around perennials, shrubs and trees. Mulch provides the same function as taller grass does, it shades the soil and reduces evaporation. Too much mulch can be counterproductive, however, because it soaks up too much of light rains which never reach the soil and during wet periods can support mold and mildew. I think one to two inches of mulch is ideal. And once the mulch is in place, there will be fewer weeds to pull, and less watering to do, so again, less work.

As one whose cars are perpetually dirty, I find it easy to forgo the habit of washing cars. During times of water restrictions, everyone can have a dirty car with a clean conscience. And we can all certainly refrain from washing driveways, patios, etc., during these times.

Of course, rainwater harvesting, even if it is just a few rain barrels, is the ultimate water- saving practice and something we should all think seriously about. That subject is discussed in a later essay.

Benjamin Franklin said it best, "When the well is dry, we know the worth of water."

How to Conserve Water AND Save Your Plants

Well, the drought continues with no real end in sight. We cannot and should not waste water, but we don't want our plants to die either. So what are homeowners to do? Fortunately, there are a number of things we can do that might help.

As the drought continues, different plants will suffer to different degrees. In general, the least xeric and most recently planted plants will suffer the most, followed by established plants native to higher rainfall areas, followed by well-established native plants, and finally xeric (drought-tolerant) plants from more arid areas such as West Texas.

So, for instance, shade-loving plants such as American beautyberry and wild red columbine, or plants native to wet areas such as buttonbush, will be the first to become stressed, as will any newly planted tree or shrub. Most established native trees and shrubs may have put out less growth and smaller leaves than usual, but will likely survive with little if any attention. Cacti and succulents and plants such as cenizo and zexmenia will likely survive without any help from us.

Since we live in an area that has, and will continue to have, limited water availability, we need to do everything we can to conserve water. That means using the water we do use in the most efficient manner possible. One of the first things we can do is to know how much water a plant needs and where, when and how often to water it. There are some rules of thumb to go by here.

Small trees, especially newly planted ones, should have 6 to 8 gallons of water per trunk diameter inch per week. So a tree with a 2-inch diameter trunk should have 12 to 16 gallons of water each week. These are optimum amounts for good growth. When water is limited, you can probably get by with half that amount and still keep it healthy. Larger, more established native trees can go longer between watering, maybe only once every 2 or 3 weeks in dry summers, and no extra water other times.

For smaller shrubs or perennials, decide how much water you think they need based on how large they are, and water them for the appropriate time. Then check a few days later. If they are wilting, you need to water them longer.

Assuming you are using a hose-end nozzle to do the watering, you need to know how much water it puts out. You can get an empty gallon milk jug or five-gallon bucket and time how long it takes to fill it, so you know how much time it takes to water each plant.

Water only once a week. Watering lightly daily or every 2 or 3 days is a waste of water (except for newly planted perennials). Also, don't water the foliage, it doesn't help and may harm the plant. Water under the dripline (the circle under the tree just under the outermost leaves), not around the trunk. The feeder roots are mostly concentrated in that area.

Don't be fooled by some of the drizzles or light rains we get. Anything less than a quarter inch is pretty much useless as far as most trees, shrubs and perennials are concerned.

If you have too much mulch, brush it away from the area you are watering so you can get the water to the mineral soil where the roots live, not just on the top mulch. You can rake the mulch back after watering. If you don't have mulch covering any bare ground, get some—it is the best thing you can do for your plants.

I'm sorry, but I have no good suggestions for lawns. The only native turf grass, buffalograss, goes dormant in times like this and looks dead, but will come back with rain. Bermudagrass probably will as well. My best advice is to have as little lawn as possible.

Drip Irrigation: Why it is Best and How to Do It

Getting the right amount of water to our plants, at the right time, without wasting water is a constant struggle for all gardeners. And even many long-time, experienced gardeners don't do it very well. Using drip irrigation is one technique that helps both to do it right and to save water.

By drip irrigation I am talking about a system of laying out plastic tubing in flower or vegetable beds or under trees that is designed to slowly emit drops of water in a pattern that covers the area to be watered. This solves several watering problems at once.

First, it puts the water exactly where it should be, directly on the ground. Watering with a sprinkler or hose-end nozzle wets the leaves of plants, which is wasted. Only after the leaves are thoroughly wet does any water have a chance to fall to the ground. And because the rate of drip is slow, all of the water soaks into the ground and none runs off, again saving water.

Also, once installed, drip irrigation can be a time-saver for you as well as allowing automatic operation during the optimum time of the day for watering, even if you are still in bed!

The type of drip irrigation I am referring to is not generally applicable for lawn watering unless the drip tubing is installed under the lawn before the grass is grown. But installation for other applications is something most home-owners can do themselves.

There are two different types of drip systems. One system involves what are called "soaker hoses" which are essentially just garden hoses that happen to be somewhat porous so that when attached to a water source they "leak" water in small drops all along the hose. These are relatively inexpensive, easy to use and can be moved around as needed.

The other system consists of light ½ inch plastic tubing which has molded into it at regular intervals (9, 12 or 18 inches) a structure that emits water droplets at about 1 gal/hr., so when laid out in a garden, water will drip at the above intervals along the tubing. The tubing is generally referred to as "inline emitter tubing." These systems are designed to be more or less permanent installations, although they can certainly be removed and reused elsewhere.

There are many accessories designed to be used with these inline emitter systems. One of the most common being what is called "mainline" tubing that does not have emitters and can be used to carry water from one tree or one bed to another without dripping water. Another is smaller ¼ inch inline emitter tubing that can be attached to either of the above ½ inch tubings if extra water is desired in a given small area. And of course there are all sorts of connectors and other things designed to be used with the system, most relatively inexpensive.

There are numerous individual small emitters that one can buy to water small individual plants. My experience with these small emitters is that they are not as reliable as the inline tubing and they are subject to plugging or air-locking. Some of these small emitters actually put out a very fine spray which to me appear to waste a lot of water to evaporation.

I would urge anyone thinking about installing such a system to first obtain a catalogue and learn about the parts available. Before installing a drip system, one needs to draw out a plan and determine the amount of tubing and number of connectors that will be needed. There are several companies that supply this equipment that can be found on the internet.

One of the advantages of a drip system is that it can be set up with a timer to go on and off automatically at regular intervals. This has a lot of advantages of watering at the best times of the day and of taking care of things when you are away. However, automatic systems can waste water by continuing to water even just after a rain, but there are moisture sensors that can tell the timers not to come on if it has just recently rained.

Rainwater Harvesting: The Basics of Why and How

I doubt that there are many Hill Country residents that are not aware that the future of our water supply is uncertain at best. It is not at all clear that governments and water-supply companies will be able in the future to find enough water for even the current population, let alone the projected increase in the population. I expect that it is highly likely that some form of water restrictions or regulations will become much more common and severe as time goes by.

There might not be much that individuals can do about any of the above, but there are some things individuals can do to take matters in their own hands. Individuals can choose to use less water for landscapes, especially water-hungry non-native lawns, as well as to conserve water in many other ways. But harvesting rainwater is something many landowners can do that is a benefit to the landowners themselves as well as to society as a whole.

Among the reasons for harvesting rainwater are:

To avoid drilling a well.

Current water source is unreliable or of poor quality.

To have purer, soft water free of chemicals, pesticides and hormones.

To be able to water plants during water restrictions.

To not use more than your fair share of a scarce resource.

So what is required to harvest rainwater? In its simplest form, what is needed are gutters on your roof, downspouts from the gutters to a tank of some kind, and a faucet near the bottom of the tank. Such a system will capture and store rainwater that you can use to run a hose or drip tubing to flowerbeds or vegetable gardens.

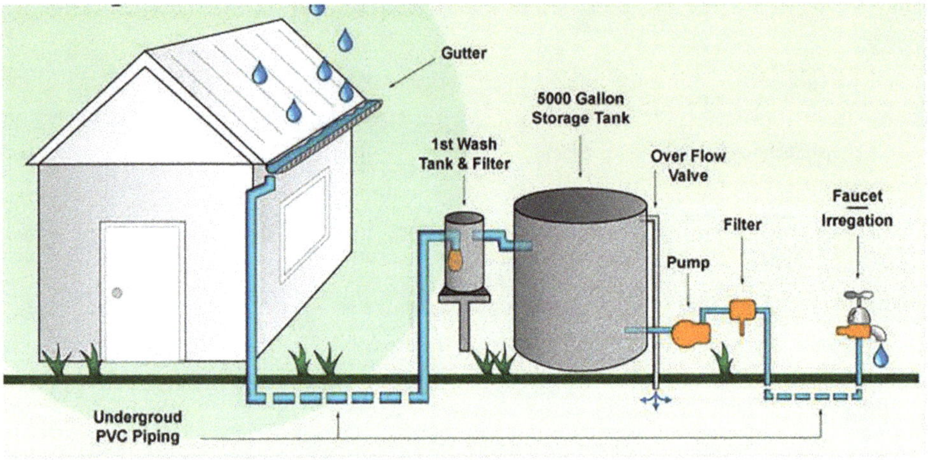

Schematic of a rainwater harvesting system at Riverside Nature Center"

In a more complicated system that can furnish all your water needs inside the house including drinking, cooking and bathing, you still need the gutters and downspouts, piping to carry the water to larger storage tanks, several filters of various kinds, a pump to pump the water to all the places in your house, and a UV sterilizer to make the water safe for drinking.

And there are all kinds of systems in between these two extremes. The accompanying drawing is of an intermediate system used for irrigation. You can view the actual system by visiting Riverside Nature Center in Kerrville or Cibolo Nature Center in Boerne.

What kinds of materials are used? While metal roofs are preferred, composition asphalt shingles are acceptable. Most all piping is inexpensive PVC pipe which is one of the materials now used in new construction. Storage tanks are either plastic (polyethylene—the same as is used in milk bottles and gallon water jugs), fiberglass or, for larger tanks, a metal shell with a rubber liner. All other components are as used for regular water systems.

How much water can you capture? One thousand square feet of roof area will capture 600 gallons of water in a one-inch rain. A typical 2000 square foot house is likely to have at least 2300 square feet of roof footprint, so a one-inch rain will capture almost 1400 gallons of water in a one-inch rain. Even in a less than "average" rainfall year of 25 inches, that is a total of 35,000 gallons, or nearly 100 gallons a day!

One point should be made because it is a common question. If everyone captured rainwater, won't the river dry up? The answer is "No" for several reasons. First, even if most people captured rainwater, the area of roofs, at least in Hill Country cities, is a small fraction of the total land area. Furthermore, we use water, we do not destroy it. Currently, the city takes water from the river or the aquifers and you use it in your house or on your lawn.

The water used outside either soaks into the ground and flows downhill toward the river or evaporates from the ground or vegetation. The water you use inside goes to the sewer system, is treated, and then either used on golf courses or is returned to the river. When you capture rainwater, you are just holding it for a time, but you are using it in the same way as city water, so its fate is the same as city water, except that the storm water amounts are reduced, thus lessening the effects of floods.

It's not magic. It works. Many of us are doing it.

Are We Polluting Our Water?

A few weeks ago I attended an all-day presentation by the Texas Watershed Steward Program. It was presented by a group from the Department of Soil and Crop Services at Texas A & M. I have attended literally dozens of programs having to do with the many aspects of water, its capture, conservation and use, but this program had a slightly different emphasis.

Just so everyone understands the term: A watershed is the area that, if a raindrop were to fall anywhere in that area and run downhill to a creek or river, all of that area would be the watershed area for that creek or river. In some other countries, this is called the watercatchment area because it is the area that catches the rainfall that replenishes the river.

Folks in the Hill Country tend to think most often about the quantity of our water. This program also included water quality as something we should think about. What comes to mind when I mention water quality? Is it clear? Does it have an odor? A bad taste? These are all certainly issues related to the quality of water, but not everything associated with water quality can be described that simply. Perfectly clear, odorless, tasteless water can be severely polluted.

Here in the Hill Country we are spoiled, I guess, by the usually clear, odorless, tasteless water in our creeks and rivers and in our groundwater. We tend to think of pollution as something around big cities, on the coast, near industrial facilities, etc., but it is not necessarily so.

Pollution is characterized as coming from either a point source or non-point source. Point source pollution can be thought of as entering the water body from a pipe as a discharge from a specific facility such as a factory, refinery, sewage treatment facility or feed lot. Non-point source pollution enters the water from many different places.

It is relatively easy for federal and state agencies to find and regulate point-source pollution because where it is coming from can be easily identified. Not so with non-point source pollution.

What are the types of non-point source pollution and where do they come from?

One type of pollution is bacteria, coming from livestock, pet waste, wildlife (feral hogs, ducks and geese) and failing septic systems. Another type of pollution are nutrients (nitrates and phosphates) which can also come from livestock, pet wastes, and septic systems, but in addition can come from fertilizers washed from farms and lawns.

Another type of pollution is sediment (soil) washed off of farms, overgrazed rangeland, construction sites, road maintenance, gravel operations, etc. Finally, toxic and hazardous substances can be washed from landfills, junkyards, parking lots, streets, underground storage tanks, and may include gasoline, oil, pesticides and herbicides.

Bacteria can obviously introduce disease-causing organisms to both surface and ground water and can make for hazardous swimming, drinking, and polluted shellfish beds. Excess nutrients can cause algae blooms which deplete oxygen levels, killing fish and causing turbidity. Sediment can silt in lakes and ponds and cause turbidity reducing plant growth and killing aquatic organisms. Toxic materials can be carcinogenic or mutagenic and can accumulate in the tissues of fish and ultimately humans.

So anyone who has property with livestock or pets or a septic system or uses fertilizers or herbicides or pesticides or drives a car may contribute to polluted surface water and in some cases even groundwater.

What can we as individuals do to reduce non-point source pollution? We can manage our land to capture rainfall and have it soak into the ground, not run off. We can make sure our septic systems are functioning properly. We can keep livestock from concentrating near lakes, creeks or rivers. We can pick up pet waste. We can use as little pesticide, herbicide and fertilizer as possible and as infrequently as possible. We can dispose of all toxic and hazardous materials properly, certainly not pouring them down the storm drain or house drain.

Most importantly, we can educate ourselves about the causes of pollution, how we might be contributing to it, and then change any harmful practices we might have been doing in the past.

Everyone who lives in a watershed, which is every one of us, owes it to ourselves and our neighbors to help keep our precious water clean. Just because we live here in the Hill Country, far from the most serious sources of pollution, doesn't mean we can ignore the problem.

What Should We Do When There is Not Enough Water?

A couple of recent events have prompted the question, "What should we do when there is not enough water?"

In a recent article in Texas Parks and Wildlife magazine, Jenna Craig describes the dilemma faced by the Lower Colorado River Authority in allocating the decreasing amount of water in the river and lakes among the various demands of municipalities (more than 1 million people), businesses, industry, agriculture, wildlife and the environment. Lakes Travis and Buchanan are currently at 37 percent of capacity and inflows have been near historic lows for several years.

Back during higher rainfall times and when the population of the area was lower, water flowing into the lakes was more than was needed by municipalities and the lakes were full so the excess water flowed down the river to industries near the coast and was diverted (as it had been for over 100 years) to rice farmers. And still there was enough water flowing into Matagorda Bay to reduce the salinity and make for ideal habitat for young shrimp, oysters and fish, as well as for ideal migratory waterfowl habitat.

But now, LCRA has had to suspend sending water to the rice farmers with the devastating effect you can imagine. And unless the lower Colorado River basin receives substantial rainfall soon to provide the environmental flows necessary for the health of the Gulf fisheries and migratory waterfowl, that habitat will be severely damaged. Municipal water users trump agriculture and the environment by virtue of sheer numbers of people.

The second event that I recently became aware of is a plan by the Texas State Soil and Water Conservation Board that has as its goal to increase the amount of water flowing off the land and to decrease the amount infiltrating into the ground. The idea is to get rainwater off the land as quickly and efficiently as possible and to have it run into lakes and reservoirs where it will be available for municipalities.

This turns out to be an example of a simple solution to a complex problem that is fundamentally wrong. Most experts would define an ideal functioning Hill Country ecosystem as one with a diversity of native vegetative species from the ground to the tree crown with little bare ground. Good native grass cover slows down the flow of water and easily absorbs the rainwater where the water can infiltrate into the shallow aquifers, flow downhill to the riparian areas where it is stored in the riparian sponge along the sides of the creeks providing the base flow for the creeks.

But the goal of the TSSWCB is just the opposite of the above-described ideal ecosystem. In order to maximize the amount of rainfall that runs off the land, they would subsidize landowners to remove cedar, but without any requirement, or even any encouragement, that the land be well-managed thereafter. The maximum amount of runoff means the maximum amount of erosion and the minimum amount of vegetation. As more water runs off and less soaks into the ground, the amount of vegetation decreases and as the amount of vegetation decreases more runoff will occur and less recharge of the shallow aquifers and riparian creek-banks will result. In time the land will have less soil, less vegetation, more rocks and fewer springs and seeps. The land will become less and less productive, for either livestock or wildlife, and the process of desertification will begin.

In short, managing for maximum runoff would destroy our Hill Country landscape and leave us, and the cities, with even less water in the future and the landowners with less useful and valuable land.

Back in 1947, Lyndon Johnson said, "Saving the water and the soil must begin where the first raindrop falls." He understood back then that a healthy, functioning ecosystem was essential not only for the health and productivity of the land, but for efficient capture and storage of rainwater. The TSSWCB plan will result in muddy water flowing into the lakes after every rain, but nothing flowing in between rains. A healthy system will capture the rain on the land and release it slowly as clear, pure water fed by the base-flow of the creeks and rivers.

But these are complicated concepts and people can easily be misled by simple answers to complex problems. There are lots of different demands on our limited water supply. Will we be smart enough to figure out the correct policies and optimal allocation? Only time will tell.

Where Can We Get More Water?

Recently, Charlie Flatten, Water Policy Program Manager for the Hill Country Alliance spoke to our local Native Plant Society of Texas chapter on the subject of water. Among the things he discussed was a list of possible sources of "new" water, that is, water that we currently don't have available to us.

Before I discuss the options we have available to us, I should point out a few things. There is no such thing as "new water" from a global perspective—what we have is what we have always had and all that we will ever have. Further, the amount of rain that falls on Texas, which is the source of all of our fresh water, both ground and surface, is, if anything, more likely to decrease in the future rather than to increase. And the population of people demanding water will certainly increase in the future. Where will the water that these new people will demand come from?

One suggestion is to build new reservoirs. But there are several problems with this idea. First, all of the best places to build dams to create new reservoirs are already taken. Building a reservoir means condemning people's property and destroying native habitats. In the western half of the state, evaporation from reservoirs far exceeds the rate of rainfall—the evaporation from lakes Buchanan and Travis exceeds the amount of water used by Austin! And finally, but not insignificantly, building dams and reservoirs is an exceedingly lengthy and expensive process.

Desalinization is the closest thing to actually "creating" new water. But it doesn't actually create any new water, but simply removes the salt from sea water or brackish water to make it potable. This process is certainly doable—El Paso is doing it; San Antonio is building a facility to desalinate brackish water from deep underground aquifers. But the process creates mountains of salt and/or highly-saline water that must be disposed of safely and it requires huge amounts of energy, so it is expensive water.

Reuse of all municipal waste water is a process that puts many people off, but in a way we have been doing it for centuries. Cities have always been taking water from rivers, then treating the waste water to varying degrees, and pumping the "used, treated" water back into the river, where each downstream city does exactly the same thing. If the treatment process were much more robust and did a much better job of really cleaning up the water, then it could be put back into the city's municipal water supply. Wichita Falls has recently been doing this, but at significant expense.

Conservation is the cheapest form of new water. Any water that is not used today is free "new" water that is available for tomorrow. It is estimated that 17 percent of all the water put into city water systems is lost to leaks! In many older cities, water mains can be 100 years old. In the summer, 50 percent of the water used in Texas is to water exotic grass lawns! Harvesting rainwater can be considered conservation because when you use water that fell on your roof, you are not using water from the aquifer or the municipal system.

One attempt by individual cities to obtain "new" water for their use is what is called an interregional transfer where cities or commercial water companies build huge pipelines long distances, sometimes at a million dollars a mile, to "purchase" water and pump it to the cities. But where are they getting that water?

Frequently they are buying the water from individuals or companies who own the land. Because in Texas the landowner "owns" all the water in the aquifer(s) below the surface and can legally (sometimes requiring permits) pump all the water they want from the aquifer and sell it. There are, however, legal, ethical, and philosophical issues at play here when someone pumps so much water from the aquifer under their land that it depletes their neighbor's aquifer water. Water in aquifers is not stationary, but flows from one place to another. The people of Texas will eventually have to decide what is and what is not allowable in these situations.

This has been just a very brief summary of some of the issues that will be facing all of us for years, no, decades, to come. All Texans owe it to themselves and to their offspring, to learn as much about our options so we, collectively, make the right decisions. Water will cost us more in the future.

— SECTION V —

LAND MANAGEMENT

LAND STEWARDSHIP

What do I mean by "Land Stewardship?" My simple answer that I used to give to that question was taken from a part of the Texas Master Naturalist mission statement, namely, "the beneficial management of natural resources and natural areas," with the important word here being "beneficial." However, the longer I am involved with natural areas, and the more I listen to my friend Steve Nelle, I think a better, deeper, definition begins with what is in the heart and head of the land manager.

And, since Nelle and I are both Aldo Leopold devotees, I will let Leopold's words describe what I believe is a better view of land stewardship. He said, "We abuse land because we regard it as a commodity belonging to us. When we see land as a community to which we belong, we may use it with love and respect...That land is a community is a basic concept of ecology, but that land is to be loved and respected is an extension of ethics... A land ethic, then, reflects the existence of an ecological conscience, and this in turn reflects a conviction of individual responsibility for the health of the land."

To me, having an "ecological conscience" and a "conviction of individual responsibility for the health of the land" defines what a land steward is.

How land is managed matters more than just to the landowner. It matters to society as a whole. Healthy, well-managed land is better habitat for native animals, more productive for livestock production, better at capturing rainwater, more resilient at withstanding droughts, floods and diseases, is more valuable, and more beautiful than land that is not well managed.

We are losing agricultural land to "development" (roads, parking lots, shopping centers, suburbs, etc.), both in Texas and nationwide at an alarming rate. We are also, especially in the Hill Country, seeing land fragmentation in which larger ranchers are broken up into many smaller properties resulting in many more people, houses, water wells, septic systems, roads, free-ranging dogs and cats on a piece of land, greatly degrading the native habitat. And we are expecting the population of the state and the Hill Country to double in a few decades. This makes every acre of native habitat increasingly every more precious and deserving of being preserved.

Specifics of what practices constitute land stewardship will vary from place to place and on the condition and past management practices of the land. But the attitude, the goals, the priorities or land ethics of the landowner are what really determine how their land is managed. My goal with these essays and this book as well as my previous books is to help to instill in all landowners an "ecological conscience," to use Aldo Leopold's term. I have no doubt that everyone who has an ecological conscience will be good stewards of the land.

One final note here for landowners with 100 or more acres. All of your good land stewardship work can be easily undone by a future owner. The only way to prevent that is to put a Conservation Easement on the property to conserve it the way you left it into perpetuity. I highly recommend you contact a local land trust in look into doing this.

Aldo Leopold's Land Ethic Philosophy: An Outlook on Land Management We Should Follow

Aldo Leopold (1887-1948) was a forester, a conservationist, a teacher, a hunter, a naturalist and a prolific writer who lived in the first half of the twentieth century. He is most famous for writing *A Sand County Almanac*, although he also wrote a textbook on game management and over 500 articles, essays and papers on all aspects of conservation and the natural world. He co-founded the Wilderness Society and served on many state and national boards and commissions as well as the boards of several conservation organizations.

Leopold spent most of his time and energy on various aspects of native habitat conservation and game management. Perhaps his most important contribution to land and wildlife management and conservation was a philosophy he called the "Land Ethic."

To very briefly oversimplify his ideas, it would be that mankind is part of a community made up of the soil, the water, the plants, and the other animals and that all components of that community are important to the overall health (or condition) of the community (or land). Leopold didn't mean to imply that man does not occupy a special place in this community, or that his needs don't take priority—just that the condition of the soil, water, plants and other animals should also be considered.

Today, we tend to think of ethics as what is right or wrong in the way one treats his fellow man, although I think most people have a sense that cruelty to animals is ethically and morally wrong. But Leopold was asserting that there are ethically right and wrong ways men treat not only animals, but the soil and water and plants as well.

Obviously, there are subjective judgments involved in determining which land management practices are ethically right or wrong, and economics and man's survival must be part of that judgment.

In Leopold's time, this attitude was far from being generally accepted. It was not uncommon for farmers and ranchers back then to use up and abuse the land until it was no longer profitable and then to simply move to a fresh piece of land and repeat the process.

But today a lot of landowners who may never have heard of Aldo Leopold or the Land Ethic have also adopted an attitude that is certainly similar. Most landowners want to, "Leave the land in better shape than I found it" or to "Conserve this place for posterity." I don't know of anyone who buys a piece of land today that intends to "ruin it," or "degrade it" or "use it up."

Modern man has a huge impact on the ecosystem, on the health of the community of the soil, water, plants, animals and himself. It behooves us all to try to minimize that impact in every way we can, whether we own a large ranch, a small ranchette, a city lot or live in an apartment, we all impact the Natural World. And it is the Natural World, however degraded or compromised, that provides us with food, water, shelter, space to raise our children and a beautiful place to live.

So if we could all just give some thought to Leopold's ideas before we make decisions about what to do on or to our land, or what we consume, or what our impact on the land will be, we will be practicing good land ethics. We can all consume less and conserve more. We can adopt habits that conserve water and all other natural resources. We can learn how to live with less fertilizer, fewer pesticides, and all other non-essential things.

They are not making any more land, or water, or other natural resources. And we are using up natural areas in the name of "development" at an alarming pace. Leopold was ahead of his time. We need to pay attention to his ideas.

Is Our Land Healthy?

Healthy may not be a word commonly used to describe land these days, but the great conservationist Aldo Leopold used it in a lot of his writings in the 1920s, 30s and 40s. Leopold was also the first to use the term "land ethic."

Today, we might be more likely to use terms like ecosystem, or native habitat, to talk about what Leopold meant by "land." Modern range scientists do sometimes rate the condition of a native habitat as being either healthy, at risk, or degraded.

So what are the characteristics of a healthy native habitat? I would say that the two most important characteristics are diversity and sustainability. Diversity refers to the number of native species of plants and animals in a particular area and sustainability means the collection of plants and animals can live together in the area long term without significant changes in the numbers of any one species.

Diversity is almost the primary requirement of any well-functioning habitat. The opposite of diversity would be a monoculture in which only one species of plants is growing. Think a wheat field or bermudagrass pasture. These places are poor habitat for most all native animal species, especially year round.

An ideal native habitat would be composed of as many different species of plants and animals as historically lived in that area as possible. It would also be free of any non-native species. Probably no place in Texas remains as a perfect replica of what it might have been before European man arrived.

The greater the number of species of plants, the greater the variety of food they provide for a greater variety of animal species. A diversity of blooming plants means something is blooming throughout the spring, summer and fall. This provides for a variety of pollinators which in turn provide food for many species of birds and small animals. The greater the diversity of grass species the greater the diversity of soil microorganisms, the greater the porosity and fertility of the soil. Different vegetation from low-growing vines to the top of trees provide homes for many species of animals.

Such a diverse habitat is only healthy long term if it is sustainable. Sustainable means that year after year the diversity as well as the numbers of the various species is relatively stable. The number of animals that eat a certain species of plant does not become so great that it wipes out that plant or so few in number that the plant becomes invasive and chokes out other species of vegetation. The number of predators does not increase to the point of exterminating any species of prey, nor does the predator population drop so low as to allow prey species to overpopulate and destroy certain vegetation. Mother Nature manages to balance all of these things better than we do.

There is no question that there have been major changes in our native habitats since European man began to arrive in Texas, although the changes in the Hill Country and far west Texas are probably less obvious than other parts of the state that are more heavily farmed. But the parts of the Hill Country that are still in native pasture land would probably still be recognized by some of the early Texas explorers.

Certainly, most all parts of the Hill Country have been overgrazed in the past, and many are currently being overbrowsed as well. Cedar encroachment is certainly a problem for many properties. And the deer population is greater in most areas than 200 years ago. But much of the Hill Country is still an oak/juniper savanna and, not all, but most of the plants and animals that were here 200+ years ago are still here.

The good news is that there are many properties in the Hill Country that we would judge to be "Healthy," that are well-functioning native habitats with a diversity of flora and fauna not too unlike what it was in 1800 and with a demonstrated sustainability managed by good land stewards. And these land stewards are examples for all landowners to emulate.

Why the Condition of Hill Country Rangeland Matters to All of Us

I have written about the changes that have taken place in the Hill Country habitat since settlement, the conditions of current Hill Country properties and how these conditions could be improved. Many readers who do not own rural property may have been thinking none of these issues are a concern to them. They would be wrong. The condition of the rangeland around us matters to all of us.

My main point is that severely overgrazed, overbrowsed properties with no vegetation below the browse-line are undesirable and unproductive as are properties that have been taken over by cedar to the point of the exclusion of all other vegetation. A more ideal habitat would be one that is not overgrazed, overbrowsed or cedar-covered, but one with good stands of native grasses as well as a variety of native shrubs and trees that provides food, water and shelter for livestock and native wildlife.

Healthy, diverse, native, Hill Country habitats are a benefit to all of us, even to apartment dwellers in the city.

Healthy habitats are capable of producing more vegetation for both grazers as well as browsers on a year to year basis, because the plants are fundamentally healthy. That means that these properties are more productive both in terms of the capability of producing livestock and income for the owner as well as providing habitat for native white-tailed deer which can also increase the owner's income.

Healthy, productive rangelands mean more money in the local economy, more tax revenue to the local city and county governments, more employment and in general a better, more vibrant society that benefits us all.

Properties with good stands of native grasses and limited amounts of cedar are much better at capturing rainwater and allowing it to infiltrate into the soil where it nourishes the vegetation, but also seeps into local water tables and in some cases into deeper aquifers as well. It is water in the shallow water tables along the riparian areas of all of our creeks and streams that provide the base flow in times between rain events.

Properties with little grass cover and a lot of bare ground allow the water to runoff during a rainstorm, down into the creeks and downstream toward the Gulf of Mexico, taking a lot of our Hill Country soil with it, which also pollutes our surface water. Properties with excessive cedar cover also have extra losses of rainfall to interception by the leaves of the junipers and evaporation back into the air so that the amount of rainfall reaching the ground is somewhat less than where it falls on a grassland.

Given the scarcity and importance of water for all of us, we need the surrounding landscape to capture as much rainfall as possible.

When shown pictures of degraded landscapes or dense cedar-covered properties or grass and tree covered savannas with a diversity of vegetation types, most people choose the latter as the most beautiful. And let's face it, one of the things that has drawn many of us to the Hill Country is its beauty. But it is not just the beauty of such a habitat, it is more sustainable, long term and more resilient in terms of being able to survive droughts, floods and disease or pest infestations.

The healthy habitat described above is also a better wildlife habitat. Good wildlife habitat means the ability to sustain many different species of native wildlife including the insect pollinators that keep our gardens and orchards alive as well as provide food for all of our native songbirds. A healthy native wildlife community means one where there is balance among the species so that no one species gets out of control and none are extirpated either. Most everyone likes to be able to see our native critters occasionally.

Finally, as the human population increases and consumes more and more of our native habitat to make more roads, parking lots, shopping centers, etc., more and more of our native habitat will be gone. We need as much as possible conserved so that the increasing urban population has a chance to see it, if only from a car.

So yes, we all have a stake in how rural property is managed.

Our Future Depends on How Rural Property is Managed

I was having a casual conversation with someone recently who lives in the city and I happened to say something to the effect that it matters to everyone how rural property is managed. To which the person I was talking with responded, "Why does it matter to me? Doesn't everyone have the right to do whatever they want to on their property?" And the answer is, of course everyone does have the right to manage their property however they see fit—this is Texas! But that doesn't mean that how they do it doesn't affect the rest of us.

Some readers may be thinking I am referring to unsightly junk yards or other industrial facilities that affect others, but that kind of thing is just a small part of what I am referring to.

In the 25 years between 1982 and 2007, the U.S. lost 23.1 million acres of agricultural land to "development" (houses, roads, parking lots, shopping centers, etc.). That's about the size of Indiana! Texas lost the most of any other state, by a large margin—2.9 million acres! That is about the size of Bandera, Gillespie, Kendall, Kerr and Kimble counties combined! (*American Farmland*, Fall/Winter 2010 pp 13-16)

"Agricultural land" as used above means cropland, timberland or rangeland. So as the population of the state increases, the amount of available land to produce the food, fiber, wood and paper that the increasing population requires is decreasing. It should be obvious to all that this is not something that can continue indefinitely.

Now, project that thought to the next 25 to 40 years when the population of Texas is projected to double.

The amount of native areas (rangeland, grassland, savannas, woodlands, and riparian areas) is shrinking fast. But that land is important to all of us, because as Lyndon Johnson said back in 1947, "Saving the water and the soil must start where the first raindrop falls," and the first raindrops fall on these shrinking native areas.

So one of the reasons why we care how native land is managed is because we are losing it at a rapid rate. Given the current trends in our human population and our current and future projected water situation, we need to consider every acre of our native land as precious. In the future, we will have fewer acres of unspoiled native habitat per person than we do now, so it just makes sense to protect and conserve as much of it now as we can. Our grandkids will thank us for it.

So, yes, landowners have the right to manage their land however they wish. The hope is that all landowners, regardless of size, will come to see themselves not as the final owners of their property, but as the custodians of the land that they will sometime pass along to future generations. Simple courtesy and common sense will dictate that they pass it on in at least as good a shape as they found it.

Erosion: Where an Ounce of Prevention is TRULY Worth a Pound of Cure

When most people look at a piece of property with the idea of buying it, living there, retiring there, they usually consider the terrain, the trees and shrubs, the grasses, maybe whether there is a creek or pond or perhaps a beautiful view. But almost no one thinks about the most important aspects of any property—the soil.

Without soil, you can't have plants, without plants you can't have animals. Without soil, plants and animals, you just have a pile of rocks. If you have soil, even the most overgrazed, overbrowsed, abused land can, in time—perhaps a lot of time—be made into a healthy, functioning landscape.

Much of what used to be soil in Texas now resides in the Gulf of Mexico, due to erosion. A certain amount of erosion has to be considered a natural geologic process that has gone on for millions of years—it's what reduces mountain tops and fills in lowland areas with deep soil. It's the accelerated, human-caused erosion that we have to be concerned about.

Soil is composed of a mixture of air, water, dead organic matter, living organisms and mineral matter. The mineral component of soil is the largest component and it comes from the degradation of rocks caused in part by the natural forces of erosion, so soil is actually created by natural erosion, but this process is extremely slow. An inch of soil takes thousands of years to form. So replacing soil once lost is not going to happen in our lifetimes.

But we can lose the soil in a very short time. It may be difficult for us now to think back to the last good rain, but one heavy rainstorm can cause significant loss of soil. If you think this is a new discovery, consider this: "For the fact is that a single night of excessive rain now washes away the earth and lays bare the rock. Now the land is losing the water, which flows off the bare earth into the sea." -Plato, 400 B.C.

When many people think of erosion, they tend to think of drainage ditches along country roads, creek banks, gullies and other features where water runs during rainstorms and where there is or has been loss of soil. While these are not unimportant areas of erosion, some amount of this kind of erosion is inevitable—you can't fight the terrain. And many of the attempted solutions just make matters worse.

The type of erosion we should be mostly concerned about is called "sheet erosion," and it consists of thin layers of water flowing across the land picking up soil and flowing downhill into the creeks and gullies mentioned above. This is where the erosion starts, this is where the general loss of soil takes place, and this is where we can stop it.

Erosion generally starts with bare ground. Raindrops are said to hit the ground at about 20 miles per hour, which is enough force to dislodge small particles of soil. These soil particles then become suspended in the water and as the shallow sheet of water flows downhill it carries the soil with it. If there were no bare ground, the raindrops would fall on vegetation or leaf litter, so the soil particles would not be dislodged and the amount of soil carried away would be many times smaller.

The suspended soil particles will not stay suspended indefinitely, but are kept in suspension due to the motion and turbulence of the flowing water. If the water were slowed down in its flow downhill, then at least some of the soil particles would drop out of suspension. Native bunch grasses are really very effective in slowing down the sheet flow of water across the land, so they greatly reduce the amount of erosion.

It turns out that a good stand of native grasses is the best thing you can have to prevent erosion. The grasses intercept the raindrops, reducing the amount of soil dislodged, they slow down the flow of water, further reducing the amount of soil carried off, and furthermore, water infiltrates into the soil better under native grasses, thus reducing the amount of water runoff and therefore the amount of erosion. Any vegetation is better than nothing, but native grasses are the best to prevent erosion.

So, grow more grass and prevent erosion.

Which is More Important, Plants or Animals? Answer, Both

A while back I was giving a talk to a group of people about the condition of our Hill Country habitat when a woman, obviously peeved about my suggesting the overabundant population of deer was damaging the habitat and needed to be reduced, blurted out, "Well, you just like plants more than animals." My initial thought was that it was just a reflex response to my suggestion that some of her beloved deer should be shot.

On further reflection, I think that at least part of her response was based on her view that deer were important, but plants were not. Well, that is a bit like saying chickens are important but eggs are not (or vice versa if you wish). It is not either/or, it has to be both.

Many years ago, Aldo Leopold observed that animals can't live in a habitat that provides "only kitchens or only bedrooms" any more than we could. Stating what should be the obvious, you can't have animals without plants which provide both food and shelter.

Plants came into existence before animals, and it is true that a few plants can live without animals, but in fact most plants need animals for the species to survive. Most terrestrial plants need soil to grow in, and the soil provides micro-organisms (bacteria and fungi) as well as macro-organisms (earthworms, beetles, other animals), which are essential for the functioning of the roots and the health of the soil.

In addition, most flowering plants require animals of one kind or another in order to reproduce either by providing pollination (birds, bats, bees, butterflies, moths as well as other animals) or transport of the seeds. All animals that eat seeds contained in fruit, berries or beans then transport the seeds to other locations where the seeds are deposited in their droppings. Animals that carry acorns or nuts from under the trees to other locations are also responsible for propagating the plant species. And it is not just squirrels that do this, rats, mice and even occasionally woodpeckers disperse acorns as well.

Finally, some plants benefit from being grazed or browsed lightly because it helps remove or prevent excessive buildup of dead leaf-litter.

So plants need animals, and it is obvious that no animals would exist without plants. It is, therefore, a fallacy to think about only plants or only animals as if they could exist without the other.

One of the most fundamental principles of modern biology is the idea that an ecosystem is made up of multiple individuals of multiple species and that each individual coexists with all of the others and there are innumerable interactions among the individuals. These interactions mean that all individuals are interconnected and are dependent upon each other for the health and well-being of the ecosystem as a whole.

Put another way, the deer are dependent on all of the plants that provide them food, shelter and cover. If too many deer eat too much of the plants, then the deer will suffer as well as the plants. Also, if there are too many deer, then their least favorite plants may crowd out their favorites, again to the detriment of the deer.

Modern wildlife biology and range science looks at the entire ecosystem as a whole, never at just one species or one class of individuals. Ranching is not just raising cattle, but is equally concerned with growing grass and harvesting it prudently by using the cows as harvesters. Raising deer is not just providing food, but managing a habitat that provides them with all of the requirements for a healthy population.

Raising animals without consideration of the condition of the habitat is essentially maintaining a feed lot or a zoo, the difference between the two being mainly the density of animals. Most of us would rather see a proper, healthy population of ALL wildlife living in a healthy natural habitat.

It turns out that a healthy habitat is also the best at growing abundant vegetation and of capturing rainwater and preventing erosion. In other words, what is good for plants and animals is also good for soil and water and therefore for us humans as well. It is not either or, it is all of us.

Land Fragmentation Part I: What Are We Doing to the Hill Country?

Those of us who chose to live on small properties in the country all have any number of reasons for doing so, and I suspect nearly everyone really loves being in the country. But some of us don't like the consequences of what we are doing to the Hill Country. Let me explain.

Let's consider a rancher who inherited 1000 acres from his father and has been ranching all of his life on that property. He raised two kids and put them through college, but it is getting harder and harder to make a living ranching these days. Furthermore, his kids have good jobs in the city and little interest in ranching or living in the country.

Then a developer offers him way more money per acre for his property than he can ever make ranching, and as much as the rancher and his wife hate the idea of leaving their ranch home and moving into the city, the economics of the situation can't be ignored.

So then the developer divides the 1000 acres into 100, ten acre lots and sells each lot for a handsome profit, but still at a price that many of us were glad to pay to get our little piece of Texas. So what happens to the land now?

Over the years, at some time in the past the ranch was almost certainly overgrazed and the deer population has probably grown beyond healthy levels, but the rancher has cut back on the number of cows and kept the cedar to manageable levels. But other than those things, the rancher and his family have had a very light footprint on the land; only one house, a barn or two, one water well and a couple of windmills, one septic system, no paved roads, only a short utility line to the house, two dogs and a barn cat. And in recent years, hunters have helped keep his deer population down somewhat.

But once the 100 lots are sold and built on, that thousand acres will look very different. Instead of one house, one water well and one septic system there will now be 100 of each. Instead of 2 barns there will now be maybe 30, most with RVs in them. Instead of 4 to 6 people there will now be over 300. Where there were no paved roads, now there will likely be 5 to 8 miles along with 3 to 5 miles of utility lines. Where there were at most about 6,000 square feet of impervious cover, there may now be close to 1 million sq. ft. And where there used to be hunters, there are now regulations preventing hunting, plus a good number of residents actively feeding the deer.

The impact of all these changes on the native habitat, native flora and fauna is substantial and probably irreversible. The effect of this increased human population is not just on the thousand acres of the subdivision but also on neighboring properties in terms of storm-water flow, aquifer drawdown, septic system overflow, increased deer population, free-roaming dogs and cats, etc. And the general public will notice that where there used to be scenes of beautiful Hill Country hills, now those scenes are spoiled by views of numerous mega-mansions on hilltops.

It would be easy to blame the developers. But when you think about it "We have met the enemy and he is us!"

So what can we do about it? Short of building a wall around the Hill Country and locking the gate, not much. But what we can do is to make sure that as rural landowners, we manage our activities and land in the most environmentally and native habitat friendly way possible.

We can minimize impervious surfaces and/or install rainwater catchment facilities. We can refrain from overgrazing with livestock or pets and encourage the growth of understory plants. We can control dogs and cats and prevent them from running free to chase and kill wildlife. We can refrain from feeding deer and work to find ways to control the deer population. We can refrain from introducing any non-native vegetation.

If we have creek or river frontage, we can manage the riparian area in the best way possible, maintaining good creek-side vegetation. We can support organizations seeking to protect the Hill Country ecology by advocacy, by accepting conservation easements, by creating preserves, etc.

Given the increasing population, these things are the least we can do.

Land Fragmentation Part II: Is There Enough Room for All of Us?

Land fragmentation is the term used to describe what happens when a larger ranch is broken up onto many smaller "ranchettes," giving rise to many more people living on an area of land that previously only had one or two families on it. It is a common thing that has happened and continues to happen at a faster pace throughout much of the Hill Country. It is where many of us are now living, and when I say us I am certainly including my wife and I.

So I certainly understand the attraction of being able to buy a small piece of land and live out in the "country," away from the noise and crowds of the city and to be surrounded by a, relatively, native habitat with native flora and fauna.

The problem is that when we do that, we are degrading that native habitat we wanted to live in—too many people living on too few acres means we are essentially "loving it to death."

I did a little research. According to Google, the total land surface area of the earth is a bit over 57 million square miles, of which about 33 percent is desert and 24 percent too mountainous for habitation, which leaves about 24.6 million square miles of *habitable* area on the Earth, which is a little less than 16 billion acres.

There are now about 7.5 billion people on Earth, so roughly 2 acres of livable land for every one of us. Or, if the average family, worldwide, is 4 people, that means 8 acres available for every family on Earth.

Obviously, the population distribution across the globe is not uniform, which is fortunate for those of us in the Hill Country, even those in the big Hill Country cities like Kerrville. If most of the world's population didn't live stacked on top of each other (literally, in high-rise apartment buildings), those of us in the Hill Country would be feeling really crowded right now.

But if there are only two acres of livable land on the planet for every person, one of the obvious things is that those two acres have to provide each person with all of the food, water, shelter, energy and minerals that person needs throughout his/her life. Think about that for a while. (OK, some of the food and energy we use comes from the ocean, and with desalination, we could get some water too, but you get the idea.)

One could ask, what difference would it have made if instead of all of us moving out into the country on small properties, we had stayed in the cities or had moved into the cities of the Hill Country? The cities would obviously be larger, both in area as well as in population. The countryside would have many fewer people living there and there would probably be more large ranches still functioning.

But would those areas be better native habitat? Possibly, but not necessarily. If the economy was such that the large ranchers had to overgraze their ranches in order to make a living, or that they could not afford to manage cedar, then the habitat might be no better than if it had been broken up into ranchettes. It is hard to know, "What would have happened if?" And it is an academic question anyway, because I am pretty sure that in the future more and more of the Hill Country will be broken up into "developments."

So, dealing with where we are in the beginning of 2017, I can only offer one suggestion. And that is for all of us current and future ranchette owners to become the best native habitat land stewards we can be so that the impact of our presence on our little pieces of native habitat will be minimal.

How can we do that? We can design our homes to be as minimally intrusive on the landscape as possible, minimize the amount of impervious cover, capture rainwater, refrain from planting any non-native plants, prevent our cats and dogs from free-ranging, manage the cedar and the deer, and live with and enjoy our native animals.

Let's enjoy it, not destroy it.

How to Best Manage Hill Country Rangeland

I have discussed what the Hill Country looked like before European settlement and the changes that have occurred in the last 200 years. I have also discussed the functions an ideal habitat should perform.

These functions can be summarized as: 1. Provide food, water and shelter for reasonable populations of livestock and native wildlife. 2. Be able to replace the vegetation eaten by animals year after year so the amount of vegetation does not decline. 3. Be healthy, meaning be able to survive droughts, floods and disease and to recover over time. 4. Capture rainwater by infiltration into the soil instead of letting it run off, and 5. Prevent erosion, by both wind and water.

A very important point to remember is that the condition of a property is only partially determined by its location (rocky hilltop or creek bottom), but is mostly the result of previous activity, or lack thereof, on that property in the past. In other words, the conditions of one's land is mainly the result of the way it has been managed, currently and earlier, sometimes going back many decades.

Virtually all of Texas has been overgrazed in the past, and many properties are still being overgrazed. Ranching is a constant compromise between raising as many animals as possible to make money this year or reducing their numbers to allow the grass cover to increase and have better quality grass species to return to improve future productivity. The result of this compromise is that most properties with livestock are, or were, stocked with too many animals to allow significant improvement in the condition of the range in most years.

This compromise is complicated, especially for small landowners, by the need to raise more animals than their land can accommodate in order to maintain their Agricultural Tax Valuation.

But to provide food, water and shelter for wildlife as well as livestock, a property needs more than just good grass cover, but also reasonable amounts of browse (tree and shrub leaves) which also provides cover for many species of wildlife. Excess deer, goat and exotic populations have produced browselines on most woody plants in the Hill Country, which not only have eliminated important vegetation below about 5 feet, but also greatly reduced the number of replacement hardwoods of many species.

The overbrowsed condition of many properties greatly limits the population of many birds and small animals as well as providing too little vegetation for healthy deer populations. Unfortunately, especially for small landowners, managing the numbers of deer and exotics can be very difficult as these animals move freely from one property to another. High fences can keep out the neighbor's deer and exotics, but that presents another very significant problem. Once you high fence your property, you are totally responsible for managing the deer/exotic population inside the fence forever. High fences also present other problems for native wildlife.

In order to create or maintain an ideal Hill Country habitat, there are at least three management actions that need to be practiced by good land stewards: Prevent overgrazing, overbrowsing and cedar encroachment. Accomplishing these objectives is obviously much easier said than done.

If the land is not being grazed by livestock, or grazed only occasionally, then the first of the big three actions is already being practiced. But the property might very well still be suffering from previous overgrazing so that the native grass cover is sparse with too much bare ground and/or is composed of smaller, less-desirable grass species which frequently result from past overgrazing.

If this is the case, then many folks' first impulse is to plant native grass seed. There are times and conditions where that is indeed the best way to improve the pasture, but native grass seed is expensive and may be unnecessary. Before spending money on seed, I would suggest the landowner consult some knowledgeable experts (AgriLife Extension, NRCS, Master Naturalist).

If a property is currently being overgrazed, then the most obvious action would be to reduce the number of grazers or grazing days, perhaps significantly. For small landowners, replacing a cow-calf operation with stocker calves or leasing your land with restrictions on how many animals can be grazed for how long can be possible options that result in less severe grazing.

Rotational grazing is another important practice that can significantly improve the condition of the grass by allowing it time to recover after grazing. Inexpensive electric cross-fencing may work well for separating pastures.

If you have goats, then you need to consider them not only as grazers but also as browsers, their preferred food. Thus the combined effect of goats, white-tailed deer and exotic ungulates on all vegetation below the browseline needs to be considered. If your property has a distinct browseline with little vegetation below 5 feet, except perhaps cedar and agarita, then the habitat will not improve significantly until the combined populations of those animals is reduced. Reducing the goat population is easy. Reducing the deer and exotic population is an obvious solution, but one many landowners find to be very difficult. At the very least, don't attract deer to feeders as that just increases the population of them on your property and thus the amount of damage they do.

If you have dense cedar on steep slopes, most people would advise you to leave it there as trying to remove it almost always results in severe erosion before you can get anything else established on the slope. On flatter areas, removal of cedar cover down to some relatively small percentage can certainly improve the habitat for wildlife and increase the grazable acres and productivity of your range.

Current thinking about removing cedar is to do so in small patches a little at a time over several years so as not to expose large areas of bare ground at once. Not having a program to remove cedar will result in a continual increase in cedar cover and subsequent decrease in other more desirable vegetation. Bare ground caused by cedar removal or burn piles can be recovered more quickly if planted in mixtures of native grass seed.

Improving the native grass cover, increasing native vegetation below the browseline, allowing replacement hardwoods to mature, and controlling cedar will all, in time, make for a more ideal native habitat and a more productive rangeland that also captures rainwater and prevents erosion.

Finally, the one thing an ideal habitat does not have is significant amounts of exotic, invasive plants, especially along riparian areas, such as Chinaberry, Chinese tallow, vitex, *Arundo donax* (Giant reed) and salt cedar.

An Example of Good Land Management

I have previously written about how land management affects us all. Here, I want to give you an example of what I was referring to.

Back in 1969, J. David Bamberger bought about 6000 acres of what he, and others, described as "the sorriest piece of land in Blanco County," just south of Johnson City. The land had been seriously overgrazed with cedar cover over much of the area and there was no water, not even a windmill, on the property.

Madrone lake on the Bamberger Ranch Preserve after years of good land management.

Bamberger set out to restore the property to what he thought was its previous, natural condition before European settlement. Back then there was not nearly as much known about how best to restore and manage Hill Country rangeland and not nearly as many knowledgeable or experienced government agents or university people to guide Bamberger in his efforts. Fortunately, he was an exceptionally gifted observer of nature and managed to figure out for himself, and by trial and error, how best to accomplish his goals.

Over the years Bamberger removed a lot of cedar, planted huge amounts of native grasses and hundreds (perhaps thousands) of native trees and laid cedar limbs and rocks across the slopes to slow down water during rainfall events and everything else he could think of that might help to restore the land. And when cattle were reintroduced, their stocking rate and management was carefully controlled to best contribute to the restoration.

As the years went by and all of the above activities began to show results, springs started flowing where none had been seen for decades. The flow was slow at first, but eventually significant amounts of spring flow resulted in a small perennial creek. This creek was eventually dammed to make a small lake, the outflow of which flows off the ranch into a creek which flows into the Pedernales River and eventually into Lake Travis.

This flow of water off the Bamberger Ranch benefits everyone downstream who now have increased stream flow 24 hours a day, 7 days a week, 365 days a year and all of that extra water eventually is available to the people of Austin, most of whom have never heard of J. David Bamberger or the Bamberger Ranch Preserve and who certainly didn't pay a cent for the extra water they have from his efforts.

Over the years David Bamberger and the Preserve have been a model and a teacher and an inspiration for all Texans, landowners, conservationists, naturalists, range scientists and biologists alike. He has certainly made the path to land stewardship and restoration clearer and easier for all of us.

I tell this story not only to acknowledge the many contributions of David Bamberger and the Bamberger Ranch Preserve, but as an example of how land management matters and how healthy native habitat has benefits for all Texans. Most of us don't have the land or the resources David has, so whatever we do will have to be done on a smaller scale. But if enough of us small landowners do our part to improve and protect our little piece of land, the overall results can still be significant.

I would be remiss if I didn't point out that not everyone who makes similar improvements to their property will necessarily have all the same results as David had, especially people with much smaller properties.

All properties are different with different problems requiring different solutions. And in spite of our best efforts, some changes to the landscape take many years to show real improvement—Mother Nature doesn't always work on our human time scale.

For those readers who live in town and don't own any rural property with native habitat, I would suggest you can still make a contribution to the overall health of the land. First, be a conservationist—use water as if it were the scarce commodity it is. In fact, don't be wasteful in anything you consume and don't pollute with fertilizers and insecticides or introduce exotic plants or animals. Be supportive and involved with all nature and conservation-related organizations and educate yourselves about nature and native habitats and policies that affect them. An informed citizenry is the best defense our native lands can have.

As the population of Texas continues to increase at a high rate and more and more native habitat is lost, the more precious the remaining natural areas will be.

NATIVE HABITAT

Habitat—It's Where We All Live

My Webster's dictionary defines habitat as: "1: the place or environment where a plant or animal naturally or normally lives and grows, or 2. the place where something is commonly found." I think that is fine, but I think a more practical definition is a place that provides all of the elements needed for a given species to live and reproduce. For animals, we tend to think of a habitat as something that provides both food and water obviously, but also possibly, nesting areas, cover from predators, shelter from the weather, and space to move about.

Most ranchers may never use the term habitat, but they know very well all of the needs of their livestock and work to provide them with a good habitat. Knowledgeable landowners who seek to raise deer, either for hunting or just for enjoyment, soon learn that the most important thing they can do is to provide a good habitat. Likewise, folks who like to have birds around their house are most successful if they concentrate on providing a good habitat for the birds.

Of course different species require different kinds of habitat. The ideal habitat for a deer (1/2 to 1 square mile, lots of woody plant leaves and weeds and wildflowers within a short distance from cover) is very different than habitat for a jackrabbit (large areas of short to medium tall grasses without too much brush so he has space to outrun his predators) or a little 3" skink (leaf litter), or a black-capped vireo (brush 3 to 6' tall without too many tall trees).

So if every species wants something different, what would be considered the ideal habitat in the Hill Country? The answer is simple, diversity.

The most important characteristic for a healthy, functional ecosystem is diversity. Diversity in plant species, diversity in animal species, diversity in type of plants (trees, shrubs, vines, forbs (weeds and wildflowers) and grasses), diversity in age of woody plants...you get the picture. The more diverse the habitat, the greater the number of plant species, the greater the number of insect species, the greater the number of animal species.

When people think about diversity they usually think of places like the Amazon rain forest, where the greatest number of species are found. But most people are surprised to learn just how diverse some areas of the Hill Country can be, areas where the grazing and browsing pressure from livestock and white-tailed deer are well controlled can have literally hundreds of species of plants on a single acre, especially if the acre also covers a riparian area near water. The key to diversity in the Hill Country is control of the numbers of the large grazers and browsers; where those animal numbers are low, plant diversity is high.

One interesting characteristic of diverse habitats is that they are less likely to be devastated by a dry spell or a cold snap and are thus better able to sustain the animals that depend on them.

So what would be the ideal Hill Country habitat? Different folks will come up with different descriptions, and they may all be right.

Here is mine: An ideal Hill Country habitat would have a mixture of native trees, grasses and forbs containing some tall mature hardwoods such as oaks, cherries, cedar elms, and hackberries plus some young saplings as well. In addition, it would have a collection of shrubs including cedar and many hardwood berry-producing species. These woodland areas would be interspersed with native grasses in open areas, and forbs would be dispersed throughout both the woodland and the grassland areas. The result would be native vegetation of all types from the shortest to the tallest, dense vegetation and open spaces as well.

Why do I consider this the ideal habitat? Because it contains the most diverse vegetation I can think of. It also happens to be a good description of what we think the Hill Country looked like 150-200 years ago, and it is a pretty good description of many areas, both large and small, that we can find in the Hill Country today which have been well managed for some time.

Do We Really Have Any "Natural Areas" Anymore?

Part of the mission statement of the Texas Master Naturalists is "...to provide education, outreach and service dedicated to the beneficial management of natural resources and natural areas..." But the question is sometimes asked, "Are there any natural areas left?" And the answer, like the answer to most questions about Nature, begins with "It depends..."

If your definition of a natural area is an area that has been completely unaffected by modern man, then the answer is probably no. There are no areas in Texas that are completely unchanged from the time before the first Europeans arrived. There are no areas that could be accurately described as "wilderness." And of course, even the Native Americans altered the landscape somewhat.

Could we return places to their prehistoric condition? Again, I think the answer is no. To do so would require that we eliminate all livestock, since none of these animals are native, take down all fences, bring back the bison, the wolves, the bears and all other native animals, convert farmland and cut-over forests back to their original condition, and probably the hardest of all, replace all of the soil lost to erosion caused by man. Then of course we wouldn't all have enough to eat!

So we don't have any truly natural areas left, at least by prehistoric standards. But we do have natural areas by today's standards. And these modern habitats, while not exactly the same as the earlier habitats, can nonetheless be healthy, sustainable and productive. Most all ranchland and other rural land not converted to farmland could be considered a natural area.

Good land stewardship today involves applying basic principles of land management to produce habitats as close as possible to the theoretical ideal habitats that existed here before Europeans arrived.

These basic principles have to do with diversity and sustainability.

Diversity, in its simplest form, means having as complete a collection of native flora and fauna as possible. Aldo Leopold described this as "keeping all the cogs and wheels" before we begin tinkering with nature. In theory, that means that if a certain plant or animal was part of the local ecosystem before settlement, a healthy habitat today would also include that species. Obviously, we can't quite get there as some species are now extinct or nearly so and others would not be acceptable to us today, e.g. wolves. But the principle still holds, that a healthy habitat today would contain as many of the original plants and animals as possible.

What does not count as healthy diversity is the addition of species that were not present in earlier times, exotic plants and animals. The introduction of non-native species into an ecosystem can be as destructive, if not more so, as the elimination of a species. Introduction of one exotic species into an ecosystem in which it did not evolve often results in the species having nothing to control its numbers, and thus becoming invasive.

Sustainability means consumers of all kinds, carnivores and herbivores, never consume more of their food source than can be replaced, and no species is eliminated, and no species becomes invasive. A habitat cannot be healthy if it cannot exist over a long period of time. The bison, the wolves, and the prairie grasses coexisted for a very long time.

What we know is that landowners who make management decisions based on these principles and with an eye on what the land could potentially look like, who avoid the common problems of overgrazing, overbrowsing, cedar encroachment, erosion and exotic invasion, that in time their property becomes a truly healthy natural area. A sustainable, productive native habitat.

So most all rural property in the Hill Country either is or can indeed become a healthy natural area in time if managed properly. Farmland and non-native pastures would not be considered natural areas, but of course they provide an important service...we all like to eat.

Browselines: What They Tell Us About Our Habitat

A browseline is the area below which browsers can reach to eat all of the vegetation, usually about 4 ½ to 5 feet off the ground. By browsers I mean animals that eat browse (woody plant leaves) which in this area refers to goats, white-tailed deer, and exotic ungulates. While cattle will occasionally take browse and sheep will certainly eat some browse if available, these animals are primarily grazers and do not generally eat enough to cause a browseline.

A live oak in an overgrazed, overbrowsed pasture showing the lack of understory vegetation.

When we look over an average Hill Country pasture what we typically see is a bare area below all of our native oaks and other hardwoods, where nothing else is growing except perhaps small cedar bushes. Because cedar (Ashe juniper) is about the last thing a deer or anything else wants to eat, the cedar bushes usually escape being browsed, but in areas with really high browser populations, even it will be browsed out as well.

The mental picture we have formed in our minds from seeing pastures with heavy browsing is that our native hardwood trees don't grow any leaves down near the ground. But that is not true. Whenever an oak tree or other hardwood is protected from browsers by an exclosure, the bottom, outer limbs begin to grow longer and closer to the ground until eventually there will be limbs with green leaves reaching the ground. In other words, many trees would "naturally" grow leaves to the ground where they receive sunshine.

Of course, the vegetation being eaten by the browsers is only partially mature hardwood leaves. Much of what is being eaten are the leaves of small root sprouts or saplings of the larger trees, or shrubs or vines, all of which make up the natural vegetation below the browseline.

The loss of all of this forage below the browseline of course affects the animals that depend on it. The white-tailed deer are most affected, because they cannot digest enough grass to survive, and the only other form of food for them, forbs, may only be available seasonally and sometimes in very limited supply. The other browsers, goats and exotics, are capable of surviving on grass alone if there is no browse available.

But it is not just the large herbivores that utilize the vegetation below the browseline. Many small animals and birds find berries on the vines and shrubs, or seeds on some of the forbs that normally grow in this level of the habitat or insects that call that area home.

And this level of the habitat also provides vital cover and protection for all sorts of wildlife, from rabbits and field mice to lizards, snakes, frogs, toads, skunks, possums, armadillos and foxes.

The endangered black-capped vireo likes to build its nest about 3 or 4 feet off the ground. Rangeland with severe browselines offers little adequate habitat for them. Quail need brush cover to hide from predators, and it is believed that much of the reason for the decline in our quail populations is loss of habitat (mostly native grassland habitat for nesting and feeding chicks, but lack of cover may be partly responsible).

Of course the populations of goats and exotic ungulates being raised as livestock can be easily controlled, and on ranges where the number of these animals plus the number of deer is below the carrying capacity, the browseline is not distinct, and both browse forage and cover are available to the animals. But controlling the white-tailed deer and the feral exotic populations is much more difficult, so many landowners (especially small landowners) have a hard time preventing their property from being overbrowsed.

Without some limit on the populations of these browsers, the habitat below the browseline will continue to be severely impaired and few if any replacement hardwood saplings will survive to become mature trees. But since nothing eats much cedar, that is the one woody species which will continue to increase in size and numbers.

If you own property without a browseline, then you are fortunate to have a sustainable population of browsers. If the only plants below the browseline are the least favorite deer foods (cedar, agarita, prickly pear) then you obviously have too many browsers. If you have some plants that are only moderately preferred (live oak, shin oak) but none of their favorite foods (Spanish oak, blackjack oak) then your browser population is in between.

Habitat Changes in the Hill Country

We know enough about what the Hill Country looked like before European settlers arrived to be able to describe it fairly well, and we certainly know what changes have taken place in the 200 years since that time. It is interesting to compare the past to the present.

Prior to European settlement, we know that the Hill Country had relatively more open grassland areas, especially on the flatter, higher portions, and somewhat fewer trees, both hardwoods and junipers (cedars). We know that on the slopes and in the creek bottoms there were plenty of junipers as well as all of the hardwood species we still have.

We know that buffalo, elk and pronghorn grazed the grasslands heavily, but were somewhat nomadic or migratory so that once they had passed by an area and grazed it down, they would not come back until the grass had recovered. We know that the deer were numerous in the woodlands and hardwood savanna areas, and we know that there were large predators (wolves, mountain lions, bears) that preyed on all of these larger herbivores.

And we know that there were relatively frequent grass fires that burned most upland areas every 3 to 10 years, which was responsible for keeping the open grasslands and savannas from becoming more dense woodlands. These fires were caused by Native Americans (intentionally or accidentally) and lightning, and they burned such large areas because the denser, taller grass provided ample fuel to carry the intense fires.

European settlement changed the environment of the Hill Country in several ways. First, they grazed the land continuously with their livestock so the grass never had a chance to fully recover. This changed not only the amount of grass but the species of grasses as well. Europeans killed the buffalo, elk and pronghorn, drove off the Native Americans and fought every grass fire they could. And they killed off most of the large predators in order to protect their livestock.

Much of the land was cleared and plowed in order to grow crops, both for themselves and for their livestock. Once barbed wire was available in the 1880s, most properties were fenced. Especially in hard economic times, most of the remaining rangeland was severely overgrazed, allowing erosion to deplete the soil and the productivity of the land decreased significantly.

Without fire there was, and still is, nothing to prevent junipers from encroaching on most all areas, because natural plant succession in the absence of fire would make this area a woodland or at least a heavily-wooded savanna. Junipers are better at spreading than most hardwoods because they make more seedlings and grow faster, and in recent years' hardwood regeneration has been reduced by our high deer population.

While a cedar brake (dense cedar thicket) may be a "natural" result of modern man's overgrazing, suppression of fire, and the overabundant deer population caused by man's eliminating most predators, that doesn't mean that the resulting cedar habitat would be considered good, or healthy, or beneficial or diverse. In other words, we are faced with a situation in which "letting Nature take its course" is no longer a desirable land management option since man has so altered the native habitat that it cannot "go back to the way it was."

The result has been the establishment of a wide varicty of different rangeland habitats on different properties around the Hill Country. On one extreme are continuously, severely overgrazed habitats with virtually nothing growing below the 5 foot browseline. Another common habitat results from land being left unmanaged and is best described as dense cedar brakes with little vegetative or wildlife diversity. A third type of Hill Country habitat results from landowners limiting the numbers of grazers and browsers to a healthy level as well as controlling the amount of cedar cover.

This latter habitat is clearly the most desirable from the standpoint of diverse vegetation providing habitat for diverse wildlife species, good grass cover preventing erosion, and good rainwater capture. This type of habitat does not very closely resemble what the land was like before settlement, and we cannot ever go back to that earlier condition. But it does represent the best we can do given the current human population and what has taken place on the land since settlement began. In other words, our goal should be for all properties to be like the third type of habitat.

What Is the Ideal Hill Country Habitat?

As discussed previously, we have three distinct types of habitat extremes in the Hill Country, with many intermediate combinations of these types. Type 1 are habitats that have been severely overgrazed (cattle, sheep, goats, some exotics) and overbrowsed (too many deer, goats and exotics) for some time resulting in virtually no vegetation below the 5 foot browseline, little or no grass and lots of bare ground and rocks on the surface due to erosion.

Type 2 are habitats where the junipers have been allowed to encroach to the point where they now have crowded out much of the earlier vegetation and the individual junipers are touching or almost so. There is little grass in between the junipers and travel through the area is difficult. In short, the habitat has turned into a cedar brake. Native oaks may have been or are declining due to competition from the junipers.

Type 3 habitats are areas where the grazer and browser populations have been controlled for some time and there are numerous species of native trees, shrubs, vines forbs and grasses scattered throughout the area. There is little bare ground. There may be scattered juniper bushes but, except on steep slopes, no dense cedar brakes.

Most Hill Country properties have habitats that fall somewhere between the above three extremes. Maybe there are too many grazers and browsers, but still some grass and browse is left uneaten, some excess cedar, but some cleared areas as well.

But the real question is, what should the best, ideal Hill Country habitat be like? No one can describe what all properties should be like, because all properties are different. Property on a rocky hilltop or southwest-facing steep slope will of course have to be different from a property along a creek or river bottom.

But rather than try to describe what an ideal habitat should look like, it is more meaningful to describe what the functions of an ideal habitat should be. An ideal habitat should: 1. Provide food, water and shelter for reasonable numbers of livestock and native wildlife indigenous to the area in sustainable numbers. 2. Be sustainable, meaning able to continue year after year to produce replacement amounts of forage and wildlife so that the population of neither declines or increases beyond recoverable bounds. 3. Be healthy, meaning able to withstand droughts, floods, pest outbreaks, etc. and recover to a sustainable level over time. 4. Capture rainwater by having it infiltrate into the soil to not only nourish the vegetation but to seep deeper underground to feed local water tables and aquifers. 5. Prevent loss of soil to erosion even during heavy rains or windy droughts.

Any property which can do all of that would indeed be considered to be an ideal habitat. The property in the creek bottom will almost certainly have more biomass of vegetation as well as more species and greater numbers of wildlife than the property on the rocky hilltop. The amount and quality of the soil has a lot to do with the potential productivity of the land as measured by the above criteria.

Judged by the above list of functions of an ideal habitat, Type 1 above would obviously fail on all counts and would be considered not only degraded and non-functional, but, for all practical purposes, probably unrecoverable by natural forces in any reasonable time frame.

Type 2 above would also fail at providing any of the above functions, although with significant expense, very careful, gradual removal of much of the cedar over several years and several years of recovery, such a property could be significantly improved.

Type 3 above obviously would be the closest to ideal habitat and the easiest to improve to achieve all of the above functions in most cases. And all of the many properties that are in some in-between condition, with more or less effort can mostly also be improved at least somewhat, with time, effort, and, of course, money.

What a Difference a Fence Makes

I have written about my observations from along a nature trail around our little piece of a larger rangeland (see "Walking the Nature Trail" in the next section). This rangeland has been overgrazed by cattle and over-browsed by deer for some time, and the flora and fauna that is and is not present is a result of these conditions.

But when we built our house, we high-fenced a one-acre area around the house so that we could grow whatever we wanted without interference from our local herbivores. Now, 16 years later, the difference inside and outside the fence is striking.

Of course, some of what is growing inside the fence we intentionally planted (native plants), but a significant number of volunteer species have also found their way inside the fence. We of course water the flower beds more or less regularly and the planted trees and shrubs occasionally as well, using our rainwater, but we don't water the native volunteers. We had a small patch of planted buffalograss "lawn" although it really isn't a lawn anymore as we only mow it once a year and allow wildflowers to grow up in it wherever they wish.

An escarpment black cherry, "planted" by the birds, grows up under an old live oak inside a fence where the browsers couldn't eat it.

To me the most striking feature inside the fence is the number of volunteer woody plants that we did not plant. We have mature post oaks, blackjack oaks, live oaks and junipers inside the fence, and all of these have given rise to root sprouts or seedlings—the most common being post oaks and blackjacks. But we also have volunteer escarpment black cherry, hackberry, gum bumelia, prairie flame-leaf sumac (one almost 18 feet tall), Virginia creeper and grape vine, all native but not growing anywhere near the house.

We planted a single possumhaw, but now have almost a dozen more scattered inside the fence, all planted by the birds—none outside the fence. Likewise, we have two mesquite bushes we planted, but we now have a volunteer mesquite. We had a beautiful goldenball leadtree that died, but left behind several little ones.

Several things have spread, some more than we wanted. Rough-leaf dogwood root sprouts to form thickets—one, we have cut back, one we have let grow. The creek plum is also a prolific root sprouter, but the Mexican plum is less so. The Blanco crabapple is beginning to form a thicket also. Shrubs that have not produced any progeny include both the Texas and Mexican redbuds, Carolina buckthorn, Mexican buckeye, retama, yaupon, Mexican silktassel, amorpha, Texas mountain laurel, American beautyberry and buttonbush.

Walking around looking for things in bloom at the end of June, I came up with the following list. Indian blanket, Engelmann daisy, pink evening primrose, greenthread, horsemint, Mexican hat, American basket-flower, Illinois bundleflower, retama, rose pavonia, purple coneflower, woolly ironweed, Texas lantana (the native one), winecup, common sunflower, yarrow, Mexican oregano, Simpson rosinweed, and Gregg's mist flower covered in queen butterflies.

Native grasses seeding out included sideoats grama, Texas grama, switchgrass (2-3 feet tall), silver bluestem (2 feet tall with 4-foot-tall seed heads), eastern gamagrass (in beautiful bloom), and KR bluestem. Grasses having just finished their seed production include Canada wildrye, rescuegrass, Japanese brome, and Texas wintergrass.

Obviously the plant diversity and habitat are much different inside the fence than outside, mainly because of the protection from the grazers and browsers outside. But also because of the variety of native plants we have planted as well as the volunteers that have successfully established themselves inside the fence.

This vastly improved native habitat, coupled with a small shallow recirculating water feature, several bird feeders and bird houses also makes for a greatly increased number of birds and small animals frequenting the yard than would be seen in any equal-sized area outside the fence.

So, other than the enjoyment we derive from living in the middle of this improved habitat, is this small area providing any benefit to the larger surrounding area? The answer is yes, somewhat. The plants that produce seed inside the fence provide a local seed source of native plants that can propagate outside the fence and beyond if not eaten. Some of the native plants we have planted are declining in the wild (such as the Blanco crabapple and rusty blackhaw viburnam) and we are helping to maintain their genetic viability. And finally, the birds and other animals that use our yard even occasionally have easier lives due to the existence of our yard.

So, make your space a native habitat and help preserve our Hill Country flora and fauna.

The Dos and Don'ts for an Inviting Backyard Wildlife Habitat

There are lots of things a small landowner can do to make your backyard a better native habitat. There are also some things you should avoid doing if you want to encourage our native birds and small animals to visit your property where you can enjoy them. Here is a partial list.

Things you can do to help out our native critters:

Provide supplemental food. Lots of folks have bird feeders, most of which are filled with sunflower seeds or mixtures which attract a wide variety of seed eaters. But other kinds of feeders are also important to attract a wider variety of birds, such as thistle feeders for finches, suet feeders for woodpeckers, and sugar-water feeders for hummingbirds.

Provide reliable, fresh water. Many bird baths are poorly designed and are often allowed to go dry. Small shallow water sources that are constantly replenished, especially if they have dripping water, are best, and can be at ground level like their natural water sources are.

Be especially mindful of keeping feeders and water sources clean and filled full time—you don't want the birds to get accustomed to your food and water and then not have any when you go away or during the winter when they especially need your help.

Berry-producing native vegetation can be very important as these plants attract birds that do not eat seeds and winter berries are needed by insect eaters when insects are hard to come by. Berry-producing shrubs also provide cover and possible nest sites for birds.

A variety of native plants, from grasses and wildflowers to shrubs and vines to small trees all help provide the kind of habitat our songbirds are looking for. The greater the variety of vegetation, the greater the variety of birds you will see, and birds attract other birds.

Providing nest boxes certainly encourages those species that are cavity nesters to raise their families in your yard. Different birds require different size entrance holes, so put up a variety.

You can plant nectar-producing wildflowers and shrubs to provide hummingbirds and butterflies with their natural food source.

Like real estate, there are three key things to keep in mind when thinking about native habitats: diversity, diversity and diversity. Diversity in terms of species of vegetation, diversity in terms of plant size or age, and diversity in terms of food types available. Monocultures of even very desirable plants are not as useful as many different types.

Here are some things to avoid in your backyard habitat.

Don't use outside pesticides. Not only will they kill beneficial insects such as pollinators, but all birds need insects as part of their diet for protein and to feed their young. Let the birds control the insects the natural way. Native plants evolved with our native insects without any pesticides.

Don't plant non-native trees and shrubs, as most of these are not utilized by our native wildlife. Some can be toxic, and many can be invasive, which crowd out our native vegetation.

Non-native grass lawns are poor habitat for native critters and utilize inordinate amounts of water. Keeping such lawns to a minimum size and using the space that would otherwise just be lawn to establish more native vegetation will make your yard better native habitat and use less water.

Don't place bird watering features or feeders near vegetation that can hide predatory cats. When these features are out in the open, the birds can more easily avoid the cats. Also, don't place hummingbird feeders at a height that cats can reach.

Keep your cats indoors and don't feed stray cats in your yard. Dogs don't seem to be very successful predators, but they can certainly keep some wildlife out of your yard.

The best thing about establishing a native habitat in your backyard is that you can enjoy it even without the wildlife, but wildlife completes the picture and make all the effort worthwhile. If you build it, they will come.

Our Changing Native Habitat

Most non-migratory animals grow up, live and die in the same general area in which they were born. If that area was not capable of providing food, water, shelter and a place to reproduce, then the parent of the animal would not have survived to live there and reproduce in the first place. So, by definition, if a non-migratory species exists for multiple generations in a given area, that area must be providing suitable habitat for that species.

Migratory animals, in general, travel from areas of low quality or unsuitable habitat to areas of better habitat on a seasonal basis. But even migratory species return to the areas where they were born in order to raise their own young.

Terrestrial plants, because of being anchored by their roots to a given place, live out their whole lives, be it a few weeks or a year or centuries, in the same place.

But habitats are not unchanging. An area that provides good habitat for some species in good rain years may be much less suitable, or even completely unsuitable in dry years. The elimination of wolves and greatly reducing the number of mountain lions, as well as hunters only taking bucks has greatly increased the number of deer which in turn has allowed them to overbrowse and greatly reduce the available food sources, thus reducing the quality of the habitat for themselves and for other species as well.

Secondary plant succession, where one group of plants takes over dominance in a given area from the previous group of plants, can change the nature of the habitat. This can happen with the introduction of invasive exotics such as *Arundo donax* (giant reed), Chinese tallow, or buffelgrass. It can also happen when conditions change such as when European settlers fought wildfires which had previously kept grasslands free of cedar. In a fire-free environment, native cedar can crowd out other native vegetation, creating a less suitable habitat for most species.

As humans we have destroyed native habitat to create farmland, roads, houses, parking lots, shopping centers, school grounds and parks. Homeowners destroy native habitats by cutting down trees and shrubs, removing native grasses and forbs and replacing them with non-native lawns which are not good habitat for much of anything.

The smaller the animal the less food and water it needs to survive and thus the less the habitat has to provide for its survival. Animals that are highly mobile can travel long distances to satisfy their needs and thus food and water sources can be spread out over long distances. Animals that are not very mobile require all of their needs to be met in a smaller area.

For an area to be suitable habitat for an insect-eating bird, the area must provide roughly 10 ounces of insects for every ounce of insectivorous birds. Therefore, for an area to be suitable habitat for insectivorous birds, it must also be suitable habitat for 10 times as many ounces of insects as well. Thus an area routinely sprayed with insecticide will not be habitat for the birds and lizards that need to eat insects. And if the birds and lizards can't live there, then the higher predators that normally prey on birds and lizards will not find the area suitable either, and so on and so on…

Of course the food web in nature is much more complicated than the simplistic description I just gave, but the point is that any alteration in a natural, well-functioning native habitat can have repercussions far beyond the specific species in question. Remember in the early 1960's when we discovered that spraying DDT to kill mosquitoes was killing bald eagles? We know a lot more now than we did back then, but we are still a long way away from being able to predict all of the long-range effects of our actions.

But we know enough to know that the less we tamper with nature and the better we are as good stewards of the land and protect diverse, natural, healthy habitats, the greater the number of species we will be protecting and the less likely we are to do any harm. Nature may be able to get along without us, but we couldn't get along without nature.

SOIL

I guess the saying, "out of sight, out of mind" applies to the topic of soil. It is certainly correct to say that it is the most overlooked, and ignored, but most valuable part of the land. It is also a part of our land that we have the least control over—we have what we have and about the only thing we can do is to try to keep everything we have and help it to be as fertile and healthy as possible. And we do that by doing everything we can to grow good stands of native grasses.

Soil: Too Valuable to be Called Dirt

I have heard it said that dirt is what you get under your fingernails, but soil is what your trees and grass and flowers grow in. It is probably true that when people look to buy a piece of property, they may look at what trees or other vegetation is growing on the property, the view, whether or not there is surface water, etc., but they seldom even think about what is arguably the most valuable thing on the property; the soil. Without soil you can't grow plants, without plants you can't raise animals, and it would be a barren landscape indeed.

So what exactly is this valuable commodity we think so little about? Soil is actually a mixture of a number of components; the mineral component, which can be classified as sand, silt or clay depending on particle size, an organic component made up of mainly dead plant debris, a collection of living organisms from bacteria and fungi to earthworms and beetles, and water and air. It is the relative amounts and the chemical and physical properties of these components that determine the characteristics of soils throughout different parts of the country.

In terms of mineral soil constituents, sand has an average particle size of about one millimeter, silt about 0.025 millimeter and clay about 0.0001 millimeter. (Note: these greatly oversimplified sizes are generalizations just to give you an idea of how different they are). Clay particles are not only very small, but they have a very high surface area per unit weight which allows them to absorb and hold tightly much more water than sand particles. Furthermore, when they adsorb water they swell, and when they dry out they shrink, which is what causes the cracking you see when mud puddles dry up.

The relative amounts of sand, silt and clay are what determine the characterization as sandy loam, sandy clay, silty clay, etc. (The term loam usually refers to the desirable properties of loose, friable soil that both adsorbs moisture easily and drains well and generally contains a significant amount of sand.)

The organic component of soil mostly starts off as either dead leaves on the surface or dead or dying roots. This dead organic matter becomes food for all of the living organisms in the soil, either being directly eaten by the larger organisms, or by the decay products being consumed by microorganisms. This process helps recycle nutrients and make various nutrients available to the roots of the higher plants.

The living organic component of the soil is a collection of microscopic organisms (bacteria) slightly larger organisms (fungi) and nematodes, in addition to beetles, ants, and earth worms. Some of the bacteria associated with the roots of legumes are called rhizobium that can "fix" nitrogen and make it available to the plants. Some of the filamentous fungi associated with plant roots are called mycorrhizae and help make phosphorus more available to the plants.

Other soil organisms digest the protein in leaf litter and convert it into ammonium or nitrate ions, otherwise the plant roots would not be able to take up the nitrogen. Nitrogen is the most commonly limiting nutrient in Hill Country soils, so without the soil organism's, the productivity of Hill Country soils would be much lower.

The fact that the soil contains water and that it is an essential ingredient in plant growth is probably a surprise to no one. Water is necessary not only to keep the living plant cells alive and functioning and transporting material from the roots to the leaves and vice versa, but it is actually a reactant in the chemical reaction of photosynthesis to make carbohydrates from carbon dioxide.

That air is also a necessary ingredient in the soil may be surprising to some people, but the roots need air too. When normally porous soil is compacted by vehicle or cattle traffic, or when an area is flooded for a long period of time, the cause of the subsequent plant death is usually lack of air to the roots. Compaction also makes it difficult for the roots to grow.

You as a landowner can't do much about the mineral composition of your soil, but you can do a lot to create and maintain the healthiest soil possible. Healthy soils need to be able to adsorb rainwater easily, and the best way to achieve that is to grow native bunch grasses which produce porous "sponges" beneath the grass plants. Good grass stands also produce large amounts of leaf litter which in turn feeds high populations of soil organisms making the soil productive. A good stand of grasses and other vegetation also protects soil from raindrops dislodging soil and creating erosion and it shades the soil, reducing water evaporation and maintaining good soil organism growing conditions.

The Nitrogen Cycle: Essential, Complicated, and Altered by Man

Mother Nature, unlike humans, recycles everything. Just how various things are recycled is illustrated by the Water Cycle or Hydrologic Cycle, the Carbon Cycle, the Nitrogen Cycle and the Phosphorus Cycle. Every farmer and every successful gardener needs to know something about these natural cycles.

Other than water, the most commonly limiting component of plant growth is nitrogen. This may seem strange, since almost 80 percent of our air is nitrogen and it is one of the more common elements. But the nitrogen in the air, molecular nitrogen, (N2) is relatively inert and cannot be utilized by either plants or animals to satisfy their requirements for this essential element. (Nitrogen is necessary for amino acids, proteins, nucleic acids, DNA, chlorophyll and numerous other components of our bodies and plant tissues.)

Legumes are plants that have associated with their roots bacteria called rhizobia that have the ability to "fix" nitrogen. That is, to convert molecular nitrogen into forms that plants can take up and use to make nitrogen-containing compounds. In addition, there are nitrogen-fixing bacteria in healthy soil. These nitrogen-fixing bacteria are the first step in the nitrogen cycle, and they convert molecular nitrogen (N2) into ammonia (NH3).

Other bacteria in the soil then convert the ammonia into nitrates (NO3-), which is the form plants can best use.

Animals then obtain their essential nitrogen-containing nutrients from these plants when they eat the plants, or from animal tissues when they eat animal products. When we digest either animal or plant proteins, these proteins are broken down into their constituent amino acids and then reassembled into proteins for our bodies.

When animals eliminate waste this material contains high levels of nitrogen-containing compounds. And when plants or animals die, their tissues contain nitrogen in many forms. Another group of bacteria and other simple organisms, called detritivores, then decompose this plant and animal material further and make the nitrogen contained in these materials available for new plants to take up.

Finally, some nitrogen-containing materials in the soil are converted back to molecular nitrogen and it returns to the air, thus the cycle continues.

This nitrogen cycle has been in existence for millions of years, altered only by the relative numbers of plants, animals, bacteria, etc. But humans have significantly changed the cycle in the last 100 or so years since the discovery of the Haber process for artificially (chemically) converting molecular nitrogen into ammonia, and the subsequent conversion of ammonia into urea and ammonium nitrate, all "chemical" fertilizers now made on a huge scale. The tragic explosion in West, Texas a few years ago was at one such facility. (As a chemist I dislike the use of the term "chemical" in that way—all matter is chemical, and the nitrogen-fixing bacteria process is certainly chemical.)

Modern agriculture, and the ability to feed as many people as we do, world-wide, is largely attributable to the use of nitrogen-containing "chemical" fertilizers. Unfortunately, the use of manufactured fertilizers has been and is still being greatly overused, and much of these highly-soluble fertilizers, instead of being recycled, are washing away from the farm fields, golf courses, and suburban lawns and into our creeks and rivers and into the ocean.

This causes lakes and parts of the ocean to grow vast quantities of algae because of the fertilization effect. The algae then die and the decay process of the dead algae then uses up the dissolved oxygen in the water, killing fish and other marine organisms in a process called eutrophication. The "dead zone" in the Gulf of Mexico off the Louisiana and Texas coasts is one example.

I read an astonishing statement in a recent National Geographic magazine that, "Almost half of the nitrogen found in our body's muscle and organ tissues started out in a fertilizer factory."

One of the goals of "organic farming" is to eliminate the use of "chemical" fertilizers and instead rely on recycled nitrogen in the form of compost made from animal and plant waste and a more extensive use of legumes to fix nitrogen the natural way. We can help by doing essentially the same thing in our gardens and lawns. Native plants, having evolved before man-made fertilizers existed, do not need any "chemical" fertilizers. Collecting lawn clippings and throwing them away is throwing away nitrogen.

The Carbon Cycle: Another Way Mother Nature Recycles Everything

The carbon cycle is another very important natural recycling process which we should all understand.

Like the nitrogen cycle, the carbon cycle is best described in two stages; the first being the purely natural process that has been taking place for eons before mankind came along, and the second is the effects that industrialized man has had on that cycle.

The natural carbon cycle begins with the fact that there are huge amounts of carbon in the atmosphere in the form of carbon dioxide, even though on a percentage basis it makes up a very small percentage of the air. And, like molecular nitrogen, we cannot use any of the carbon dioxide in the air to build and fuel our bodies.

We have to rely on other forms of life to make that carbon available to us. And that, of course, takes place when green plants undergo photosynthesis in which the carbon in the carbon dioxide in the air is transformed into carbohydrates and from there into proteins, fats and all of the other components of plant and animal tissues. We are all, as Star Trek fans know, "carbon-based life forms."

The photosynthesis process converts carbon dioxide and water into carbon-based compounds. And when we use these compounds to fuel our bodily processes, to build tissues and to do work, these compounds are said to be "burned" and they indeed are then converted back into carbon dioxide and water. This is part of the carbon cycle.

Another part of the carbon cycle takes place in the ocean. Carbon dioxide dissolves in the ocean and there marine plants carry out the same photosynthesis as do land plants. And marine animals get their carbon by eating marine plants or other animals.

But in addition to that part of the cycle, carbon dioxide also becomes part of the mineral content of the ocean and becomes part of many marine organisms (oyster, mussel and clam shells, coral, etc.) as calcium carbonate. When these carbonate-containing animals die, they become part of the sediment at the bottom of the oceans. This is the process which, millions of years ago, formed the limestone over which most of us in the Hill Country live.

When plants and animals die, their tissues eventually degrade and return back to carbon dioxide which returns to the air, thus completing the carbon cycle. Also, when plants burn in natural forest or grass fires, the carbon is returned to the air as carbon dioxide. Some dead organisms settle into deep ocean areas and other places where there is little or no oxygen, and over eons of time and after being covered with deep sediments, the carbon in these plant and animal tissues is converted to hydrocarbons: coal, oil and methane.

Mankind has introduced another pathway for organic carbon to be returned to the air as carbon dioxide: burning forests and fields to make new cropland, and burning the fossil fuels which were formed millions of years ago. These activities, which have greatly accelerated since the industrial revolution, are increasing the amount of carbon dioxide in the atmosphere. Carbon dioxide, methane and other gases which strongly absorb infrared radiation capture the heat radiating from the Earth that would otherwise be lost to space, and thus contribute to increasing Earth's temperature.

Efforts, worldwide, to reduce the destruction of forests and to reforest cut-over land help to capture large amounts of carbon dioxide in the cellulose of the trees. This is called "carbon sequestration" (having nothing to do with Congressional budget policies a few years back!) and it traps carbon from the air and holds it in the trees until they die or are burned, thus reducing the amount of carbon dioxide in the air. It is not clear if these efforts are making a significant difference.

Farmers, gardeners and anyone managing land have another reason to want to capture as much carbon as possible. Especially in the Hill Country, our soil is generally lacking in the amount of humus, or organic matter in general, and it is largely this soil organic matter which contributes to the soil health by feeding soil organisms, capturing and holding water, and generally making the soil more productive.

So grow more plants and return organic matter to the soil. You will be better off and so will our atmosphere.

Bare Dirt: What You Don't Want on Your Land

I noticed a lot more bare dirt in the pasture in early 2012 than in previous years. Because of last year's (2011) drought, there was very little new grass growth. This means for the most part, the only grass on the landscape was growth from 2010, and it is decaying and disintegrating, leaving the soil bare where it used to be covered with green grass leaves and/or dead grass litter.

There are several problems caused by having bare ground. First, not having any vegetation covering the soil means that raindrops fall directly on the ground, with nothing to break their fall. It is estimated that raindrops hit the ground at about 20 miles per hour. I don't know that that is true, and it probably depends on the size of the raindrops, but I do know that they hit the ground hard enough to dislodge small particles of soil. I have demonstrated this by making a "raincloud" out of a five-gallon bucket with tiny holes in the bottom, held only about 6 feet above a patch of bare ground and watched the dirt particles dislodge and bounce up to adhere to a white foam board and turn it quite brown.

There are two consequences of raindrops dislodging soil particles and neither is good. First, the dislodged particles can become suspended in the water and thus they can then be carried downhill with the water flow. This is the first step in erosion. The second step in erosion is that the soil particles suspended in the flowing water give the water stream a much more erosive force to abrade other soil particles from the surface and thus carry off even more soil.

Furthermore, as water with suspended solids flows over the land, it is in patches of bare soil where the most erosion takes place. Under normal conditions, native grass and the dead leaf litter associated with it trap and slow down the water, causing it to drop out the suspended solids, thus preventing further erosion. But with the absence of the usual grass covering, more bare soil is exposed and there is less to slow the flow of water.

Another aspect of not having vegetation to break the raindrop's fall is that the small particles that are dislodged can fall into the small surface pores of the soil, plugging up the pores and slowing down the rate of water infiltration into the soil. I have discussed the decrease in porosity of bare ground versus ground under native grass roots in other essays.

The general results of what I have just described are probably known to everyone. We know that when construction lays bare the soil on a hillside, severe erosion can take place before enough grass grows to hold the soil, thus the practice of placing straw or fiber mats on the slope to protect the soil and hold it until grass can grow.

Bare ground causes another problem. Bare ground that is not shaded by vegetation soaks up a lot more heat from the sun, and in the summer can be easily 20 degrees hotter than soil under grass or other vegetation. In the summer this can make the ground hot enough to kill many of the soil microorganisms that are essential for healthy soil. Furthermore, the hotter the soil, the more moisture is lost from the soil by evaporation, and this becomes a cycle as the drier the soil, the hotter it gets.

In the summer, bare ground can get so dry and hot that the small feeder roots of some trees and other plants can die, obviously with negative consequences for the plants.

Soil for Water???

I recently attended the first in a symposia series entitled "Soil for Water: Maximizing the potential of healthy soil to catch and hold rainwater." The symposium was sponsored by the National Center for Appropriate Technology, the Hill Country Alliance and the Dixon Water Foundation. When I first saw the title it made me think of the book on the history of J. David Bamberger and the Bamberger Ranch Preserve, which is entitled "Water from Stone."

I have always assumed that the title of the Bamberger book was a play on the old saying, "you can't get water from stone," which I have always interpreted to mean you can't get something if it is not there. In the Bamberger case, it referred to the fact that by applying many good land management practices, Bamberger was successful in getting springs to flow where none had for many years.

I can't say I learned anything at this meeting I had not known before, but sometimes that in itself is satisfying. The principles expressed by the speakers, however, are important for everyone to understand as they relate to land management and our water supply.

The basic premise of the symposium was that, "Healthy soil acts like a sponge: holding rainwater for long periods of time and slowly releasing it to plants, springs, creeks, rivers and aquifers."

It takes healthy vegetation to make healthy soil, and vice versa for that matter. Healthy vegetation has a healthy root system, and that in turn requires a healthy collection of micro and macro organisms from bacteria and fungi to nematodes, earthworms, beetles and ants. A symbiotic relationship exists among the soil organisms and plant roots in which the roots provide food for the other organisms and the other organisms make certain nutrients available to the roots.

This relationship is not static but dynamic as some roots die and others grow, as do all components of the living organic matter, all of which makes the soil porous. As the living organisms die and as dead leaf litter degrades and becomes incorporated into the soil, the organic matter in the soil increases. This is important because the porosity of the soil and the organic matter determine how easily water soaks into the soil and how much water the soil can hold.

Healthy vegetation with healthy soil can capture and hold a lot of water. Bare soil has no vegetation, nor roots, very little other organisms and of course very little organic matter and it is not porous. Around 80 percent of the rainwater that falls on an oak mote or native bunchgrass infiltrates into the soil, whereas only about 25 percent soaks into the soil under bare ground.

The above-ground vegetation is also important because it shades the soil surface with its leaves, both living and dead, thus lowering the temperature of the soil. When the soil temperature is 70 degrees or lower, virtually all of the water that infiltrates into the soil is used for plant growth or seeps deeper underground to feed springs and aquifers. When the soil temperature is over 100 degrees, (as in unshaded areas) a large amount of soil moisture is lost to evaporation. And when the soil temperature is over 115 degrees (as bare soil can be), the soil microorganisms begin to die.

So, healthy vegetation above the soil is capable of growing healthy roots as well as slowing down the overland flow of water (allowing it more time to infiltrate) and shading the soil surface. A healthy root structure is capable of forming symbiotic relationships with soil organisms for the mutual benefit of the plants and the organisms, and this in turn makes the soil porous and the soil organic matter high. All of which allows the capture and beneficial use of rainwater, either for vegetation of feeding springs and aquifers.

One final point. I have written in the past about the importance of biological diversity. One of the reasons diversity is desirable is that diversity in above-ground vegetation means diversity in soil organisms, some of which will be better able to withstand drought, hard freezes, etc., so that even if some species are lost, some will survive.

— SECTION VI —

NATURE

We couldn't completely understand our Hill Country habitat and the many interactions among the various plants and animals without some basic understanding of nature. Most of the properties of native plants and the behavior of native animals and the interrelationships among them are common everywhere, not just in the Hill Country, but in East Texas, West Texas, California or Maine.

Everything that goes on in the Natural World without the help or interference of man can be thought of as part of "nature." A simple walk through a Hill Country savanna, or time spent along a Hill Country creek would reveal many interesting and wondrous things about nature. In fact, even city dwellers can observe some little bits of nature from their windows. I would argue that anyone who observes and appreciates nature in this way is more likely to want to conserve it and protect it, and to also enjoy it.

You can't really appreciate the Hill Country without first being able to appreciate nature.

MOTHER NATURE

As I discussed much earlier, I am writing this book as a layman or "educated amateur," and thus my descriptions of complicated biological principles are somewhat oversimplified compared to the descriptions a professional might give, but I hope they are still accurate and clear without too much scientific jargon.

Diversity: A Key Concept in Biology, Ecology and Ecosystems

When scientists study a natural area, be it a farm or ranch, a field, a woodland, a grassland, or a riparian area, one of the features that they will take note of is the diversity, or more correctly, biodiversity of the area. The term biodiversity was first used by E.O. Wilson in 1983.

Diversity has to do with variety, in terms of both numbers of plant and animal species and ages of the longer-lived species. One can think of diversity of woody plants, or grass plants or forbs, or of mammals or birds or insects or of young individuals or old individuals or breeding pairs. And in one context or another, each of these has meaning to biologists. But in most contexts, when we think of biodiversity, we are really thinking of the diversity of all of the above.

And why does diversity matter? Because diversity is an indication of the health and sustainability of the ecosystem and the functioning of all of its components. One characteristic of what scientists would consider pristine or near-pristine ecosystems or habitats is that they are very diverse. Said another way, a diverse habitat is a requirement for a healthy, sustainable and functioning habitat. The greatest biodiversity is usually found in tropical rainforests.

Consider the opposite. The least diverse habitat could be a cotton field, or a corn field, or a pure bermudagrass pasture. The cotton field can provide food for only a few species of insects, fewer still species of birds to eat the insects, no nest sites for most birds. Only an occasional rabbit will nibble young cotton plants. And during much of the year when the field lies fallow, it is even less of a habitat for anything.

Now consider an ideal Hill Country habitat. It will contain several species of grasses, some producing seeds early in the year, some throughout the year and some in the fall, so that seed-eating birds and small animals can find food throughout the year. It will also contain several species of wildflowers, some blooming early in the year, some later so that there is always something blooming for pollinators, which also means food for insect-eating birds. This ideal habitat will also contain several species of woody plants, some vines, some low shrubs, some larger shrubs and some major trees, so there will be berries, fruit, nuts and acorns at some point during the year as well as nesting sites for various birds from the ground to the crown.

The bottom line is the more different plant species in a given area, the more species of insects, birds, mammals and reptiles can live there, and the more insects means more birds and more birds attract more reptiles, etc. The more vegetation, the more herbivores, the more herbivores the more carnivores and omnivores, the more of all kinds of animals the more detritivores (decomposers), and so on.

The more different species of plants growing in an area, the more likely the soil organisms will be healthy and productive, which makes for more porous soil and thus better capture of rainwater, and the better capture of rainwater and the more fertile the soil, the healthier the plants and the greater the amount of biomass.

Diversity is what drives the food web and the water cycle.

People can help to manage and improve on the diversity in several ways. First, not introducing non-native plants that may become invasive and which the native insects, pollinators and animals did not evolve to utilize will help to maintain a healthy native habitat. Second, controlling native invasive species, such as juniper (cedar) will prevent it from crowding out other native vegetation and thus reducing the plant diversity and therefore the animal diversity as well.

Another way people can improve the habitat is to encourage native plant diversity by either planting more different species of native plants and/or protecting any volunteer native plants to allow them to mature and prosper.

Remember, for a habitat to be suitable for any non-migratory animal, it must provide food, water, shelter, and cover for the animal. Year around. A corn field might feed a raccoon just fine in the summer and fall, but where will it hide and find food after the corn is harvested and the stubble is plowed under in the winter?

"The Earth Is Full"

I was struck by an article recently in the New York Times by Thomas Friedman, concerning how some of the ecology principles that I have previously discussed in these columns as they relate to the Hill Country are also applied to the Earth as a whole.

As I have discussed before, the term "carrying capacity," applies to the capacity of a given property to support wildlife and livestock, long term. Carrying capacity is defined as the number of animals that the property can provide food, water and shelter for, long term, without degrading the habitat. The idea is that a particular piece of land can grow only so much forage, capture and hold only so much water, and provide only so much shelter. If the animals on the land consume more than the property can produce in the next growing season, then the habitat will be degraded because they are taking more than the land can replace.

I have also applied the idea to the human population of the Hill Country as a whole, arguing that as more and more people move here, buying up small pieces of ranches, using more water, polluting more, and mismanaging the landscape, the capacity of the land to accommodate the increasing population will diminish. The long term result of this land fragmentation will be a decrease in the qualities of the Hill Country that many of us came here for in the first place.

In his Times article, Freidman relates how a group of scientists have calculated how much land area and water area we need to produce the resources we consume and absorb our waste, using current technology. Their calculations show that we need 1.5 Earths! Friedman quotes Australian environmentalist Paul Gilding as saying, "The Earth is full. We are now using so many resources and putting out so much waste into the Earth that we have reached some kind of limit, given current technologies."

My interpretation of all that is that we humans have exceeded the carrying capacity of the Earth and we are now degrading our habitat, worldwide, just as I argued that we may be doing with land fragmentation here in the Hill Country.

My solution for the Hill Country is, that if we are to continue to put more and more people onto a fixed amount of land with a fixed amount of available water, we need to do so in ways that minimize the impact we all have on the land. This means managing our landscape for the most healthy, productive habitat possible. In short it means not allowing grazing or browsing animal numbers to exceed the carrying capacity of the land. It means not allowing cedar to take over the grasslands. It means minimizing our use of water and managing the land to better absorb rainwater without runoff. It can also mean minimizing our use of energy, recycling to reduce waste accumulation and harvesting rainwater. It means landscaping with native plants, minimizing lawn areas and utilizing cacti and succulents to conserve water.

The parallel between what we need to do in the Hill Country, and Gilding's thoughts for global solutions is striking. He states, "The economy is going to have to get smaller in terms of physical impact.....To do that you need a growth model based on giving people more time to enjoy life, but with less stuff." And he believes it will happen, stating "We may be slow, but we are not stupid."

I would put it another way, when we manage our own property in ways that best preserve a healthy habitat and conserve water, we not only benefit ourselves, but also our Hill Country neighbors, and even the planet as a whole.

The older I get, the more I believe there is no correlation between the amount of stuff I have and my quality of life. We need to save more, conserve more and consume less. Think about it. Together we can make a difference.

Energy and the Natural World: How Energy is Passed Up the Food Chain

All living things require energy to live, to grow, and to reproduce. With the exception of a few rare species that live near deep ocean vents or a few species of bacteria living around hot springs, the ultimate source of all of that energy is the sun. All plants, except for various types of fungi which obtain energy from other plants, use energy absorbed from sunlight to produce all of the chemicals that make up the plants. This is accomplished by using the electromagnetic radiation (light) from the sun as the energy to convert carbon dioxide in the air and water into chemical energy (the chemical bonds that hold the plant's molecules together) by a process called photosynthesis, using chlorophyll as a catalyst.

Fortunately, the Earth gets lots more light energy than is needed for that process. In fact, most of the light energy that reaches the Earth is absorbed by the land and the seas or reflected back to the upper atmosphere or to outer space. And a lot more energy reaches the Earth than we can see. We only see light in the visible wavelength range, but the Earth receives radiation from many other wavelength ranges, so the visible light range is only a small part of the total amount of energy we receive.

It is estimated that only about 1 percent of all of the visible light received by the Earth is converted into chemical energy by plants. That may not seem like a lot, but it is enough to produce about 170 billion tons of biomass every year! It also means that all of the living world has to live on that amount, or less, every year.

The plants use the chemicals they produce in this energy transformation, the carbohydrates, proteins, oils, etc., as the building blocks for the structures of the plants themselves. The plant growth and all of the flower, seed, fruit, etc. production comes from the chemicals produced, initially, by photosynthesis and further biochemical reactions.

And all of the above is also the source of energy for all animals. All animals either consume plants directly or indirectly if they consume other animals. Animals use the chemicals they get from plants (fuel) to "burn" in their cells (producing carbon dioxide and water) which powers all of the functions of a living animal.

When an animal eats a plant it is only able to convert about 10 percent of the energy in the plant tissues into energy for itself. If another animal then eats the first animal, it again is only able to convert about 10 percent of the energy in the first animal into energy for itself.

So if an insect (grasshopper, caterpillar) eats the leaf of a plant, 90 percent, on average, of the energy in the plant chemicals are lost to heat or not digested. If an armadillo or lizard then eats an insect, the same loss of energy occurs, and then if a hawk eats the lizard or a vulture eats the armadillo, another 90 percent of the energy is lost.

Plants are considered primary producers because they produce the chemicals that store the energy from the sun. The insects, in the example above, would be considered primary consumers, the lizard a secondary consumer, and the hawk a tertiary consumer. Put another way, to supply the hawk with one unit of energy (say 1 kcal), requires 10 kcal of energy at the lizard level, 100 kcal at the level of the caterpillar, and 1000 kcal at the plant level.

All of this explains why some people who are concerned that the human race is using too many of the Earth's resources, advocate we all become vegetarians. When we eat meat, we are functioning as a secondary consumer, getting only 10 percent of the energy in the animal, which is only 1 percent of the energy in the plants. But if we ate only plants, then we would be primary consumers and we could get 10 percent of the energy in the plants and thus we would require only 10 percent as much biomass as we do when we eat meat. We would be eliminating one consumer level. The fewer consumer levels, the more efficient the whole process.

All of this also explains why it takes many primary consumers and secondary consumers to support a single tertiary consumer, *i.e.* it takes many prey animals to support a single predator. And likewise, it takes many plants to support a single herbivore.

Bugs: We Couldn't Live Without Them

I know, a lot of folks might be saying to themselves right now, "Well, I could certainly live without them." It is interesting how much animosity we have toward some of the smallest critters in our world. It has even crept into our language. When something bothers us or gives us some concern, we don't say that it "birds us" or "fishes us," or "mammals us," we say that it "bugs us."

So, let me try to set the record straight about bugs, or more properly, insects. There are an estimated 30,000 species of insects in Texas. With so many species, only a professional entomologist would be able to identify many insects down to the species level, and in fact most people are happy if they can identify the order of the insect, or possibly the family, and they don't worry so much about the genus or the species. Depending on the book and when it was written, there are over 30 orders of insects and similar invertebrates.

In spite of how some people think about them, insects perform some exceedingly important services for mankind. The most obvious of which is pollination. While some plants, including grasses and many trees, are fertilized by wind-borne pollen, the majority of blooming plants require pollen to be spread by an animal, and most of this is done by insects. And a very wide variety of insects indeed, including not only the bees, but many wasps, flies, beetles, moths, butterflies and ants can transfer pollen from one flower to another. Without pollination, most of our fruits and vegetables could not be produced, as well as most wildflowers and flowering shrubs. Adequate pollination is so important to agriculture that a whole industry has developed to bring bee hives to farmers' fields at considerable costs.

Perhaps a less obvious benefit to having insects is that they provide food for so many other animals. Frogs, toads, lizards, snakes, fish, armadillos, skunks, and most other small mammals including foxes and coyotes eat insects for at least part of their diet. Most birds need insects as at least part of their diet. All songbirds, including hummingbirds and seed eaters, need insects to feed their young. Without insects, many species of higher animals would not exist, and all of these animals are in fact food sources for other predators. So for a large part of the animal world, insects represent the initial harvesters of photosynthesized food sources and are the base of the food chain.

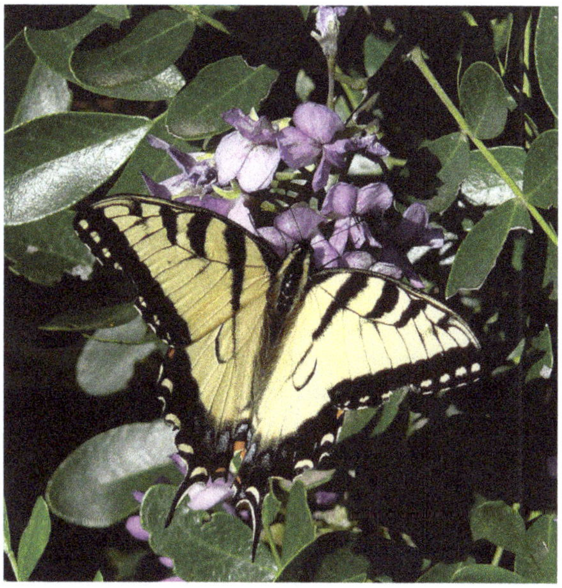
A tiger swallowtail butterfly on a Texas mountain laurel bloom.

Finally, it is also true that many insects feed on other insects, and therefore help to control the numbers of the prey species. This is especially beneficial to humans when the prey species is a pest that damages our crops and garden plants.

Soil-living insects help to contribute to the fertility and porosity of the soil.

Some of the more common orders of insects include: dragonflies and damselflies, mantids and walkingsticks, grasshoppers and crickets, cicadas and aphids, true bugs (Yes, there is an order called true bugs), beetles, butterflies and moths, true flies, and wasps, bees, and ants. The definition of an insect is that they have three distinct body parts (head, thorax, abdomen) and six legs. There are a number of insect-like invertebrates that are not true insects, and these include spiders, ticks, chiggers, scorpions, centipedes, millipedes, and pill bugs. They all have eight or more legs.

For such small critters, insects can have very complicated life cycles. Many insects such as butterflies have a larval stage that looks totally different from the adult, then a pupal stage where a complete metamorphosis takes place before emerging as an adult. Other insects skip the pupal stage, and still other species hatch from an egg looking like a small adult.

Given the importance of insects to our world as we know it, I would suggest we all try to limit the use of insecticides as much as possible, at least outside of our homes. We can keep insects out of our homes without killing every one on the lot, and the flowers and the birds and the lizards and the frogs and the toads will thank you very much.

There are two field guides to insects I would recommend: *A Field Guide to Common Texas Insects*, by Drees and Jackman, and *Kaufman Field Guide to Insects of North America*, by Eaton and Kaufman.

Bacteria and Fungi: Essential Organisms for Life as We Know It

Yes, I know, certain bacteria and fungi can cause disease, both in animals and plants, and it is these detrimental aspects we normally think of first. But there are also many species of beneficial bacteria and fungi that we very much need and want to keep healthy. We have all seen the ads that tout the beneficial effects of bacteria (although the ads never use that word) in the proper functioning of our digestive systems.

We all know that the ultimate source of everything we eat is plants, either because we eat them directly, or indirectly when we eat animals.

While the great majority of the mass of a plant comes from the carbon dioxide in the air and the water in the soil, there are certain other essential nutrients that plants need in order to grow and reproduce. The three nutrients needed in largest amounts are nitrogen, phosphorus and potassium, and fungi and bacteria play critical roles in providing the plants with these nutrients.

Most all plants grow very thin "root hairs," almost microscopic feeder roots, along the surface of larger roots and this is where most of the water and nutrients are taken up by the plant. Most plants are aided in this process by microscopic fungal threads or filaments covering the surface of the root hairs. These associations of root hairs and fungi are called mycorrhiza. The fungal filaments provide an enormous surface area which absorbs water and inorganic ions, especially phosphate, and some of the water and ions are transferred to the root hairs. The fungi obtain sugars and starches from the plant's root hairs in exchange for the service they provide.

Nitrogen is the most commonly deficient nutrient in the soil and the one needed in greatest amounts by the plants. Elemental nitrogen, (N2) in the air or in the soil is not a form that plants can use; plants need nitrogen in the form of nitrates or ammonium ions, and this is where bacteria come into the picture.

Healthy, fertile soil contains bacteria, along with other micro-organisms as well as larger species such as nematodes, earthworms, beetles, ants and other insects, and decomposing organic matter called "humus." Healthy soil also contains water, oxygen and elemental nitrogen.

There are three types of bacteria in healthy soil that convert elemental nitrogen into nitrate and ammonium ions which the plants can take up and use. Nitrogen-fixing bacteria convert elemental nitrogen into ammonium ions. Ammonifying bacteria convert organic matter from decaying plant and animal tissues into ammonium ions also. Plants can take up ammonium ions, but do much better with nitrates, and there is a bacterium, nitrifying bacteria, that convert most of the ammonium ions to nitrate ions. Thus the plants get the nitrogen they need to make proteins, DNA, enzymes and even chlorophyll.

Some types of plants, specifically legumes, naturally have nodules (small round growths) on their roots that actually have nitrogen-fixing bacteria living inside the plant. The bacteria get carbohydrates from the plant and the plant gets ammonium ions from the bacteria.

Since we and all other animals can't make amino acids, the building blocks of proteins, from ammonium ions or nitrate ions or elemental nitrogen, we have only two ways to get these essential nutritional components: either from plants directly or indirectly from eating animal material.

In humans world-wide, protein deficiency is one of the most common forms of malnutrition, partly because not all types of plants have enough protein containing all of the essential amino acids humans need. Strict vegetarians must eat a variety of plant materials in order to obtain all of the necessary amino acids, a difficult task for many people in some parts of the world.

The protein content of plants depends on the nitrogen availability in the soil, and commercial inorganic fertilizers containing nitrates have helped to produce more nutritious food, worldwide. But inorganic fertilizers have environmental issues during production and can be leached out of the soil into the water table and into creeks and streams. Recycled organic material containing nitrogen from vegetative sources is better overall for the land and soil fertility.

Small Changes in the Environment Can Have Large, Unexpected Consequences

A few years ago it was fashionable for people, wanting to sound familiar with the then-new theory in mathematics and physics called the "Chaos" theory, to talk about how a butterfly flapping its wings in Brazil could be the cause of a tornado in Texas. This was not really a serious thought but rather an attempt by some to explain a complex theory for laymen, the theory being that small changes in initial conditions could result in large changes far removed in time and space, and weather predictions were frequently cited as an example. But in thinking about the consequences small changes in the environment can have on future conditions, the butterfly analogy seems appropriate.

A balanced, highly-interconnected ecosystem can be thought of as a bit like the old Rube Goldberg cartoons where sunlight (a) coming through a window (b) shining on a magnifying glass (c) burns a string (d) that drops weight (e) slamming door (f) thus pulling string (g) and yanking out a man's tooth. Here are some real-life ecological sequences where a change in one thing brings about unanticipated changes elsewhere.

Shoot a wolf, kill a fish: Shooting wolves in one area allowed the deer population to increase. The hunters were excited, which is why the wolves were shot in the first place. But as the deer population increased, they began to exhaust their favorite foods, then their less-favorite food, then most of the remaining vegetation. With no vegetation covering the ground, erosion began to take place, causing rainwater to run off the land carrying heavy loads of silt and soil and exposing rocks which increased the flooding. This silted in creeks, rivers, lakes and ponds, killing fish.

Settlers cause trees to grow in the grasslands: As settlers of European ancestry moved into the Hill Country, they caused two changes in the ecosystem. Their livestock continually overgrazed the land and reduced the amount of grass. The settlers moving in caused the Native Americans to be displaced or to spend less time in the area. Both of these changes reduced the frequency and extent of wildfires, frequently set by Native Americans. With fewer fires burning less intensely in shorter grass, more woody plants survived from not being burned up and became established in grasslands.

Introducing wolves to Yellowstone increases the number of ducks: The introduction of wolves into Yellowstone National Park had the expected effect of reducing the elk population. But then the reduced elk population, being afraid of the newly introduced predators, tended to spend more time in open areas where they could better see and flee from the predators. This meant they spent less time along the stream banks eating willows. The number of willows then increased, which is a favorite food of beavers. This allowed the beaver population to increase and build more dams, which are actually beneficial for many different forms of wildlife, including ducks.

Eliminating screw-worm flies reduces hardwood trees: The elimination of the screw-worm fly not only saved many thousands of ranchers' livestock, but it also removed the last natural predator of the white-tailed deer. The deer population has increased significantly since then. The higher deer population means there is not enough browse (woody plant leaves) for the population, so that every leaf of most all woody plants below the browseline is eaten, thus preventing any replacement hardwood trees from surviving to become mature trees. Without replacements, the number of hardwood trees will continue to decline. Since Ashe juniper is about the last thing deer will eat, cedar is not declining and continues to encroach on most Hill Country properties.

The point of all of this is that, as Aldo Leopold said, "we don't know enough about Nature to tinker with it." There are unintended consequences to just about every action that we take in terms of the Natural World, so that our goal should be to make as few changes as possible and to make them as small as possible.

The folks that dumped the giant salvinia from their aquarium didn't intend to for it to choke out whole lakes, but it did. Similarly, when people imported and starting planting Vitex, Chinese tallow, Chinaberry, giant reed and salt cedar, they didn't intend for any of these species to take over whole creek sides and crowd out the native vegetation. But that is what happened.

Nature's Clean-Up Crew: Vultures Help Mother Nature Recycle

I have written about the nitrogen cycle and the carbon cycle as illustrations of how Mother Nature recycles matter. One of Nature's helpers in this regard are vultures. This may not make for the most appealing discussion, but it is important to understand this essential process.

I recently came upon what appeared to be a rather fresh jackrabbit carcass in the middle of the road not far from our house. I moved it under a tree in the pasture where I could watch from my window. It was less than an hour later that I noticed the first turkey vulture on the carcass. Only a few minutes later he had the company of 4 or 5 black vultures. A little later a crested caracara came down to try his luck, but quickly felt he was out-numbered and took off. A little more than an hour after the first vulture was seen, all the vultures had departed, and a search of the area found only a couple of leg bones identifiable.

A black vulture guards a nest under a log.

Here in the Hill Country we have two species of vultures: black vultures and turkey vultures. Black vultures have a shorter wing-span and shorter tail than turkey vultures, and they are heavier and less-agile flyers than turkey vultures. Black vultures have black or dark gray heads while turkey vultures have red heads. Black vultures are year-round residents of the Hill Country, while turkey vultures are most often seen in the summer.

Both vultures find their food by soaring over the landscape looking for dead animals. Black vultures tend to spend more time higher above the tree-level than turkey vultures because the latter are better flyers and can maneuver around trees better. Interestingly, turkey vultures are unusual in the bird world, they can find food by their sense of smell as well. This frequently results in turkey vultures finding a carcass first, but then being chased off by a group of heavier black vultures. We have noticed more than once that when we fire up the Bar-B-Q outside we see turkey vultures appearing overhead, attracted by the odor apparently.

Crested caracaras are not related to vultures, and are in fact raptors in the same family as falcons. While carrion is their main food, they are perfectly capable of catching live prey. The Hill Country is probably about the northern extent of their range.

Other raptors, including bald eagles also eat carrion, but usually in much smaller amounts than caracaras. And many small omnivorous animals also eat carrion when they find it.

I expect it is probably safe to assume vultures are not on your "favorite-bird" list. The service these animals provide places them in a biological category as detritivores, species that decompose organic matter making the nutrients contained therein available to plants and other soil organisms. In so doing, they help to maintain or increase soil fertility and aid the growth of all vegetation.

It doesn't take much imagination to think of what things would be like without species that perform these services, so maybe vultures should be on your favorite-bird list.

So what happens to the material the vultures eat? With apologies for a less-than-appealing discussion, what they eat gets degraded and decomposed in their digestive tract. Some of the nutrients are used in the bird's body to maintain temperature and provide energy, some become part of the bird's tissues, some is fed to their young, and some becomes excrement and is spread around as the bird moves about. And when the bird dies, its tissues will be eaten or decomposed by other organisms and the cycle continues.

A healthy ecosystem is one that has healthy recycling processes taking place, the overall result is more fertile soils and a more productive landscape. We humans would probably be better off if we did a better job of recycling everything possible, and would be better stewards of the land if we helped Mother Nature take care of our land.

Detritivores and Decomposers: Nature's Recyclers

When plants and animals die, what happens to the carbohydrates, fats, proteins, and bones in their bodies? Or when the animals eliminate waste what happens to that? And how does it happen?

Well, in addition to the herbivores and carnivores of the animal kingdom, there are things called detritivores, and these species eat dead plant and animal material, and animal waste, in order to build their own bodies, and they in turn produce waste. Eventually all of the larger complex chemicals that made up the plants and animals are broken down into simpler chemicals or elements which then become the nutrient building blocks of the next generation of living things.

Vultures were discussed in the previous essay. But there are a lot more species that either live almost exclusively or partially on dead things. Ravens and crows of course, but most omnivores such as coyotes, foxes, raccoons, skunks, opossums, rats and mice will all eat dead animals when given the opportunity.

There are also fish that will eat almost anything (e.g. catfish). The young of many animals and insects will eat small bits of dead plants because they are not yet large enough to eat other animals. Earthworms, dung beetles, ants, centipedes, crawfish, and tadpoles are other examples.

Many species of flies lay their eggs in dead animal carcasses as well as on manure, and the larva feed on that material when they hatch.

Thus much of dead plant material and animal bodies and waste are recycled into other organisms, all of which perform a service we can all appreciate. If something didn't take care of all of the dead leaves and animal bodies and waste, the forest floor would be many feet deep in these materials. And of course if these raw materials were not being recycled, we would eventually, if we had not already, run out of things.

But the process doesn't stop there. Organisms frequently called "decomposers," usually bacteria and fungi such as mold and mushrooms, further break down dead organic material into its simplest molecules and elements and return these simpler materials back to the ecosystem as carbon dioxide and water, plus various minerals such as nitrates, calcium, phosphorous and potassium. And it is these organisms that decompose organic litter on the surface of the soil into small enough particles to be carried into the soil by rainwater and where other bacteria and fungi convert many of these minerals into forms that can be taken up by the roots of plants.

Mother Nature doesn't waste anything! Everything is recycled. Atoms are essentially indestructible.

Every gardener knows that the component of our soil that is most lacking is organic matter and it is organic matter that helps make the soil porous, light and airy as well as being a source of important nutrients. When gardeners compost dead plant material and then put it on their vegetable gardens or flower beds they are simply using Nature's process to break down organic matter into simpler compounds and making it available for their living plants, as well as maintaining their soil in a healthy, fertile state.

Life and Changes on an Acre of the Hill Country. Part I

We first saw this acre of land in 1996 when we bought the land that included this one acre. For some time, we thought it would be the backyard of the house we intended to build. For the first few years we lived far away and only visited the place a couple of times a year. One of those visits was after good rains and there was taller than usual grass. I spent all day walking around planning for the location of the house. That night, I rediscovered chiggers!

This acre is a gently sloping savanna with a lot of surface rocks. On it were 9 live oaks, 13 shin oaks, 7 blackjack oaks, one large old-growth cedar, two Spanish oaks, a large grape vine and a really old twisted, hollow prairie flameleaf sumac with bees in it. One of the live oaks was a really large one with spreading branches, and one of the Spanish oaks was a large double-trunk tree with one trunk growing out at an angle.

This property is part of a working ranch, and what we didn't appreciate at the time was just how overgrazed and overbrowsed the property was. We fell in love with the trees.

We eventually changed plans and built our house a couple of hundred yards away, but we can still take walks to that one-acre area and do so frequently. This allowed us to observe the life and the changes of this little piece of the Hill Country. We don't have control of the management of the property, so it is still overgrazed and overbrowsed, and while certainly not good habitat, it is typical of much of the Hill Country today.

Changes have occurred on this acre. Since we first saw it we have lost one of the Spanish oaks several years ago to hypoxylon, and we have also lost two of the blackjacks to the same fungus. We have lost three of the shin oaks, and the old prairie flameleaf sumac has died and the bees have left.

A few years ago, after understanding that the high deer population was preventing any new woody plants, except cedar, from growing, we put a few wire cages around some of the trees to protect any root sprouts that might come up. The urge to do this came one spring when we discovered a Spanish oak sprout near the double-trunk Spanish oak that the deer had not yet found. Inside the wire fence we put around that Spanish oak we now have one 10 foot Spanish oak (the original root sprout) an 8-foot escarpment black cherry and a 5-foot hackberry, plus now three other small oak sprouts.

Inside the other wire cages, we put around some other trees we now have a cage full of three-foot-high shin oak sprouts, a three-foot live oak, and some greenbrier.

One half of the double-trunk Spanish oak broke off in a windstorm 4 or 5 years ago. It was, as are most oak trees in the Hill Country, partially hollow. The other half of the tree and the root sprouts are doing fine so far.

A view of an overgrazed, overbrowsed, pasture in the Hill Country.

A recent walk around found 5 species of grasses, 4 are native grasses, 9 native forb species and a few shin oak sprouts not in cages that have escaped being totally eaten. There are three species of cacti on that acre, (the large and small pad prickly pear (*Opuntia engelmannii* and *Opuntia macrorhiza*) and lace cacti.

I recently discovered that feral hogs have been working the area, (rooting up the *macrorhiza*) to get at the fleshy root.

This is not by any means a healthy Hill Country habitat. It has too few plant species total as well as almost no vegetation below the browseline (outside of the few small cages we put up), it has poor quality as well as poor quantity of grass, and most of the forbs are smaller than normal. Part of this may be because it is a very rocky, shallow soil site which will never be as productive as sites with better soil.

So of the 34 trees on that acre 16 years ago, we have lost 7 and a half, and had we not caged some small areas, we would have no new saplings as replacements.

Below, I will contrast another acre where we built our house and built a high fence to keep the grazers and browsers out.

Life and Changes on a One Acre Piece of the Hill Country: Part II

Above, I discussed the conditions and changes I have observed on a one-acre piece of property we have owned for 20 years. That acre, part of a larger property of an overgrazed, overbrowsed working ranch is a rocky savanna with a few trees showing a distinct browseline and little grass or forbs. I described how, after placing some small wire cages around some of the trees, woody plant sprouts have appeared inside the cages where the animals can't get to them.

As I discussed last week, we built our house about 200 yards from the acre described above, on a site with slightly better soil and more trees. We immediately built a high fence around one acre surrounding the house about 16 years ago. Other than slightly deeper soil, more trees, and some post oaks not present on the above acre, the two sites were similar and had been part of the same ranch management for over thirty years.

The acre around the house, inside the fence, had 40 hardwood trees (live oaks, blackjack oaks and mostly post oaks) and 10 cedar trees when we fenced it. Since that time we have lost one blackjack oak to hypoxylon and the top of another.

A view of a similar area fenced form the grazers and browsers where "volunteer" plants have been allowed to grow.

I recently walked around the yard counting the small shoots and saplings of hardwood trees and vines that have come up on their own in the past 16 years. It was not an exhaustive search and I undoubtedly missed some, and there have been others that we have either removed, dug up to grow in pots or died, so the numbers are certainly low. I found 108 hardwood tree and shrub sprouts and saplings that we had nothing to do with their being there. In other words, these were all "volunteers" and represent what Mother Nature put there by herself.

Many of these sprouts (37) are live oaks, post oaks and blackjack oaks that may well be root sprouts of mature trees. But the rest are of species that are growing no closer than a few hundred yards away and some we have no idea where the closest source of seeds is. All of these young trees range from about a foot tall to 6 to 8 feet tall. We have blackjack oaks, escarpment black cherries, hackberries and prairie flameleaf sumacs in the 6 to 8-foot range, and one of the sumacs which is over 15 feet tall, and one cherry over 12 feet tall.

We also have over 50 native vine plants which have established themselves around the yard, including greenbrier, grape, Virginia creeper and trumpet creeper.

We have planted a number of native shrubs which have grown to produce berries which have been the source of new plants scattered around the acre, presumably by birds and small animals, such as possumhaw, and some of which also produce root sprouts, including roughleaf dogwood, Blanco crabapple, and trumpet creeper.

In addition, numerous native grasses and wildflowers planted in specific places over the years have produced seeds that obviously traveled to other places in the yard and reseeded themselves.

It is worth noting that none of these new plants can be seen outside the high fence.

The point of all of this is just to illustrate how Mother Nature propagates her plants and establishes replacement plants for her trees, shrubs, vines, forbs and grasses, and to note that it means that this process is still operating even in areas that have been seriously overgrazed and overbrowsed for some time. All that is required is to protect the young plants from overabundant herbivores, native and non-native, out there.

Of course, not all of the woody sprouts will make it to maturity, and in areas not fenced, but having lower (more "normal") animal numbers, some would certainly be eaten, but some would escape and that is how the diversity of Hill Country vegetation is perpetuated.

We will not be able to allow all of the 108 woody sprouts to become mature trees or vines because the place would become an over-shaded jungle. But to the extent we can allow many of these new plants to survive, we help to maintain the seed bank for native species and to maintain a more healthy habitat for native birds and animals.

Plus, it is just fun to watch Mother Nature do her thing.

A Lifetime Involved with Nature

I generally only write about topics related to the Hill Country or Edwards Plateau, both because this is the area I know best and because it is the area I love the most. But a recent series of TV specials on PBS by and about David Attenborough gave me a different perspective.

I have been an Attenborough fan all my life. He was 89 years old at the time of the TV special and started making nature films in the 1950s, before I ever had a TV! I have watched his nature films from literally pole to pole and all around the equator and marveled at the experiences he has had over all these years.

The latest three-hour series details some of the early experiences he had in filming nature around the world, how the world and our technology have changed over his lifetime and some of his insights into the future. So today I want to write about some of the things I took away from Attenborough's perspectives on 60+ years of wildlife filming.

Roaming the world filming nature in the '50s and '60s, was, by current standards, primitive in terms not only of the technology available at the time, but also in terms of the attitude and knowledge about nature that they had. Most of the "expeditions" in the early days were to "collect" specimens of rare, unusual, or unknown animals, and to bring them back (dead or alive) to "civilization" and to show the film to the world.

And in those days, the idea of "conservation" was largely about how to capture threatened species to bring them back to zoos and game preserves and raise them in captivity in order to "save" the species.

But also in Attenborough's early days, his visits to various remote places in the world were to places with pretty much pristine, unaltered habitats. As time went on, however, more and more of the habitats he visited were showing signs of human destruction of habitat and the subsequent destruction of wildlife. Attenborough commented that more habitat and wildlife destruction has occurred during his lifetime than had occurred in *all human history before that!*

Gradually, the thinking among scientists was that the idea of "saving the species" by captive breeding and confining animals to zoos was not only ineffective and ultimately impractical, but also questionable from a moral standpoint. What was necessary was to save native habitat where the animals had evolved to live and that this was far preferable than saving a few individuals in captivity.

The problem that was occurring at the same time that the importance of native habitat began to become more widely held, was that it was also the time when the greatest destruction of native habitat was occurring, worldwide. And it is still occurring.

Most habitat destruction takes place because an ever larger worldwide human population needs a greater and greater supply of food, which requires more and more native habitat destruction for farm land and to raise livestock. It is also true that many of the most remote native habitats are home to people with very little resources and for whom feeding their families will always be more important than conserving habitat for wildlife.

The good news, from Attenborough's standpoint, is that we finally know how to conserve native habitats and the wildlife that inhabit them, and we are also, as a population, becoming more desirous of doing so. There is a greater awareness of the importance of native habitat and wildlife, and a willingness to do what is necessary to protect our natural areas.

So while we may have become enlightened belatedly, better late than never, and so there is some hope that some places will indeed be protected and/or restored.

Interestingly, I have maintained that we are lucky in the Hill Country. This area has not been very conducive to farming, and as a result we have more potentially native habitat than most of the rest of the state and much of the country as well. This is even more reason, I believe, to do everything we can to conserve as much native Hill Country habitat as possible.

For over 60 years, Attenborough has been trying to teach the world about wildlife and has in the process been witness to evolving knowledge and attitudes about the natural world. He concluded by saying "We now have a much better understanding of how to protect it. I can only hope that we will."

Nature's Calendar

I am often fascinated by many aspects of nature, native animals and plants and their interactions with each other. One of the things that fascinates me the most is how both plants and animals tell time, or more specifically, days of the year.

It was the changing of the leaf color in our trees that got me to thinking about this recently. The fact that plants respond to something in the environment differently at different times of the year is obvious. All deciduous flowering plants put up new leaves in the spring and then the leaves turn color and drop off in the fall. How do the plants know when to do this? Is it temperature? Rainfall? Daylight? All of the above? None of the above?

It turns out that while temperature and rainfall have some effect on the timing of various plant processes, the most important environmental condition that determines when a given plant will do certain things (grow leaves, bloom, set fruit or turn color) is called the "photoperiod" which is the relative length of day and night. However, the most strictly correct answer to the above questions is "none of the above." It is in fact the number of nighttime hours.

For instance, plants that bloom in late fall to early spring when the days are short and the nights are long require a certain length of darkness before they will bloom. If their nights are interrupted by a short period of light, they will not bloom. Plants that require a short period of darkness before they will bloom (such as plants that bloom in late spring to early fall) can be induced to bloom in the winter by turning on the lights for a brief period in the night. I guess, like people, some plants need more sleep than others.

But then the question is, how do plants know if it is day or night? They don't have eyes. But all plants have a pigment called "phytochrome." Well, actually, two closely related pigments called phytochromes that are slightly different in structure. To greatly oversimplify things, I will call the one that persists throughout the nighttime Pn and the one that is mostly present in daylight Pd. So when sunlight hits a leaf, it converts Pn to Pd, but when it gets dark, Pd reverts back to Pn, and thus the plant can "tell" when it is daylight and when it is dark by which phytochrome is in abundance.

So the phytochromes act like hormones which turn on or off certain other processes that cause the plants to respond by growing leaves, putting up flowers, etc.

All of the above is pretty well established by science, but that still leaves a number of questions. Even if the cells in a leaf "know" it is daylight or nighttime by the structure of the phytochrome, plants don't have watches so how do they "know" how long the light and dark periods are. And how do individual plants "know" how long a nighttime needs to be before it begins to bloom?

Plants don't have a brain or a nervous system so that one part can communicate with another. Growing leaves or blooms requires more water, nutrients and carbohydrates to be brought up from the roots. How do the roots "know" to respond? It is dark all the time for the roots.

Also, in every year there will be two times when the same length of nighttime occurs (for example once in the spring and once in the fall, an equal number of days before and after the longest day of the year). So without a brain, how can a plant "know" that a certain length of nighttime means it is early spring and not late fall?

Regardless of how much we understand about how things work in the Natural World and how thoroughly fascinating it is to learn what science has discovered, almost every new discovery just raises more questions. While we humans will continue to strive to understand everything in nature, we will probably never answer all the questions we will have.

And maybe that is a good thing. Not understanding the why and the how of everything just adds to the mystery of nature and the awe we have that never goes away when we seek to understand nature. Nature will always keep us humble.

ENJOYING NATURE

The Joy of Watching Nature

As I sit at my computer writing this, I can look past my monitor and watch the queen butterflies literally flocking to the blooms on Gregg's mistflower, or the hummingbirds probing each bloom on the columbine, both of which are growing just off the porch only a few feet from where I sit. Or I can watch the lesser goldfinches at the thistle feeder under the porch overhang. The entire view out my window is a collection of native trees, shrubs, flowers and grasses, and being able to see it all on a regular basis makes whatever I am doing here on the computer much more enjoyable.

And when I take my coffee cup and go out on the porch and sit quietly to watch all of the goings-on it is even more enjoyable. I never get tired of watching the squirrel climb over the back gate, run down the path, up the old cedar tree and jump over onto the post oak and down to the ground to see if the birds spilled any sunflower seeds. Or watching the cardinals taking a bath in the recirculating stream.

This year it has been interesting to watch the old agave, with its only chance at immortality, put up an 18-foot tall flower stalk with huge flat yellow and green flower structures, all in a matter of a few weeks.

The point of all of this is just to describe what to me is one of the real joys of life, simply watching, observing and studying nature. And all of what I just described occurs every day in an area of about a half-acre. The reason I am writing about this is to remind folks with busy, distracted lives, to figuratively, "stop and smell the roses."

The nature purist will have noted that much of what I described above is not truly "natural," because the bird feeders and the water feature were obviously something we added, and to be fair, the Gregg's mistflower and the columbine, while native wildflowers, were planted. But my point is that you don't have to be in a true wilderness to experience nature. You don't have to drive to a distant park or hike miles up a trail or book some "outdoor adventure." For most people you don't even have to leave your back yard.

A Queen butterfly on a Gregg's blue mist flower.

Baba Dioum, an environmentalist from Senegal said, "In the end, we will conserve only what we love, we will love only what we understand, and we will understand only what we are taught." I have been fortunate to have witnessed a number of instances where people have learned something new about the natural world around them and almost immediately came to value it more and were more inclined to conserve it.

So one of my goals in life is to try to interest as many people as possible in becoming more educated about and involved with nature in whatever way works for them. The more people know about nature, the more they will care for their little piece of it, and the better off the Hill Country will be for all of us.

If you are an adult and nothing I have written above about viewing nature appeals to you, then I feel sorry for you because I believe you are missing out on a really important part of life. If you are a parent, I hope that among the many gifts you give to your children will be an appreciation of and a love for the natural world.

I think just getting the kids out of the house and away from all their electronic gadgets, away from texting and Facebook and out into the real world will be good for them, both mentally and physically. And some of them may even discover a love for real live things that is unmatched by anything that they see on a little screen.

The future stewardship of the Hill Country will rest in the hands of today's kids, and if they don't care about it, its future will be in jeopardy. If a generation grows up thinking the natural world around them is unimportant and fails to conserve it, they will regret it when it is too late to save it, and may blame us for not teaching them about it.

A Naturalist's Walk Around the Yard

A few days ago I took a walk around the house to see what I could see.

The first thing I saw as I walked out was one of our Texas spiny lizards. We haven't seen a fully grown one in a while, but seem to have a couple or more medium- sized ones. They are usually on the ground, on the house or sidewalks or in the flowerbeds, but they really blend in well on a tree trunk.

Then I looked at the Turk's cap growing on the south side and thought about the several times lately that we have seen Baltimore and Orchard orioles pecking at the little fruits that these perennials produce.

I also noticed that the KR bluestem, which unfortunately makes up a significant portion of our "lawn" around the house, was growing quite well around the shrubs that we have been watering occasionally this summer to keep them alive. I am glad to say that most all of the native shrubs seem to be doing OK, but I had hoped that the KR would not fare as well in this drought as our native grasses, but it seems to be competing quite well.

I almost stepped on a ground skink wiggling through the leaf litter under the post oaks. They seem to thrive, even in dry times, living in leaf litter. Since they are so tiny, they can only be eating small insects, maybe pill bugs. If you haven't seen one, they look like very little (less than 3-4 inches long) skinny brown lizards with very short legs.

We had a couple of decent rains a few days ago, and I noticed in more than one place that the rain had run off even in fairly level areas and carried with it a lot of grass litter and probably soil as well, which piled up in little debris dams. We don't normally see this because when there is a normal amount of grass growing and less bare ground, it holds the water and litter back and slows down any runoff and actually allows the water to soak into the ground faster than the bare ground. Since we haven't had much of any grass growth this year, the dead grass is wearing out and we have much more bare ground than in "normal times." Rain hitting bare ground causes soil particles to plug up the pores in the soil and slow down water infiltration and begin erosion.

When I walked by the outside of the bathroom window, I remembered a few nights ago when I looked out at the window ledge and saw a baby Blotched water snake, maybe 9 inches long and about half the diameter of a pencil. He was probably waiting there for bugs that are attracted to the night-light. A few weeks earlier, Priscilla had found him, or one of his hatchlings, in one of her potted plants.

I noticed the Autumn sage seemed to be in full bloom after the rains 8 to 10 days earlier and it made me think that we will probably see the cenizo (Texas sage) blooming in a few days.

As I walked around I also noticed that virtually all of the "volunteer" native shrubs and trees we have inside our deer-proof homestead fence, none of which have been watered this year, seem to be doing relatively well in spite of the drought. We have lots of escarpment black cherries, hackberries, possumhaws, flame-leaf sumacs, Virginia creepers and grapes, as well as lots of root-sprouts of post oaks, blackjack oaks and live oaks, none of which we planted and none of which were here before we built the high fence. The interesting thing, however, is that virtually all of these small woody plants are growing under large trees where they are at least partially shaded, and, so far, they are surviving the drought without being watered. Of course the root sprouts get water from the mother tree's roots, but all of the others were "planted" by the birds sitting in the trees.

You don't have to have a huge ranch to find interesting things in Nature, just step outside and look.

Life Around the Backyard "Creek"

A number of years ago I built a small recirculating stream or "creek" on a slight slope in our backyard. There were several reasons for wanting this rather than a bird bath. First, I wanted to have the sound of running and/or dripping water as that attracts birds. I wanted it at ground level to make it available to small animals, and I wanted it in an open area without any bushes or tall wildflowers so the birds would be able to see any predators approaching. And I wanted it to be able to fill automatically in times when we were not at home.

At the top I dug out a very shallow, saucer-shaped "pool" and then a long, shallow "creek" about 6 or 7 feet long. At the bottom I dug a hole about a foot deep and two feet in diameter. All of this was then lined with a single piece of heavy-duty black plastic sheeting. I then placed a heavy rubber "tub" in the hole at the bottom.

Inside the "tub" was placed a float valve and a small submersible pool pump inside a mesh bag with foam filter material. At the top around the small pool were stacked several large rocks in such a way as to make a support for a very large rock that would hang over the pool. Then the entire area around the pool and the creek was covered with rocks to hide and hold down the plastic sheeting and large gravel was placed in the pool and the creek.

A small water line was connected to the float valve and it was adjusted to maintain the tub nearly full. The outlet from the pump was connected to ½ inch plastic tubing which was buried under the plastic sheeting up to and up on the very large rock above the pool. The top of the tub was covered with several large flat rocks to prevent any animals from having access.

So the water circulates from the tub up to the top of the big rock, falls down into the shallow pool and then runs down the "creek" and back into the tub. The water running down the "creek is not more than about ½ inch deep and about 2 to 3 inches wide. There is a shallow depression in the large rock at the top that has water running through it as well.

Robins drinking from a recirculating backyard "creek".

The creek runs unattended for months at a time. I usually clean out debris that accumulates in the tub about every 3 months.

Our permanent resident birds include cardinals, titmice, chickadees, house finches, lesser goldfinches, scrub jays and woodpeckers which make frequent use of the creek on a daily basis, both for drinking as well as for bathing. Seasonal or less frequent visitors include various sparrows, finches, flycatchers, summer tanagers, painted buntings, robins, cedar waxwings, roadrunners, American goldfinches and hummingbirds.

We had a turkey nest in the front yard one year and she made daily visits to the water in the backyard, and individual turkeys as well as small groups will sometimes fly into the yard looking for food, but always stop at the creek as well.

Water attracts birds which are not attracted to seed feeders so you see species you might not see without water. You might think that hummingbirds would not need to drink, given their liquid diet, but it is amazing how often the hummingbirds like to bathe in the ¼ inch deep water running over the rock.

Our feathered friends are not the only critters that like the creek. The resident squirrels stop at the creek at what seems to be several times a day (if you have ever tasted the tannin in an acorn, you would probably want a drink too!) We also occasionally have a visit by a cottontail.

We know we occasionally have visits by skunks and raccoons and other night critters, and have seen them use the creek as well, but we probably only see a small fraction of the visits during the night.

Two of the most fascinating animals to use the creek are frogs and toads. We have a collection of several leopard frogs living in and around the tub under the rocks. As I said above, we are over a half mile from permanent water, so it is amazing and somewhat mysterious as to where they came from and how these animals got here, and when they were no longer to be found, where they went. We have observed many tadpoles in the tub as well as small frogs, so we obviously have an ongoing population in our tiny "creek."

We also have at least two Gulf Coast Toads. These animals are not always seen around the water, but also in flowerbeds and nursery pots where the vegetation and soil is usually moist.

Both frogs and toads lay eggs in water which hatch into tadpoles and then undergo metamorphosis to adult animals, so the water in the tub and the pool at the top of the creek is essential to their reproduction.

A question I have always had is what is the difference between a frog and a toad? Here, apparently, is the answer: Frogs are slim and fast, toads are fat and slow. Frog skin is usually smooth and toads have "warts." Frogs usually live in or near water, toads can live in drier habitats. Both animals can burrow into the mud and go into a state of hibernation and survive for long periods of time.

If you like to watch wildlife, you should have some form of permanent, shallow, moving water. If you build it, they will come!

Enjoying Watching Nature and How to Spread the Joy

A little while back one morning after a rain the previous day I looked up from my computer and saw a swarm of flying ants rising from the grass outside. They were back-lit by the early morning sun so their wings made a dazzling display of flapping wings against the dark background of the green shrubs. I was pretty sure they were fire ants, and went out and confirmed that they were indeed.

New ant colonies are established from old colonies when at certain times of the year the colony produces many winged males and a few winged females. As they emerge (usually after a rain), the males will search for a female to fertilize, the females will then search for a suitable place to start a new colony, lose her wings and begin digging a new nest.

A little bit later I looked out again and saw that the ants were still flying up to catch the breeze, but then I also noticed that there were at least two large dragonflies that were flying around among them, presumably having a feast—I was too far away to actually observe an ant being caught, but my friend Bill Lindemann says that dragonflies are one of the most voracious predators and I am sure they had plenty to eat that day.

A few days later while sitting on the back porch enjoying the fall weather I noticed two dragonflies (same two?) embraced in a tandem mating flight and flying over my artificial creek. The bottom one of the two dipped her tail into the water occasionally to deposit an egg in the water. My first thought was how neat it is that the dragonflies could use my little creek to lay their eggs in. My second thought was how I expect the frogs to get the larva when they hatch.

A couple of days ago, late in the afternoon, we noticed not one but three Texas spiny lizards on one of our window screens. Early the next morning, they were still there, but soon took off. The next evening one was back to spend the night on the screen. I have seen at least one around that side of the house several times now.

I tell all of these little anecdotes because they illustrate a point. None of these observations would have been nearly as interesting and fun to watch if I didn't know something about ants and dragonflies and frogs and lizards. The more you know about a subject the more interested you are in engaging in it, in watching, participating, talking, reading and learning about it. There is nothing unique to nature about this. If you are an expert in quilting, then you will be interested in looking at quilts and learning how the maker made it and in appreciating what you see more than someone who knows nothing about quilting.

I admit to a desire to get everyone more interested in and engaged with Nature, for two reasons. First, I get so much enjoyment out of Nature that I think others will also. And the more you learn, the more you will want to learn and the more fun you will have with Nature.

Native Wildlife can be Interesting and Entertaining

Being naturally more interested in what is going on outside than inside, I find myself gazing out the window at the vegetation and especially the critters out there. And frequently one of those critters does something really interesting, surprising, or even funny. Here are a few of the incidents I have seen recently.

One morning while working on my computer I kept hearing a tapping noise from the room across the hall. Going to investigate, the noise stopped. The next day the same thing happened. It finally occurred to me that it might be a bird at the window, so the next time I heard it I was much more careful going into the room quietly and slowly and there it was, a flycatcher on the window sill pecking at the window. Over the past few weeks, this little bird came pecking on several occasions.

My friend, Bill Lindemann, tells a story of a turkey doing the same thing and ascribed it to the bird seeing its reflection in the window and attacking the reflection. A few years ago we had a titmouse that was waging war against that titmouse he saw in the rearview mirror of my pickup—it went on for weeks!

Speaking of titmice, not long ago I caught some activity out of the corner of my eye out on the porch that seemed strange. It looked like a titmouse had flown onto a branch of a large potted plant, carrying a large object. Well, titmice are seed eaters and it seemed to be past nesting time, so a titmouse carrying any large object seemed strange. Through binoculars it looked like the titmouse was pecking something it was holding with its foot on a branch, but I also saw something that looked like a hummingbird just below the branch. Going out to get a better look, as I approached, the titmouse flew away empty-handed (empty beaked?) in one direction and a hummingbird flew away in another direction. I can only conclude that the titmouse had the hummingbird by the wing and was pecking at it.

But predators can be prey too. One day I saw a roadrunner on a path in our yard bashing something in its beak on the ground. The view from my binoculars showed it to be a titmouse! A few days later I heard a commotion on the porch and looked up to see a roadrunner jumping up into a small shrub just off the porch. Putting two and two together, I realized that the titmice and cardinals like to land in that bush and then hop down from there to drink in the saucers under some of the plants on the porch (this is in spite of the perfectly good water feature I provide for them a few yards away!). That was probably where the roadrunner had caught the titmouse earlier.

I have always been amused to watch hummingbirds bathing in the thin sheet of water that flows over one of the rocks in our recirculating "creek," especially early in the morning. Lately, after watering some perennials and shrubs, I have noticed the hummingbirds bathing on the wet leaves—kind of a hummingbird "sponge" bath I guess.

We have two bird feeders in our backyard and the birds spill some of the sunflower seeds on the ground below. Some of the birds, as well as the squirrels, spend a lot of time on the ground picking up spilled seeds. But they apparently don't get all of them because we sometimes see a raccoon in the early evening doing the same thing. It amazes me that they can distinguish whole seeds from hulls, but apparently they can. The raccoons and squirrels appear to do it with their "hands."

A few weeks ago I was watching a raccoon doing this when I saw a gray fox slowly creeping toward the raccoon. Then all of a sudden the fox rushed the raccoon, obviously surprising and scaring it, and the raccoon raced a few feet up a tree. The raccoon obviously outweighs the fox by quite a bit. The fox then began to search for seeds himself. But shortly, the raccoon, apparently recovered from its surprise, rushed the fox and chased it away. No blows, no bites, but the raccoon established its dominance and the little fox didn't return.

The Lightning Tree Fell Down!

Several years ago my wife and I were sitting on our front porch enjoying a thunderstorm when suddenly a lightning bolt struck a post oak a couple of hundred feet in front of us.

Lightning generally travels down a tree through the vascular bundles underneath the bark. Sometimes it boils the fluid therein and the steam blows off the bark, which is what happened to parts of this post oak. It was about 15 to 18 inches in diameter and 30-35 feet tall. In the next few weeks it became obvious that at least 80 percent of the tree was dead—only one limb on what appeared to be the least damaged side of the trunk remained green.

As the months and years went by, first the smaller twigs and later larger limbs decayed and fell off so that what remained was a skeleton of a tree with several dead limbs here and there and one live limb, the latter having grown considerably from its original size when the lightning struck.

I have no doubt that the tree, which could be seen from the street, was a subject of discussion or displeasure to some passersby who undoubtedly thought the tree should have been taken down for aesthetic reasons. I have a different philosophy about these things. First, when considering what to do or not do in terms of managing our property, my first thought is "What would Mother Nature do?"

The trees and all of the other native vegetation in the area evolved to take care of themselves quite well without any "help" from humans. That fact alone is reason enough for me to leave any dead trees that do not threaten the road or our house. I know that dead trees provide insects for woodpeckers and other birds and animals as well as cavities for birds and squirrels to nest in. Finally, the last thing I would ever do is cut down a tree and haul it off or burn it since allowing the tree to decompose by natural forces returns important organic matter and nutrients to the soil.

Anyway, over the years the lightning tree (we don't generally name our trees, but this one seemed to be an exception) gradually lost more bark and more limbs, but at the same time the one live limb grew bigger and bigger.

Then, a few months ago after a night of rain and wind, I noticed that the tree had fallen down. When we went out to take a look, we first noticed that the trunk was not fully down on the ground, but was supported by a couple of large limbs. Then as we stood looking at the tree, a squirrel poked its head up over a limb and looked back at us. The next thing we saw was a pair of Carolina wrens hopping around the leaves of the live limb. Then upon closer inspection we saw that the deer had already found the tree and had eaten all of the leaves they could reach on the one living limb.

I don't know what the squirrel was doing on the tree. The wrens gave the appearance of having a nest close-by, but we couldn't locate it. Only time will tell if there are enough living roots to support the one live limb in its now-semi-prone state (now, several months later, it is still alive).

We have lots of healthy trees for which we are quite thankful. We certainly enjoyed the lightning tree for as long as we had it, and even in its current state it represents just one more part of a fascinating piece of Hill Country native habitat we are lucky to have.

Watching Whooping Cranes in Texas

My wife and I recently spent some time on the Texas coast near Rockport. We like to visit places like Aransas National Wildlife Refuge and the Laguna Madre National Wildlife Refuge.

One Whooping Crane displays for another in Aransas National Wildlife Refuge.

Aransas NWR is well-known as the wintering grounds of the endangered whooping cranes. The parts of the refuge that are accessible by car represent only a small fraction of the total area, most of the refuge is either shallow bays or marshes, and these are the areas most frequented by the cranes. This is where the blue crabs live, which are the favorite food of the whooping cranes.

Whooping cranes, the tallest bird in North America at 5 feet, were almost wiped out in the early 20th century, mainly due to loss of habitat. The cranes nest and raise their young in spring and summer at Woods-Buffalo National Park in the Northwest Territories of Canada. Then in the fall the cranes and their young begin a 2,500-mile migration to the Texas coast northeast of Rockport. In 1941 there were only 16 birds left! The draining of marshes and playa lakes along the migration route was primarily the reason for the decline in the population, although hunters and loss of habitat on the Texas coast also played a part.

Since the 1940s there has been a tremendous effort on the part of the United States, Canada and several states and their biologists to restore the population so that today the migrating population is approximately 250 birds. There are perhaps another 250 in several non-migrating populations in the United States. This is a huge success in restoring a highly endangered species which also happens to be one of the most spectacular birds in the country.

But 250 birds are still a very small number of individuals to sustain a healthy population. Whenever the entire population of a species lives in a small area, especially if the population is small, any number of events could spell disaster. What if a late-fall hurricane were to hit the Texas coast as the entire population arrived? Or more likely, what if something happens to their food source, either in Canada or Texas?

The main food of the whooping crane at the Aransas refuge is blue crabs, but they also eat shrimp, crawfish and wolfberries. But the population of crabs, shrimp, and other aquatic critters depends on the conditions in the bays, estuaries and marshes along the coast, and in the Aransas area, that in turn depends on the amount of fresh water from the Guadalupe and San Antonio rivers flowing into the bays. Currently there are court actions, appeals, and controversy as to whether the Texas Commission on Environmental

Quality is allowing too much of the river waters to be used by farmers and cities and too little allowed to flow into the bays, in what are called environmental flows. The lack of fresh water decreased the crab and other aquatic species populations substantially, stressing the cranes. If this issue is not resolved in favor of the cranes, they could be threatened again.

We knew from past experience that the best way to see whooping cranes is from a tour boat, not from the roads in the refuge. This year we again took a tour and were treated to a great sight. We spotted a single crane feeding in a marsh only about 25 yards from the edge of the Intercostal Waterway, and the bird allowed us to pull up close to the shore and watch. We watched this bird for probably 20 minutes, taking dozens of pictures.

Then another crane was spotted flying in our direction, just off the surface of the water. We watched as the second crane flew up and lit not 20 yards from the first crane and proceeded to find itself a couple of crabs. While the second bird seemed to ignore the first, the first bird quit feeding and seemed somehow agitated. Then we were treated to a fantastic display in which the first bird jumped into the air and spread its wings numerous times, showing its black primary wing feathers, all similar to a mating display in what appeared to be an attempt to either chase away another male or impress a female (we were not sure of the sex of either bird).

In spite of over 70 years of efforts to save the species, it could still be lost to a single natural or man-made event. Once a habitat is lost, it is lost for decades or forever. Once a habitat is conserved, however, its conservation has to be continued by every generation.

Fears of Nature Are Greatly Exaggerated and Mostly Unfounded

I recently read an article by a woman who described her visit to a tall grass prairie remnant in Kansas, and the utter joy she felt by simply walking among the grasses and wildflowers and experiencing what much of the middle of the country used to look like. But then she described a conversation she had with a waitress at a diner just down the road from the prairie. She asked the waitress if she ever goes there, and her answer was, "Oh no! My high school biology teacher showed us photos of what chigger bites look like!"

Of all people, it was her high school biology teacher who forever put the fear of wild places in that young girl's mind. And of course the media sensationalize every incident of anyone being injured, chased or just scared by anything in nature. Just today I saw, on TV, for the umpteenth time, the video of a woman, fishing from a 10-foot high pier and having a small shark grab her fish as she was reeling it in—the screams went on for some time. The San Antonio Zoo is now advertising their "Cold-Blooded Reptiles" in the manner that one might advertise a Halloween visit to a Haunted House.

Parents inadvertently instill in their children certain fears just by the act of protecting them from harm. When a mother sees her child getting too close to a hot stove or a fireplace, or picking up a knife, her actions, words and tone of voice tell the child this is something they should fear. And of course, when she sees her child pick up a bug or a lizard she may react the same way and the child gets the impression of danger. But the child will grow up to no longer fear a hot stove or a knife, but may forever fear wild things.

The reality, of course, is that there are far more dangerous things in your kitchen, or your garage, or your workshop, than there are in the local fields or woodlands. People cutting themselves with knives in the kitchen, or hitting their thumbs with a hammer, or falling off a ladder, seldom make the news. And then of course, there are all the sports we play. Most things that threaten us are man-made.

In 15 years of walking many miles over the hills, pastures, or creek bottoms of over 400 Hill Country properties, plus hiking the trails of most all of the Hill Country State parks, my wife and I have yet to see a poisonous snake in the wild. Or encounter any threat from any animal. Or be bitten by any insect more serious than chiggers or occasional fire ants. The Hill Country is just not a dangerous place.

On the other hand, in that same period of time we have experienced two scorpion stings and one paper wasp sting, all either in the house or on the porch.

I guess the critters that most people are afraid of are snakes. Of course, nothing can be more harmless than non-venomous snakes, which make up the very high percentage of all snakes in the Hill Country. But since most people cannot, with confidence, tell the difference between harmless and venomous snakes, all snakes strike fear in many people. People are almost always startled when seeing one, even if it is a little rough green snake or a tiny ring-necked snake. In 15 years of living in the Hill Country, I have seen only one rattlesnake—and it wasn't out in the pasture, but in our garage!

My concern about people being afraid of Nature is that they will therefore avoid spending any time with nature or learning about it. And to me that means they are missing out on one of life's greatest joys—experiencing Nature. It also drives some people to want to surround themselves with as little vegetation as possible, to cut the grass as short as possible, and to eliminate any wild animal, from a caterpillar to a mouse to a rabbit to a raccoon.

The "wild animal" I have the most concern for is the brown recluse spider. My wife was bitten many years ago and the subsequent wound was very painful and slow to heal. You are very much more likely to encounter one in your closet or under furniture or in your storage shed than in the wild.

WALKING THE NATURE TRAIL

A Nature Walk to Observe Seasonal Changes Around Us

A few months ago a friend gave me a book she thought I would like, *The Forest Unseen: A Year's Watch in Nature* by David George Haskell. The author is a biologist, and he embarked on a year-long project to observe a small patch of forest in southeastern Tennessee every week or so for a year and record whatever he saw that interested him.

Sometimes he would just sit silently for an hour or so and watch and listen to whatever there was to see and hear. Sometimes he would lie flat on his stomach and observe tiny animals and plants in the leaf litter with his magnifying glass. Sometimes it was bright and sunny, sometimes it was raining, and sometimes it was snowing.

I find the whole idea fascinating and would like to do something similar. But Haskell had two advantages that I don't have and was obviously willing to work harder at the project than I can see myself doing. He lives in an area near mature eastern forests that inherently have a much greater biodiversity of plants and animals than our part of the Hill Country, and he is a well-trained professor of biology, much more knowledgeable about both plants and animals than I am: he could identify just about everything he saw. He also had access to an area that has been very little affected by man, whereas the area most easily accessible to me has been significantly overgrazed by cattle and blackbuck antelope and overbrowsed by too many white-tailed deer for a long time.

Rather than concentrate on a small area and everything I could see, hear, smell or feel from that one location, I am going to attempt to establish a nature walk that begins and ends at our driveway and attempt to take that walk every ten to fourteen days, making note of everything I see of interest and any changes noted. The area in question is best described as a somewhat heavily-wooded savanna located on a relatively flat (by Hill Country standards) upland site.

My study area is a rather irregular oblong-shaped route covering about a third of a mile. There are wooded areas, there are open grasslands, there are dead trees, there are rocky areas, and there are patches of cedar. The entire area is active rangeland with cattle grazing several months every year, several blackbuck grazing constantly, and many white-tailed deer as permanent residents.

Native trees include live oaks, post oaks, blackjack oaks, Spanish oaks, shin oaks and cedar. There is a severe browseline on all of the oaks and some of the cedar. The only unprotected vegetation below the browseline is agarita, prickly pear and cedar.

Grass cover varies with soil type and tree cover. In open areas, short native grasses such as Texas grama, curly mesquite, buffalograss and oldfield threeawn can be found as well as introduced King Ranch bluestem. Also, purple threeawn patches are common. The prominence of these grasses is usually an indication of overgrazed pastures. On the positive side, there is relatively little bare ground.

In more shaded areas and areas of better soil, some populations of better grasses can be found. Specifically, two cool season grasses; Texas wintergrass is common and occasional Canada wildrye can be seen. In addition, plains lovegrass, Hall panicum and meadow dropseed can frequently be found. Occasionally, a few less-than-robust little bluestem plants can be observed.

There are occasional prickly pear plants along the path, both Texas prickly pear (*Opuntia engelmannii*) and the smaller plains prickly pear (*Opuntia macrorhiza*) and in a rocky place some lace cactus. I also noticed one small mammillaria cactus.

Unlike Haskell's patch of undisturbed native habitat, my nature walk is certainly not a representative sample of undisturbed native Hill Country habitat, but it is, unfortunately, not an uncommon sample either. The most striking thing missing from this area is vegetation diversity below the browseline, which is not only the natural food source for many animals including white-tailed deer, but is the preferred habitat for many of our small native animals.

But maybe by closely observing things in this kind of area I can learn something about how nature is coping with these man-made disruptions. Our native creatures are, if nothing else, resourceful. I will let you know what I see.

First Observations Along the Nature Trail

March 1, 2014. This was my first nature walk along the path I laid out earlier and which I described in the essay above.

At the very beginning of the path just off the driveway I encountered a blackbuck antelope dung pile. A dominant mature male marks his territory with dung and urine and defends his territory against all other males. He does this so that whenever a doe herd passes through as they graze, if any of the does are in season, he has a chance to mate with them. Sometimes, however, he has to spend a lot of time trying to convince her that he is the one, and by then they may have drifted into another male's territory and a fight ensues. Meanwhile, the immature bucks watch and wait.

A little further along I saw a flycatcher. Last year ash-throated flycatchers built their nest in my new bluebird box just off the path, so that may happen again if the bluebirds don't lay claim to it soon.

Next I came to the top half of a large blackjack oak on the ground. I know exactly when it broke off, it was the big ice storm we had back around Thanksgiving when there were still leaves on the trees. We lost the top of another blackjack not far from this one at the same time.

As I observed the top of the tree on the ground, I noticed the tell-tale signs of hypoxylon with large patches of bark having fallen off and a grayish color on the trunk where the bark had been. Hypoxylon is a fungal disease that is somewhat related to oak wilt but with very different properties—it does not travel from one tree to another through the roots like oak wilt does and thus only affects individual trees.

Another difference between oak wilt and hypoxylon is that while oak wilt can and often does attack perfectly healthy trees, hypoxylon usually infects only stressed trees. Of course the severe drought of 2011 and subsequent less-than-needed rainfall years since certainly stressed this tree as well as many others.

In fact, we have lost about a half dozen large trees, mostly blackjack oaks and a few post oaks, to the drought of 2011. Nearly all of these trees also showed signs of hypoxylon, but it is not clear if the trees ultimately died from the drought stress and just happened to contact hypoxylon as well, or if the fungus was the proximal cause of the tree's death. Of course, that is all sort of academic, either way we lost nice trees.

A lot of folks would see these dead trees, either upright or lying down and think about all the work required to cut them up and haul them away or burn them—in other words to "get rid of them." But in times like these, I ask myself "What would Mother Nature do?" And Mother Nature would leave them alone, right where they are, and that is exactly what I will do.

My reason is not just because of what Mother Nature does, but because it is good for the ecosystem. Allowing dead trees to stand where they are or lie where they fall makes for good wildlife habitat for everything from insects to birds and most all of our other small animals. The insects help the decay process of the trees and they provide food for other wildlife. The hollow trunks provide dens for lots of critters.

As the wood decays, bacteria and fungi degrade the cellulose into tiny particles that then work into the soil adding organic matter to the soil, something which Hill Country soil is usually lacking. So the body of the trees in time decays and becomes food for new vegetation, the carbon cycle is complete and the soil is more fertile.

Further along the path I noticed a lot of lace cacti in a rocky area, some of which appeared about ready to start showing buds, some of which didn't look so healthy and some of which were clearly dead. I used to think cacti were long-lived plants, but more recently, I have begun to think of them as having rather short live spans.

Animal count for this walk was: one flycatcher, one wren, two titmice, three sulfur butterflies, one deer and one fox squirrel.

March and April Walks Along the Nature Trail

Continuing my observations while walking along my nature trail between March 20 and April 12, here are some of the things I recorded.

On March 20th I noted that the Lacey oak we planted several years ago, and which is caged from browsers, has large swollen buds. This is a great tree that is endemic to our area of the Hill Country and was first identified as a separate species by rancher Howard Lacey on his place near Lower Turtle Creek in Kerr Co. in the late 1800s. The tree is most often seen growing on the upper reaches of hills even on very rocky soils, so it is pretty tough.

I noticed a number of insects on this day, from a tiger swallowtail butterfly, to several sulfur butterflies to a number of grasshoppers. There were a lot of tiny bees swarming on the flowers of the agarita bush. This is an important shrub in the Hill Country. It is evergreen, and it is generally not browsed by anything, so it is one of the few shrubs that one can find on almost any property. Because the leaves are so stiff and sharp- pointed, these shrubs can also serve as very effective "nurse" plants that allow other species to grow up within their protection and escape browsing. It is not at all uncommon to find hackberry or escarpment black cherry saplings growing up inside an agarita bush.

On this walk, I also observed a big turkey gobbler displaying for a group of six or so hens.

On March 30, one of the first things I noticed was that some of the ball moss on various live oak trees was blooming. Most of the time ball moss is just kind of ignored, but the blooms make it slightly more noticeable. It also reminds us how remarkable this epiphyte is, obtaining all of its nutrients from the air and rainfall and not taking anything from the live oaks except for a place to live.

Along one part of the walk, the trail passes a large live oak that we once thought would be outside our bedroom window of our yet-to-be-built house. But only now, after over a decade of walking around under this wonderful tree did I notice that up on a big limb about 15 feet up, there was a Texas prickly pear growing! It is not really rare to find prickly pear growing up in trees or even in rain gutters sometimes, as all sorts of wildlife like prickly pear tunas and deposit the seeds everywhere, but I couldn't believe I had missed it all these years.

I noticed more wildflowers on this walk than before, including low verbena, low bladderpod, and prairie verbena.

I also noticed three turkey toms displaying—this time for each other as best I could tell!

On the April 12th walk, I decided to check on the bluebird house just off the trail. The last time I checked it was totally empty. This time I discovered a nest with at least one bird in it. I very quickly closed the box and walked away, so I didn't yet know what kind of bird it was. But later I went out with my binoculars and hid in the trees to watch for any activity at the bird house. Sure enough, after less than 10 minutes I was able to confirm that a pair of titmice were obviously feeding a brood.

Just a little further along my trail, I noticed that one of the large blackjack trees that died of drought and/or hypoxylon in 2012, and is still standing, had lost a very large (about 1 foot in diameter) branch in a recent windstorm. That is generally the fate of trees that die—they usually lose several limbs to wind damage as the weakened wood can no longer support the weight, but it is always a little sad to see it happen.

We have a small of grove of maybe a dozen shin oaks that have a slightly different- appearing bark than the rest of the shin oaks, and previously I had noticed they were also later in greening up than the other shin oaks. But on this walk they were indeed leafing out nicely.

There is always something new and interesting to see, even on a familiar 30-minute walk.

A Fun Morning Sitting and Watching Nature

My previous visits to the nature trail have been walking. But as every hunter, birder and naturalist knows, you can't walk through the woods without most all of the critters knowing you are there long before you ever see them, so you miss a lot when you are walking.

I decided, therefore, to just sit still at various places along the trail and see what I could see. So off I went with my milk crate, binoculars and notebook, stopping along the way and sitting quietly for a time just watching nature.

My first stop was not that far from our yard and I could see activity along the fence around the yard, a bird house on the fence and another out in the open pasture. The first activity that caught my eye was a jackrabbit out in the open pasture casually grazing on the newly sprouted grass. He would bite off some grass, chew it, then stretch a bit to reach another clump of grass, chew it, then make a slow-motion lazy hop and begin the process all over.

The next thing I noticed was a fox squirrel climbing down a branch of a post oak and jumping from the branch to the top of a bird house on a fence post. From there he did a high-wire act of balancing by switching his tail back and forth as he walked along the top fence wire until he got close enough to jump to the nearby blackjack oak. Nothing about this was new. I had watched this kind of activity from the house many times. But then another squirrel followed the first one only a few seconds later, then another, then another. At least some, if not all four squirrels appeared to me to be juveniles—this year's litter.

Over the next 20 or 30 minutes I watched numerous squirrel antics, jumping from tree to tree and back again, up this trunk and down the next, chasing, then being chased. These squirrels were obviously not searching for food as they never stopped to eat anything, and they were certainly not hiding from predators, so it is difficult to think they were doing anything but playing—much like human children would do. They were, of course, honing their survival skills.

I watched a wren search around a coral honeysuckle near the bird house, then up on the fence, then onto the bird house and then, hanging upside down, it looked into the bird house. At this point a male English sparrow appeared and chased off the wren.

English sparrows are among the earliest exotic species introduced into the US, being brought to New York around 1850. Normally, I would not want any exotics nesting around the house. But, growing up in near-treeless west Texas, English sparrows were about the only birds I regularly saw as a kid, so I couldn't bring myself to evict these from the nest box.

At my next stop, as I was looking at the live oak sprouts around me, a sparrow flew down in the grass not 8 feet away (I believe it was a rufous-crowned sparrow, but I could be wrong) and it proceeded to rustle through the grass looking for seeds and/or bugs for some time.

An alert jackrabbit sits ready to take off at the first sign of danger.

At the next stop, a little while after I sat down, a jackrabbit came hopping up to within about 50 or 60 feet and sat, posed with his ears up and the sun shining through his ears so that I could see every vein. Then the wind blew the paper in my notebook and he took off. I don't know, but I don't think this was the same jackrabbit I saw earlier.

Sitting and watching takes more time than walking, but you see a lot more.

Sitting Around the Nature Trail in Mid-July

I took my milk crate and my notebook and went out to sit in various places along my nature trail to see what I could see. It was mid-July and things were beginning to show the lack of rain.

I did notice, however, on my first stop that the grass still had enough green in it, especially the grass under the live oaks, to give the area a nice green hue when viewed from a distance. At this same stop, I noticed what looked like dead leaves on a post oak. When I walked over I was able to confirm that this lower limb was indeed dead, having died this year as the dead leaves were clearly this year's growth.

At the next stop I noticed a good example of the "nursery effect" of a dead limb on the ground. A sizeable limb had fallen some time ago, and the grass growing up in amongst the dead branches was much taller with many more seed heads than the grass growing everywhere else. Downed branches and limbs protect newly sprouted woody plants as well as grass and forbs from being grazed or browsed. This protection allows for the production of more seeds and the establishment of forbs and woody plants, thus improving the condition of the range and the diversity of the habitat.

I also noted something I already knew, but hadn't thought about for some time. Because of the browseline (caused by deer) most vegetation from about 5 feet down was missing so one can see much farther under the trees when sitting down.

When sitting at my next stop, I suddenly noticed a very large, black feral cat moving with some purpose somewhat towards me. It appeared to be careful where it put each paw as it was walking through the grass. When it got to within about 25 feet, it suddenly turned its head and looked at me for maybe one second before it bolted off. In less than a minute, I saw it again about 250 yards away, still moving with a purpose.

Feral cats are a real problem for our native fauna, killing very many birds and small animals. The problem, other than they are not native, is that their population is very much higher than would naturally be the case for any apex predator, and therefore their effect on the ecosystem is proportionately greater. Their population is so high because humans keep adding to the population by releasing unwanted animals and also by providing them with food and even shelter in some cases.

Moving on to my next stop I came upon a relatively fresh "cow pie." And low and behold, it was being worked on by several dung beetles. For some years, I never saw a single dung beetle around here, apparently because the cattle were being given anti-worm medication that killed the dung beetles. Dung beetles provide a service of not only helping to disperse the manure, but by burying the balls of manure with their eggs inside, they help to aerate and fertilize the soil.

Wildlife seen this trip: cardinal, white-wing dove, sparrow, white-tailed deer, swallow, golden-fronted woodpecker, pipevine swallowtail butterfly and a queen butterfly.

A friend of mine used to talk about his visits to the woods behind his house to sit on a log and smoke a cigar and how relaxing it was. It took me a while to realize that it really wasn't the cigar he was going to the woods for, it was the woods themselves, and the relaxation that he experienced. I thought of my friend when I was out in the pasture. Try it, you will find it relaxing too.

More Time Spent on the Nature Trail

It had been about six weeks since I had been out on the Nature trail and about two weeks since the last rain, so I was interested in seeing if there was anything new. It is always interesting to just sit alone in the pasture and look and listen. I never lack for something to catch my eye and hold my attention for a time.

On my first stop, I got to looking at the various rocks lying on the ground and the variety of rock types. I know from basic geology that they are all limestone and that they all were formed in shallow seas that periodically covered this area several million years ago. And I know that, being on an "upland" site that is relatively flat and about 2000 feet above sea level, this area was not likely part of a river or creek bed—those types of areas are to the north and south of where I was sitting. So I found the variety of rocks, given their similar origin and environment, interesting.

Some of the rocks are almost pure white, others gray, still others reddish. Some were smooth in texture, some rough and irregular shaped, some contained obvious small fossils. Some displayed tiny quartz crystals and others showed areas of chert. So just looking at the rocks is fun, and if you pick up enough of them, you will almost certainly find a scorpion!

Some of these rocks may have been laid down in clean water seas while others may have been formed in muddy estuaries of runoff from mountain erosion. Some areas along the trail are pretty much free of surface rocks, some areas show numerous surface rocks making walking difficult, and still other areas show the tops of bedrock protruding from the soil in places.

So rocks help make the trail interesting and diverse.

Further along the trail I noticed that the top had broken off of the "baobab tree." Of course, it was not a real baobab tree, but that is what we called it when we first saw it nearly 20 years ago, because it had an unusually wide trunk and relatively few branches or leaves—just like the real baobab trees we had seen in Africa many years before.

Actually the tree was a post oak and if you walked around it you would find that the trunk was really just a shell that was totally hollowed out and there was even a small hole through what was left of the trunk. The top died a few years ago from hypoxylon, so it was not surprising that the top would break off.

Wildlife noted on this visit included 3 or 4 turkeys off 200 yards or so away, a white-tailed doe walking out of the cedar, a red wasp hunting along the tips of the grass, hovering now and then, but never landing, and a bumble bee that zipped past my face on what appeared to be an important errand.

Not much was blooming on this visit at the end of August. The only actual blooms I saw were on two-leaved sennas, a toxic native wildflower that nothing eats much of and a single low vervain, both responding to the rain two weeks ago.

Watching Deer and Grass on the Nature Trail

I went out on my previously-described, nature trail, on Oct. 10th. It was the first time I had been out on the trail since the very welcome rains (about 5 inches) in September, and I was interested to see what changes I could find.

As I sat down on my milk crate at my first stop, the first thing I noticed was green Texas wintergrass under my feet. This is a cool-season grass that usually doesn't start growing until later in the year, but all the rain last month plus the fact that it was in the shade of a tree meant it was taking advantage of the ideal conditions to get started on next year's foliage. This is an important grass to have on a range as it provides grazers with nutrition in the spring when there isn't much else to eat.

Next to the Texas wintergrass was plains lovegrass with a full seedhead, a warm-season grass that provides good forage. At other stops I found Hall panicum, a fair forage grass, as well as Texas grama, hairy grama, red grama and old-field threeawn—all poor forage grasses.

I didn't have to go out on the trail to notice the KR bluestem that suddenly sprang up everywhere with prominent multiple seed heads. From a car driving by, one might conclude that we suddenly have lots of tall grass, as the seed heads are 18 to 24 inches high and from a distance it looks like the range is covered with lots of "amber waves of grain." Unfortunately, it is just the stems and the seed heads that are sticking up like that, and they provide very little nutrition for grazers. Later in the year, the seed heads will drop off and the stems will turn yellow.

Just to see how much edible foliage was present, I pulled up a small KR bluestem plant that had 6 stems and seed heads. It turns out that it was really two plants, but the total amount of foliage down low on the plant was fairly minimal—this introduced, invasive, ubiquitous grass is not the best forage grass.

Sitting on my crate at one stop I noticed a white-tailed doe doing what I can best describe as a hesitation/stomping gait that I have observed numerous times when a deer is uneasy about something it sees and wants to investigate instead of simply bounding away. The doe would pick up one of her fore feet (and sometimes her opposite hind foot as well), hold it motionless in the air for maybe a second, then stomp it down with some force.

I don't know if the stomping was aimed at me, trying to scare me away, or at other deer, trying to warn them of something to be concerned about. Stomping is something other animals do to try to drive away something they consider a possible threat.

At any rate, the doe continued this behavior for several minutes, moving through somewhat brushy cover that was dense enough to partially hide her from me and vice versa, but not dense enough for me to lose sight of her. Then when she walked out of the brush and into a clearing, she continued this hesitation/stomping as she turned toward me and came to within about 50 feet of me, with both of us being in the open. Then we had a starring contest for a couple of minutes when neither of us moved. Eventually, although I never moved or turned my head, I turned my eyes to one side for a moment and she bounded off, showing her white tail flag briefly.

Deer in our area are so numerous and live among so many people and their cars that they scarcely ever look up when you drive by, even within 10 feet of them, but I suspect they usually see humans, even out of their cars, being in motion. So maybe my complete lack of motion made her more curious than scared, at least for a while.

Sadly, I found another blackjack oak which showed signs of hypoxylon and the two main limbs had broken off from the hollow trunk about six feet off the ground. This was yet another casualty of the drought that started in 2011. The rains we got in September came much too late to save this one.

More Views from Stops Along the Nature Trail

This visit to my nature trail was on a bright sunny morning at the end of November. It was a treat just to sit and watch as each gust of wind brought down a shower of leaves from the post oaks and blackjacks. Intermingled with the leaves was an occasional plains lovegrass seed head that had been picked up by the wind and was being dispersed as nature had intended. All sure signs that fall is ending and winter is not far away.

Another sign was watching two squirrels searching under an oak for any acorns the deer and the turkey have left. But sometimes, with squirrels, it is difficult to tell the difference between searching for food and just chasing around for the fun of it.

At my next stop I set my box down amid a patch of mealy blue sage. This is one of my favorite wildflowers, partly because of its beautiful blue flowers and partly because it is not eaten by livestock or deer, so it can survive even in heavily grazed and browsed pastures. Sadly, the nursery trade now sells a version of this flower which may or may not be a true native that is referred to as Henry Duelberg sage. It is making the native version harder to find. It is not clear if this new version will be eaten by anything or not.

As I was sitting amongst the mealy blue sage, I noticed a young blackbuck fawn standing alone in the grass looking around, presumably for its mother. After a while it laid back down and even in the short grass it was well camouflaged. Blackbuck antelope, having evolved to live in a warm climate nearer the equator where seasonal differences are less pronounced, don't have the strict breeding and fawning seasons that our white-tailed deer do. Thus it is not that unusual to see young blackbuck fawns this time of year. As I left this spot I gave the fawn a wide berth and it stayed motionless—just as its mother told it to I suspect.

It was interesting walking around the woods this time of year to see the difference in the leaf color and the stage of fall color between different individual trees of the same species. One would expect that all the post oaks, for example, in a given area that appear to be roughly the same age would have very similar genes and to be closely related—more so, at least, than they would be related to post oaks a few hundred miles from here or many decades different in age. But clearly, there are still variations in the genes of individual trees of the same size growing next to one another.

On several places along the trail, mainly in the shade of large trees, I noticed obvious feral hog activity. We had noticed significant rooting and other signs not far from the house recently. I found a place on the back fence where the hogs had forced apart the strands of barbed wire and were coming onto the ranch through that hog-made opening. I fixed it so they could not come in at that point, but all the while I knew they would just find another place to break through.

The blackbuck antelope have been on the ranch for decades and there has been some success in controlling their numbers. In the previous 14 years we have lived here, however, we have only seen an axis deer on the ranch on two or three isolated occasions. But in the past two or three months, I have seen two different axis deer around our house. Clearly, feral, exotic animals are a real and growing problem for Texas landowners.

Winter Along the Nature Trail

I had not been on the Nature Trail in a while and it was the middle of January, approaching the middle of winter. It is not a time when one expects to see a lot of activity, and in terms of wildlife, and other than a flock of turkeys and a couple of squirrels, I didn't see too much.

I did watch a buck slowly searching for acorns and forbs among the grass, and as he stepped over a log it reminded me of something I have often wondered about four-legged critters—how do they know where their back feet are? The buck smoothly stepped over the log with his front legs and then just as smoothly with his back legs as well.

Can he see where his back feet are? I doubt it, but he certainly didn't turn his head to look. And I know that predators (think cats and dogs) can't see their hind feet when they are walking straight ahead, but their brains clearly "know" how to step over things with their back feet. What really amazes me is to see a deer running through the pasture with downed tree limbs and rocks strewn everywhere and they seem to almost never stumble even in areas where I would have to be careful not to stumble while only walking on two legs.

At one stop where I set my box down, I examined the grasses around me. The Texas wintergrass stood out because it is green and growing, and I could see that grazers had already found the grass around me. The yellow stems of the KR bluestem are beginning to fall over and decay. I could also identify small tufts of Hall panicum and curly mesquite. I found a single triangular seed of Texas grama.

I noticed several newly broken limbs of some of the blackjack oaks that died as a result of the drought in 2011 and 2012. These trees seem to be falling apart faster than I expected, and I found it puzzling because a little further along the trail I came to a live oak that has been dead for over 10 years and even though it had lost a lot of its bark, it is still standing and still had most of its big limbs.

Some may consider all of these dead limbs to be unsightly, but Mother Nature doesn't think of it that way. The dead and decaying trees and limbs make for habitat for insects and the birds and critters that feed on them, as well as "nurse areas" to protect grass and forbs from being eaten. This allows the grass and forbs to set seed and for the seed to be distributed around the area, thus improving the seed bank, the vegetative cover and the native habitat.

Ten or fifteen years ago I noticed a small live oak about a foot or so tall in an area too far from the nearest live oak to have been a root sprout, so it obviously came from an acorn. The reason I noticed it was that it is very unusual to find small shoots of any hardwood trees in this overgrazed, overbrowsed pasture. So I put a wire cage around it to protect it, and it has been growing, slowly, inside that cage ever since—it is now about four feet tall.

A few months ago I noticed the cage was gone. I assumed that a buck caught his antlers in the wire and ran off with it, but the live oak seemed to be OK. I kept intending to replace the cage, but didn't. Well, on this last visit I noticed it had been browsed and a buck had been rubbing on it as well. So, better late than never, I hope, it now has a new cage.

Stop, look and Listen: One Year of Visits to the Nature Trail

About a year ago I started taking this series of nature walks on a trail that I set out on the pasture around our house. The idea for such a study came from a book I read, *The Forest Unseen: A Year's Watch in Nature* by David George Haskell. The author is a biologist, and he embarked on a year-long project to observe a small patch of forest in southeastern Tennessee every week or so for a year and record whatever he saw that interested him.

I found the whole idea fascinating and wanted to do something similar. Rather than concentrate on a small area and everything I could see, hear, smell or feel from that one location, I established a nature walk path that begins and ends at our driveway and attempted to take that walk every ten to fourteen days, making note of everything I could see of interest and any changes noted.

Since I like nothing more than spending time in a native habitat, I found each visit to be both fun and informative. Even though it was an area I was thoroughly familiar with, there were some surprises (some good, some bad), and it was never dull.

It has been a year since I started making these periodic visits along my so-called nature trail, and I have learned something very important. I have been interested in nature all my life, and over the years I have had the pleasure to hike along the trails of some of the most spectacular places in the country, from Arcadia National Park to the Everglades, to Big Bend to the Grand Canyon, to Mount Rainier, to Denali in Alaska and to the Hawaiian Islands. But I obviously missed a lot of really interesting nature observations by just hiking.

About half way through the year on the nature trail, I began taking a milk crate with me and instead of just walking the trail I would periodically stop, and sit on the crate for a while and just look around—more like Haskell did his visits. What I learned was, if you really want to begin to understand nature and observe it as it is, not as it reacts to a human walking through it, you need to go alone, sit quietly and just look and watch and listen. Sometimes it causes you to focus on little things up close, but sometimes you focus on the bigger picture in front of you.

But sitting in one place causes you to study and to learn about what you are seeing. Billy Kniffen, a former AgriLife Extension agent and expert on range science and land management likes to say that his father used to tell him, "Boy, you need to learn to see what you are looking at." Sitting on a box in the pasture has taught me the essential truth of that statement.

So the next time you are out in a natural area, don't focus on how far you can hike or how fast you can get to the end of the trail, take your time and concentrate on what you see in front of you.

SEASONS

Part of observing and enjoying nature involves observing it with the changing seasons. We are fortunate in the Hill Country to have four seasons that are mild enough to be outside and have interesting things happening around us all year.

Winter is Coming

It is just a couple of weeks before winter officially arrives. The two times of the year that show the greatest changes in the local landscape are the beginning of winter and the beginning of spring. As humans, we tend to view the former with dread and the latter with hope and enthusiasm. Mother Nature views it all as part of the process of life on Earth.

For deciduous trees and shrubs and other perennial plants, losing their leaves and becoming dormant is just their way of coping with freezing weather and preparing for spring. Annuals have produced seeds that will survive the winter and begin a new generation in the spring. Even evergreens cease growing although their leaves are capable of surviving sub-freezing temperatures.

Some animals hibernate. Many animals in this part of the country don't actually hibernate, but may remain in burrows or nests during the more severe winter storms. Some of our birds fly south for the winter, but then other birds migrate from the north to spend winter with us. Most insects die in late fall but leave behind eggs, larva or cocoons, but some adult insects actually live over the winter in a dormant state, some underground and some just curled up in vegetation or leaf litter.

Winter of course brings us humans lots of outdoor chores. My philosophy on this is simple; grow native plants that have always been here and think about what happened to them during all those winters before we got here. Nobody raked the leaves from under the trees, and out in the woods, even today, no one does. So why do we consider that such an essential activity? I admit that a pile of leaves on non-native turf grasses might not be good for the lawn, but leaves falling in flower beds or scattered over the native grasses is just mulch for the winter and organic matter to be mixed into the soil later.

Mother Nature doesn't cut the seed heads off grasses, wildflowers or perennials during the fall either, but leaves the seeds for the birds and small mammals when there is little else to eat. Mother Nature doesn't mow the native grasses short either, but leaves the leaf litter to cover the ground, reducing evaporation and protecting the soil microorganisms.

Winter is a stressful time for most all animals, because not only is it cold out, but there is generally less food available. About the only protection many species of wildlife have during the winter are evergreen trees and shrubs, and yes, that includes cedar. So protecting or planting some native evergreen shrubs will be appreciated by the wildlife.

Maintaining bird feeders throughout the winter is certainly important, and even more so if there aren't many native sources of seeds nearby. Insect-eating birds are particularly affected in the winter and have to switch to berries. If you don't have berry-producing shrubs around, you might consider providing suet or fruit as possible food for these birds.

One thing that some folks don't think about is the need wildlife have for water in the winter. Our coldest spells tend to also be the driest, so small birds and animals can easily become dehydrated. And it is also usually at those times when many people's bird baths are frozen. So if you can work to provide fresh water on those mornings, your feathered friends will appreciate it.

On a recent cold morning, my wife watched birds coming and going from our small recirculating stream in the backyard and said, "It looks like the air traffic around Houston Intercontinental Airport." Sometimes water is more important than food.

We have on occasion had a few hummingbirds overwinter here, and they seem to really appreciate our feeder since little else is blooming in the winter. We have also been amazed to see sulfur butterflies out and about even after Christmas on warm afternoons. You have to wonder; how can those little things survive the cold nights we have had? But then, monarch butterflies winter in the high mountains of Mexico after migrating from Canada, and they will be back in Texas to lay eggs in the spring! It makes me feel just a little guilty when I complain that the thermostat is set too low!

So bundle up and go out and enjoy the natural world, even in winter.

Nature is Interesting Even in Winter

A non-naturalist friend of mine remarked the other day that, "This must be a slow season for you naturalists," which I guess seemed like a reasonable statement given the fact that we were looking out at a rather bare, drought-stricken, winter landscape. But in fact, it is a lot more interesting than my friend realized. Here are just some of the interesting things I have observed in the past few weeks.

First, not everything is brown and leafless. In addition to live oaks and cedar (Ashe juniper), we have Texas mountain laurel, evergreen sumac, cenizo and all the native cacti and succulents (yuccas, agaves). The rosettes of many of our favorite wildflowers such as bluebonnets, Engelmann daisy, standing cypress and big red sage are green now just waiting for longer days to begin their growth spurt.

Where the grazers haven't eaten it faster than it can grow, our Texas wintergrass (some call it speargrass) is responding to our December rains and is greening up nicely. This year I have not seen the rescuegrass and other bromes that usually begin growing this time of year.

As I watch our lesser goldfinches at our thistle seed feeder, I reflect on the fact that I haven't seen any American goldfinches this year, and didn't see any last year either, although they have been abundant in previous years. We had lots of pine siskins a few weeks ago, but they seem to have moved on for now.

Just a few days ago we had our usual winter flock of cedar waxwings attacking the cedar berries. They are always fun to watch as they descend on a bush in mass and depart together the same way, chattering to each other the whole time.

Flocks of robins seem to come and go. They were challenging the cedar waxwings a few days ago for the cedar berries, but the robins also spent a lot of time on the ground finding fallen berries, while the waxwings stayed in the trees. The robins appear to love the re-circulating stream to bathe in, sometimes crowding each other for the best bathing spots.

I noticed a male cardinal bathing in a spot that was apparently a favorite spot of the robins also, as several robins appeared to be standing around watching the cardinal splash around. But the cardinal stood his ground and the robins had to wait their turn.

I also rediscovered how much titmice really love peanut butter. I have a hanging piece of cedar with holes drilled in it that I can fill with peanut butter or suet, especially in cold weather. A few days ago I decided to refill the holes that had been empty for several weeks, and then noticed that within 5 minutes of returning from filling the holes with peanut butter, a titmouse was eagerly pecking away at it.

I was driving past a friend's house the other day and noticed him standing out by his car, so I pulled in to chat. As I drove up, he never turned his head to look at me, although I know he knew who it was, and even when I stopped, he remained motionless looking ahead in front of his car, finally pointing to the front of the car. As I followed his point, I saw a roadrunner, not 5 feet in front of him just slowly turning her head back and forth obviously looking for something to eat. Then, after perhaps spying something behind us, she took off at a moderate pace almost stepping on my friend's toes.

The peak breeding season for our white-tailed deer is November, so the rut should be over by now, the third week of January. But I just saw a buck with his head down sniffing the ground in the usual posture when they are stalking a doe. I guess his calendar didn't show him the season was over for now.

Finally, yesterday we noticed a bat roosting on our porch, hanging from the limestone rock near the ceiling. I don't know for sure what kind of bat it was (probably a Mexican free-tail), but I am told that some bats overwinter here and can be active on warmer nights. We wished we could have communicated to the little critter that we had just put up a bat house out front. Maybe he found it as he didn't return the next morning.

For a naturalist, the Natural World is always interesting.

Greenery Even in Our Hill Country Winters

When most people think of the winter landscape, they tend to think of brown, dead-looking foliage. While a lot of our trees, shrubs and perennials do in fact lose their leaves in the winter, we in the Hill Country have greener winters than folks in many other parts of the country.

Most of the greenery we see in the winter is due to our two most common woody plants, juniper and live oaks, and since these two species make up so much of our landscape, our winters are not as dreary as some other places. Mexican white oak, which is not locally native but grows in Val Verde County and into Mexico, and is commonly planted in this area, has leaves that persist into the spring.

But those are not the only evergreens we have, so sprinkled among the junipers and live oaks are many other green shrubs. Here are some of them.

Texas mountain laurel, also called mescal bean, is an evergreen shrub usually 4 to 8-feet tall with compound, dark-green leaves with shiny leaflets 1 to 2-inchs long. It has large showy purplish flowers in the early spring that smell like grape Kool-Aid. Deer will avoid this plant.

Cenizo, or Texas sage, is a 4 to 10-feet tall shrub with very small silver-grey leaves. It usually flowers around 7 to 10 days after a good rain, covering the whole shrub with lavender blooms that attract hordes of native bees. Cenizo is not a deer favorite.

Evergreen sumac is another plant with shiny green compound leaves. It produces tiny white blooms in clusters in the summer, especially after good rains.

Agarita is a common Hill Country shrub with compound leaves consisting of three very stiff leaflets, each with 3 to 5 very sharp points. Agarita produces small, fragrant, yellow flowers in early spring that are a favorite with native bees. The red berries ripen in late spring and some people make jelly from them. The birds like them too.

Texas madrone is a distinctive shrub or small tree with peeling bark revealing a smooth reddish or tan bark. Its leaves are dark green and leathery, its flowers are white clusters in early spring followed by small red berries.

There are two common Hill Country shrubs that are not, strictly speaking, evergreen, but are classified as having persistent leaves, meaning they survive into the winter, and in mild winters or in slightly more southern locations, may indeed be evergreen. They are the Texas persimmon and willow baccharis.

Texas persimmon is characterized by peeling bark, small, velvety leaves that curl under slightly and 1-inch round persimmons. The green fruit turns black when ripe. The fruits are a huge favorite with most all wildlife and many humans as well. Poverty weed or willow baccharis is a common, somewhat-invasive, multi-trunked shrub with airy fine foliage. It is commonly seen colonizing roadsides and disturbed areas of bare soil.

Mexican silktassel is another multi-stem shrub with oblong leathery leaves that are evergreen. Yaupon holly which has tiny leaves and produces red berries for the birds is more common in the eastern part of the Hill Country.

In addition to the above shrubs are the vines, greenbrier with leathery leaves with prickles and coral honeysuckle with red tubular flowers from February to November. Also, prickly pear and all other cacti, and the succulents, Buckley and twist leaf yucca, and two species of nolina are all evergreen.

In contrast to all of the above greenery is the yellow or straw-colored King Ranch bluestem seen along many roadsides and many pastures this time of year. The seed heads fall off and in late fall and early winter the stems take on a straw-colored appearance that gives the appearance of a healthy wheat field or an abundant grass-covered range, especially as it blows in the wind. Unfortunately, these stems contain almost no nutrition for animals.

Be careful pulling off the road in tall grass as a hot muffler can ignite the grass and start a fire.u

Winter Butterflies

If the phrase "winter butterflies" sounds strange to you, it is probably because, like most of us, you associate butterflies with summer and blooming wildflowers. And we always think about winter as a time when most all insects have either died or are in an egg or pupae stage or have become dormant underground or are otherwise unseen. But, when it comes to nature, nothing is quite that simple.

Several years ago we planted an elbow bush (*Forestiera pubescens*), on the south side of our house. It is now about 6-7 feet tall and about that big around. It always begins to bloom on the last few days of January or the first week or so of February, which is why it is also called the "spring herald." This year I noticed it in near full bloom on February 7, so I went out to look at it and the critters it attracted. I found four different species of butterflies and a number of bees taking advantage of a rare resource—nectar in the middle of winter!

I also went over to our Rosemary bush which is loaded with blooms and found the same species of butterflies and again a collections of bees. Rosemary is not a native plant but it is not invasive and is easy to grow and it blooms several times a year. But don't plant one close to your house or any other building—in a wildfire, it is very flammable.

The species of butterflies I observed were the red admiral, painted lady, variegated fritillary, and orange sulphur (aka clouded sulphur), all fairly common local butterflies. So seeing them was not in itself unusual, but seeing most of these butterflies active in winter, especially just three days after we had a cold (23 deg.) morning was somewhat surprising. Actually, seeing sulphur butterflies flitting around the yard on warm winter days is not unusual. A few days later I saw a snout butterfly on the elbow bush.

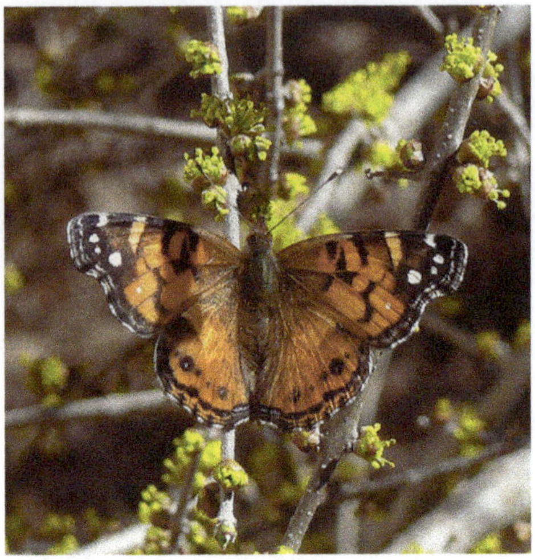
Painted Lady on the elbow bush.

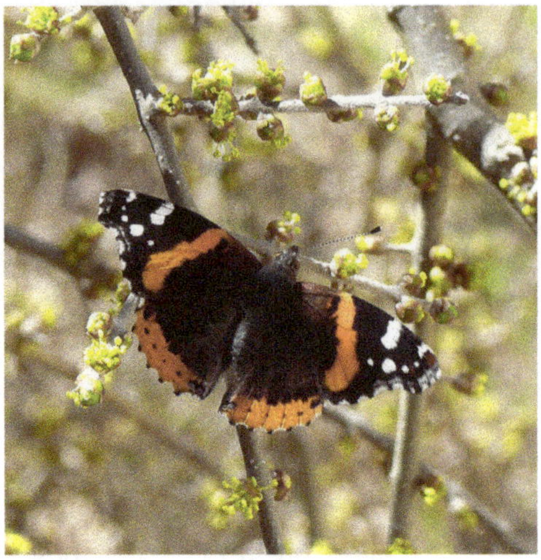
Red Admiral butterfly on the elbow bush.

Orange Sulphur on Rosemary.

Variegated Fritillary on Rosemary.

What is amazing to me is how these critters survive winter when it gets well below freezing. I know insects are technically "cold-blooded," but it also means there is often very little if any food available to them, so they obviously have to go into some kind of dormant state but then come out of it on warm days.

And then there is the aspect of how does the plant let the butterflies and bees know that it is blooming and it would like to be pollinated? And how do the pollinators find the plant that is blooming? The obvious answer is that the blooms produce molecules which tell pollinators that there are blooms around and by following the trail of these chemicals they find the blooms. As a chemist with a lot of experience working with very small amounts of material, I am still in awe that such a process works as well as it does.

This whole process of how a plant decides when to bring carbohydrates and other materials up from the roots to produce blooms and/or leaves, which kind of bloom and leaves to make, which chemicals the blooms produce, and then how the various pollinator species recognize the chemical and can follow the trail back to the bloom so they get their nectar and the plant gets pollinated to reproduce the species is really amazing.

How can anyone not marvel at how Mother Nature works?

After I finished writing the above, I was out in the back yard doing some maintenance on our water feature and I saw a butterfly floating in the water. I gently scooped it up and put it on a rock for it to dry out although I suspected it was dead. But a few minutes later I noticed it had flown away. It was a painted lady.

Changes Observed as Winter Turns into Spring

This year my New Year's resolution was to do a better job of recording my daily nature observations in a notebook or journal in order to document the progression of spring. The results so far are not perfect, but much better than previous years. Here are some of my observations:

As expected, the first sign of spring occurred on the last day of January—the elbow-bush was blooming and full of butterflies, tiny bees and wasps. The elbow-bush didn't show any signs of leaves for another month.

The next thing to bloom around our place was the Mexican plum in mid-February, followed by the creek plum in early March and the Mexican redbud a few days later. I didn't record the first blooms of the Texas redbud, but they are usually a week or two after the Mexican redbud.

Our possumhaw began showing leaves the first week of March, followed by breaking buds on one of our blackjack oaks a few days later.

We saw our first hummingbird of the year on March 4th. A few days later, I was working one evening in my office when I heard a strange noise at the window. It was an opossum, catching moths on the window that were attracted to the light. Occasionally we see a raccoon doing the same thing.

By the second week in March the rusty blackhaw viburnum had leaves and its first bloom. The blackjack oak was also in bloom. I observed the first leaves on the rough leaf dogwood, yellow buckeye, creek plum, wafer ash, cedar elm and gum bumelia the second week of March.

The third week of March saw the post oaks beginning to bloom, the blackjack beginning to leaf out as well as the fragrant sumac, switchgrass, Eve's necklace, mesquite and Vasey oak. This was also the week that the first bluebonnets began to bloom, as did the Spanish oaks, and the volunteer peach trees that came up adjacent to the compost pile a few years ago. I know the coral honeysuckle began blooming before the third week in March, but that was the first time I noticed it.

By the third week in March, the live oaks had lost most of last year's leaves in their spring leaf exchange and were beginning to bloom and to show new leaves. Also, the bald cypress was beginning to make cones, the bois d'arc and Texas persimmon began to show leaves, and the shin oak's buds were breaking.

By the fourth week in March, the Carolina buckthorn, Mexican buckeye, desert willow, fragrant mimosa, acacia, hackberry, amorpha, escarpment black cherry and Blanco crabapple were all showing leaves.

Toward the end of March, I observed the first leaves on the retama, kidneywood, flame-leaf sumac, greenbrier, Virginia creeper, trumpet creeper, black dalea and walnut.

Also, by the end of March we had not only bluebonnets blooming, but also rosemary, four-nerve daisy, columbine, prairie verbena, low verbena, Engelmann daisy, pink evening primrose, blackfoot daisy, prairie phlox, spiderwort, gaura, and I am sure others I didn't write down. Grasses showing new leaves included switchgrass, Eastern gammagrass, Texas wintergrass, rescuegrass, cheatgrass, little barley, Scribner's dichanthelium and big bluestem.

Interestingly, not all individuals of a species bloom and leaf out at the same time, even when they are in close proximity. About 6 years ago we had two blackjack oaks come up in our back yard, both the same year and about 8 feet apart. Given the distance these new oaks were from the nearest mature blackjack, I assume they were planted by the squirrels.

On March 19 I noted that one of the blackjacks was totally leafed out with almost full-size leaves, but the other had only begun to show the first tiny leaves. Not until the end of March did the second blackjack grow nearly-mature-size leaves.

Similarly, I noticed our mature Spanish oak had leafed out about 2 weeks ahead of a couple of Spanish oaks that we had planted.

The point is that plants are just like animals and humans, no two are exactly alike, and their DNA has enough variation to make them different from each other just as we are. And I am sure that the plants around your place didn't match those at our place in terms of timing of bloom or making new leaves. And all will be different next year.

Ahhhh....Fall

Ever since I escaped the winters of the northlands to come back to Texas, fall has been my most favorite time of the year. (In the north, fall just makes you look forward with dread to the winter; spring, so long awaited, is the time for joy and optimism.)

Fall also has to be one of Mother Nature's busiest times. All sorts of things are happening. Maximilian sunflowers, goldenrod, gayfeather, fall asters, mountain sage, cowpen daisies and common sunflowers are all taking advantage of the cool sunny weather to bloom and produce seeds before the winter.

Many plants are maturing their seeds or acorns or nuts. Walnuts and pecans are maturing, with the pecans splitting their husks to release the nuts and the walnuts dropping their husks so they can rot and release their nuts.

All of the various oaks are dropping their acorns. By the way, did you know that white oaks produce mature acorns in the fall after flowering in the spring, but red oaks (Texas red oak/Spanish oak and blackjack oak) require another year for the acorns to mature?

Many of our native grasses are taking advantage of the rains a few weeks ago to flower and make seeds. I know, most people don't think much about grasses making flowers, and some of them are pretty small and don't last very long, but when you see eastern gamagrass or yellow Indiangrass in flower, they are really beautiful. And beginning in November, when the little bluestem begins to turn an orange-red and open its fluffy seed head and you catch it with the light shining through the stems, it is a wonderful sight.

Soon, as the leaves begin to turn, all the hillsides will be transformed into paintings. Spanish oaks and flame-leaf sumacs turning red, cedar elms and escarpment black cherries turning yellow, cypress trees turning copper, all contrasted by the continued green of the live oaks and the cedars, give the Hill Country a whole new look. I know, it doesn't exactly compare to parts of the Midwest and Northeast, but these are OUR fall colors and we don't have to go anywhere to enjoy them.

Not all of the activity of fall is taking place with the plants. The animal kingdom is pretty busy also. With many species of migrant birds stopping by on their way south, we get to see species we don't usually see around here, even if it is just for a few days. Around our place, most of the hummingbirds seem to have already departed, but we still have a few late migrants that are enjoying our flowers and feeder. The lesser goldfinches are taking advantage of some sunflowers that bloomed earlier and are now just, apparently, delicious brown seeds. If people were not so eager to cut down dead flower stalks, the birds would really love to have the seed heads to play with into the winter.

The white-tailed bucks have lost their velvet by now and are showing renewed interest in the does. They need to fatten up for the rut and also to survive the winter. Fortunately, they have the acorn crop to give them the extra energy for the coming months, but they will certainly have to share the acorns with the turkeys, squirrels, and other critters. Unfortunately, mast (acorns, nuts, fruits) only lasts so long, and usually runs out as winter intensifies, leaving the animals with the least supply of food when they really need it.

As soon as the leaves begin to fall, the squirrels will begin to think about making nests for the winter. Every hollow log, tree or limb, or underground burrow, will be investigated by every little creature in the area before they all find suitable homes.

The raccoons are having to compete with the deer, the skunks, the squirrels and who knows what other critters for the Texas persimmons, Mexican plums, and other fruits. But as they enjoy their fall fruits and wander around, the seeds of the next generation will be planted.

Humans can get in on the act also, as this is the best time of the year to plant trees or shrubs or perennials as well as wildflower seeds. So enjoy this nice weather and get out and join Mother Nature and all the goings on.

Fall in the Hill Country—Like a Second Spring

This year, most of us were fortunate enough to have good spring rains, adequate summer rains and welcome September showers—a huge contrast to last year when we endured the worst single year drought in a hundred years.

This spring and early summer we were fortunate in having spectacular drifts of native wildflowers just about everywhere, some of which were of species and numbers not seen in years. Again, a huge contrast with the previous year.

Right now it seems like everything is responding to the September rains. I have even seen the rare sight of an oak tree putting out new leaves the first week of October!

I took a pad of paper and walked around our yard recording the things that were blooming right now. The following are my lists.

Shrubs and small trees: Autumn sage of various colors, kidneywood, cenizo, retama, rose pavonia, evergreen senna, mountain sage, black dalea, and rosemary.

Perennial forbs: Lindheimer's senna, Maximilian sunflower, gayfeather, tall goldenrod, zexmenia, prairie verbena, indigo spires, yellowbells, corona de Cristo, obedient plant, gaura, Mexican bush sage, fall aster, Gregg's mistflower, rainlily, Navaho tea, straggler daisy, Mexican red sage, Mexican mint marigold, tropical sage, purple coneflower, giant blue sage, Turk's cap, and snapdragon vine.,

Annual forbs: common sunflower, eryngo, hierba del Marrano, and cowpen daisy.

Grasses having just put up a fresh seed head or still in bloom: Indiangrass, switchgrass, big bluestem, little bluestem, sideoats grama, silver bluestem, blue grama, buffalograss, meadow dropseed, plains lovegrass, Lindheimer muhly, canyon muhly, and seep muhly.

Just outside the yard we see frostweed and snow-on-the-mountain.

The point of all of this is that we are fortunate in the Hill Country to have so many native plants that bloom in the fall. Needless to say, the butterflies and hummingbirds are happy about all of the flowers and especially the diversity of species.

This collection of plants wasn't always here and it obviously didn't just happen overnight. I can take no credit for all of the planning, planting and tending my wife did to achieve this diversity, but I can certainly attest to the beauty and enjoyment we get from it. And the butterflies, bees and other insects that evolved with these mostly native plants certainly appreciate having their foods available. And of course, the frogs, toads and lizards that live on these insects appreciate it too.

So much of what might have been called "natural areas" in the past have been lost to development, farms and overgrazed and overbrowsed ranches that much of the vegetation that was the base of the food chain for all native Hill Country animals is now disappearing.

Gardeners like my wife are working to restore native habitat to our gardens to create an oasis where both native plants and native animals can find conditions more like they had both evolved with. As the human population continues to increase and development takes increasingly more of our natural areas, the backyard oases will become more and more important.

So I urge all landowners to grow a great diversity of native plants, eliminate the non-native ones, and do your part to preserve and restore native Hill Country areas.

And get out and enjoy this wonderful Hill Country Second Spring!

— SECTION VII —

HELP FOR HILL COUNTRY RESIDENTS

Many new residents of the Hill Country are attracted to the beauty of the landscape, the climate, and perhaps the people, but they arrive here not knowing much about where to go for information about many aspects of the Hill Country. This section is designed to help landowners find the experts and the information they need.

In addition to the books listed in the essay below and in Appendix I, there are essays about various experts in the following section. In addition, contact information for government agents and nature-related organizations can be found in the Appendix II. And finally, in the section on Parks, there is a list of state parks in the Hill Country where people can go to view native habitat and to learn more about the Hill Country flora and fauna.

I encourage everyone, especially new residents to take every opportunity to visit natural areas and attend as many functions as possible where our native habitats will be discussed.

BOOKS

I guess it labels me as "old fashioned" in this age of electronic gadgets, but I still like books printed on paper—even though both of my previous books are also available in electronic form.

I urge all readers interested in nature and Texas natural history to look over my list of recommended books in Appendix I where I have arranged the books by general topics, including: Life in Texas, Natural Philosophy and Land Stewardship, Woody Plants, Grasses, Forbs, Animals, Birds, Geology, and Insects.

My List of the Most Important Books for Hill Country Residents

I would strongly suggest that all Hill Country Residents, especially new residents, consider at least the following books.

If someone were to ask me what single book I would recommend to help them to understand the basics of how a naturalist or a conservationist views the world, I would first protest that no one book can do that. But if pressed for just one, it would have to be Aldo Leopold's *A Sand County Almanac*, published in 1949, a year after his death. Leopold has to be considered at least on a par with Thoreau and John Muir and is usually credited as being the father of modern land and wildlife management thinking.

To help you, and/or your friends and relatives learn about and how to identify the native Hill Country plants around them, I would highly recommend these three books: *Trees, Shrubs, and Vines of the Texas Hill Country* by Jan Wrede, *Wildflowers of the Texas Hill Country* by Marshall Enquist, and *Grasses of the Texas Hill Country* by Brian and Shirley Loflin.

I would add to the above three books, three very recent new books that I think are exceptional.

Texas Master Naturalist, edited by Michelle Haggerty and Mary Pearl Meuth, is a very large, heavy (763 pages) training manual for the Texas Master Naturalists now made available to the general public. This book contains the greatest breadth and depth of coverage of a long list of topics about nature and the ecology of Texas.

Attracting Birds in the Texas Hill Country: A guide to Land Stewardship, by W. Rufus Stephens and Jan Wrede is an exceptionally well-written, detailed book about managing property for wildlife with special emphasis on birds.

There is a useful book by Ricky Linex, USDA Natural Resources Conservation Service, entitled *Range Plants of North Central Texas. A Land User's Guide to their Identification, Value and Management.* This book contains descriptions for the layman of over 300 forbs, grasses and trees as well as multiple color photographs of each plant. Don't be put off by the title, as probably 90 percent of the species discussed are also found in the Hill Country. (All of the other books listed here can generally be found online, but for this one contact the nearest Soil and Water Conservation Service office.)

Finally, but I hope not the last on your list, is my book, *Hill Country Landowners Guide*, which I hope will help bring all of the above into perspective and to help landowners understand the interrelatedness of all the other topics.

EXPERTS

I have always been keen on getting the best expert advice I could on anything and trying to avoid advice from non-experts or from anyone who has a financial stake in any decisions I might make. I guess that is part of why I chose a scientific field for my education and vocation.

The problem is that it is not always easy to know who is the unbiased expert and who isn't. But in the case of topics about land management, nature and native habitat, the experts on these subjects tend to be folks with some kind of biological or agricultural education and who work for, or have worked for, some of the government agencies and/or universities. And, especially for most of these folks who work for government agencies, it is their job to help you, and your taxes have already paid for it.

Appendix II contains the contact information for the various government agencies that have trained individuals whose job it is to help landowners with all kinds of questions and issues with their land management.

In addition, the contact information for various nature- and conservation-related organizations in the Hill Country is listed. Most of these organizations have meetings open to the public and also have knowledgeable individuals willing to help residents answer their questions. I urge everyone to become involved with these organizations and take advantage of the information they have.

Listening to the Experts

I still remember the first exposure I had to experts talking about land management in the Hill Country. It was in January of 2002 in an all-day symposium on land management in one of the local hotels in Kerrville. The speakers were all college professors or government agency people from Texas A&M AgriLife Extension, Texas Parks and Wildlife Department, Texas Forest Service and the USDA Natural Resources Conservation Service.

I still remember vividly my impressions from that day. I was surprised at the near unanimity of opinion of the different speakers representing different disciplines, as well as different agencies with different missions and experiences as to what constitutes good land management for the Hill Country. I was also inspired by the passion and dedication of these folks for the work they were doing and its importance.

I had grown up in the country in the high plains of Texas and had worked on a farm and hiked and hunted the open pastures as a kid. And I had spent a lifetime of vacations in State and National Parks being interested in wildlife and conservation. But I had no formal academic training in the disciplines most of the speakers at the symposium represented.

What I learned from that first symposium was that nature, native habitats, ranching, wildlife and conservation are much more complicated than I thought and some of what I thought I knew was probably wrong. But that symposium was truly a life-changing event for me. Since then I have been learning everything I can about all of these topics, and working to help others learn about them as well. This has become my full-time "job" in retirement.

In the intervening years since that first symposium I have had the opportunity and privilege to attend nearly a thousand hours of presentations and demonstrations by scores of experts on many different topics having to do with the land and the flora and fauna of the Hill Country. Many of those opportunities were facilitated by my becoming a member of the Hill Country Chapter of the Texas Master Naturalists, but many of those opportunities were events sponsored by various government agencies and other organizations.

Almost without exception, I have found these agency and university people to be eager to share their knowledge and experience as well as their time to help landowners and other interested folks better understand the natural world around them. Some of the government agents will even visit a landowner's property to discuss various management issues and in some cases there is even government money available to assist some landowners with specific problems.

I can say that I have been able to get to know many of these experts and can count many of them as friends. I have to thank all of them for not only sharing their knowledge and experience, but for their encouragement and guidance as I have tried to do my part in educating folks in the Hill Country about the natural world around them and how they can become better stewards of the land.

The Texas Master Naturalist organization, which is jointly sponsored by the Texas AgriLife Extension Service and the Texas Parks and Wildlife Department, is a program that not only facilitates the education of interested Texans on all topics related to the natural world around us, but also provides trained naturalists to volunteer for hundreds of projects involving education, outreach and service dedicated to the beneficial management of natural resources and natural areas. This program also would not be possible without the involvement of many government agents.

When I was 10 years old, I started to work for the cotton farmer near our house. I remember a time when the AgriLife Extension agent (we called them County Agents back then) came out to count boll worms to tell the farmer if he needed to spray them. That same county agent helped me choose my first 4-H lambs and later my calves and hogs and he taught me how to take care of all of them and how to show them. I have more fond memories of that agent and my animals and 4-H than I do of going to school in those years.

My experience is that too few people avail themselves of the free advice, knowledge, experience and help from these government agents when it comes to land management. And their advice is free of any economic interests in the decisions you make.

A Visit with Kerr County Extension Agent Roy Walston

In the above essay I wrote about how much I have learned from government agents and A&M professors about the natural world in the Hill Country and how everyone can benefit from their knowledge and experience. I have known Roy Walston for well over 10 years and have always found him friendly, helpful, and knowledgeable.

I sat down with him recently to get his view of his job and to introduce him to the people of Kerr County. Roy has been with the Texas A&M AgriLife Extension for 28 years. When asked to describe this job, his first words were "education," followed by youth development and agriculture and natural resources. AgriLife Extension is part of the Texas A&M University system which was one of the original land-grant colleges established by the Republic of Texas back in 1839.

Roy's list of duties is long, including anything having to do with agriculture and natural resources, new landowner education, range management, management of brush, crops and forage, anything involving helping farmers and ranchers and 4-H kids. 4-H activities are a major part of Roy's job, with 350 4-H kids in Kerr County in 8 different clubs—everything having to do with helping kids and their families select animals, learn to care for and show the animals, and actually showing their animals at stock shows. Roy points out that he couldn't do his job without a great staff and many volunteers.

Whenever any of the 4-H kids are showing their animals at any local or district stock shows (San Antonio, Ft. Worth, Houston, Austin, San Angelo, Dallas), Roy will accompany them and help them in many ways. For instance, there were 45 kids who were showing their animals at a recent San Antonio stock show.

It is important to note that there are many other 4-H activities that do not involve raising or showing animals, such as: clothing/textiles, photography, food & nutrition, wool and mohair judging, shooting sports, veterinary science and leadership. Roy is deeply involved in all of these activities.

Other duties of the County Extension Agent are to be the advisor and sponsor of the local Master Gardeners chapter and an advisor for the local Texas Master Naturalist chapter.

The Master Gardener Program is a volunteer program designed to increase the availability of horticultural information. Master Gardeners aid AgriLife Extension by conducting school garden projects, answering telephone requests for horticultural information, as well as establishing and maintaining demonstration gardens.

When asked about the most fun part of his job, Roy answered without hesitating, "Working with kids and ranchers."

When asked what changes he has seen in Farming and Ranching in Texas over the course of his career, Roy described the decline in the number of old-time ranchers and more and more new landowners on smaller pieces of property, most with much less experience in managing rural property.

The County Extension Agent's office is a joint partnership between the county and A&M, with funding coming from both. One thing that Roy wanted to make sure everyone knows is that his office will try to get the answer to any question anyone has about agriculture, land management and natural resources. To do that he can rely on the vast resources of the various departments of Texas A&M as well as their research stations and the experts in those facilities and the literature available from them.

One of the disappointments Roy expressed, and that I and others that I know have expressed, is that too few people avail themselves of the knowledge, literature, advice and help they could obtain from the AgriLife office and some of the many educational programs that are put on by that office and others every year. While people who have been ranching or farming for a living for many years are well acquainted with the services of the AgriLife office, many new small landowners, the people who could most use expert advice, frequently are not aware of the service. I urge them to think about doing so. Your local AgriLife office can be found on the state website listed in Appendix II.

At one point in our conversation, Roy expressed what I think is the essence of how he approaches his job. He said, "It is not about doing a job, but doing it to make a difference."

A Visit with Rufus Stephens of Texas Parks and Wildlife Department

The Texas Parks and Wildlife Department (TPWD) has three divisions that most impact folks in the Hill Country: Parks, Law Enforcement (Game Wardens) and Wildlife. Rufus Stephens is the Wildlife Division's District Leader for the Edwards Plateau. Wildlife biologists of different specialties in this district work in 25 counties.

Stephens holds a BS degree in wildlife ecology and has worked for the Noble Foundation in Oklahoma. He also did deer research in Missouri and was a wildlife biologist in Kansas before becoming an urban wildlife biologist with TPWD in San Antonio in 1994. I first met Rufus when he spoke to our first Hill Country Master Naturalist chapter in 2002 and I have considered him to be one of my go-to experts with questions about deer and native habitat ever since.

Stephens defines his job as being mainly in support of the many biologists in the Edwards Plateau district in their efforts to help manage wildlife species, aid private landowners to better manage their land, manage the state's natural resources and conduct wildlife research. The main constituents and beneficiaries of this work are private landowners, hunters and fishermen.

Rufus describes the best part of his job as being able to get out into the field with landowners and wildlife. He adds that education of landowners and the general public, both one on one and in groups, is a major part of his job.

One of the things that makes his job harder is the fact that many new small landowners are unaware of the information about land, wildlife and native habitat management that TPWD provides, at no cost to them, and therefore they do not avail themselves of this service. The result is that many new landowners may do things on their land that are unnecessary or even detrimental to the native wildlife.

The biggest problem, from a biological or ecological standpoint, in the Hill Country or the Edwards Plateau, is the overabundant deer population. Stephens points out that many people hear that statement and assume that for some reason TPWD doesn't like deer or doesn't want many deer. In fact, it is not the number of deer per se that is the problem, but rather the effect they have on the habitat. The goal of their efforts is to try to maintain a healthy deer population and quality habitat for the benefit of both hunters and landowners.

Too many deer consume too much native vegetation. When the deer population is such that they eat about every green leaf below the browseline (from the ground up to as high as a deer can reach—about 4.5 to 5 feet) they destroy a segment of native habitat used by many other species of animals as food, cover and nesting sites. Furthermore, since just about every hardwood tree in the Hill Country is browsed by deer, we no longer have the replacement hardwoods coming up to replace the older trees when they die. The number of trees in the Hill Country is declining, and it is because of excessive deer numbers. Ironically, the deer are destroying their own habitat.

Here are three additional important things that Stephens has done and continues to do to help the public and landowners in particular.

Rufus was instrumental in getting the Texas Master Naturalist program organized in 1997, and now there are over 10,000 Master Naturalists in 44 chapters in the state! Thus his work contributed greatly to all of the education, outreach and service provided by all those Naturalists. He has continued to be a great resource for our Hill Country Chapter as well as other chapters in the area.

Stephens gives presentations to numerous groups on the do's and don'ts of creating native landscapes as well as explaining the abundant deer situation, especially in urban settings.

Rufus has recently coauthored a great book, with Jan Wrede, *Attracting Birds in the Texas Hill Country: A Guide to Land Stewardship.*

Stephens may be contacted at his office on 309 Sidney Baker South in Kerrville. Phone, 830-896-2500.

A Visit with Laura Broyles of the Natural Resources Conservation Service

The Natural Resources Conservation Service (NRCS) is an agency within the U.S. Department of Agriculture which is a conservation leader for all natural resources, including soil, water, air, plants and animals. Its primary focus is to ensure that private lands are conserved, restored and made more resilient to environmental changes.

The agency was established near the end of the Dust Bowl in 1935 as the Soil Conservation Service (SCS) and was renamed to NRCS in 1994. The SCS was largely responsible for teaching landowners how to better manage their farmland to prevent erosion and the fact that even in the drought of the 1950s the extent of erosion was nowhere near as bad as in the 1930s is a testament to their work.

Laura Broyles is the District Conservationist in charge of the local NRCS office, and there are four other specialists that work with her. Broyles is also the Resource Team Leader for four other offices in the six county area of Kerr, Kendall, Bandera, Real, Edwards and Kimble counties.

The main function of Broyles and the people who work with her is to help landowners better conserve and manage their land for the protection of all its natural resources. The NRCS folks can help landowners better understand their land by providing conservation plans, plant identification, forage measurements, GPS coordinates, aerial maps, and education for the landowner as well as, in some cases, provide financial assistance for various projects to help improve the land.

NRCS employees are particularly good at plant identification, range management, grazing systems, water management and erosion control. The assistance provided by these experts is available to all landowners and it is especially advised that all new landowners avail themselves of this service. The mission of the NRCS is "Helping People Help the Land," and landowner education is a big part of that.

One of the programs available to some landowners, called Environmental Quality Incentives Program (EQIP), provides financial assistance to correct or treat a resource concern or problem. The agents visit the property, assess the condition and write a management plan for the landowner to follow. Projects such as piping water for livestock from one place to another, perhaps construction of cross fencing, or brush control can be considered.

Another program is the Conservation Stewardship Program (CSP) that rewards individuals who have proven to be exceptionally good land stewards for the past few years. There are a number of other programs that address specific issues. The NRCS can also provide landowners with recommendations for native seeds and seed mixtures for help in restoring rangeland.

The NRCS maintains a very useful website, called the Web Soil Survey, www.websoilsurvey.nrcs.usda.gov, where landowners can get aerial maps of their property, soil descriptions and plants that historically would have likely been growing on the property. It is a free web site and the data can be downloaded for free, but if people have trouble getting the information they want, they can get help in the NRCS office.

Broyles says the main ecological problems she and her coworkers face is degraded and poor utilization of rangeland. One of the limitations on how much good the NRCS employees can do for landowners is that many new landowners have limited experience or knowledge of managing native habitat and they are unaware of the free services NRCS can provide.

Sharing an office with NRCS is the Kerr County Soil and Water Conservation District (SWCD), and, as in many counties in Texas, there is a partnership between the two organizations as there is some overlap in their activities. The Kerr SWCD has an excellent book for sale, called *Range Plants of North Central Texas.* It has many photos and descriptions of grasses, forbs and woody plants, 95 percent of which grow in the Hill Country—I recommend it.

STATE PARKS

Everyone who is even a little interested in nature, our natural world, and preserving as much of our natural world as possible should be very supportive of our state parks. Or, as Carter Smith, Executive Director of Texas Parks and Wildlife Department often says, "State Parks: they need you now more than ever." Many new residents have little experience with the native habitat other than on their own property, and may have a very distorted view of what healthy native habitat should look like, so many of the parks are places where they can gain a better perspective of Hill Country habitat.

Local State Parks Are Great Places to Go, Even in Winter

I have urged everyone, especially those with kids, to spend more time outdoors enjoying and learning about Nature. But recently, someone said to me, "But there is nothing to do in the winter." I beg to differ. There are 18 State Parks and Wildlife Management Areas in the Hill Country.

Some may think things are not as "pretty" when everything is not green, and the rivers that run through many of these places are too cold for swimming or tubing, but Mother Nature is still there. The trails are open, the rivers are flowing, the birds are singing. There are things to do and things to see in all of them. And best yet, they are not nearly as crowded as in the summer.

Most all of these places have hiking trails, some moderately strenuous, most fairly easy. The sights and sounds and smells are different in the winter, but no less interesting. You can sometimes see more in the winter without the leaves. For bird watchers, both serious and casual, there are opportunities to see species that are not here year round. For photographers, there are always interesting things to photograph.

Best of all, you get to experience and learn from Mother Nature. Here are some of my favorite places:

South Llano River State Park just south of Junction is a great place to watch birds from any of the several blinds the park has built. There is a large "pecan bottoms" area filled with huge pecan trees and a long expanse of the South Llano River. Adjacent to the park is the Walter Buck State Wildlife Management Area with 18 miles of hiking trails.

Garner State Park, 10 miles south of Leakey on the Frio River has about 7 miles of hiking trails and a long stretch of the river, and they have both cabins and campgrounds.

Lost Maples State Natural Area on the Sabinal River 4 miles north of Vanderpool is justifiably famous for the fall color of its Bigtooth maples, but it is a great place to visit anytime. There are over 10 miles of hiking trails, some short and easy, some more strenuous, but with beautiful views. There is a campground and some primitive camping sites.

Hill Country State Natural Area about 10 miles outside of Bandera is well known to folks that like to go horseback camping, but most trails are also open to hikers. It is a really beautiful, undeveloped expanse of hills and woodlands. It is closed on Tuesday and Wednesday.

Enchanted Rock State Natural Area 14 miles north of Fredericksburg on RR 965 is one of my favorite Hill Country places. While famous for the granite dome which rises 450 feet above the valley floor and affords a striking view of the surrounding countryside, there is also a great 4 mile trail around the domes and shorter trails along beautiful Sandy Creek.

Pedernales Falls State Park 9 miles east of Johnson City contains numerous hiking trails, a great stretch of the river flowing over interesting rock formations, and is an excellent birding location.

A painted bunting taken from a bird blind in South Llano River Sate Park.

Other Hill Country State Parks and Natural Areas are Lyndon B. Johnson, Devil's Sinkhole, Kickapoo Cavern, Colorado Bend, Inks Lake, Longhorn Caverns, Blanco, McKinney Falls, Guadalupe River/Honey Creek, and Government Canyon, all very much worth a trip.

Two of the local Wildlife Management Areas are also recommended. Kerr Wildlife Management Area is open to the public and is a favorite with seasoned birdwatchers. It is about 13 miles west of Hunt on Rt 1340. Then in the spring through fall when the bats are present, everyone should experience seeing the bats exit the tunnel for their nightly flights at Old Tunnel Wildlife Management Area between Comfort and Fredericksburg.

Texas has a smaller percentage of public land than any of the other states in the west, so all of the 115 State Parks and Historic Sites are playing a critical role in maintaining and protecting Texas' native habitat. So take advantage of these places, enjoy your visits and become better acquainted with our native ecosystems.

For more information, phone numbers and directions, visit the Texas Parks and Wildlife website at www.tpwd.state.tx.us.

New Public Land for the Hill Country

Texas is a big state, but that doesn't mean we have a lot of land area for the citizens to enjoy. Only 2.6 percent of the land area in Texas is in some form of municipal, county, state or federal government park, natural area, wildlife management area, forest, or Defense Department land. While most all of these areas, except for Defense Department land, are at least somewhat accessible to the public, we are still way behind many states in the amount of land area devoted to state parks. Texas ranks only 28th among all states in the percentage of land area devoted to State Parks—0.35 percent.

Projections are for the population of Texas to double in the next few decades. But where will these people live? We are not going to have any more land for these new Texans to live on, so the percentage of land occupied by human habitation will certainly increase. Some of our parks are already so crowded that people have to be turned away on busy week-ends. The availability of natural areas for people to camp, hike, fish, hunt, picnic and just experience Nature will be severely strained. Every unspoiled or even slightly spoiled piece of natural area will become more and more precious.

That is why I think we should celebrate something that occurred a few years ago. At that time, the Albert and Bessie Kronkosky Foundation donated the 3,800 acre 3K Ranch between Boerne and Pipe Creek to the state. This is especially important because that is an area that is growing fast with many ranches and natural areas being broken up for "developments" and "ranchettes." It is in an especially geologically and ecologically sensitive area on the Balcones Escarpment, and it contains an astonishing number of important species of native vegetation.

For the past two years, Texas Parks and Wildlife Department biologists and various volunteers, many of them Master Naturalists, have been studying, surveying and inventorying the various features of this property, especially the vegetation. And it is the diversity of vegetation and the number of uncommon, special species that make this property so valuable.

I have had the privilege of accompanying Superintendent James Rice and volunteers on a number of study trips on the property and have seen bigtooth maples in the canyons and sycamore-leaf snowbells along the creeks. The list of identified plants compiled by the best botanists in the state is truly amazing.

This is an especially rugged property, being near the Balcones Escarpment, with elevations ranging from 1400 to 2000 feet. The ranch had not been grazed for some time before the land was donated to the state, and the only roads on the property are extremely primitive, rocky ranch roads requiring high-clearance, four-wheel drive vehicles. The one problem with the property is that Ashe juniper has encroached in many areas to a level that is detrimental to healthy native habitat.

In the two years while this initial study has been going on, it has been concluded that the property will be called the Albert and Bessie Kronkosky State Natural Area, or ABKSNA for short. Volunteers and TPWD agency personnel will continue to study the property, to fight back cedar in selected areas, and to begin to make the area suitable for public visitation in the future. This process is still going to take a few years of hard work, but agency folks and volunteers are exceedingly enthusiastic about preserving the property and sharing it with the public.

Aldo Leopold advocated that governments should maintain wilderness areas as examples of unspoiled nature and protection of threatened species. ABK is certainly not an unspoiled wilderness, but it may be close to the best we can do in the 21st century. As the population of the Hill Country continues to increase and more and more such properties are broken up for individual housing and the natural habitat is destroyed, the more precious places like ABK become.

Everyone who enjoys parks, natural areas and wildlife refuges should strongly support the Texas Parks and Wildlife Department and thank the Albert and Bessie Kronkosky Foundation for this gift to the people of Texas.

Will Our Parks Become Obsolescent?

I recently read a quotation in National Geographic, from Jonathan Jarvis, the director of the National Park Service. He said, "Young people are more separated from the natural world than perhaps any generation before them." He went on to say, "The national parks risk obsolescence in the eyes of an increasingly diverse and distracted demographic."

Obsolescence? Our National Parks? Often called "America's best idea"? For those of us who love and cherish our national and state parks and all of our native habitats and the plants and animals in the natural world around us, that is a frightening thought! And this in spite of the fact that a record 307 million visits were made to our parks last year.

But it is not a new or original thought. I have written before about the acclaimed book, *Last Child in the Woods,* by Richard Louv, in which he coined the phrase, "Nature Deficit Disorder" to describe the many children who grow up with little or no experience or contact with a native habitat or a natural area.

When shown a beautiful large photo of the Grand Teton National Park taken in evening light to a group of inner-city kids, they described the photo as "scary, empty, forbidding, not welcoming." They asked "Where are all the people?" A group of city kids were taken out to Death Valley to look at the stars they could never see in Los Angeles, but when they got there, they wouldn't get out of the van. The felt threatened by the quiet and darkness!

I don't imagine our Hill Country kids would react in quite the same way, but they might be just as unnerved at the lack of internet connectivity in many parks.

Visitors to the national parks are older and more white than the general population. I don't know if the same applies to our state parks, but I suspect it does. Minorities and the young are just not as interested in visiting parks, for whatever reason. Sally Jewell, secretary of the interior, said they have learned some of the reasons. "We learned...for blacks and Latinos there were cultural barriers to enjoying the outdoors...For the young, in many cases it was about technology."

Here are some of my observations. First, as the years go by, a larger and larger percentage of the population lives in the cities so the kids grow up completely removed from rural life, unlike those of us who grew up in the country. In addition, certainly in the last 20 years or so, electronic gadgets have occupied an increasingly important part of the lives of young people, leaving less time to spend with nature or even just in their backyard. Finally, it seems to me that school curricula are designed primarily for city schools and much more time is spent teaching more "advanced" topics such as molecular biology, and little or no time teaching about the local native habitats and plants and animals.

The consequences of this, I believe, should be of concern to all of us. It is the young and the growing numbers of minorities who will have to protect and preserve the parks for all future generations. If they feel the condition of the land, rural land, and our parks and natural areas have no connection to the quality of their lives, they will be much less vigilant in their stewardship of them. As the author of the National Geographic article wrote, "A conservation constituency in a newer generation will be needed to protect wild places through the next hundred years."

So what can we do about this? One thing we can do is to make sure every child in our world is exposed to some form of nature outdoors on a regular basis, something that does not involve any electronic screen. We can make an effort to take them to nature centers and natural areas and give them time and space to observe nature even if it is just a bug on a leaf or a flower, or a lizard. Try to steer them to want to go to parks on vacation rather than Disney World or Sea World.

We can provide them with books that help them identify plants or animals. Or, and I hate to say this, but "there are apps for that" as well.

For older kids and young adults, try to get them involved in organizations like nature centers, NPSOT and Master Naturalist meetings, star-gazing parties, etc. Teach them what you know and be a role model. They will thank you for it in the future.

We Should Listen to Teddy Roosevelt

We have all heard of Teddy Roosevelt, the 26th President of the U.S. from 1901 to 1909. He was at one time or another during his life considered a statesman, author, explorer, soldier, naturalist and reformer. He rode with the Rough Riders in Cuba in the 1890s, served as Governor of New York, Vice President under William McKinley, and became President when McKinley was assassinated.

He can be considered the nation's foremost naturalist and conservationist for what he accomplished during his tenure as President. He established the U.S. Forest Service, 5 National Parks, 18 National Monuments, 51 Bird Preserves, 4 Game Preserves, and 150 National Forests totaling 230 million acres of government land with some form of protection.

In 1916, Roosevelt wrote the following:

"Defenders of the short-sighted men who in their greed and selfishness will, if permitted, rob our country of half its charm by their reckless extermination of all useful and beautiful wild things, sometimes seek to champion them by saying 'the game belongs to the people.' So it does; and not merely to the people now alive, but to the unborn people. The 'greatest good for the greatest number' applies to the number within the womb of time, compared to which those now alive form but an insignificant fraction. Our duty to the whole, including the unborn generations, bids us to restrain an unprincipled present-day minority from wasting the heritage of these unborn generations. The movement for the conservation of wildlife and the larger movement for the conservation of all our natural resources are essentially democratic in spirit, purpose and method."

For the record, Roosevelt was a Republican.

The "short-sighted men" he was referring to were those who opposed early hunting restrictions and the establishment of wilderness areas designed to protect all wildlife, game and non-game species. It should be noted that Roosevelt was widely known as an avid hunter throughout his life, so hunters could hardly have had a more kindred spirit as President.

Back in the late 1800s and early 1900s there were subsistence hunters (people who hunted as a major part of their food source), sport hunters and commercial "hunters," (most of the latter were probably better described as "harvesters"). Many people believed that any predator of game animals should be killed to increase the number of game animals for hunting, but at the same time many also resisted any effort to limit the number of animals, the season or the method of hunting or any restrictions as to where animals could be hunted. There was even a view that because, as stated above, "game belongs to the people," it was OK to pursue game onto anyone's property without permission.

Some of these attitudes led to, or contributed to, such things as the near extinction of the buffalo, the near extinction of many egrets and herons (for feathers for ladies' hats), the extinction of wolves in many areas, and, two years before Roosevelt's quote above was written, the extinction of the passenger pigeon.

We have come a long way since then. Few of us need to hunt in order to eat. Commercial hunting and trapping has largely disappeared and is now limited mostly to nuisance species such as feral hogs and other exotics. And today, sport hunters and current regulations are mostly a force for good for managing wildlife and their habitats. But now there are a lot more of us and we have to work harder at, as Roosevelt said, the "conservation of wildlife and the larger movement for the conservation of all our natural resources."

What struck me most about Roosevelt's quote above was the idea that we should be thinking not so much about ourselves, but about the unborn generations. And how would we feel if 50 or 100 years from now those generations looked back at the early 21st century with the same disappointment, and sorrow at how we managed our natural resources, our native habitats and our wildlife as we do now when we look back at the late 1800s and early 1900s.

In 1947 Aldo Leopold wrote, "Men still live who, in their youth, remember pigeons; trees still live who, in their youth, were shaken by a living wind. But a few decades hence only the oldest oaks will remember, and at long last only the hills will know."

Let us keep future generations in mind and treat our native lands and waters, plants and animals as if our successors are looking over our shoulders.

— SECTION VIII —

MISCELANEOUS TOPICS

Here are some essays that don't exactly fit in any of the other sections, but are about interesting things that I believe folks will enjoy.

Screwworm Fly Eradication: Local Lab Played Major Role in Eliminating the Pest from Texas

Ever hear of the screwworm fly? If not, you can thank the local USDA-Animal Research Service Knipling-Bushland U.S. Livestock Insects Laboratory on route 16 just north of I-10 in Kerrville. Ask anyone who was ranching in Texas before the mid-1960s and they can tell you about the screwworm fly.

In 1935, in the middle of the Great Depression and the middle of the Dust Bowl, Texas ranchers were faced with yet another economic disaster, the loss of an estimated 160,000 head of cattle due to the screwworm fly. During all of these depressed times, in the 1930s, Texas ranchers had losses of many millions of dollars due to this insect.

The screwworm fly is about twice the size of a house fly. It likes to both feed on and lay its eggs on blood, open wounds or soft tissue of animals. The eggs then hatch and the larva (maggots) then feed on the flesh, keeping the wound open and subject to infection. And the wound that attracts the flies can be as small as a tick bite, so all wild animals, pets, livestock and even humans are susceptible.

Research conducted by scientists at the Kerrville lab, and facilities associated with the Kerrville lab, especially by Drs. Edward Knipling and Raymond Bushland (for whom the lab is now named), in the late 1930s up into the 1950s demonstrated a way to eradicate the fly. These researchers found that if the male pupa were irradiated with radioactive isotopes they could be made sterile, and further that the female screwworm fly would only mate once in her life, so that if she mated with a sterile male, no eggs would be produced and the population of flies would decline.

So, if a way to produce huge numbers of sterile male flies could be found, and these flies were released into the wild populations, many of the wild, fertile females would mate with the sterile males and not be able to produce eggs. If this process were repeated over several life cycles of the flies (3-6 weeks), then the population would decrease drastically.

The problem with this idea, however, was that it required the production of very large numbers of sterile flies being released into the wild fly population. This required learning how to raise, feed, sterilize, transport and release literally tens of millions of sterile flies at the right place and the right time. Much time and effort by many researchers was required to learn how to do all of this, but that is exactly what was done.

The principle of eradicating a wild screwworm fly population was successfully demonstrated on the island of Curacao in 1954. In 1955-1957 the technique was applied to 2000 square miles around Orlando, Florida, and by 1959, screwworms had been eradicated from the southeastern U.S.

In 1962 the program to eradicate the flies from the Southwestern U.S. was begun using flies produced in the Kerrville Lab. Subsequently, a mass production facility was built in Mission, Texas. By 1966 the USDA declared screwworms eradicated from the Southwest U.S. There were several outbreaks that occurred between 1966 and 1982, caused probably by cattle imported from Mexico where the fly had not been totally eliminated.

Since then, sterile screwworm fly production facilities have been moved to Mexico and to Central America. By 1991 Mexico was declared screwworm free, followed eventually by all of Central America down to Panama by 2000.

One consequence of this work, other than the prevention of hundreds of millions of dollars in losses to American ranchers, and now Central American ranchers, is the effect this program has had on the white-tailed deer population. It has been said that the screwworm fly was the last remaining effective natural predator (other than man) for the white-tailed deer in Texas.

The elimination of the screwworm fly from Texas corresponds to the beginning of a significant increase in deer populations. Now these increased deer populations are responsible for the decline in the number of hardwood trees and shrubs and the reduction in understory habitat in the Hill Country.

Thanks to Dr. Steven Skoda, Research Leader in the Screwworm Research Unit of the Kerrville lab for supplying me with some of the facts for this article.

How to Protect Your Home from a Wildfire

We have all heard the reports and seen the pictures of the many wildfires burning throughout the state. Many homes have been lost. Fire officials frequently point to situations where a home has been lost, but the home next to it is untouched. Sometimes it is just luck that protected one home and not the other, but often is has to do with the surviving home being better prepared to withstand a wildfire.

If you live on the edge of the city, in the country, or anywhere surrounded by, adjacent to, or within a half mile of a natural area, your home could be involved in a wildfire. What you do now, to anticipate and to prepare for such an eventuality, can make all the difference in whether your home, and your family, survive a wildfire.

People often think if they have a wildfire near them, the fire department will take care of it. Not necessarily. Not if every fireman and fire truck have been out all night fighting a wildfire and trying to defend more homes than there are defenders. Under low humidity and high wind conditions, wildfires move too fast and burn too intensely to be contained. Your fate is in your hands.

There are two levels of wildfire preparedness. What you can do to make your home less likely to catch fire, now before any wildfire threatens, and what you can do when a wildfire is threatening.

To help homeowners prepare their homes to survive a fire, the Texas Forest Service has instituted programs to educate landowners on what they can do. Go to www.firewise.org/usa to access some of this information, or to my website, www.hillcountrynaturalist.org and open the HC Ecology page.

Basically, what you need to do is to walk around your house and think about how fire from the surrounding pasture/woodland might catch your house on fire. The idea is expressed as a fire ladder. For example, if a grass/brush fire were to catch your wooden privacy fence on fire and it in turn burned up to your wooden deck and the deck caught the soffit area of your roof on fire, the house would likely be lost. You need to make sure there is some nonflammable break between native vegetation and your house, garage, deck, etc., so that if there is a wildfire, it won't get to your home.

Homes located on hills above steep cedar-covered slopes, homes with raised wooden decks open underneath or homes open underneath are especially susceptible. Homes with wood roofing or siding, single-pane windows, open soffits, etc., are also at greater risk. Providing non-flammable barriers, such as sidewalks, gravel paths, and low-growing green vegetation around the house help keep a wildfire away.

But it is a bit more complicated than just the above, because an intense wildfire can send burning embers flying a half mile or more and if they land on your roof, on your porch, against a fence, etc., your home could still be in danger. You can't do a really good job of preparing your home to survive a wildfire until you learn the many ways homes can be at risk, and how to mitigate these risks. The above websites can lead you to much of that information.

The second part of what you need to do is to formulate a plan of what to do if a wildfire is moving toward your home. You need to have thought about that situation in advance and made a plan that everyone in the household understands.

There is a program initiated by the International Fire Chiefs Association called "Ready Set Go" which outlines the steps each homeowner should take before any fire is approaching. It prepares the residents so that if such a situation should arise, everyone in the home can react appropriately, ready the home for evacuation and leave early enough to escape danger. For more information, go to www.wildlandfireRSG.org, and/or, better, http://www.montecitofire.com/resources/pdf/Public_Education/ReadySetGoMFD2Single.pdf

One thing I can't emphasize enough. Many folks think that if a fire should approach, they would stay and defend their home. That is exactly what most people who have died in these fires thought. Don't even think about defending your home with a garden hose! Get out!

Even if it rained yesterday, think about this and plan now.

Grass and Trees and God

For a change of pace, enjoy this fable.

Overheard in a Heavenly conversation between God and St. Francis...

> GOD: St. Francis, you know all about gardens and nature. What in the world is going on down there in the USA? What happened to the colorful flowers I started eons ago? I had a perfect, no-maintenance garden plan. Those plants grow in any type of soil, withstand drought and multiply with abandon. The nectar from the long lasting blossoms attracts butterflies, honeybees and flocks of songbirds. I expected to see a vast garden of colors by now. But all I see are these green rectangles.
>
> ST. FRANCIS: It's the tribes that settled there, Lord. The Suburbanites. They started calling your flowers weeds and went to great lengths to kill them and replace them with grass.
>
> GOD: Grass? But it's so boring. It's not colorful. It doesn't attract butterflies, birds and bees, only grubs and sod worms. It's temperamental with temperature. Do these Suburbanites really want all that grass growing there?
>
> ST. FRANCIS: Apparently so, Lord. They go to great pains to grow it and keep it green. They begin each spring by fertilizing grass and poisoning any other plant that crops up in the lawn.

GOD: The spring rains and warm weather probably make grass grow really fast. That must make the Suburbanites happy.

ST. FRANCIS: Apparently not, Lord. As soon as it grows a little, they cut it, sometimes twice a week.

GOD: They cut it? Do they then bale it like hay?

ST. FRANCIS: Not exactly Lord. Most of them rake it up and put it in bags.

GOD: They bag it? Why? Is it a cash crop? Do they sell it?

ST. FRANCIS: No, sir—just the opposite. They pay to throw it away.

GOD: Now, let me get this straight. They fertilize grass so it will grow. And when it does grow, they cut it off and pay to throw it away?

ST. FRANCIS: Yes, sir.

GOD: These Suburbanites must be relieved in the summer when we cut back on the rain and turn up the heat. That surely slows the growth and saves them a lot of work.

ST. FRANCIS: You aren't going to believe this, Lord. When the grass stops growing so fast, they drag out hoses and pay more money to water it so they can continue to mow it and pay to get rid of it.

GOD: What nonsense. At least they kept some of the trees. That was a sheer stroke of genius, if I do say so myself. The trees grow leaves in the spring to provide beauty and shade in the summer. In the autumn they fall to the ground and form a natural blanket to keep moisture in the soil and protect the trees and bushes. Plus, as they rot, the leaves form compost to enhance the soil. It's a natural circle of life.

ST. FRANCIS: You'd better sit down, Lord. The Suburbanites have drawn a new circle. As soon as the leaves fall, they rake them into great piles and pay to have them hauled away.

GOD: No. What do they do to protect the shrub and tree roots in the winter and to keep the soil moist and loose?

ST. FRANCIS: After throwing away the leaves, they go out and buy something which they call mulch. They haul it home and spread it around in place of the leaves.

GOD: And where do they get this mulch?

ST. FRANCIS: They cut down trees and grind them up to make the mulch.

GOD: Enough! I don't want to think about this anymore....... St Catherine, you are in charge of the arts. What movie have you selected for us tonight?

ST CAHTERINE: Dumb and Dumber, Lord, it's a real stupid movie about....

GOD: Never mind. I think I just heard the whole story form St Francis.

Author Unknown.

What Happened to All the Critters I Used to See?

Growing up in the country in the Permian Basin between Lubbock and Midland, I spent a lot of time roaming the pastures around our house, although much of it was being plowed up to make new cotton fields back then. But the time I spent in the mesquite/shinnery/short grass prairie was so much fun because of all of the critters I could see.

I lived away from Texas for a number of years, but when I returned several years ago I was saddened to find that many of the critters I enjoyed as a boy have become much less common. Some are even quite scarce and becoming more so.

As a kid I could almost always walk around for a little while and find a Texas horned lizard. We called them "horny toads" back then. They were easy to catch and fun to play with, and I always let them go where

I found them. They were fun to watch picking ants from around a harvester ant hill. Both the harvester ants and the horned lizard have largely disappeared from most of Texas.

A Greater Short-Horned Lizard in the Davis Mountains

Cottontails and jackrabbits used to be much more numerous. A short walk through the pasture in midday when they were resting in the shade could always result in flushing at least one of my favorite animals. A drive down a country road at night would frequently show more than one in the headlights at once. They are still around, of course, and they are not threatened like the horned lizard, but their numbers are much reduced.

At one time when I was a kid I collected 13 box turtles and kept them in a pen my father had used to raise pheasants. One of them even laid eggs and I had several baby turtles. Box turtles are nowhere near as common as they used to be.

My favorite bird used to be the mourning dove. I think it was because I learned to mimic their call and could sometimes call one up. Back then mourning doves were quite common, but if people wanted to hunt white-winged doves, they had to travel to Mexico to do it. Now it appears that white-winged doves have expanded their range and have out-competed our native mourning doves.

Quail of all species, especially scaled and bobwhites have declined dramatically in the past years, to the point where seeing, or even hearing one is a rarity for most of us. You don't have to be a hunter to mourn their loss.

I have seen many fewer field mice and rats in recent years than I remember from when I was a kid, nor do I see any sign of either of them very often.

I had always assumed that the Hill Country would be ideal habitat for rattlesnakes, and expected to see a lot of them when we moved here. But in fact I have seen very few, in spite of walking many miles over hundreds of properties in the past several years. I know there are localities where they are relatively abundant, but I don't think they are nearly as abundant as they were where I grew up.

Coyotes also seem to be less plentiful now than in the past, at least as judged by the few sightings or hearing their calls or seeing roadkills. This may be due largely to trapping that occurs to protect sheep and goat raisers.

So what caused the changes in these and other animal populations? I think the short answer is "us."

As the human population has increased we have begun to occupy more and more of the habitat these animals used to have available to them. We have also destroyed or degraded otherwise native habitat by our land use practices. Overgrazed ranges are less favorable wildlife habitat. Increased cropland acreage as well as cultivated "improved" pastureland are poor habitats for just about everything.

Removing predators has increased native deer populations which have destroyed or damaged habitats for other wildlife. Introduction of alien species from fire ants, to exotic ungulates to feral hogs and cats certainly have had some negative effect on some wildlife.

The bottom line is that by far most of the decline in the numbers of most of these native animals, just like the cause of most species extinction, is loss of habitat caused by humans. I think it is sad that today's kids can't experience the number of wild critters that I did.

Cochineal Bugs: Tiny Cactus Bugs with an Interesting History

A reader recently asked me what were the small cotton-like balls on her prickly pear pads? The answer is Cochineal (*Dactylopius coccus*), a scale-like insect that lives on cactus pads. The insects attach themselves to the cactus and live off the juices they suck from the pads. They secrete sticky web-like filamentous wax which is what we normally see as white cotton-like balls or coatings on the cactus, possibly as a defense mechanism to ward off predators or to protect themselves from dehydrating in the sun.

Cochineal bugs on a Texas prickly pear.

While it is easy to notice the white coating, one might never see one of the actual insects unless you are carefully looking for one. They are flat, oval-shaped and less than a quarter of an inch long, and once attached to the cactus, they don't move about.

While these insects are in fact parasites, and in very large numbers can damage the cactus, in the numbers seen around here they seldom cause significant damage to the cactus.

What makes these insects so interesting, however, is none of what I just described, but what is inside the bugs. Over 20 percent of the weight of the insect is an acid that deters predators called carminic acid. This acid is easily converted to a bright red dye called carmine, and it has been known and used since the Aztecs and Mayans in the 15th century!

When Cortes invaded Mexico in 1519 he found Montezuma wearing clothes dyed a bright, vivid red, unlike anything they had in Europe at that time. He also found bags of the dried cochineal in present day Mexico City which he sent back to Spain. This soon resulted in a huge demand for the dye in Europe, resulting in it being extremely expensive. It was used for the robes of Roman Catholic Cardinals as well as Kings and Queens.

Eventually it was also used to make the British military "Redcoat" jackets, and in addition to taxes on tea, the British also imposed high taxes on cochineal imports on the colonies.

There were numerous early attempts to grow both prickly pear and cochineal in various parts of North Africa and Europe, with only some successes, mainly in Spain, Portugal and the Canary Islands. One attempt by the British to create a source of the dye in the British Empire occurred in 1788 when a ship's captain collected cochineal-infected cacti in Brazil and introduced them to Australia where they were trying to establish the first European settlement there. The bad news and the other bad news was that the cochineal bugs died off in Australia, but the prickly pear did not—it eventually covered 100,000 square miles of eastern Australia!

In more modern times synthetic dyes have been produced that are much cheaper than the natural one, although cochineal is still better as a dye for wool than most synthetic dyes.

Cochineal dye is mainly used today as colorants for food and beverages and for medical applications. In ingredient lists it is likely listed as "cochineal extract," "carmine," "natural red 4," or "natural coloring." One reason it is preferred for some applications over many synthetic dyes is that some of the latter are carcinogenic. Cochineal color is also more light- and heat-stable with time than many synthetic dyes.

Cochineal is still produced and exported from Peru (200 tons/year), the Canary Islands (20 tons/year) and small amounts from Chile and Mexico. In order to appreciate those numbers, it takes 70,000 insects to make one pound of cochineal dye. In 2005 when synthetic food dyes were selling for $10-20 per kilogram, cochineal was selling for $ 50-80 per kilogram.

Today cochineal dye can be found in many types of foods, especially desserts, beverages, sauces and sweets. It is safe for use in eye cosmetics, hair- and skin-care products, including lipstick and face powder. It is also used as a medical tracer and for microscopy stains. It is the only natural food coloring approved by the FDA.

So the next time you walk by a prickly pear, look for little white patches of what looks like little pieces of cotton. Then carefully, trying to avoid the spines and glochids, mash one of the fuzzy balls and then look at the color of your finger. Or if you are less adventurous, use a small stick. Isn't Nature fun?

"Society Has an Indoor Kid Issue"

A recent issue of *Texas Wildlife* (the magazine of the Texas Wildlife Association) carried an article with the above title. It was a quotation by Margaret Lamar of the Children & Nature Network, an organization working to connect children, families and their communities to nature, speaking at a recent gathering of conservationists.

The organization was founded by Richard Louv, author of *Last Child in the Woods* in which he first used the phrase "nature deficit disorder" to describe the situation today that most kids spend very little time outdoors and even less time in any environment that would be considered "natural." Lamar stated that, "Kids today do not understand nor do they care where their food and water comes from."

A recent survey found that 8-year old kids spend 8 hours a day on electronic media, and that teenagers, similarly, spend 11 hours a day. Another survey found that kids are only spending 2 to 7 minutes a day on outdoor constructive play.

I remember a few years back when the paper carried a front page picture of a man with a trailer and a milk cow and a milking machine. He pulled the trailer and the cow around to various schools so that he could show kids the cow being milked. Many kids, even in Kerrville, didn't know that was where their milk came from.

Lamar described her own efforts to teach her children about nature, saying, "We're trying to make the land really meaningful for not just me and my family but for my children's children. That doesn't come from understanding the real estate value of the land. It comes from having the knowledge needed to take care of it."

This lack of connection to the land by today's Texans (86 percent of all Texans now live in urban areas) is not just the younger members of the population. Many, probably most, urban adults are pretty much unaware of their dependence on natural areas.

Neal Wilkins, a Texas Wildlife Association member and another speaker at the same meeting, related a story about an urban woman in San Antonio. She was telling him about a drive she took through the Hill Country and specifically on the road from Comfort to Fredericksburg.

And Wilkins said, "She talked about seeing all this vacant land, and she wondered what they were going to do with it. She had no idea that it wasn't vacant land, that it was actually owned by someone." He said, "She went on to ask why they keep people out."

Wilkins said, "Most people do not understand what we mean when we talk about private lands with public benefits…a dangerously large number don't know what we're talking about when we say private land."

I would like to highlight two programs that I believe do a terrific job of helping to fight nature deficit disorder and teach kids about all aspects of nature and wildlife in Texas. One is a series of "summer camp" type activities sponsored by several state agencies, as well as TWA, called the Texas Brigades, in which kids are taught not only about various nature topics, but how they should treat nature, wildlife and each other.

The TWA sponsored L.A.N.D.S. program (Learning Across New Dimensions in Science) is a program in which whole classes of school children are taken out to a rural ranch for a day and taught many things about nature, wildlife, ranching and rural living. These programs require many educated volunteers (as well as volunteer landowners) to conduct such a program for, often, hundreds of school kids. I am especially happy that many of the volunteers report the activity is one of the most meaningful activities they participate in. And the kids say the same thing.

But activities such as these can only do so much. Parents need to work to see to it that their kids are exposed to some form of a nature experience as often as possible. That may include walks in the woods or by the river, taking them to programs on nature at nature centers, or to state and city parks. Buy them books about nature and how to identify critters and plants (and yes, there are apps for that!).

You don't want your child to grow up like the woman who thought the land was "vacant."

Nature's Recovery After the Bastrop Fire

I heard a fascinating presentation about the recovery of the vegetation after the Bastrop Complex Fire in the fall of 2011. It was presented to the Fredericksburg Native Plant Society and the speaker was Bill Carr, a friend of mine and someone whom I and many others consider to be one of the most knowledgeable botanist in Texas.

It turns out that Texas Parks and Wildlife had scheduled Carr to do a routine botanical survey of the park for 2012. The timing of the survey proved to be very fortunate. The fire started in early September of 2011, during the region's worst drought since the 1950's. It started on a windy day when power lines sparked and ignited fires in three places. Thanks to tinder dry vegetation and strong winds, the fire spread very quickly from the ground into the woodlands' understory shrub layer, made up mostly of yaupon, a highly flammable native evergreen shrub, and in turn into the canopy of loblolly pines.

The fire eventually burned over 34,000 acres, including over 1,600 homes with an insured cost of over $ 325 million. Two people lost their lives. It is considered the most destructive wildfire in Texas history. Photos just after the fire showed huge areas with just standing dead tree trunks and white ash covering the ground—nothing green could be found. So from a human standpoint of lives and property lost, it was truly a disaster. Many people feared it would be a biological disaster as well.

Carr started surveying the area in early spring of 2012 and has been back periodically since. Before the fire, much of the area had been just loblolly pine and yaupon and very little else underneath the pines because of the lack of sunlight and also the thick cover of pine needles, so it was not the healthiest native habitat.

Following the fire, during fall of 2011 and winter of 2012, the Bastrop area received record rainfall, and in spring of 2012 Carr found large expanses of wildflowers and grasses in many parts of the park, blanketing areas that had previously been just dead trees and ash. Among the wildflowers seen were tradescantia, lazy daisy, coreopsis, gaillardia, helianthus, snake cotton, Mexican hat, horsemint, coneflower, rock rose, palafoxia, snoutbean, dalea, sensitive briar, butterflyweed, pokeweed, and many others I had never heard of. Carr's pictures were full of spring color where there had been nothing living visible just a few months earlier.

Wildflowers blooming where none had been before, just eight months after the Bastrop fire, Photo by Bill Carr.

As the years have progressed, more species were found including eastern cottonwoods and willows—trees with seeds carried by the wind from outside the park. And of course, loblolly pines. These pines need fire to make the hard seeds germinate and Carr found them in many areas. By 2013 new pine regrowth was 4 feet high and by 2014 some were 8 feet tall. Interestingly, Carr's observations were that nature was being much more successful at regenerating the pine forest than the deliberate planting that was done by Texas A & M.

One of the most surprising findings was the vast number of species and numbers of individual plants that came up so quickly—species that had not been seen in the area for many years. Obviously the seed bank was in the ground for many years but the shading by the trees and the cover of pine needles prevented these flowers from germinating. We have learned enough from prescribed burning to expect burning to bring back species not seen in years, but the scale of this regeneration was totally unexpected.

Another really surprising thing was that, contrary to what was feared by many folks, there have so far been almost no new exotic species observed in the burned areas. Many of us are accustomed to seeing many exotics such as thistles colonize disturbed areas, and we feared the worst, but apparently no seeds of exotics were among the seed bank in the soil underneath the loblolly pine forest.

The one sad discovery from a nature standpoint is that it is likely that the Houston toad, an endangered species, is no longer alive in the burned area.

The take-home message here is that nature really does repair itself. The destruction to human life and property was devastating, but nature lives on. It may not come back exactly in the same form as it was before the fire, and it will certainly take many years for the pines to make a mature pine forest, but it will probably be a more healthy native habitat than it was before.

— APPENDIX I —

SUGGESTED BOOKS ON VARIOUS HILL COUNTRY ECOLOGY TOPICS

AUTHOR	TITLE	YEAR	PAGES	PRESS	COMMENTS
LIFE IN TEXAS, 1500s TO 1970					
Cyclone Covey, Ed & Translator	Cabeza de Vaca's Adventures in the Unknown Interior of America	1961	151	U of NM	Incredible story of de Vaca's 10 -year journey from Florida to Mexico in the 1500s, mostly on foot and naked
Jones, C. Allen	Texas Roots. Agriculture and Rural Live Before the Civil War	2005	256	TAMU Press	Detailed accounts of life, mainly in South and East Texas, from the earliest Spanish missions to Mexican rule, to Texas Independence, to Statehood
Roemer, Ferdinand Translated by Oswald Mueller	Roemer's Texas	1967	301	Texian Press	Ferdinand Roemer's account of his travels in Texas, mostly in the Hill Country in the mid-1800's, when European settlement was just beginning on a large scale. Many interesting stories, observations
Weniger, Del	The Explorer's Texas. the Lands and Waters	1984	224	Eakin Press	Compilation of quotations from early explorers about early Texas
Weniger, Del	The Explorer's Texas. The Animals They Found	1997	200	Eakin Press	Compilation of quotations from early explorers about early Texas

Web, Walter Prescott	The Great Plains	1931	520	U of Nebraska	The author draws on history, anthropology, geography, demographics and climate to explain the differences in life on the plains and areas further east, and how the invention of the revolver, barbed wire and the windmill helped mold life there.
Jordon, Gilbert J	Yesterday in the Texas Hill Country	1979	171	TAMU Press	Description of life in the early to mid 20th century in a German settlement in Mason Co.
Kelton, Elmer	The Time it Never Rained	1973/1984	377	TCU Press	Historical novel based on the authors personal experience with the drought of the 50s in West Texas
Graves, John	Hard Scrabble. Observation on a Patch of Land	1974	271	SMU Press	Acclaimed author describes his life and the land in the early to middle 20th century in Central Texas
Graves, John	From a Limestone Ledge	1977	228	SMU Press	A collection of essays on a wide variety of topics about rural Texas
Graves, John	Goodbye to a River	1960	306	Vintage Books	Thoughts and observations on a float trip down the Brazos River in the 1950s before dams were built
Sitton, Thad Ed.	Harder than Hardscrabble	2003	297	UT Press	Description of life in the first half of the 20th century from families who were being displaced for the formation of Fort Hood
Duval, John C.	Early Times in Texas	1936	284	U. Nebraska Press	A story of a young man who came to Texas to fight for Independence, survived the massacre at Goliad, and made his way back to Houston dodging Indians and Mexican soldiers

Olmsted, Frederick Law	A Journey through Texas	2004	539	U. Nebraska Press	A detailed account of a horseback trip across Texas from the Louisiana border to the Mexican border and back to New Orleans in the 1850s, by the man who would later design Central Par in New York
Mathews, Sally Reynolds	Interwoven: A Pioneer Chronical	1982	230	TAMU Press	An account of living on ranches in Throckmorton and Shackelford counties in in the mid-to late- 1800s.
Jordan, Terry	German Seed in Texas Soil	1966	237	UT Press	Account of the life of German immigrants in Texas in the 1800s
Campbell, Randolph B.	Gone to Texas: A History of the Lone Star State	2003	500	Oxford University Press	A detailed, but very readable, history of Texas from the first inhabitants through the 20th century.
Herring Jr., Joe	Kerrville Stories	2012	181	Herring Pri9nting Co.	A history in pictures and essays of Kerrville, TX from pre settlement times to present
Clothier, Patricia Wilson	Beneath the Window	2005	167	Iron Mountain Press	A story of growing up in the Big Bend area before it was a park in the 1930s and 40s
Goyne, Minetta Altgelt	Live Among the Texas Flora: Ferdinand Lindheimer's Letters to George Englemann	1991	236	TAMU Press	Lindheimer, often called the "Father of Texas Botany" collected plant samples in Texas and sent them as well as the letters from the 1840s in this book to George Englemann of the Missouri Botanical Garden.
Doughty, Robin W.	Wildlife and Man in Texas. Environmental Change and Conservation	1983	237	TAMU Press	Discussion of the wildlife in Texas and man's interactions with them, from early settlement times until well into the 20th century
Egan, Timothy	The Worst Hard Time	2006	340	Houghton Mifflin	Great story of those folks who survived the Dust Bowl in the 1930s

NATURALIST PHILOSOPHY AND LAND STEWARDSHIP					
Books by and About Aldo Leopold					
Leopold, Aldo	A Sand County Almanac	1949	295	Ballantine	Often put on the same level as Thoreau and John Muir, Leopold might be described as the first modern naturalist. One reads this and wonders at how prescient he was and also at how little has changed.
Leopold, Aldo	Game Management	1933/1996	479	Natraj Publishers	Leopold's classic text, the first of game management. It is not completely consistent with his later views.
David Brown & Neil Carmony, Eds.	Aldo Leopold's Southwest	1990	250	U of NM	Twenty-six early writings by Leopold. It is interesting to read the evolution in Leopold's thinking about SW Forest Management in these twenty-six early writings.
Ledopold, Luna B. Ed.	Round River. from the Journals of Aldo Leopold	1953/1993	173	Oxford U. Press	A collection of stories about various hunting trips Leopold took with his sons and/or brothers from the early 20's to the late 30's.
Callicott and Freyfogle, Eds.	Aldo Leopold. For the Health of the Land	1999	243	Island Press	A collection of Leopold's essays mainly about land management
Flader.and Callicott, Eds	The River of the Mother of God and other Essays by Aldo Leopold	1991	384	U. of Wisconsin	A collection of essays by Leopold that stretches from his first essays as a teenager until a year before his death.
Flader, Susan L.	Thinking Like a Mountain. Aldo Leopold and the Evolution of an Ecological Attitude toward Deer, Wolves and Forests	1974		U. of Wisconsin	Chronicles the evolution of Leopold's thinking in a holistic, ecological way about the land and wildlife management.

Meine, Curt	Aldo Leopold. His Life and Work	1988	635	U. of Wisconsin	This biography of Aldo Leopold is not just dates and places but the issues he faced and his responses and philosophy.
Meine and Knight	The Essential Aldo Leopold: Quotations and Commentaries	1999	362	U. of Wisconsin	A thorough collection of quotations from Leopold's writings, organized by general topic, each topic introduced by a different scholar
Books by Other Authors					
Bedichek, Roy	Adventures with a Texas Naturalist	1947	327	UT	The Texas version of Leopold, Bedichek was both a contemporary and friend of J. Frank Dobie. Again, one is amazed at how long ago our problems began and in many cases how little has changed.
White, Matt	Prairie Time	2006	251	TAMU Press	A vivid description of Tall Grass Prairies in NE Texas and the author's relationship with them and his efforts to save them
Louve, Richard	Last Child in the Woods. Saving our Children form Nature-Deficit Disorder	2008	391	Algonquin books	The author decries the lack of experience, knowledge and interest children of today have for nature , and the consequences for the future.
Louve, Richard	The Nature Principle	2011	317	Algonquin books	The author expands the Nature-Deficit Disorder idea to adults as well, arguing that a better connection with nature would have beneficial effects on our own well-being.
Holechek, Pieper and Herbel	Range Management. Principles and Practices	1995	526	Prentice-Hall	College text, very thorough, covers issues/ practices worldwide

Butterfield, Bingham & Savoy	Holistic Management Handbook: Healthy Land, Healthy Profits	2006	248	Island Press	A detailed handbook discussing the "How To" of the Holistic Range Management Philosophy
Bartlett, Richard C.	Saving the Best of Texas	1995	221	UT	Essays about the different eco systems of Texas by the Chairman of The Nature Conservancy of Texas.
Hart, Garland, Barr, Carpenter, Reagor	Toxic Plants of Texas	2003	243	TCE	Written primarily for livestock managers, it has excellent photos and range maps for over 100 range plants.
Schmidly, David J.	Texas Natural History. A Century of Change	2002	534	TTU	The author was President of Texas Tech and probably the foremost mammologist in Texas. The first half of the book is a reprint of Vernon Bailey's account of his Biological Survey of Texas from 1889 to 1904, which in itself is fascinating reading. The second half is Schmidly's discussion of changes since then.
Lewey, Sky-Jones Ed	Your Remarkable Riparian	2010	92	Nueces River Auth.	A field guide to riparian areas and plants, this is a must for every landowner with a riparian area.
Nelle, Steve	Managing Riparian Areas	2010	34	Nueces River Auth.	Companion to Your Remarkable Riparian but with specific land management instructions
NRCS Technical Reference 1737-20	Grazing Management Procedures and Strategies for Riparian-Wetland Areas	2006		NRCS	Thorough discussion of managing riparian lands
Hart, Rector, Hanselka, Lyons and McGinty	Brush and Weeds of Texas Rangelands	2008	100 species	TX AgriLife Extension # B-6208 09-08	Multiple, good quality photos for about 100 species, with discussion about each

Haskell, David George	The Forest Unseen: A Year's Watch in Nature	2012	170	Penguin Books	The author visited a small patch of Tennessee forest every week for a year and wrote about his observation of Nature, both large and small.
Tallamy, Douglas	Bringing Nature Home	2007	358	Timber Press	Great advocate for gardening with nature in mind, how to sustain wildlife with native plants
Gunter, Pete and Oelschlaeger, Max	Texas Land Ethics	1997	156	UT Press	Ethical discussion about how we are not taking very good care of Texas and her natural resources
Stanley, Jim	Hill Country Landowner's Guide	2009	204	TAMU Press	Discussion of the changes to the Hill Country caused by settlement, the land management problems, and solutions to those problems
Stanley, Jim	A Beginner's Handbook for Rural Texas Landowners	2014	185	Outskirts Press	What rural Texas landowners need to know about their land and how it is important that they be good land stewards
Haggerty & Meuth	Texas Master Naturalist	2015	763	TAMU Press	The curriculum for the Texas Master Naturalist—Introduction to all of the topics taught in that program.
WOODY PLANTS					
Vines, Robert A.	Trees,. Shrubs and Woody Vines of the Southwest	1960	1104	UT	Out of print, but excellent, comprehensive reference work, very good illustrations, used copies can be expensive
Stahl, Carmine and Ria McElvaney	Trees of Texas	2003	287	TAMU Press	Organized by leaf shape and type, so good for tree identification, and photos of leaves are life size, but in black and white....too big to carry into the field

Vines, Robert A.	Trees of Central Texas	1984	405	UT	many of same excellent black and white illustrations as in larger book, organized by family, good field identification remarks
Wrede, Jan	Trees, Shrubs and Vines of the Texas Hill Country	2005	246	A & M	Newest book on the subject by Cibolo Education Director. Organized by family, excellent photographs, useful discussion of local ecology
Simpson, Benny J.	A. Field Guide to Texas Trees	1999	372	Lone star	organized by family, color photos in center, removed from brief description and map with ranges
Cox, Paul and Patty Leslie	Texas Trees, A Friendly Guide	1988	374	Corona	organized by families, less detailed drawings than some other books, more discussion of tree habit and uses, also shows ranges
Tull, Delena and George O. Miller	A. Field Guide to Wildflowers, Trees and Shrubs of Texas	1991	344	Gulf	small photos in center not much help in identification, but organized around dichotomous key, good for distinguishing similar species
Correll and Johnston	Manual of the Vascular Plants of Texas	1970	1881	TX Research Found.	Reference book listing over 5000 species of plants, includes trees, shrubs, forbs, and grasses and has detailed descriptions of each species, no illustrations. It is out of print.

Diggs, Lipscomb and O'Kennon	Illustrated Flora of North Central Texas	1999	1626	Botanical Research institute of TX	This is an excellent reference book for the area from the Red River south almost to Austin. Obviously many of the same species as are found in the rest of the Hill Country except for the more xeric species of the south and west. Excellent illustrations and some color photos. It is for trees, shrubs, forbs, and grasses,
Sibley, David Allen	The Sibley Guide to Trees	2009	426	Alfred A. Knopf	Written in the same format a The Sibley Guide to Birds with several excellent illustrations and good descriptions, also shows maps of areas for each species
Linex, Ricky L.	Range Plants of North Central Texas	2014	345	USDA/NRCS	It is a detailed discussion of the identification, value and management of 161 forbs, 58 grasses and 103 woody species with numerous excellent photos of each. The great majority of all species also occur in the Hill Country.
Taylor, Richard	Common Woody Plants & Cacti of South Texas	2014	204	U Texas Press	Good photos and a description of the 50most common species of woodies and cacti in South Texas
Gustafson, Mark	A Naturalist's Guide to the Texas Hill Country	2015	349	TAMU Press	Collection of photographs of most common trees, forbs, animals, birds, insects, reptiles, etc. of the Hill County, with a brief discussion of each.

GRASSES					
Shaw, Robert	Guide to Texas Grasses	2012	1080	TAMU Press	Latest, most complete list of over 700 species in Texas. Has drawings and some photos, range maps, but only brier descriptions or discussion about each grass. Newest plant names
Gould, Frank	The Grasses of Texas	1975	652	TAMU Press	Before Shaw, this was the "bible" of Texas grasses. It has detailed descriptions, good illustrations, over 500 species of grasses, older names.
Gould, Frank	Common Texas Grasses	1978	267	TAMU Press	Covers the 150 most common grasses, same descriptions and illustrations as in the Gould's previous book. Indexed by common name—easier to use for beginners than the above two books
Loflin, Brian and Shirley	Grasses of the Texas Hill Country	2006	195	TAMU Press	Best "first book" for Hill Country grasses, arranged by seed head type, photos instead of illustrations, covers over 70 grasses including grasses introduced since Gould's books were published
Hatch, Stephan and Jennifer Pluhar	Texas Range Plants	1993	326	TAMU Press	Illustrations and easy to read descriptions of common grasses, forbs and some shrubs of Texas ranges
Powell, A. Michael	Grasses of the Trans-Pecos and Adjacent Areas	2000	377	Iron Mountain Press	Detailed discussions, small illustrations, grass key. Many species common to Hill Country, but many are not
Coffey, Chuck and Russell Stevens	Grasses of Southern Oklahoma and North Texas: A pictorial Guide	2004	120	Noble Foundation	Excellent, multiple photos of 116 grasses, many of which are common to the Hill Country as well

Rector, Barron	Know Your Grasses	2003	94	Texas AgriLife Extension	Illustrations and brief descriptions of 80 Texas grasses
Linex, Ricky L.	Range Plants of North Central Texas	2014	345	USDA/NRCS	Detailed discussion of the identification, value and management of 161 forbs, 58 grasses and 103 woody species with numerous excellent photos of each great majority of all species also occur in the Hill Country
Allred, Kelly W.	A Field Guide to the Grasses of New Mexico	2005	388	New Mexico State University	Very detailed drawings of most grasses of New Mexico and maps of their ranges
Everitt, Drawe, Little and Lonard	Grasses of South Texas	2011	321	Texas Tech University Press	Descriptions, color photos of 175 native and 75 non-native grasses
Nicholson, Robert A.	Pasture and Range Plants	2006	175	Fort Hays State University	Beautiful full page color drawings of grasses and forbs.
FORBS					
Enquist, Marshall	Wildflowers of the Texas Hill Country	1987	275	Lone Star	The "bible" of Hill Country Flowers to most Hill Country Naturalists. Excellent color photographs of over 200 wildflowers, arranged by families
Ajilvsgi, Geyata	Wildflowers of Texas	1984	414	Shearer	Over 350 Excellent color photos, but covers the whole state not just the Hill Country.
Niehaul, Ripper and Savage	Southwestern and Texas Wildflowers	1984	449	Houghton/ Mifflin	A large number of flowers covered, arranged by color of flower and then shape, some color and some black and white illustrations.
Loughmiller, Campbell and Lynn	Texas Wildflowers, A Field Guide	1999	271	UT	Color photos of 300-400 flowers arranged by family.
Everitt, Drawe and Lonard	Field Guide to the Broad-Leaved Herbaceous Plants of South Texas	1999	277	Texas Tech	Good color photos, well organized descriptions

See also Diggs, Lipscomb and O'Kennon under "Woody Plants"	See also Correll and Johnston under "woody plants"				
ANIMALS					
Tekiela, Stan	Mammals of Texas Field Guide	2009	416	Adventure Publications	Good, small, fact-filled guide based largely on Schmidley's book below
Kays, Roland and Don Wilson	Princeton Field Guides: Mammals of North America	2002	240	Princeton	Field guide with brief description, range maps, and color drawings
Martin, Zim and Nelson	American Wildlife and Plants. A Guide to Wildlife Food Habits	1961	500	Dover	Range maps, discussions and food graphs for birds and animals
Schmidly, David J.	The Mammals of Texas	1994	501	UT	Probably the best book for Texas mammals only. Thorough descriptions, range maps by county. Most photos B & W, but major animals in color.
Schmidly, David J.	Texas Natural History. A Century of Change	2002	534	TTU	The author was President of Texas Tech and probably the foremost mammologist in Texas. The first half of the book is a reprint of Vernon Bailey's account of his Biological Survey of Texas from 1889 to 1904, which in itself is fascinating reading. The second half is Schmidly's discussion of changes since then.
Nora Bowers, Rick Bowers & Kenn Kaufman	Kaurman Field Guide to Mammals of North America	2004	351	Houghton Mifflin	Well illustrated with good photos

Burton,	Principles of Zoology and Ecology: Fish and Wildlife	2003	470	Delmar	A low-level college or advanced high school) text which mixes ecological principles with specific species discussions. It is easy to read.
Tennant, Alan	A Field Guide to Texas Snakes	1998	291	Gulf	Half page color photos grouped together in the center, full page descriptions and range maps for each species
Conant and Collins	Reptiles and Amphibians, Peterson Field Guide	1998	616	Houghton/ Mifflin	Good field guide with color photos, maps and illustrations
Halfpenny, James C.	Scats and Tracks of the Desert Southwest	2000	144	Globe Pequot Press	Black and white drawings of tracks, walks and scat for many animals
Mungall, Elizabeth C.	Exotic Animal Field Guide	2007	285	TAMU Press	Photos, discussion and origin of many introduced exotic mammals introduced to Texas ranges.
BIRDS					
There are so may good bird books, and most everyone has one that any list will omit a favorite, but here are two that deserve listing.					
Sibley, David A.	The Sibley Guide to Birds (National Audubon Society)	2000	544	Alfred A. Knoph	A little big to carry in the field, but excellent color illustrations and with similar species on the same page to aid in distinguishing
Rylander, Kent	The Behavior of Texas Birds	2002	431	UT	Kent Rylander is a Professor at Texas Tech/Junction and Fredericksburg, President of Fredericksburg Native Plant Society. This book doesn't help you identify birds, but it is great to help you understand them.
W. Rufus Stephens & Jan Wrede	Attracting Birds in the Texas Hill Country: A Guide to Land Stewardship	2016	498	TAMU Press	An excellent discussion of managing native habitat for native birds and for good land stewardship.
GEOLOGY					

Lambert, David	The Field Guide to Geology	1998	256	Checkmark	Good beginners book, lots of drawings, concise discussion
Spearing, Darwin	Roadside Geology of Texas	1991	418	Mountain Press	Basic discussion of Texas geology plus discussion of what you are looking at on many roadside cuts across the state.
Fensley, Charles	A Field Guide to Fossils of Texas	1989	209	Gulf	Lots of photos, detailed discussions
Turner, Hester, and Roemer	A Field Guide to Stone Artifacts of Texas Indians	1993	393	Gulf	Hundreds of drawings of arrowheads and other stone tools
INSECTS					
Drees, Bastiaan, and John Jackman	A Field Guide to Common Texas Insects	1998	359	Gulf	Organized by order, good descriptions and small color photos
Jackman, John	A Field Guide to Spiders and Scorpions of Texas	1997	201	Gulf	Organized by order, good descriptions and small color photos
Brock, Jim and Kenn Kaufman	Butterflies of North America	2003	384	Houghton/ Mifflin	Very large number of butterflies described and small photos of each
Glassberg, Jefffrey	Butterflies through Binoculars. The West	2001	374	Oxford	Very many good descriptions and color photos, also range maps.
Opler, Paul	Peterson First Guides. Butterflies and Moths	1994	128	Houghton/ Mifflin	A concise field guide to the most common butterflies and moths of North America
Wright, Amy Bartlet	Peterson First Guides. Caterpillars	1993	128	Houghton/ Mifflin	A concise field guide to 120 common caterpillars of North America
Eaton and Kaufman	Kaufman Field Guide to Insects of North America	2007	391	Houghton/ Mifflin	Well illustrated with good photos
MISCELLANEOUS					
Elpel, Thomas J.	Botany in a Day. the Pattern Method of Plant Identification. 5th Ed	2006	222	HOPS Press	Illustration and descriptive discussions of the structural characteristics of plant families

Capon, Brian	Botany for Gardeners	2010	267	Timberline Press	Basic Botany is discussed and illustrated for laymen
Kohnke & Franzmeier	Soil Science Simplified	1995	162	Waveland Press	The basics of soil science and its importance in land management
Loflin, Brian &Shirley	Texas Cacti	2009	287	TAMU Press	Excellent photos of over 200 species as well as discussion about cactus types and how to identify
Powell, A. Michael James Weedin & Shirley Powell	Cacti of Texas, A Field Guide	2008	383	Texas Tech	Detailed descriptions and good photos
Allred, Lance	Enchanted Rock. A Natural and Human History	2009	296	UT Press	Very thorough discussion of Enchanted Rock and probably over a thousand photos of the rock, the plants, the insects, etc. that live there
Turner, Nichols, Denny, and Doron	Atlas of the Vascular Plants of Texas—Vol 1	2003	649	Botanical Research Institute of Texas	A graphic listing of the counties in which each of the approximately 6000 species of dicots have been verified.
Turner, Nichols, Denny, and Doron	Atlas of the Vascular Plants of Texas—Vol 2	2003	239	Botanical Research Institute of Texas	A graphic listing of the counties in which each of the approximately 750 species of monocots have been verified.

— APPENDIX II —

EXPERTS LIST

CONTACT INFORMATION FOR HILL COUNTRY LANDOWNERS

Your Local Government Agents:

Texas Parks and Wildlife Department, http://tpwd.texas.gov/ Click on "Wildlife" or "Find a Biologist," or "Find a State Park."

Texas AgriLife Extension Service, http://counties.agrilife.org/ Click on "County Offices," You can sign up for newsletters.

Texas Forest Service, http://txforestservice.tamu.edu/default.aspx Click on "Oak Wilt," or "Wildfire Preparedness," or "Contact Us," then "landowner Assistance," or "County." Also, for detailed information about Oak Wilt, go to www.texasoakwilt.org/ .

USDA/Natural Resources Conservation Service, http://offices.sc.egov.usda.gov/locator/app click east or west Texas and then click on your county, then Natural Resources Conservation Service.

Nature/Conservation related organizations:

Hill Country Master Naturalist, http://txmn.org/hillcountry/, Covers much of the Hill Country. The State web site is http://txmn.org/

Native Plant Society of Texas, http://npsot.org/wp/ go to "Chapters."

Hill Country Alliance, http://www.hillcountryalliance.org/ 512-560-3135

The Nature Conservancy, http://www.nature.org/ourinitiatives/regions/northamerica/unitedstates/texas/

Hill Country Land Trust, www.hillcountrylandtrust.org, 830-997-0027

Nature Centers:

In Boerne, www.cibolo.org 830-249-4616

In Fredericksburg, www.fredericksburgnaturecenter.org 830-660-7592

In Kerrville, www.riversidenaturecenter.org 830-257-4837

For help with plant identification and properties:

Trees, Shrubs and Vines of the Texas Hill Country, Jan Wrede, Texas A&M Press.

Grasses of the Texas Hill Country, Brian and Shirley Loflin, Texas A&M Press.

Wildflowers of the Texas Hill Country, Marshall Enquist, Lone Star Botanical.

Range Plants of North Central Texas, Ricky Linex USDA/NRCS, Available at Soil and Water Conservation Districts.

Free iPad/PDF plant ID books, Sandra and Scott Magee, http://csmapps.webs.com/

Grass and Tree ID aids on Jim Stanley's website, http://www.hillcountrynaturalist.org/ecology

http://www.wildflower.org/plants/ Type in name of native plant

http://plants.usda.gov/ Type in name of native plant

http://csmapps.webs.com/ Free iPad App/PDF

Places to visit to see native habitat:

Kerr Wildlife Management Area, 13 miles from Hunt on 1340. 830-238-4483

Bamberger Ranch, south of Johnson City, www.bambergerranch.org 830-868-2630

All State Parks in the Hill Country

Miscellaneous contacts:

Jim Stanley: 830-257-2094, jstmn@ktc.com.

Native grass and forb seeds, range restoration, www.seedsource.com 1-800-728-4043

Jim Stanley's website, previous Kerrville Daily Times columns, Plant ID, Book lists etc. http://www.hillcountrynaturalist.org/

Books about land management:

Hill Country Landowners Guide, Jim Stanley, Texas A&M Press.

A Beginners Handbook for Rural Texas Landowners, Jim Stanley, Outskirts Press.

ABOUT THE AUTHOR

Jim Stanley grew up in the High Plains of Texas. After degrees in chemistry, a B.S. and M.S. from Texas Tech and his Ph.D. from Indiana University, and a career as a chemist in both academia and industry, he retired, with his wife Priscilla, to Kerrville in 2000. Jim was in the first class of the Hill Country Chapter of the Texas Master Naturalists in 2002, which led to the following 15 years of his studying, learning and eventually teaching about the Hill Country ecology and land stewardship.

He is the author of *Hill Country Landowner's Guide,* published by Texas A & M Press in 2009 for which he was awarded the Carroll Abbott Memorial Award for writing by the Native Plant Society of Texas. For the past seven years Jim has written the weekly column, "Hill Country Naturalist," for the *Kerrville Daily Times.* His second book, *A Beginner's Handbook for Rural Texas Landowners: How to Live in the Country without Spoiling It,* was published in 2014.

www.ingramcontent.com/pod-product-compliance
Lightning Source LLC
Chambersburg PA
CBHW061225270326
41928CB00024B/3340
9781936449743